D0891396

READINGS IN THE CONCEPT AND MEASUREMENT OF INCOME

READINGS IN THE CONCEPT AND MEASUREMENT OF INCOME

Edited with an introduction by

R. H. PARKER

Professor of Accountancy
University of Exeter

G. C. HARCOURT

Fellow of Jesus College, Cambridge

G. WHITTINGTON

Professor of Accounting
University of Bristol

Second Edition

PHILIP ALLAN

Originally published by Cambridge University Press 1969

This Edition first published 1986 by

PHILIP ALLAN PUBLISHERS LIMITED
MARKET PLACE
DEDDINGTON
OXFORD OX5 4SE

This Selection and Introduction © Philip Allan Publishers Limited 1986

British Library Cataloguing in Publication Data

Readings in the concept and measurement of
income.—2nd ed.
1. Income distribution
I. Parker, R. H.   II. Harcourt, G. C.
III. Whittington, Geoffrey
339.2'01   HC79.15

ISBN 0-86003-536-0

Reprinted in 1987

Printed in Great Britain by
Antony Rowe Ltd, Chippenham, Wiltshire

Contents

Contents

Acknowledgements

We are greatly indebted to all the authors, editors and publishers who have so kindly allowed us to reprint the papers included in this book. We are especially grateful to Ray Chambers, Charles Kennedy and Maurice Scott for adding to or revising their original papers especially for this edition. A number of our academic colleagues (notably Emeritus Professor W. T. Baxter of the London School of Economics, Professor P. A. Bird of the University of Kent at Canterbury, Professor W. Birkett of the University of New South Wales and Professor D. Solomons of the Wharton School of Finance and Commerce, University of Pennsylvania) read drafts of the introduction to the first edition and gave us good advice, as did Professor P. W. Bell of Rice University in the case of the second edition, but we are, of course, solely responsible for the final result.

References in square brackets in the introduction to the first edition refer to the reprints in this book, not to the originals. Where such a reference does not give page numbers it indicates that the reading referred to is in the first edition but not in the second.

Introduction to the second edition

RELATIONSHIP TO THE ORIGINAL PARKER AND HARCOURT
COLLECTION*

The purpose of this book, like that of its predecessor, is to bring together some important writings on the concept and measurement of income, drawing from both the economic and the accounting literature. The central theme of the selection, and of this introduction, is the measurement of business income at the level of the individual firm. The debate on inflation accounting has raged vigorously, under the influence of the rapid inflation of the 1970s, since the original Parker and Harcourt volume was produced and we have therefore, with considerable regret, had to excise the selections on National Income Accounting and on Depreciation and to forego the temptation to add material on the measurement of income for tax purposes (with the exception of a valuable but brief contribution in the postscript by Kennedy), in the cause of giving adequate coverage to the views on business income of the major participants in the inflation accounting debate (Section III).

The Introduction to the First Edition (Parker and Harcourt 1969) has been referred to frequently in the accounting literature. We have therefore reproduced this intact (apart from the changed pagination), although some of the papers to which it refers have been omitted from this new edition. The following is a complete list of papers from the first edition which have not been included in the new edition.

S. H. Frankel: 'Psychic' and 'accounting ' concepts of income and welfare. (pp. 83–105)

P. H. Wueller: Concepts of taxable income. The German contribution. (pp. 141–160)

P. W. Bell: Price changes and income measurement. (pp. 185–192)

F. W. Paish: The estimation of business profits in periods of changing prices. (pp. 193–200)

W. T. Baxter: The accountant's contribution to the trade cycle. (pp. 215–229)

* R. H. Parker and G. C. Harcourt (eds), *Readings in the Concept and Measurement of Income* (Cambridge University Press, 1969).

Introduction to second edition

The papers which we have added are those by Fisher (The economics of accountancy), Beaver and Demski, Kennedy, Scott, Baxter (on sale price versus replacement cost), Edwards, Bell and Johnson, Gynther, and Chambers. The papers retained from the original edition are those by Fisher (Income and capital), Lindahl, Simons, Hicks (two papers), Hayek, Pigou, Kaldor, Solomons, and Mathews and Grant.

The net effect of these changes is that we have retained ten papers (and the original Introduction), deleted fourteen, and added nine (plus this Introduction). We are acutely aware that, in narrowing the field, we have sacrificed coverage of some important areas and some excellent papers. Moreover, even within our chosen field, we are aware of some extremely good work which we have been unable to include. However, we hope that the relative compactness of what remains will further our central purpose of bringing some important literature to the attention of a wide audience.

PLAN OF THE NEW EDITION

The book has three sections. The first two of these deal with fundamental concepts, and the writings of economists predominate. The third section concentrates on measurement, and here the writings of accountants predo-

2

minate. although it is pleasing to be able to include contributions from economists, such as Kennedy and Scott.

Section I, Concepts of Income in Economic Theory, includes a series of classic writings by Fisher, Lindahl, Simons, Hicks and Kaldor, on the fundamental concept of income. The second of Fisher's papers provides a useful overview of the classic but somewhat indigestible book by John B. Canning, *The Economics of Accountancy*, which was a pioneering attempt to evaluate the income measurement procedures of accountants in the light of economic theory, particularly the theory of Irving Fisher, who was, not surprisingly, well disposed towards Canning's work.

The remaining papers in this section deal with the definition of income in the context of economic theory and have no particular concern with accounting or the measurement of business income. It is particularly important to remember this, as the papers by Fisher and Hicks are sometimes misinterpreted by accountants. Fisher insisted on consumption as the measure of individual income, but he did not extend this to the measurement of business income*, as is sometimes believed (although he defined the income measure which would apply to business as 'earnings'): his review of Canning shows this clearly. Hicks was writing in the context of neoclassical economic theory and concluded that 'we shall be well advised to eschew *income* and *saving* in economic dynamics. They are bad tools, which break in our hands'. However, these strictures are applied specifically to *ex ante* income as required by the economic theorist, whereas the accountant is often concerned with *ex post* income, which Hicks describes as 'almost completely objective', providing 'a useful measuring rod of economic progress'. Moreover, Hicks writes with approval of 'the sort of estimation [which] is normal statistical procedure' for the practical measurement of social income, and he would presumably approve equally of accounting procedures as practical estimates of business income or 'rough approximations, used by the business man to steer himself through the bewildering changes of situation which confront him'.

Section II contains three classical papers by Pigou, Hayek and Hicks on income and the maintenance of capital intact. The central concern of these papers is with social income, but the same issue of choosing a physical concept (Pigou) or a value-based concept (Hayek) has been debated in the context of business income: the paper by Gynther, in Part III of the book, provides a partial suvey of this debate.† The section

* However, Fisher did believe in consumption rather than income as a basis for taxation. He was author of a pioneering book on expenditure taxation. Simons, on the other hand, was an advocate of income as a tax base: our extract is from his classic book on income taxation.
† Gynther's paper was published in 1974. A more recent survey is R. R. Sterling and K. W. Lemke (eds), *Maintenance of Capital: Financial versus Physical* (Scholars Book Co.,

concludes with Kaldor's survey of the concept of income in economic theory, which draws together many of the themes in the earlier papers by economists. Kaldor's main ultimate concern is with income as a tax base and he makes the important point that even *ex post* income relies on subjective estimates. He concludes that income is too subjective to provide a sound basis for taxation and prefers expenditure as a tax base (thus reaching the same conclusions as Fisher, but by a different route).

The problems of assessing the value of end-of-period assets and the capital value which will maintain beginning-of-period well-offness have, of course, been central concerns of accountants, and this is reflected in the papers in Section III, which attempt to provide a cross-section of leading contributions to the debate on the measurement of business income. The first paper in this Section, by Solomons, provides a link with the earlier sections, by comparing and attempting to reconcile the economist's and the accountant's concepts of income. This paper reaches the pessimistic conclusion (written in 1960) that 'so far as the history of accounting is concerned, the next twenty-five years may subsequently be seen to have been the twilight of income measurement'. Whether Solomons' prediction was fulfilled is a matter which we are content to leave to the judgement of the reader and of subsequent historians. There has certainly been much controversy about the role of income measurement in accounting since 1960, as many of the papers in Section III testify. A fundamental theoretical issue which has been clarified during this period is the distinction between income as a unique 'true' measure of performance and income as a useful summary item of information which might be combined with other information in a somewhat subjective and imprecise measure of performance, or in other uses of accounting data. The former approach ('true income') is feasible only under highly restrictive conditions, but its elegance and apparent simplicity have exercised a powerful influence on accounting theorists. The latter approach (income as one item of information) is less tidy in its implications, but probably more realistic, and it is expressed in the language of modern neoclassical general equilibrium theory by Beaver and Demski, in the second paper in Section III. Beaver and Demski point out that the accountant usually operates in a world characterized by imperfect and incomplete markets, in which all goods do not have unique and unambiguous market prices. Thus, the processes of asset valuation and income measurement are subjec-

---

Houston, 1982). A recent analysis and extension of the Pigou–Hayek–Hicks debate is provided in 'Maintaining Capital Intact', by M. FG. Scott, contained in D. A. Collard, D. R. Helm, M. FG. Scott and A. K. Sen (eds), *Economic Theory and Hicksian Themes* (Oxford University Press, 1984).

tive, and the accountant's role is to provide 'noisy communication' rather than precise measurement. The role of 'noisy communication' is to provide an input into the subjective estimation processes carried out by users of accounts. A useful 'income' number is one which aids these processes, not one which claims to provide a unique 'true' measure of income. The third paper in this section, by Kennedy, surveys the recent debate on inflation accounting in the UK and concludes with a recommendation for providing an information set, in the form of an appropriation statement, which provides a range of income measures, and their components, which may be useful for different purposes: this approach is consistent with Beaver and Demski's 'noisy communication' approach. Kennedy's postscript also provides a critical commentary on the relevance of taxation to recent developments in the UK. The fourth paper, by Scott, examines the influential Sandilands Report in the light of the Hicksian standard stream concept of income, pointing out the deficiencies of the Sandilands proposals from this standpoint, and suggesting some remedies to provide a better measure in the spirit of Hicks's 'rough approximations used by the business man'. Hick's 'rough approximations' are, of course, a less formal but perhaps clearer equivalent of 'noisy communication'.

The remainder of Section III is devoted to contributions by leading advocates of various forms of current value accounting. Baxter, in a critique of Chambers's realizable value approach, states elegantly the case for selecting what Bonbright* called value to the owner which, under the guise of 'value to the business', was adopted by the Sandilands Report and has subsequently (in amended form) become the basis of current cost accounting in both the UK and the USA.† This is followed by an extract from the pioneering book by Mathews and Grant, which advocated replacement cost as the basis of measuring business income; one of the authors, Mathews, subsequently acted as chairman of a government committee whose report‡ had an important influence on the current value accounting debate in Australia, in addition to its main purpose of proposing reform of the tax system. There follows a paper by E. O. Edwards, whose classic book, co-authored by P. W. Bell, *The Theory and Measurement of Business Income* (California, 1961), has probably had more influence on the theory and practice of business income measurement

---

* J. C. Bonbright, *The Valuation of Property* (two volumes) (Charlottesville, Va., 1965; first published in 1937).

† *SSAP16, Current Cost Accounting* (Accounting Standards Committee, 1980) is the relevant UK standard. *FAS33, Financial Reporting and Changing Prices* (Financial Accounting Standards Board, 1979) is the US standard.

‡ Committee of Inquiry into Inflation and Taxation, *Report: Inflation and Taxation* (Australian Government Publishing Service, 1975).

5

than any other book published in the last 25 years. The Edwards and Bell approach consists of reporting a reconciliation of various income measures and their constituent components. Perhaps their most important distinction is that between operating gains and holding gains, but they also distinguish between real and nominal gains and between realized and unrealized gains. This approach yields a set of information which is consistent with the Beaver and Demski approach to income reporting. The Edwards and Bell approach is elaborated in the Bell and Johnson paper, where it is compared with alternative approaches. This paper uses value to the business as the valuation base, whereas the original Edwards and Bell book preferred replacement cost. In the next paper, Gynther, a noted advocate of the pure replacement cost approach (similar to that of Mathews and Grant, having replacement cost as the capital maintenance concept, as well as the valuation base) gives a controversial critique of general purchasing power adjustments and surveys alternative methods of capital maintenance. Finally, Chambers, the outstanding advocate of current value accounting based upon realizable market values (i.e. selling prices rather than replacement costs) elaborates upon some features of his continuously contemporary accounting system (CoCoA). Chambers's paper is supplemented by a brief note on his views on the specific issue of income measurement, and this note uses the notation for accounting income measurement which he developed and which is used (he would say 'abused') in the Introduction to the First Edition of this book.

We hope that this selection of papers provides an appropriate cross-section of the currently available literature on the concept and measurement of income, with particular relevance to business income. We regret the necessary constraints on the scope of our brief, which have already been discussed, and we are conscious that we have had to omit a wealth of good papers. Our criteria for selection have been similar to those used in the First Edition. They are, firstly, the importance of the ideas expressed in the paper; secondly, the necessity of representing what we believe to be the important alternative approaches to the subject; and, thirdly, quality of exposition. We have also had some regard to the physical accessibility of the papers, although we have not allowed this to override any of the other criteria; we are particularly pleased, for this reason, to be able to include the papers by Kennedy and Scott, which we feel have not received the attention which they deserved. We have also confined our choice to papers published in English, mainly because we already had an embarrassment of riches from which to choose, and certainly not because we are unaware of the important contributions of writers in other languages, e.g. the Dutch and German writers on replacement cost accounting. We have also tended to prefer short papers to long ones, because the overall length of the book was a crucial constraint. We have tried to exercise impartial judgement within these self-imposed constraints, but our prejudices and the limitation of our own knowledge are unavoidable additional constraints.

MEASUREMENT OF BUSINESS INCOME

Having introduced the individual papers in the previous section, we shall devote this section to providing a brief but more systematic discussion of the problems of defining and measuring business income, referring where relevant to papers included in this book but also referring to some of the extensive literature which we have been forced to omit.

We start by discussing the crucial question of whether income measurement is useful and, if so, what it is useful for. We conclude that it is useful, adopting a stance broadly in line with that of Beaver and Demski (as interpreted in the previous section). We then discuss some alternative *ex post* concepts of business income and conclude that something like the Edwards and Bell or Kennedy systems (also described briefly in the previous section) would be the most generally relevant. Such a system would incorporate current asset values but would also make use of general price indices to measure the effects of inflation. It would provide a measure of 'real income' which would distinguish between 'current operating profit' and 'real holding gains': other methods of partitioning income might also be included.

Whatever the difficulties of measuring income, such measures are frequently attempted in practice. This suggests that there is some demand for them, and the existence of demand suggests an underlying utility. The uses of income measures are not difficult to find—an early attempt to define them was that by Daines*, published in 1929. Various uses are defined by the authors of the papers reproduced here: some (such as Solomons and Kennedy) indicate a variety of alternative uses. The commonly cited uses of income measures include share valuation by investors; the assessment of financial security by creditors; the appraisal of management performance by proprietors; the assessment of the prudent level of dividends by directors; the assessment of employment prospects by employees and trade unions; and the assessment of tax by government.†

---

* H. C. Daines, 'The Changing Objectives of Accounting', *The Accounting Review*, 4 (1929), pp. 94–110.
† A fairly representative list of uses will be found in *The Corporate Report* (Accounting Standards Steering Committee, 1975), para. 7.5.

Introduction to second edition

It is clear from the variety of these uses that all might not be served equally well by the same definition of income, so that if we believe that income measures are supplied because they are useful, we might advocate 'different incomes for different purposes'. Many writers on accounting do in fact subscribe to this view, although there have been few attempts to follow the prescription by defining clearly a particular use and deriving logically the particular income measure which would best serve that use.*

Of course, a theoretical purist might argue that there can be only one true measure of income and that our 'different incomes for different purposes' are not *income* measures at all (or, at most, only one of them is true income). Fisher's approach is consistent with this view. For him, true income is measured in terms of an individual's psychic satisfaction; consumption is a satisfactory measure of this for practical purposes; and what is popularly termed 'income' (consumption plus savings of the individual, or dividends plus change in net worth of the business firm) is described as 'earnings'. However, as Kaldor argues, for practical purposes we must accept that the term 'income' is widely used to define something closer to Fisher's earnings concept, the definition used by Hicks being much closer to popular usage than that of Fisher.

If we adopt the Hicksian approach, the case for multiple measures of income is reinforced by the fact that, under realistic conditions of uncertainty, income is a subjective measure. Hicks presents us with six alternative measures (three *ex ante* and three *ex post*), and each contains a further degree of subjectivity in its own measurement. Even Income No. 1, *ex post* (which Hicks describes as 'not a subjective affair, like other kinds of income') is only '*almost* completely objective' (our emphasis), because it relies upon accepting market values as an appropriate measure of end-of-year values.

Beaver and Demski extend this type of argument to demonstrate that a unique income measure can exist only in a world of perfect and complete markets, in which there are markets for all commodities in all possible future states of the world, so that all uncertainty can be traded away. In such a world it is doubtful if income measures would be needed anyway (e.g. share prices would be based upon the prospective dividend stream rather than current profits). In a more realistic setting of incomplete markets, Beaver and Demski develop the case for reporting income numbers as a form of 'noisy communication', communicating useful information

---

* This point is elaborated in G. Whittington, 'The British Contribution to Income Theory', in M. Bromwich and A. Hopwood (eds), *Essays in British Accounting Research* (Pitman, 1981). Kennedy's paper provides a brief indication of the uses which he feels would be served by various alternative income measures.

8

in a summarized form which may be more digestible than the mass of detailed facts upon which it is based. This implies that a variety of income concepts may be of some use in the reporting process: none will be a unique measurement of income, and different concepts will be found useful in different situations or to different users. This complements the case already made for reporting 'different incomes for different purposes'.

Our own preferred method of reporting income is consistent with this approach. It is to adopt a system similar to that proposed by Edwards and Bell (and illustrated in the paper by Bell and Johnson, as the 'EDBEJO' model); Kennedy's proposed appropriation statement is in a similar mould and a similar proposal is made in the Introduction to the First Edition, which follows this Introduction. Such a system would reflect costs in terms of current values, rather than historical costs, and would distinguish between operating gains (due to manufacturing and trading activity) and holding gains (due to changes in price over time). It would also reflect the effects of inflation by means of general price index adjustments, which would enable a distinction to be made between real gains (i.e. a gain in command over goods and services) and nominal gains (i.e. a gain in command over monetary units). The distinction between realized gains (realized by sale or use of the asset) and unrealized gains (reflected in the value of assets still held by the business) would also be made.

Of course, within this broad framework, there are many important matters to be resolved, particularly the valuation base, where a choice of several current values faces us. These issues are discussed and debated in a number of the papers in Part III of the book and in the Introduction to the First Edition. However, we feel that it would be a step forward for both the theory and the practice of accounting if agreement could be reached on the broad framework. This would involve the recognition that alternative income measures can co-exist reasonably within the same income statement. As a corollary of this, the 'bottom line' of the income statement would no longer be of unique importance; the components would be as important as the final total. Above all, this would end the sterile debate about which is the 'correct' way to measure business income. This debate has, in our view, done much damage to the status of normative theory in accounting. The attention of accounting researchers could then focus on establishing the most useful detailed contents to put into the broad framework*; theorists could help by deducing specific information

* The contents of the income statement would also have a bearing on the contents of other accounting reports, e.g. a current-cost profit measure is likely to lead to demand for current-cost balance sheet figures for use in rate of return calculations.

needs from specific uses and empiricists could continue to explore the perceived usefulness of different pieces of information to different users, an area of research on which a promising start has been made, but where much remains to be done. We would emphasize that theory (deduction) and empiricism (induction) are complementary and would reject the view, apparently held by Watts and Zimmerman*, that the sole function of normative theories is to provide an *ex post* justification for what practical men wish to do anyway. Every paper in this book is founded on theoretical reasoning, and so are the models tested in good empirical research papers.

SOME RECENT DEVELOPMENTS IN PRACTICE

The previous section dealt with the development of theory and research, but there have also been some dramatic developments in the practice of income measurement, due largely to the problems posed by the high inflation rates experienced by most free market economies during the 1970s. In this section, we outline some of these developments very briefly.†

The paper by Kennedy (p. 179) traces the recent history of what is usually termed the 'inflation accounting' debate (*price change* accounting might be a more appropriate description) in the United Kingdom. When inflation was first perceived as posing serious problems for accounts, the adjusted historical cost method (CPP) had an immediate appeal to the professional standard-setting body, and was recommended, as a form of supplementary disclosure, by *PSSAP7* (1974). However, before *PSSAP7* was issued, the Government appointed the Sandilands Committee to investigate inflation accounting. The *Sandilands Report* (1975) polarized the debate by proposing current cost accounting, based upon value to the business rather than historical cost, and focusing on current operating profit as the central income measure. This was to be the basis of the main accounts, and the Sandilands Committee was strongly opposed to any form of general index adjustment of accounts.

The result of this polarization of the debate was much controversy, which was resolved by the introduction of the gearing and (later) monetary working capital adjustments, which attempt to recognize a gain on borrowing or loss on holding monetary assets, as prices rise, by resort to specific

---

* R. L. Watts and J. L. Zimmerman, 'The Demand for and Supply of Accounting Theories: The Market for Excuses', *The Accounting Review*, 54 (1979), pp. 273–305.

† A much more detailed account of the developments described here will be found in D. P. Tweedie and G. Whittington, *The Debate on Inflation Accounting* (Cambridge University Press, 1984).

price changes rather than general indices. These adjustments are a feature of the current cost standard (*SSAP16*, 1980) which is, at present, in force in the United Kingdom.* Australia, Canada and New Zealand have all had a similar experience to the UK (initial professional support for CPP, followed by government intervention favouring current cost methods) and have also experimented with gearing and monetary working capital adjustments. In the USA, there was a similar history (the government intervention taking the form of a Securities and Exchange Commission requirement for replacement cost disclosures by large companies) but the compromise (in *FAS33*, 1979) took the form of reporting both specific price changes and general price index adjustments, to give a set of information consistent with the real income measure. It will be apparent from the earlier discussion that we prefer this solution and would wish to see standards in other countries evolve in this direction.

It is also worth noting that all of the countries mentioned in the previous paragraph have adopted some form of value to the business as the valuation basis of their current cost disclosure requirements. This has typically been modified so as to avoid or minimize the possibility of discounted present values being reported as asset values, because these values are obviously highly subjective. Methods involving year-end adjustments and approximations using appropriate price indices have been permitted and often encouraged. Finally, since the defeat of *ED18* in the UK, there has been no requirement in any country that current cost should be required as the basis of the main accounts. Clearly, a revolutionary development of this type must await the accumulation of much more experience of current cost valuation methods.

Such a radical change may also have to await an appropriate set of political circumstances, in which a majority of those who are influential in the accounting standard-setting process see their interests being served by such a change. Although we criticized Watts and Zimmerman's somewhat dismissive attitude to normative theory, it is clear that they and other contemporary writers have provided valuable insights into the political nature of the accounting standard-setting process and, in particular, the importance of the economic consequences of accounting standards in affecting the interests of different parties.† Thus, if we wish to understand why certain interest groups espouse certain income measures, we must look at the consequences of alternative measures for such matters

* At the time of writing (October 1984), the future of *SSAP16* was under review.
† See, for example, S. A. Zeff, 'The Rise of Economic Consequences', *The Journal of Accountancy*, December 1978.

as taxation, wage bargaining, price setting, competition policy and levels of dividend payment, in addition to the theoretical logic of the case. For example, oil company managers, faced by allegations that their profits were 'obscene', following the 1973 Oil Crisis, would naturally tend to adhere to a physical view of capital maintenance (which would exclude holding gains from profit), irrespective of their views of the relative merits of the various arguments advanced in the Pigou–Hayek–Hicks debate. However, we do feel that theoretical argument has an important role in establishing which income measures are logically consistent with which assumptions about the purpose of income measurement and the economic setting in which it is conducted. We hope that the reader will find that the papers which we have selected help to clarify the problem of business income measurement, by generating the light of understanding from the heat of debate.

Introduction to the first edition

'A man will turn over half a library to make one book',
Samuel Johnson as reported in Boswell's *Life*, 6 April 1775.

PLAN OF THE BOOK

The purpose of this book of readings is to bring together under one cover some important writings in economic and accounting literature on the concept and measurement of income. It is hoped that the book will be of interest to both economists and accountants. The papers chosen for reprinting (but not this introduction) reflect a bias towards economics rather than accounting, partly because accountants are already blessed with at least three excellent books of readings* with which we are in no way trying to compete.

We have divided the book into six sections. In the first section various concepts of income are discussed by Fisher, Lindahl, Simons, Hicks, Frankel and Solomons. Most economists (with the notable exception of Fisher) have included the 'maintenance of capital intact' as part of their definition of income. In the second section we reprint from the pages of *Economica* a discussion by Pigou, Hayek and Hicks of the meaning of this concept. In the third section we reprint two surveys of the economic literature on income. Wueller surveys the little-known nineteenth-century German contribution to concepts of taxable income and Kaldor discusses the contributions of such economists as Fisher, Lindahl and Hicks.

The fourth section is concerned with the measurement of business income. Bell summarizes the influential ideas put forward by Edwards and himself in their book *The Theory and Measurement of Business Income*. Paish and Mathews and Grant express differing ideas on the effects of changing price levels on the measurement of business income. Baxter discusses the possible contribution to the trade cycle of conventional methods of measuring business income; Edey traces the effect of accounting practice on taxable income; and Parker discusses the origins of the lower of cost and market rule of inventory valuation.

* W. T. Baxter and S. Davidson (eds.), *Studies in Accounting Theory* (London, 1962); S. Davidson, D. Green, Jr, C. T. Horngren and G. Sorter (eds.), *An Income Approach to Accounting Theory* (Englewood Cliffs, N.J. 1964); S. A. Zeff and T. F. Keller (eds.), *Financial Accounting Theory* (New York, 1964).

13

Introduction to first edition

The fifth section includes four papers on the vexed problem of depreciation. Hotelling and Wright concern themselves with general theories of depreciation; A. R. Prest discusses replacement cost depreciation; and Harcourt analyses the discrepancies between the economist's and the accountant's measures of the rate of profit which arise from their different methods of measuring depreciation and valuing capital.

The sixth and final section contains three articles on national income accounting. In an historically important paper Meade and Stone discuss the construction of tables of national income, expenditure, savings and investment. The problem of measuring economic growth is analysed in an excerpt from the Australian *Report of the Committee of Economic Enquiry*. The national accounting conventions used in Eastern Europe and the Soviet Union, which still differ widely from those currently used in the West, are surveyed in a note of the *Secretariat of the Economic Commission for Europe*.

Choosing articles for inclusion in a book of readings is an exercise of some delicacy and difficulty. How was it done in this case? Our first criterion was merit: we hope it will be agreed that all the items included make a contribution to our understanding of the concepts and measurement of income. But so, we hasten to admit, do many articles not included in this volume. Limitations of space and time have forced us to adopt certain constraints. No attempt has been made to include translations of papers in languages other than English. Other things being equal, short papers have been preferred to long ones. We have excluded some important papers because they are readily available elsewhere, e.g. Sidney S. Alexander (revised David Solomons), 'Income Measurement in a Dynamic Economy' and Ronald S. Edwards, 'The Nature and Measurement of Income' both of which are reprinted in Baxter and Davidson's *Studies in Accounting Theory*. On the other hand, their relative inaccessibility encouraged us to include Lindahl's 'The Concept of Income' (from *Essays in Honour of Gustav Cassel*) and an extract from the Australian *Report of the Committee of Economic Enquiry*. We have purposely not limited ourselves to one or two journals. Reprints are included from *Abacus, Accounting Research, The Accounting Review, British Tax Review, Economica, The Economic Journal, Journal of Accounting Research, Journal of the American Statistical Association, Oxford Economic Papers, Political Science Quarterly*, and the *U.N. Economic Bulletin for Europe*. No previously unpublished papers are included.

We have not consciously chosen articles just because we agree with the opinions of the author and we have tried hard to represent various points of view, but the fact that so many of the papers in this book were written by present or former members of the University of Cambridge, the London

School of Economics and the University of Adelaide is due no doubt not only to the excellence of those institutions but also to the academic background and prejudice of the editors.

PLAN OF THE INTRODUCTION

In the remainder of this introduction we discuss some of the problems of defining and measuring income and the solutions suggested by the authors represented in this book. We have not hesitated to make clear our own views or, occasionally, to bring in the views of some authors not represented in this book whose writings are readily available.

We first of all discuss whether income measurement is useful. Having decided that it is, we look in some detail at a number of *ex post* concepts of *business* income and conclude that the concept relevant to most situations is what we call 'real income' which is divided into 'current operating profit' and 'real holding gains'. We then consider the problem of valuing non-monetary assets and some of the practical problems of measuring the concepts we find most relevant. Finally we discuss briefly the use of current operating profit and real holding gains as tax bases.

IS INCOME MEASUREMENT USEFUL?

Why measure income? Hicks suggests that 'income', like 'saving', 'depreciation' and 'investment', is a rough approximation used by the businessman to steer himself through the bewildering changes of situation which confront him and that the purpose of income calculations in practical affairs is to give people an indication of the amount which they can consume without impoverishing themselves [pp. 102-3]. Income is, as Solomons points out [pp. 154-5], currently used as a measure of taxable capacity, as a determinant of corporate dividend policy, as a guide to investment policy, and as a measure of the success of the management of business enterprise. He would no doubt have added, if he had been writing for a different audience, that income is also used as a measure of the success of the management of an economy.

All these uses can be criticized. Kaldor's criticism of income as a measure of taxable capacity is well known;* Solomons suggests that command over capital resources is a fairer guide to ability to pay taxes and thinks that a system of direct taxation could get along quite well, and perhaps better, with no concept of income at all. In defence of income tax one might reply, first that the major industrial nations show no signs of abandoning the taxation of income (this retort carries much practical weight

* *An Expenditure Tax* (London, 1955).

but is not very convincing conceptually); secondly, that arguments in favour of taxing expenditure or capital are not necessarily arguments against taxing income as well; and thirdly, that the concepts of income and capital are so intertwined that one cannot escape the difficulties of defining income by trying to define capital instead.

Solomons rightly points out that using periodic income as a guide to corporate dividend policy may be inadequate if the losses of previous periods or the need for short-term solvency are ignored. But this does not necessrily mean that we should abandon our measure of income, although it may be that we need a better concept or a more precise measure of the concept. We must also recognize clearly that income may only be one of a number of measures which need to be considered.

It must be admitted that income as a guide to investment policy or as a measure of business or national economic success may suffer from being overmuch concerned with the past rather than the future. It is nevertheless true that the past can be of some help in forecasting the future and that shareholders and citizens need a report of stewardship from their company or government.

SOME INCOME CONCEPTS

There is no reason to suppose that there is only one useful concept of income. Even a cursory glance at the contributions to this book suggests that there are many possible concepts. Economists, mindful of Jevons's remark that 'bygones are forever bygones', have tended to define income in terms of expectations. The best-known definition is that of Hicks in *Value and Capital*: 'the maximum value which [a man] can consume during a week, and still *expect* to be as *well off* at the end of the week as he was at the beginning' (italics added). The difficulties of attaching any precise meaning to this definition are well known and are explained at some length by Hicks himself [pp. 103–7]. Kaldor argues that if we define income in terms of expectations neither income *ex ante* nor income *ex post* can be objectively measured. For if K_1 and K_2 are the 'actual' value of assets at the beginning and end of an accounting period; K_2' is the value which the assets are expected to have at the end of the period; and K_1' is the revised value of the assets at the beginning of the period as estimated at the end of the period; then

$$\text{income } ex \ ante \text{ is } K_2' - K_1$$
$$\text{income } ex \ post \text{ is } K_2 - K_1'$$

and both of these concepts depend on a hypothetical value (K_2' or K_1') [pp. 118–9].

One could, however, following Hicks, define income *ex post* as $K_2 - K_1$, whilst retaining income *ex ante* as $K_2' - K_1$. We shall discuss later some of the problems of measuring $K_2 - K_1$, but it is worth noting that these definitions are not too far away from contemporary accounting practice and are useful both for planning and control and for stewardship reporting. At the beginning of a period an individual or firm has a known set of assets, K_1, and plans to have, based on his or its expectations of the future, a set K_2' at the end of the period. By measurement at the end of the period he finds that he has, in fact, K_2. The extent to which the plans and expectations are not realized, $K_2 - K_2'$, will show up as a 'variance' (in the cost accounting sense of that word) which can be used as a guide to corrective action. For reporting to shareholders and as a base for income tax $K_2 - K_1$ is (subject to the discussion below) the relevant concept.

As Hicks has shown it is possible to construct a number of *ex post* $(K_2 - K_1)$ concepts of income. The one which he considers to be the most objective is, for an individual, 'the value of the individual's consumption *plus* the increment in the money value of his prospect which has accrued during the week' [p. 109]. This, claims Hicks, is not subjective but is almost completely objective since the capital values of the individual's property both at the beginning and end of the week are assessable quantities. It follows that the income of all individuals can be aggregated without difficulty and the same definition of income applied to the community as a whole. This concept we shall call *money income*:

a man's money income in any period is equal to the money value of his consumption plus the increase in the money value of his capital assets. For the sum of these two is the amount which he could have spent on consumption *while maintaining the money value of his capital stock intact*. [Meade and Stone]

A similar concept is put forward by Simons [p. 96]:

Personal income connotes, broadly, the exercise of control over the use of society's scarce resources. It has to do not with sensations, services, or goods but rather with rights which command prices (or to which prices may be imputed). Its calculation implies estimate (*a*) of the amount by which the value of a person's store of property rights would have increased, as between the beginning and end of the period if he had consumed (destroyed) nothing, or (*b*) of the value of rights which he might have exercised in consumption without altering the value of his store of rights. In other words, it implies estimate of consumption and accumulation.

We shall discuss in more detail later the meaning of such phrases as 'money value of his capital assets' and 'the value of a person's store of property rights'.

For a business enterprise we can, following the work of Edwards and Bell,*

---

* E. O. Edwards and P. W. Bell, *The Theory and Measurement of Business Income* (Berkeley & Los Angeles, 1961). Our debt to their book is obvious.

divide money income into (*a*) *current operating profit* (or 'current income' as Mathews and Grant, p. 250 below, call it); and (*b*) *holding gains*. Current operating profit is defined as 'the excess over a period of the current value of output sold over the current cost of the related inputs' [Bell]. A holding gain arises whenever the current market value of an asset exceeds its historical cost.

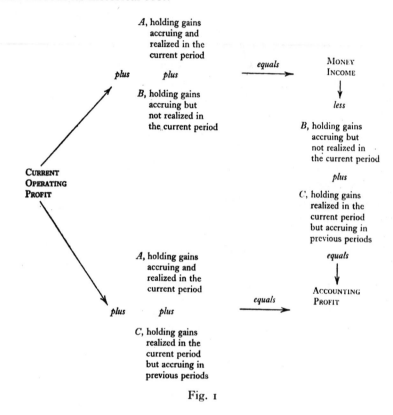

Fig. 1

Neither money income nor current operating profit is equivalent to *accounting profit* as found in business practice. This is usually defined as the difference between the historical costs of the net assets at the beginning and end of an accounting period (net of depreciation of fixed assets based on historical cost) after adjusting for new capital introduced and for dividends or other distributions to proprietors. The most important exception to this rule—the valuation of inventories at market value—is only applied when the effect is to reduce accounting profit. Ignoring this, the difference between money income and accounting profit will be made up of: (i) holding gains which have accrued during the current accounting period but have not yet been 'realized'; (ii) *less* holding gains which accrued in previous accounting periods and have been 'realized' in the current period. There is clearly one other kind of holding gain: (iii) those holding gains which have both accrued and been 'realized' during the current accounting period.

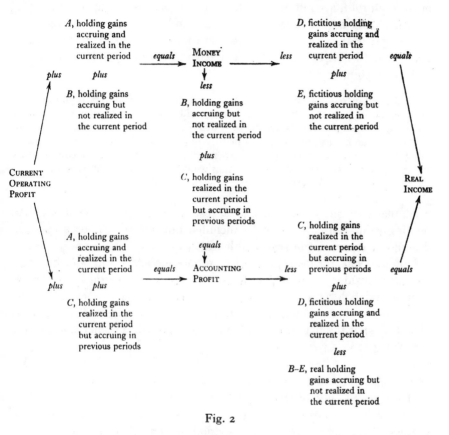

Fig. 2

A holding gain may be 'realized' either directly by sale of the asset concerned (a building, for example) or indirectly when the asset concerned (e.g. raw materials) is converted and sold in the form of finished goods.

The relationship between money income, current operating profit and accounting profit is shown in Fig. 1.

Neither money income nor accounting profit makes any allowance for changes in the general price level, both real gains resulting from changes in relative prices and fictitious gains resulting from the effects of a rise in the general price level being regarded as income. There is clearly room for a concept of *real income*. For a man this is 'the value of his expenditure

19

on consumption plus the value of any increase in the real amount of his capital assets' [Meade and Stone]. For a business enterprise, real income can be obtained by separating holding gains into their real and fictitious elements. Figure 2 shows the relationship between current operating profit, accounting profit, money income and real income.

It could be argued that holding gains and losses should be regarded not as part of income but as changes in capital. This is really a matter of definition. Fisher, for example,* defined income to exclude savings but, as Kaldor points out:

> If we defined income as consumption we should still require another term to denote as potential income the consumption that would obtain if net savings were zero. Hence apart from the trivial question of which is the right use of words, it is evident that income and consumption (as ordinarily understood) do not refer to the same thing, but to two different things; and if we reserved the term income for consumption we should still need another term for what would otherwise be called income; and we should still be left with the problem of how to define the latter [p. 114].

Similarly, if one *defines* income as resulting only from operations then holding gains can clearly not be included but one still needs a name to describe that increase in real wealth which we have called 'real income'.

Holding gains (or losses) can arise on both monetary and non-monetary assets.† Consider a firm which during an accounting period has no transactions and holds the same quantities of net monetary assets (e.g. cash *plus* debtors *minus* creditors) and non-monetary assets (e.g. land, machinery, inventories) at the beginning and end of the period. The net assets at the beginning can be written as

$$M_0 + N_0 \qquad (1)$$

where M_0 = net monetary assets, N_0 = non-monetary assets.

If during the period the general price level rises by a rate p, and the specific price level of non-monetary assets by a rate r, then at the end of the period the net assets in end-of-period market prices will be

$$M_0 + N_0(1 + r). \qquad (2)$$

M_0 has not changed because the monetary value of cash, debtors and creditors has not changed.

To discover the 'real income' of the period we must subtract expression (1) from expression (2) *after* allowing for the change in the general price level. Thus although 'money income' would be

$$M_0 + N_0(1 + r) - (M_0 + N_0) = N_0 r, \qquad (3)$$

---

* I. Fisher, *The Nature of Capital and Income* (New York, 1906).
† The next few paragraphs owe much to R. J. Chambers, *Accounting, Evaluation and Economic Behavior* (Englewood Cliffs, N.J., 1966), ch. 10.

real income will be

$$M_0 + N_0(1+r) - (M_0+N_0)(1+p) = N_0(r-p) - M_0p. \tag{4}$$

By not changing the quantities of the assets, current operating profit has been assumed to be zero, so it follows that equation (4) represents the real holding gains (or losses) accruing during the period (realized and unrealized). These arise both from the effect on non-monetary assets of the differential movement of specific and general prices, and from holding monetary assets through a change in the general price level.

Dropping the assumption that M_0 and N_0 are constant in quantity throughout the accounting period, let M_1 and N_1 be the values of net monetary assets and non-monetary assets at end-of-period prices. This means that real income will be

$$(M_1+N_1) - (M_0+N_0)(1+p). \tag{5}$$

Subtracting the holding gain element, current operating profit will be

$$(M_1+N_1) - (M_0+N_0)(1+p) - [N_0(r-p) - M_p]$$
$$= (M_1+N_1) - [M_0+N_0(1+r)], \tag{6}$$

i.e. current operating profit is equal to the difference between the current values of the net assets at the end of the period and the end-of-period values of the opening net assets.

Current operating profit is not, however, measured in practice by the comparison of two balance sheets but by the recording of revenues and expenses. Expression (5) and equation (6) need to be rewritten accordingly. Assume that non-monetary assets are divided into fixed assets (F) and inventories (I), that their values increase at a rate r during the accounting period, and that all transactions take place on the last day of the period. This ignores the problem, which we shall discuss later, of holding gains on assets acquired during an accounting period. In summary a typical period's transactions might be as follows:

(*a*) Bought goods costing P, thus increasing inventories and decreasing monetary assets.

(*b*) Sold goods whose current cost was Q, receiving in exchange monetary assets of S.

(*c*) Fixed assets depreciated (in current values) by D.

(*d*) Used monetary assets of E to pay other expenses.

From the above:

$$M_1 - M_0 = S - P - E$$
$$N_1 - N_0 = (F+I)r + P - Q - D.$$

21

Equation (6) can now be rewritten as

$$S - Q - D - E, \tag{7}$$

i.e. current operating profit = sales *less* current cost of goods sold, depreciation at current cost and other expenses.

Similarly expression (5) can be rewritten as

$$S - Q - D - E + (F + I)(r - p) - M_0 p, \tag{8}$$

i.e. real income = current operating profit + real holding gains accruing.

We have so far distinguished three *ex post* concepts of income: accounting profit, money income and real income. A fourth concept, which we shall call adjusted accounting profit (or adjusted historical cost), has been supported by a number of economists and accountants. With this concept changes in relative price levels are ignored but a general price index is used to adjust for changes in the general price level. Thus, during an accounting period in which there are changes in relative and general prices but no change in the quantities of assets held, adjusted accounting profit will be

$$M_0 + N_0(1 + p) - (M_0 + N_0)(1 + p) = M_0 p,$$

compared with an unadjusted accounting profit of zero, money income of $N_0 r$ and real income of $N_0(r - p) - M_0 p$.

ARITHMETICAL ILLUSTRATION OF FOUR INCOME CONCEPTS

As a simple arithmetical illustration of the four income concepts of accounting profit, real income, adjusted accounting profit and current operating profit (current income) consider the following example which is an adaptation of one given recently by Professor Baxter.* A firm starts with a capital of £1,300 in cash and uses £1,000 of this to buy goods for resale. Three-quarters of the goods are sold at retail for £1,500 at a time when the wholesale replacement cost of all the goods bought is £1,560 (i.e. the special index has increased from 100 to 156). During the same period, the general index has increased from 100 to only 120.

Balance sheets drawn up under four different income concepts are shown below for

(*a*) the start of the period;

(*b*) immediately after the increases in the assets' replacement cost and in the general index but before the sale; and

(*c*) immediately after the sale.

---

* W. T. Baxter, 'General or Special Index?—Capital maintenance under changing prices', *Jgurnal UEC*, no. 3 (July 1967). Professor Baxter does not necessarily agree with our conclusions.

BALANCE SHEETS

		(1) Start £	(2) Before sale £	(3) After sale £
	I **Accounting profit**			
Assets				
Cash		1,300	300	1,800
Inventory at historical cost		.	1,000	250
		£1,300	£1,300	£2,050
Proprietorship				
Capital		1,300	1,300	1,300
Profit		.	.	750
		£1,300	£1,300	£2,050

		(1) Start £	(2) Before sale £	(3) After sale £
	II **Real income**			
Assets				
Cash		1,300	300	1,800
Inventory at current value		.	1,560	390 (a)
		£1,300	£1,860	£2,190
Proprietorship				
Capital				
historical		1,300	1,300	1,300
inflation adjustment		.	260 (b)	260 (b)
Real holding gain on inventory				
unrealized		.	360 (c)	90 (c)
realized		.	.	270 (c)
Loss on holding money		.	−60 (c)	−60 (c)
Current operating profit		.	.	330 (d)
		£1,300	£1,860	£2,190

		(1) Start £	(2) Before sale £	(3) After sale £
	III **Adjusted accounting profit**			
Assets				
Cash		1,300	300	1,800
Inventory at adjusted historical cost		.	1,200 (e)	300 (e)
		£1,300	£1,500	£2,100
Proprietorship				
Capital				
historical		1,300	1,300	1,300
inflation adjustment		.	260 (b)	260 (b)
Loss on holding money		.	−60 (f)	−60 (f)
Profit		.	.	600
		£1,300	£1,500	£2,100

23

	(1) Start £	(2) Before sale £	(3) After sale £
IV *Current operating profit*			
Assets			
Cash	1,300	300	1,800
Inventory at current value	.	1,560	390 (a)
	£1,300	£1,860	£2,190
Proprietorship			
Capital			
historical	1,300	1,300	1,300
inventory	.	.	.
revaluation		.	.
reserve	.	560 (g)	560 (g)
Current operating profit	.	.	330 (d)
	£1,300	£1,860	£2,190

The income statements resulting from the various methods are given below.

INCOME STATEMENTS

	(1) Accounting profit £	(2) Real income £	(3) Adjusted accounting profit £	(4) Current operating profit £
Sales	1,500	1,500	1,500	1,500
Cost of goods sold:				
Historical	−750	.	−750	.
Inflation adjustment	.	.	−150	.
Adjusted historical	.	.	−900	.
Current	.	−1,170	.	−1,170
Current operating profit	.	330	.	330
Real holding gain (net)	.	300 (c)	.	.
Loss on holding money	.	.	−60	.
Income	£750	£630	£540	£330

Notes

(a) The current value of the goods remaining in stock, i.e. $\frac{1}{4} \times$ £1,560.

(b) The inflation adjustment is derived by multiplying the opening capital by the rate of change in the *general price level*.

(c) The unrealized holding gain on inventory is £1,000 $(0.56 − 0.20)$ = £360 before sale, and $\frac{1}{4} \times$ £360 = £90 after sale. The realized holding gain is $\frac{3}{4} \times$ £360 = £270. The loss on holding money is £300 × 0.2 = £60.

(d) The current operating profit can be derived either from a comparision of balace sheets (second and third columns),

$$(M_1 + N_1) - [M_0 + N_0(l+r)] = £(1,800 + 390) - £(300 + 1,560) = £2,190 - £1,860 = £330,$$

or by deducting current cost of goods sold from sales, £1,500 − £1,170 = £330.

24

(e) The inventory at adjusted historical cost is derived by multiplying the purchase price of the goods by the change in the *general* price index.

(f) The loss on holding money is Mp, i.e. £300 × 0·2 = £60.

(g) The inventory revaluation reserve represents the difference between the historical and current costs of inventory purchased; it is the equivalent on the credit side of revaluing the asset on the debit side.

Income concept I, accounting profit, represents conventional practice but is clearly unsatisfactory in that it completely ignores market values and changing price levels. Income concept III, adjusted accounting profit or the use of a general price index only, is an improvement but it still ignores market values and it still reflects the unwillingness of accountants to abandon historical cost. There is no real violation of the 'historical cost convention' but merely a recognition that the unit of account is elastic. For this reason it may be that this is the only method which has any chance of acceptance in practice. Certainly half a loaf is better than no bread, but it is important to recognize that a second-best solution will have been adopted. The results reflect the change in the general price level, and once agreement has been reached on the index to be used the method can be objectively applied. On the other hand, an historical cost remains an historical cost even when it has been adjusted by a general price index. It does not represent a current valuation. It is possible for the prices of particular goods to differ quite markedly from the change in the general price level. For example, Whitehead and Cockburn in their study of prices and productivity in 39 Australian manufacturing industries for the period 1954–8 point out that whilst during this period the consumer price index rose from 101·4 (September quarter 1954) to 114·8 (June quarter 1958) and the wholesale price index from 322 to 339, 14 of the industries showed overall reductions in 1954–5, 11 in 1955–6, 6 in 1956–7 and 12 in 1957–8.*

Income concepts II and IV, real income and current operating profit, are the only ones which bring current market values into the balance sheet and in fact the assets side of their balance sheets is identical. The two concepts differ only in their handling of holding gains. The latter concept ignores changes in the general price level and excludes real holding gains from income.

A possible compromise might be to produce financial statements that disclosed more than one concept of business income. It would not be difficult to combine income concepts I, II and IV (accounting profit, real

---

* D. H. Whitehead, 'Price-Cutting and Wage Policy', *Economic Record*, XXXIX (June 1963), 189. For some British data see W. A. H. Godley and C. Gillien, 'Pricing Behaviour in the Engineering Industry', *National Institute Economic Review*, no. 28 (May 1964), pp. 50–2.

income and current operating profit). The income statement would be as follows:

Sales

less historical cost of goods sold
   historical depreciation
   other expenses

equals Accounting profit

less holding gains *realized* (whether accruing or
   not) in the current period

equals Current operating profit

plus real holding gains *accruing* (but not necessarily
   realized) in the current period

equals Real income

This statement is equivalent to a clockwise movement around Fig. 2 [p. 19 above] starting at Accounting profit and going from Current operating profit to Real income in one jump instead of two.

Using our existing arithmetical illustration gives:

COMBINED INCOME STATEMENT

	£
Sales	1,500
Historical cost of goods sold	750
Accounting profit	750
Excess of current over historical cost of goods sold	420
Current operating profit	330
Real holding gain (net)	300
Real income	630

BALANCE SHEET

	(1) Start £	(2) Before sale £	(3) After sale £
Assets			
Cash	1,300	300	1,800
Inventory			
historical cost	.	1,000	250
excess of current over			
historical cost	.	560	140
current cost	.	1,560	390
	£1,300	£1,860	£2,190

26

	(1) Start £	(2) Before sale £	(3) After sale £
Proprietorship			
Capital			
historical	1,300	1,300	1,300
inflation adjustment	.	260	260
Accounting profit	.	.	750
Excess of current over his-			
torical cost of goods sold	.	.	−420
Current operating profit	.	.	330
Real holding gain (net)	.	300	300
	£1,300	£1,860	£2,190

THE VALUATION OF NON-MONETARY ASSETS

It is worth pausing at this point to remind ourselves that the 'accounting profit' which we regard as the least useful of the concepts discussed is, however, the dominant one in accounting practice. Why have accountants been so reluctant to adopt another concept? There are at least four possible reasons.

(i) Accountants are 'practical' men and like most practical men they tend to 'repeat the mistakes of their forefathers' and to avoid solving theoretical problems. One certainly gets the impression that the leading professional accounting bodies in Britain and the United States have hoped that if they waited long enough the problems of accounting for changing price levels would fade away.

For example, the Council of the Institute of Chartered Accountants in England and Wales accepts that the significance of accounts prepared on the basis of historical costs is subject to limitations and that the results shown by such accounts are (*a*) not a measure of increase or decrease in wealth in terms of purchasing power, or of the amount which can prudently be regarded as available for distribution; (*b*) not necessarily suitable for purposes such as price fixing, wage negotiations and taxation. In spite of this, the council has been unable to find a practicable and generally acceptable alternative. It has recommended that fixed assets should not, in general, be written up, 'especially in the absence of monetary stability'.*

Similarly, the American Institute of Certified Public Accountants has stated that 'accounting and financial reporting for general use will best serve their purposes by adhering to the generally accepted concept of

---

* Institute of Chartered Accountants in England and Wales, *Recommendation on Accounting Principles*, no. 15, 'Accounting in Relation to Changes in the Purchasing Power of Money' (issued 30 May 1952), paragraphs 28 and 30.

27

depreciation on [historical] cost, at least until the dollar is stabilized at some level'. In 1961, however, the Institute's Accounting Principles Board agreed that 'the assumption in accounting that fluctuations in the value of the dollar may be ignored is unrealistic'. As a result the authors of an accounting research study published by the Institute in 1963 concluded that 'recognition of price-level changes in financial statements is practical, and not misleading or dangerous' and recommended that the effects of such change should be disclosed as a supplement to the conventional statements. A single index of the general price level should be used,* i.e. the concept of 'adjusted accounting profit' should be adopted.

(ii) In most countries historical cost is used for taxation purposes. Historical cost is unlikely to be abandoned for income measurement so long as its use is compulsory for the measurement of taxable income.

(iii) The practising accountant can legitimately complain that the critics of historical cost have failed to agree among themselves as to the alternative which should be adopted.

(iv) But what makes most practising accountants (and some academic accountants also) cling to historical cost is the fear that although published financial statements might gain in relevance they would lose their present objectivity. We can be sympathetic to this plea for objectivity without accepting that historical cost is necessarily more objective than market value. It is well known that even depreciation based on historical cost is an estimate. It is perhaps not so well known that the so-called historical cost of a manufactured article depends on a number of rather arbitrary decisions about which overheads are 'inventoriable' (a useful but horrible word) and how they should be allocated between jobs or processes. On the other hand, many, though admittedly not all, assets have easily verifiable market values.

Many assets have market values which differ according to whether one is a buyer or a seller. Edwards and Bell† call these 'entry' and 'exit' values respectively. Clearly, we can subdivide our concepts of money income and real income according to whether we use entry values only, exit values only or some combination of the two. This illustrated in the table below.

	Money income	Real income
Entry values only	'Business profit'	'Real business profit'
Exit values only	'Realizable profit'	'Real realizable profit'

* American Institute of Certified Public Accountants, *Accounting Research Study* no. 6, *Reporting the Financial Effects of Price-Level Changes* (New York, 1963), p. xi. The sources of the earlier quotations can be found in ch. 9 of *Accounting Research Study* no. 7, *Inventory of Generally Accepted Accounting Principles for Business Enterprises* (New York, 1965), by Paul Grady.

† *Business Income*, p. 75.

The titles in quotation marks are taken from Edwards and Bell. They regard all four concepts as useful but develop their arguments mainly in terms of 'business profit'.

There is, however, a strong argument for a concept of income which uses both entry and exit prices.* An upper limit to the value of an asset to a firm is set by its current replacement cost (RC), for the loss which the firm suffers from being deprived of the asset cannot exceed the cost of restoring it to its former position. Other possible values are net realizable value (NRV), the present value (PV) of the expected net cash receipts from the asset where this differs from RC and NRV and the present value of the best alternative use of the funds locked up in the asset. We define NRV to be the larger of net realizable value and (in a capital-rationing situation) the present value of the best alternative investment. The six possible relationships between RC, NRV and PV can be set out as follows:

1	NRV > PV > RC		4	PV > NRV > RC
2	NRV > RC > PV		5	RC > PV > NRV
3	PV > RC > NRV		6	RC > NRV > PV

The relevant value to the firm in each case can be worked out in the following manner:

(*a*) Divide the cases into two groups according to whether the asset should be held for use or resale. This is roughly but not exactly the same as the accountant's distinction between fixed and current assets. An asset should be held for use only where PV > NRV. Thus we have:

Use		Resale	
3	PV > RC > NRV	1	NRV > PV > RC
4	PV > NRV > RC	2	NRV > RC > PV
5	RC > PV > NRV	6	RC > NRV > PV

(*b*) If we now delete all NRVs from the 'use' group as irrelevant and all PVs from the 'resale' group as irrelevant and also remember that the upper limit of value to the firm is current replacement cost, the six cases can be rewritten as follows:

Use		Resale	
3	RC	1	RC
4	RC	2	RC
5	RC > PV	6	RC > NRV

* The next few paragraphs owe much to D. Solomons, 'Economic and Accounting Concepts of Cost and Value' in M. Backer (ed.), *Modern Accounting Theory* (Englewood Cliffs, N.J., 1966). See also J. C. Bonbright, *The Valuation of Property* (Charlottesville, Va. 1965), I, ch. IV (first published in 1937).

That is to say, value to the firm is current replacement cost in all cases except 5 and 6. Case 5 is the situation where it would not be worth buying the asset were it not already held. The value to the firm is therefore, we suggest, the present value of the expected net cash receipts from the asset. Case 6 is the situation where an asset which the firm intends to sell is not worth replacing. Value to the firm is therefore net realizable value.

We are now in a position to suggest the following general rule of asset valuation:

The 'value to the firm' (VF) of an asset is its current replacement cost, with two exceptions:

(i) where the asset is held for use (i.e. PV > NRV) it should be valued at the present value of the expected net cash receipts if this is lower than current replacement cost;

(ii) where the asset is held for resale (ie. NRV > PV) it should be valued at net realizable value if this is lower than current replacement cost.

The rule can be expressed even more briefly as follows: Value to the firm = RC, except where RC > PV or RC > NRV, when VF = PV or NRV, whichever is the greater.

How helpful is this rule as a guide to valuations in practice? There is little difficulty in the case of stocks of raw materials, work in progress and finished goods. Both raw materials and finished goods will usually have reasonably easily ascertainable replacement costs and net realizable values. The present value of expected net cash receipts can be regarded for all practical purposes as equal to net realizable value.

Work in progress as such will usually have a very low net realizable value, but the present value of the expected net cash receipts calculated on the usual incremental basis (see next paragraph) may be both large and difficult to calculate. Perhaps the best practical solution is to assume, except where it is expected that the RC of the *finished product* will be greater than its NRV, the work in progress to be at least equal in value to its current replacement cost as measured by the firm's standard costing system (see next section). Value to the firm will then usually be replacement cost.

Fixed assets are by definition acquired for use rather than resale. It is rather curiously argued by some accountants that this being so we need to know only the asset's historical cost. If one of a manager's aims is to maximize the wealth of his firm this is clearly wrong. He needs to know when to scrap the asset and this point must come when NRV as defined above becomes greater than the present value of the expected net cash receipts. The relevant net receipts are those which would not be receivable by the firm if it did not own the asset. Such a figure may, of course, be very large indeed: in the limiting case *all* the receipts of the firm might cease if it did not own the asset. Happily we can escape from the rather frightening prospect of the whole firm being valued at several times the sum of its parts by falling back on our rule that an upper limit is provided by an asset's current replacement cost. But this also could be a suspiciously high figure for a machine which could only be replaced by another one specially made for the firm. It is essential therefore to interpret current replacement cost not as the cost of replacing the actual physical asset used by the firm but as the cost of currently acquiring the *services* provided by the asset.* It is even more difficult to arrive at an objective estimate of an asset's PV. Fortunately this is only relevant to income measurement when both PV and NRV are less than current replacement cost. In most cases current replacement cost will be the relevant measure of value to the firm and the remaining sections of this introduction have been written mainly on this assumption.

A. R. Prest has put forward a number of persuasive but not, we think, entirely convincing arguments against the use of replacement cost depreciation.† First, while he does not dispute that replacement cost is appropriate in the measurement of the national income he is doubtful of its relevance to business income, principally on the grounds that he cannot agree that '"the" correct *motif* of action for the individual firm is to aim at preserving intact its stock of physical assets'. This argument, however, seems to confuse income with distributable income. The supporter of replacement cost depreciation does not have to argue that a firm *must* maintain its physical assets intact, but merely that any distribution of real capital should be recognized as such and not regarded as a distribution of income.

Secondly, Prest rightly attacks loose arguments about depreciation providing funds for replacement: 'after all, if depreciation charges on a replacement cost basis were not earned then it would be possible to have no liquid resources available, for replacement despite the most conscientious accounting'. One must be careful of assuming, however, that replacement cost depreciation for income measurement purposes has any connexion with the *replacement requirements* of a firm. No method of income measurement can by itself provide funds or replace assets.

Thirdly, Prest does not believe that historical cost depreciation tends to exaggerate the trade cycle: 'the profitability of new investment must depend *inter alia* on the current costs of purchasing equipment; simple extrapolation of current profits reckoned on the basis of *past* capital costs

* For the contrary view see Edwards and Bell, *op. cit.* p. 186 n.
† See also his *Public Finance in Theory and Practice* (London, 3rd ed. 1967), ch. 16.

is a path which surely few would follow. We shall not pursue this argument here.

THE MEASUREMENT OF CURRENT OPERATING PROFIT AND REAL HOLDING GAINS

If, as we believe, current operating profit and real holding gains are elements of business income of great practical significance to both managers and shareholders it is important to tackle the problem of how to measure them. A concept of income which cannot be measured reasonably objectively is not likely to have much impact in practice.

From the point of view of management accounting it is highly desirable that changes in specific prices be integrated with a company's routine standard costing system. That this is possible in practice is shown by the experience of Philips Electrical Industries.*

Many items in a company's income statement are automatically recorded in current terms, e.g. sales and purchases of goods. The two exceptions are the stock element in cost of goods sold and the depreciation of fixed assets.

One of the incidental advantages of a system of standard costing is that the detailed stock records can be kept in quantities only. We suggest that standard costs should be calculated for each item of stock in the usual way but that price indexes should also be prepared for groups of related articles. A significant movement in an index should be followed by a revaluation. (In practice Philips do not usually revise standard prices more than once a year.) At a revaluation adjustments are made *in total* by writing up the value of stock in hand, recognizing the existence of a Real holding gain (or loss) to the extent that the specific price rise is greater than or less than the rise in the general price level, and transferring the difference to an inflation-adjusted account.

If, as in the arithmetical illustration on p. 22 above, the original value of the stock was £1,000, the specific price level had risen by 56 per cent, and the general price level by 20 per cent, then the following entry needs to be made:

		£
Stock	Dr.	560
Real holding gain	Cr.	360
Inflation adjustment	Cr.	200

---

* See A. Goudeket, 'An Application of Replacement Value Theory', *Journal of Accountancy* (July 1960), pp. 37–47; also R. S. Gynther, *Accounting for Price-Level Changes: Theory and Procedures* (Oxford, 1966), pp. 223–40.

A purchase of raw materials after such a revaluation would be recorded by debiting Stock account with the revised standard cost, crediting Trade creditors with the actual amount payable and debiting or crediting a Materials price variance account in the usual way with the difference if any between the revised standard cost and the actual amount payable. Materials would be issued to production at the revised standard cost so that the values placed on work in progress and finished goods stock would take into account significant changes in the price of raw materials.*

If the above suggestions are regarded as impracticable by some companies, end-of-year adjustments could be used instead. The usual historical figures are recorded during the year and accounting profit is calculated in the normal fashion. From this a figure for stock appreciation is then deducted. There are a number of ways in which this adjustment could be calculated:

(i) If stock accumulation *during* the year is ignored then the stock appreciation adjustment is simply the difference between the opening stocks valued at end-of-year prices and the same stocks valued at beginning-of-the-year prices.

(ii) Stock appreciation can be calculated as the difference between the historical cost of sales and the quantity sold during the year multiplied by the weighted average purchase price of the year.

(iii) A third method is based upon a suggestion made by Paish. The adjustment is calculated as the average of the appreciation on opening and closing stocks, i.e.

$$S = \tfrac{1}{2}[(O_o^c - O) + (C - C_c^o)],$$

where S = stock appreciation O = opening stocks at beginning-of-the-year prices, C = closing stocks at end-of-year prices, o = beginning-of-the-year prices, c = end-of-year prices. Changes in the physical levels of stocks are thus taken into account.

A simple example will show the relative effect of these methods. At the beginning of a year a company's stocks consisted of 1,000 units valued at £10 each. During the year it bought 3,800 units at £10·2 each and 1,200 units at £10·3 each (in that order). It sold 4,500 units at £20 each and had a closing stock of 1,500 units at which time the purchase price was still £10·3 per unit. Using the conventional first-in, first-out assumption the closing stock

---

* Readers who are not accountants are reminded that expenses and increases in assets are debits (Dr.) and that gains and increases in liabilities and proprietorship are credits (Cr.). For details of accounting and costing procedures see R. Mathews, *Accounting for Economists* (Melbourne, 2nd ed. 1965).

would be valued at £15,420 (i.e 1,200 × £10·3 + 300 × £10·2) and accounting profit can be calculated as

		£
Sales		90,000
Cost of goods sold	£	
Opening stock	10,000	
Purchases	51,120	
	61,120	
less Closing stock	15,420	
		45,700
Accounting Profit (gross)		£44,300

The various stock appreciation estimates (£) will be

(i) $1,000 \times (10·3 - 10·0) = 300,$

(ii) $(4,500 \times [51,120/5,000]) - 45,700 = 308,$

(iii) $\frac{1}{2}\{[(10,000 \times 10·3/10·0) - 10,000]$
$$+ [15,450 - (15,450 \times 10·0/10·3)]\} = 375.$$

To the extent that stock prices have risen more rapidly than prices in general the stock appreciation estimate will include a real holding gain. If for example there has been a 2 per cent rise in the general price level during the year, then the real holding gain element calculated on opening stocks only would be £100.

Practical problems also arise in the measurement of current cost depreciation.* There is little difficulty in obtaining current replacement costs for those fixed assets which are marketed continually and which are subject to little technical change. Where no market exists for new fixed assets of the type used by the firm resort must be had either to appraisal or specific price indexes (such as those prepared in the United Kingdom by the Economist Intelligence Unit).

One way of handling the necessary calculations is to incorporate them in the normal monthly entry recording depreciation expense and the increase in the accumulated depreciation of the fixed asset. So long as there are no significant changes in price the entry will be based on historical cost. If a significant change occurs the fixed asset should be written up (debited) accordingly and the Inflation adjustment and Real holding gains accounts credited.

---

* The argument of this section ignores those questions whoch arise from viewing depreciation as the change over time in the value of an asset, on the one hand, and as an arbitrary allocation of past expenditure, on the other. For a discussion of these aspects, see the papers in section v below and also H. R. Hudson and Russell Mathews, 'An Aspect of Depreciation', *Economic Record*, xxxix, no. 86 (June 1963), pp. 232–6, and J. W. Bennet, J. McB. Grant and R. H. Parker, *Topics in Business and Accounting* (Melbourne, 1964), pp. 91–4.

As an example, assume that a company bought a machine on 1 January for £12,000. Only one significant price change occurred during the year: an increase of £600 (5 per cent of £12,000) on 1 June. Assuming straight-line depreciation and an estimated life of ten years (120 months) the historical depreciation will be £100 per month. Suppose also that the general price level had risen by 3 per cent over the first five months of the year. The entry to record the increase in the purchase price of the machine will be

		£
Machine	Dr.	600
Inflation adjustment	Cr.	345
Real holding Gain	Cr.	230
Accumulated depreciation	Cr.	25

The real holding gain is £12,000 (0·05 − 0·03) × 115/120 = £230. The written-down value of the machine at 1 June should be £12,600 less the accumulated depreciation based on the new purchase price

$$(5/120 \times £12,600 = £525).$$

Since only £500 has so far been credited to Accumulated depreciation account it is necessary to place there another £25. The credit to the Inflation adjustment account represents the fictitious element in the *net* monetary increase in the asset's market value, i.e.

$$0·03/0·05 \times £600 \times 115/120 = £345.$$

By the end of the year the balance in the Machine account will be £12,600 (its current replacement cost) and in the Accumulated depreciation account £1,260 (i.e. £500 credited in the first five months, plus the £25 credited on 1 June, plus £105 per month for seven months). The machine would thus be shown in the year-end balance sheet at its written-down current replacement cost of £11,340. The total depreciation expense of the year, however, will not be £1,260 but £1,235 (i.e. five months of £100, plus seven months of £105) representing the *average* current depreciation expense of the year. The balance of the Inflation adjustment account would remain at £345 and would be shown in the proprietorship section of the balance sheet. It is important to realize that it is merely an inflation adjustment and not in any way a source of funds for replacing the machine.

Some companies may prefer to make year-end adjustments only. These are inevitably more approximate. Current cost depreciation could for example be calculated as

$$\text{Accounting depreciation} \times \frac{\text{Average current replacement cost during the year}}{\text{Purchase price of asset.}}$$

35

Introduction to first edition

If average current replacement cost is interpreted as simply the arithmetic mean of the current replacement cost at the beginning and end of the year then current cost depreciation in our example would be

$$\pounds 1,200 \times \frac{\frac{1}{2}(12,600 + 12,000)}{12,000} = \pounds 1,230.$$

The only item of real income whose measurement in practice remains to be discussed is the holding gain or loss on monetary assets. If prices are rising this item will usually be negative. It is useful to distinguish between monetary assets with a market value, which we shall call *marketable securities*, and those without a market value which we shall call *net monetary claims*.*

Examples of marketable securities are quoted investments held by the firm. Each marketable security can be treated as if it were a fixed asset. A significant change in market value should be followed by a revaluation and appropriate transfers to the Inflation adjustment and Real holding gains (or losses) accounts.

Assume, for example, that on 1 March a company owns investments quoted on the stock exchange at £10,000. During the month this value rises to £10,500 (an increase of 5 per cent) and the general price level increases by 1 per cent. The following entry should be made:

		£
Investments	Dr.	500
Real holding gain	Cr.	400
Inflation adjustment	Cr.	100

The explanation of this entry is that the investments are written up to their new market value; a real holding gain of £400 is recorded; and a 'fictitious holding gain' of £100 is transferred to the Inflation adjustment account.

Net Monetary Claims Example

	General index	Unadjusted amount	Multiplier	Adjusted amount
Opening balance	120	£10,000	140/120	£11,667
Net change (+ or −)	130[a]	+2,000	140/130	2,154
Closing balance	140	£12,000		13,821
				12,000
			Loss	£1,821

[a] The average for the period, assumed to $(120 + 140)/2$.

Net monetary claims are those whose value apparently remains constant, e.g. cash, debtors and creditors. The loss or gain from holding these through

* Net of current liabilities such as trade creditors. We do not recommend the recognition of price-change gains or losses on *long-term* liabilities. See Gynther, *op. cit.* ch. 11.

36

a rise or fall in the general price level can be calculated (from a managerial point of view, preferably monthly) as in the example opposite. The loss would be debted to a loss on Holding net monetary claims account and credited to inflation adjustment account.

CURRENT OPERATING PROFIT AS TAX BASE

We have argued in the preceding sections that current operating profit is a more useful concept than accounting profit for reporting to managers shareholders. Is it also more suitable as a tax base?

It is a basic principle of the tax system of the United Kingdom (and we shall confine ourselves to the U.K. in the discussion that follows) that taxpayers should be taxed in accordance with their 'ability to pay'. The income of the taxpayers is regarded as the most objective measure of this ability. In order to achieve this the income of different classes of taxpayers should, as far as is practicable, be measured in a similar way. The taxable incomes of wage and salary earners, and of companies in insurance, banking and finance, are measured in current terms, but when accounting profit is the tax base and the prices of fixed assets and stocks are changing the taxable incomes of manufacturing companies and farmers are not so measured. On the grounds of comparability, therefore, current operating profit is more suitable than accounting profit as a tax base. The income of all classes of taxpayer would be measured in a similar way and the taxable incomes of manufacturing firms of the same technical nature and the same replacement costs would be the same. The present use of accounting profit as the base tends to favour new firms, firms which bought plant in periods of high prices and firms which spend more on repairs than replacement.

Because companies are not persons, we have deliberately argued below in terms of comparability rather than in terms of equity, which can only apply to persons—even though it is true that what is being taxed are incomes which are attributable to the owners of companies. Prior to the recent (1965) change to a corporation tax there was no capital gains tax in the United Kingdom, and distributed company profits were taxed for the period 1947–58 at a different rate from undistributed profits. The latest changes, however, include the introduction of a capital gains tax, a corporation tax on companies' incomes as such and taxation at the standard rate on distributed company incomes. Any consideration of equity, therefore, must concern the sizes of the rates of these various taxes as they apply to individuals, not the company tax base itself, which is the concern of the present discussion.

Introduction to first edition

What are the possible objections to current operating profit as tax base? If tax rates remained unchanged there would be a fall in the total amount of revenue collected which would have to be dealt with by an increase in the rate. The relative burden of tax on different companies would, of course, change. The conditions most favourable to a company paying *less* tax than previously are moderate increases in the prices of fixed assets and moderate stock appreciation in the country as a whole, combined with severe increases in the prices of fixed assets and severe stock appreciation for the company itself. In these circumstances the difference between taxable income before and after the change will be great and the increase in the rate of tax will be small. On the other hand, severe stock appreciation and severe increases in the prices of fixed assets generally, combined with moderate stock appreciation and moderate increases in the prices of fixed assets (or, worse still, stock *depreciation* and price falls) for the particular company would lead to considerably heavier tax payments than previously.*

A second possible objection is that firms lack the necessary data to adjust for the changing prices of fixed assets and stocks and that such adjustments would increase the scope for tax evasion. We have already discussed the practicality of adjustments in the previous section. It may be objected that more objective methods should be used for tax purposes. This could be achieved if official indexes of specific categories of fixed assets and stocks were published. A company would then receive normal statutory capital allowances based on original purchase costs as at present and additional allowances (which could be negative) for changes in the prices of specific assets since the dates when they were acquired. In effect, the company would be allowed on each fixed asset an historical cost capital allowance multiplied by an 'inflation factor' P_c/P_a where P_c is the current replacement cost of the asset and P_a the purchase price at the date of acquisition. In practice, these allowances might have to be restricted to assets acquired during the post-war period. The rates of capital allowances already exist; the indexes of prices of fixed assets probably exist also, as the Central Statistical Office publishes figures of annual capital consumption valued at current replacement cost which are presumably based on an index of this sort.† (Indexes for specific categories of fixed assets are also compiled by, and available from, the Economist Intelligence Unit.) The taxpayer and the Board of Inland Revenue could decide between them the categories to which fixed assets of the taxpayer belonged, and taxpayers could be re-

* The order of magnitude of these changes for the years 1950 and 1951 will be found in G. C. Harcourt, 'The quantitative effect of basing company taxation on replacement costs', *Accounting Research*, IX, no. 1 (January 1968), pp. 1–16.
† See, for example, *National Income and Expenditure* (1967).

quired to use the official indexes when calculating their allowances for changes in the prices of their fixed assets.

A third possible objection to the use of current operating profit as the tax base is that it would mean a departure from the consistent application of generally accepted accounting principles and involve the use of arbitrary and individual judgments. This objection is implied in the rejection of revaluation schemes by the Millard Tucker Committee and the Royal Commission on the Taxation of Profits and Income.* Current operating profit, however, differs from accounting profit only by the amount of the stock and depreciation adjustments already discussed and these can be calculated in an objective manner. The construction of the price indexes would require individual judgments, but not by taxpayers.

A fourth possible objection is that it would be impossible to make retrospective tax refunds or payments when the change in the tax base was introduced.† This is true, but it is irrelevant to considerations of equity and comparability between different classes of taxpayers in the future.

The Millard Tucker Committee objected to this and similar changes in the tax base because they would give preferential treatment to taxpayers who had to replace fixed assets and stocks. But a tax base of current operating profit would, on the contrary, restore comparability to these taxpayers. The same committee argued (by implication) that a tax base of current operating profit would not encourage firms which were, or could become, of importance to the national interest, e.g. new or expanding firms.‡ (A tax base of accounting profit does encourage these firms, relative to old-established ones, in that they pay relatively less tax.) This objection could be overcome by having a tax base of current operating profit and making cash investment grants at different rates to particular firms and for expenditure on particular types of assets. (This is, of course, the current government policy in the United Kingdom.)

It is of great interest to note that in most years since 1953—and especially since 1954 when investment allowances were first introduced—the aggregate taxable incomes of companies have been *less* than their total current operating profits. In Table 1 total allowances, both investment and other, to companies by the taxation authorities are compared with the total of stock appreciation and current-cost capital consumption for the period 1953–66. The table shows that stock appreciation has often been greater than the shortfall of historical-cost depreciation allowances compared with

---

* See *Report of the Committee on the Taxation of Trading Profits*, Cmd. 8189 (London, 1951), para. 115 and Cmd. 9474, para. 354.

† Cmd. 8189, para. 105; Cmd. 9474, para. 361.

‡ Cmd. 8189, para. 132.

TABLE I. *U.K. Companies 1953–66*

£m.

	1953	1954	1955	1956	1957	1958	1959	1960	1961	1962	1963	1964	1965	1966
Initial and investment allowances	104	147	205	227	269	347	400	476	539	544	652	778	764	318
Other allowances	303	364	420	500	569	625	675	737	813	907	1,104	1,298	1,390	1,252
(1) Total	407	521	625	727	838	972	1,075	1,213	1,352	1,451	1,756	2,076	2,154	1,570
Current-cost capital consumption	429	459	516	581	637	680	706	747	813	868	914	985	1,073	1,179
Stock appreciation	−44	53	119	159	141	−18	66	89	115	100	163	271	282	273
(2) Total	385	512	635	740	778	662	772	836	928	968	1,077	1,256	1,355	1,452
(1)−(2)	22	9	−10	−13	60	310	303	377	424	483	679	820	799	118

Source: National Income and Expenditure (1967), Tables 62, 71, p. 124 for 1956–66. Earlier editions for 1953–5.

TABLE 2. *U.K. Companies 1958–66*

| Difference between Taxable income and Current operating profit as percentage of Current operating profit | | | | | | | | |
1958	1959	1960	1961	1962	1963	1964	1965	1966
12	10	11	13	15	19	21	20	3

Taxable income: company income arising in the United Kingdom, less interest payments, initial, investment and other allowances.

Current operating profit: company income arising in the United Kingdom, less interest payments, stock appreciation and current-cost capital consumption.

Source: *National Income and Expenditure* (1967). Tables 30, 62, 71; p. 124.

current-cost capital consumption. For many companies, for example woollen and worsted manufacturers whose stocks form a large proportion of their total assets, it must be even more important.

It can be seen from the table that, with the exception of 1955 and 1956, total allowances exceeded stock appreciation and current-cost capital consumption combined. From 1958 to 1965 the allowances were, in fact, considerably greater; the annual average excess for 1958–65 is £524m. Since 1960 the aggregate historical-cost depreciation allowances have been greater than current-cost capital consumption. This is explained by the fact that depreciation allowances given by the Inland Revenue are mainly on a reducing-balance basis, while those in the estimates of current-cost capital consumption are on a straight-line basis adjusted by an inflation factor. If a capital stock is growing, historical-cost reducing-balance allowances exceed straight-line ones. Evidently the rate of growth of fixed assets in the company sector in the United Kingdom has been great enough to offset, through the reducing-balance effect, the effects of the mild rates of inflation of recent years.

The degree to which the aggregate current operating profits of U.K. companies have exceeded their aggregate taxable incomes is quite surprisingly large. The difference between the two as a percentage of current operating profit is shown for the years 1958–66 in Table 2. The astonishing figures of 19 per cent, 21 per cent and 20 per cent for the years 1963–5 reflect two changes in the 1963 Budget. The first is the increase in investment allowances on certain assets to 30 per cent; the second is the increase in annual allowances on plant and machinery to 15, 20 and 25 per cent, and on industrial buildings to 4 per cent. In the development areas up to 100 per cent write-offs were allowed in the first year for the period 4 April 1963 to 17 June 1966.

Introduction to first edition

We have argued in preceding sections that real income consists of current operating profit plus real holding gains accruing and that the former is a suitable base for taxation. Should real holding gains accruing also be taxed? It would seem that if we consider them part of income and think that comparability demands that the tax laws take account of changing price levels then they ought to be taxed. We do indeed think this but doubt whether the taxation of such gains as they *accrue* is administratively and politically practicable. To avoid taxing fictitious holding gains we suggest that a suitable *general* index published by the government be applied to the historical cost of the asset being taxed and that capital gains tax be charged only on the selling price less the adjusted historical cost. In other words (using our previous notation) the gain subject to tax would not be $N(1+r) - N = Nr$, but $N(1+r) - N(1+p) = N(r-p)$, where $N(1+r)$ is a *realized* market value. A system similar to this is in force in Belgium.*

* Confederation of British Industry, *Taxation in Western Europe* (London, 1967), pp. 47–8.

42

PART I

CONCEPTS OF INCOME IN ECONOMIC THEORY

1 Income and capital[1]

by Irving Fisher[*]

I. SUBJECTIVE, OR ENJOYMENT, INCOME

Income is a series of events.[2]

According to the modern theory of relativity the elementary reality is not matter, electricity, space, time, life or mind, but events.

For each individual only those events which come within the purview of his experience are of direct concern. It is these events—the psychic experiences of the individual mind—which constitute ultimate income for that individual. The outside events have significance for that individual only in so far as they are the means to these inner events of the mind. The human nervous system is, like a radio, a great receiving instrument. Our brains serve to transform into the stream of our psychic life those outside events which happen to us and stimulate our nervous system.

But the human body is not ordinarily regarded as an owned object, and only those events in consciousness traceable to owned objects other than the human body are generally admitted to be psychic income. However, the human machine still plays a role in so far as, through its purposeful

[*] Professor of Political Economy, Yale University, 1898–1935.

[1] The Nature of Capital and Income (first published in 1906) was primarily intended to serve as a foundation for The Rate of Interest which immediately followed it. It was my expectation that the student would read the former before reading the latter.

But now, for the convenience of those who do not wish to take the time to read The Nature of Capital and Income, I have written this first chapter summarizing it. I have availed myself of this opportunity to redistribute the emphasis and to make those amendments in statement which further study has indicated to be desirable.

A friendly critic, Professor John B. Canning, suggests that The Nature of Capital and Income should have been called 'The Nature of Income and Capital' and that the subject matter should have been presented in reverse order, inasmuch as income is the basis of the concept of capital value and is, in fact, the most fundamental concept in economic science.

While it might not be practicable to employ the reverse order in such a complete presentation as I aimed to make in The Nature of Capital and Income, I have, in this chapter, where brevity may justify some dogmatism, adopted Professor Canning's suggestions. This radical change in mode of presentation may induce some who have already read that book to review it now in the reverse order employed in this chapter. I hope also that some who have not read it may be moved, after reading this chapter, to read The Nature of Capital and Income in full. I have tried, in this chapter, to confine myself merely to those conclusions most essential as a preliminary for proceeding to the consideration of the origins, nature and determinants of the rate of interest.

[2] The first writer to employ the concept of events as fundamental in interest theory appears to have been John Rae, whose book, originally published in 1834, is commented on elsewhere.

activities, it produces or helps produce other owned objects which are material sources of desirable events—food, houses, tools, and other goods, which in their turn set in motion a chain of operations whose ultimate effect is registered in our stream of consciousness. The important consideration from this point of view is that human beings are ever striving to control the stream of their psychic life by appropriating and utilizing the materials and forces of Nature.

In Man's early history he had little command over his environment. He was largely at the mercy of natural forces—wind and lightning, rain and snow, heat and cold. But today Man protects himself from these by means of those contrivances called houses, clothing, and furnaces. He diverts the lightning by means of lightning rods. He increases his food supply by means of appropriated land, farm buildings, ploughs, and other implements. He then refashions the food by means of mills, grinding machinery, cooking stoves and other agencies, and by the labour of human bodies, including his own.

Neither these intermediate processes of creation and alteration nor the money transactions following them are of significance except as they are the necessary or helpful preliminaries to psychic income—human enjoyment. We must be careful lest, in fixing our eyes on such preliminaries. expecially money transactions, we overlook the much more important enjoyment which it is their business to yield.

Directors and managers providing income for thousands of people sometimes think of their corporation merely as a great money-making machine, In their eyes its one purpose is to earn money dividends for the stockholders, money interest for the bondholders, money wages and money salaries for the employees. What happens after these payments are made seems too private a matter to concern them. Yet that is the nub of the whole arrangement. It is only what we carry out of the market place into our homes and private lives which really counts. Money is of no use to us until it is spent. The ultimate wages are not paid in terms of money but in the enjoyments it buys. The dividend cheque becomes income in the ultimate sense only when we eat the food, wear the clothes, or ride in the automobile which are bought with the cheque.

2. OBJECTIVE, OR REAL, INCOME (OUR 'LIVING')

Enjoyment income is psychological entity and cannot be measured directly. We can approximate it indirectly, however, by going one step behind it to what is called real income. Real wages, and indeed real income in general, consist of those final physical events in the *outer* world which give us our *inner* enjoyments.

46

This real income includes the shelter of a house, the music of a victrola or radio, the use of clothes, the eating of food, the reading of the newspaper and all those other innumerable events by which we make the world about us contribute to our enjoyments, Metaphorically we sometimes refer to this, our real income, as our 'bread and butter'.

These finals in the stream of outer events are what we call our 'living', as implied in the phrases 'cost of living' and 'earning a living'. The final outer events and the inner events which they entail run closely parallel or, rather, the inner events generally follow closely in time on the outer. The enjoyment of music is felt almost instantaneously as the piano or singer produces it. The enjoyment of food is experienced with the eating or soon after the eating.

These outer events, such as the use of food or clothes, etc., are like the resultant inner events in not being very easily measured. They occur largely in the privacy of the home; they are often difficult to express in any standard units. They have no common denominator. Even the individual who experiences them cannot weigh and measure them directly. All he can do is to measure the money he paid to get them.

3. COST OF LIVING, A MEASURE OF REAL INCOME

So, just as we went behind an individual's enjoyment income to his real income, we now go behind his real income, or his living, to his *cost* of living, the money measure of real income. You cannot measure in dollars either the inner event of your enjoyment while eating your dinner or the outer event of eating it, but you can find out definitely how much money that dinner cost you. In the same way, you cannot measure your enjoyment at the cinema, but you do know what you paid for your ticket; you cannot measure exactly what your house shelter is really worth to you, but you can tell how much you pay for your rent, or what is a fair equivalent for your rent if you happen to live in your own house. You cannot measure what it is worth to wear an evening suit, but you can find out what it costs to hire one, or a fair equivalent of its hire if, perchance, the suit belongs to you. Deducing such equivalents is an accountant's job.

The total cost of living, in the sense of money payments, is a negative item, being outgo rather than income; but it is our best practical measure of the positive items of real income for which those payments are made. For from this total valuation of positive real income may be subtracted the total valuation of the person's labour pain during the same period, if we wish to compare a labourer's income with that of a man who does no labour but lives on his income from capital (other than himself), a *rentier*.

47

Enjoyment income, real income, and the cost of living are merely three different stages of income. All three run closely parallel to each other, although they are not exactly synchronous in time. These discrepancies, as has been intimated, are negligible as between real and enjoyment income. So also the time elapsing between the cost of living and the living is usually brief. There is a little delay between the spending of money at the box office and the seeing of the entertainment, or between paying board or rent and making use of the food or housing facilities. In many cases, the money payment follows rather than precedes the enjoyment.

4. COST OF AN ARTICLE *v.* COST OF ITS USE

The only time discrepancy worth careful noting is that which occurs when the money spent is not simply for the temporary use of some object but for the whole object, which means merely for all its possible future uses. If a house is not rented but bought, we do not count the purchase price as all spent for this year's shelter. We expect from it many more years of use. Hence out of the entire purchase price, we try to compute a fair portion of the purchase price to be charged up to this year's use. In like manner, the statisticians of cost of living should distribute by periods the cost of using a person's house furnishings, clothing, musical instruments, automobiles and other durable goods, and not charge the entire cost against the income of the year of purchase. To any given year should be charged only that year's upkeep and replacement, which measures, at least roughly, the services rendered by the goods in question during that particular year. The true real annual income from such goods is the equivalent approximately of the cost of the services given off by those goods each year.

Strictly speaking, then, in making up our income statistics, we should always calculate the value of *services*, and never the value of the objects rendering those services. It is true that, in the case of short-lived objects like food, we do not ordinarily need, in practice, to go to the trouble of distinguishing their total cost from the cost of their use. A loaf of bread is worth ten cents because its use is worth ten cents. We cannot rent food; we can only buy it outright. Yet there is some discrepancy in time in the case of foods that keep, such as flour, preserved foods and canned goods. These we may buy in one year but not use until a later year, and in such cases the money given for the food might almost be said to be invested rather than spent, like the money given for a house. A man who buys a basket of fruit and eats it within an hour is certainly spending his money for the enjoyment of eating the fruit. But, if he buys a barrel of apples in the fall to be eaten during the winter, is he spending his money or is he

48

investing it for a deferred enjoyment? Theoretically, the barrel of apples is an investment comparable to a house or any other durable good. Practically it is classed as expenditure, although it is a border-line case.

Spending and investing differ only in degree, depending on the length of time elapsing between the expenditure and the enjoyment. To spend is to pay money for enjoyments which come very soon. To invest is to pay money for enjoyments which are deferred to a later time. We spend money for our daily bread and butter or for a seat at the theatre, but we invest money in the purchase of bonds, farms, dwellings, or automobiles, or even of suits of clothes.

5. MEASURING AT THE DOMESTIC THRESHOLD

In practice, we can estimate with fair accuracy in all ordinary cases how much of what we pay is for this year's use. That is to say, we can find out pretty nearly our cost of living for the year. We need only reckon what is spent on personal articles and services—on everything which enters our dwellings (or enters us), food, drink, clothes, furniture, household rent, fuel and light, amusements, and so on, our 'bread and butter'—exclusive of what is left over for future years, such as what we pay for securities, machinery, or real estate, or what we put into the savings bank. The domestic threshold is, in general, a pretty good line of division. The cost of almost every object which crosses it measures a portion of our real income, and few other expenditures do.

Thus, at the end of production economics, or business economics, we find home economics. It is the housekeeper, the woman who spends, who takes the final steps through the cost of living toward getting the real income of the family, so that the family's enjoyment income may follow.

6. MONEY INCOME

We have just been dealing with money payments for consumption goods, or money *outgo*. We may now go back one further step to money received by the individual spender, or money income. Money income includes all money *received* which is not obviously, and in the nature of the case, to be devoted to reinvestment—or, as the expression is, 'earmarked' for reinvestment. In other words, all money received and readily available and intended to be used for spending is money income. It sometimes differs from real income considerably. For instance, if you more than 'earn your living' of $6,000 with a salary of $10,000, you voluntarily put by the $4,000 remaining as savings. This part of your money income is saved from being turned immediately into real income. That is, instead of

49

spending all your salary for this year's living you invest $4,000 of it to help toward the cost of living of future years. And so, the $4,000 is not only credited as income but debited as outgo. With it you buy durable objects such as land or buildings, or part rights in these, such as stocks or bonds. Your money income is in this case your salary (or it may be dividends, rent, interest, or profits) and it exceeds real income by the amount of your savings. On the other hand, you may be living beyond your (money) income. This means, expressed in terms of the concepts here used, that your real income for the year is greater than your money income.

That all one spends on his living measures real income, even when he 'lives byond his income' (beyond his *money* income), may be a hard saying to some who have never attempted to work out consistent definitions of economic concepts which will not only satisfy the requirements of economic theory but which will also bring these economic concepts into conformity with the theory and practice of accountancy. But a definition of income which satisfies both theory and practice, in both economics and accountancy, *must* reckon as income in the most basic sense all those uses, services, or living for which the cost of living is expended even though such expenditure may exceed the money income.

Thus we have a picture of three successive stages, or aspects, of a man's income:

Enjoyment or psychic income, consisting of agreeable sensations and experiences;

Real income *measured* by the cost of living;

Money income, consisting of the money received by a man for meeting his costs of living;

The last—money income—is most commonly called income; and the first—enjoyment income—is the most fundamental. But for accounting purposes real income, as measured by the cost of living, is the most practical.[1]

To recapitulate, we have seen that the enjoyment income is a psychological matter, and hence cannot be measured directly. So we look to real income instead; but even real income is a heterogeneous jumble. It includes quarts of milk, visits to the cinema, etc., and in that form cannot be measured easily or as a whole. Here is where the cost of living comes in. It is the practical, homogeneous[2] measure of real income. As the cost of living is expressed in

---

[1] Later in this chapter we shall see that these three sorts of income are all of a piece, parts of the entire economic fabric of services and disservices. Which of the three comes out of our accounting depends merely on which groups of these services and disservices are included in our summation.

[2] Even this is not homogeneous as a measure of subjective enjoyment; for a dollar to the poor and a dollar to the rich are not subjectively equal. See my 'A Statistical Method for Measuring "Marginal Utility" and Testing the Justice of a Progressive Income Tax', *Economic Essays contributed in honor of John Bates Clark*, pp. 157–93.

terms of dollars it may, therefore, be taken as our best measure of income *in place of* enjoyment income, or real income. Between it and real income there are no important discrepancies as there are between money income and real income. Money income practically never conforms exactly to real income because either savings raise money income above real income, or deficits push money income below real income.

7. CAPITAL VALUE

Savings bring us to the nature of capital. Capital, in the sense of capital *value*, is simply future income discounted or, in other words, capitalized. The value of any property, or rights to wealth, is its value *as a source of income* and is found by discounting that expected income. We may, if we choose, for logical convenience, include as property the ownership in ourselves, or we may, conformably to custom, regard human beings as in a separate category.

I define wealth as consisting of material objects owned by human beings (including, if you please, human beings themselves). The ownership may be divided and parcelled out among different individuals in the form of partnership rights, shares of stock, bonds, mortgages, and other forms of property rights. In whatever ways the ownership be distributed and symbolized in documents, the entire group of property rights are merely means to an end—income. Income is the alpha and omega of economics.

8. THE RATE OF INTEREST

The bridge or link between income and capital is the *rate of interest*. We may define the *rate of interest as the per cent of premium* paid on money at one date in terms of money to be in hand one year later. Theoretically, of course, we may substitute for money in this statement wheat or any other sort of goods. But practically, it is only money which is traded as between present and future. Hence, the rate of interest is sometimes called the price of money; and the market in which present and future money are traded for that price, or premium, is called the money market. If $100 today will exchange for $105 to be received one year hence, the premium on present money in terms of future money is $5 and this, as a percentage of the $100, or the rate of interest, is five per cent. That is to say, the price of today's money in terms of next year's money is five per cent above par. It should always be remembered *that interest and the rate of interest are not identical*. Interest is computed by multiplying capital value by the rate of interest.

Irving Fisher

The aim of this book is to who show the *rate* of interest is caused or determined. Some writers have chosen, for purposes of exposition, to postulate two questions involved in the theory of the rate of interest, namely (1) why any rate of interest exists and (2) how the rate of interest is determined. This second question, however, embraces also the first, since to explain how the rate of interest is determined involves the question of whether the rate can or cannot be zero, i.e. whether a positive rate of interest must necessarily exist.

9. DISCOUNTING IS FUNDAMENTAL

But although the rate of interest may be used either way—for computing from present to future values, or from future to present values—the latter process (discounting) is by far the more important of the two. Accountants, of course, are constantly computing in both directions; for they have to deal with both sets of problems. But the basic problem of time valuation which Nature sets us is always that of translating the future into the present, that is, the problem of ascertaining the capital value of future income. The value of capital must be computed from the value of its estimated future net income, not vice versa.

This statement may at first seem puzzling, for we usually think of causes and effects as running forward not backward in time. It would seem then that income must be derived from capital; and, in a sense, this is true. Income *is* derived from capital *goods*. But the *value* of the income is not derived from the *value* of the capital goods. On the contrary, the value of the capital is derived from the value of the income. Valuation is a human process in which foresight enters. Coming events cast their shadows before. Our valuations are always anticipations.

These relations are shown in the following scheme in which the arrows represent the order of sequence—(1) from capital goods to their future services, that is, income; (2) from these services to their value; and (3) from their value back to capital value:

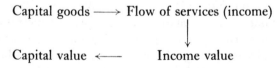

Not until we know how much income an item of capital will probably bring us can we set any valuation on that capital at all. It is true that the wheat crop depends on the land which yields it. But the value of the crop does not depend on the value of the land. On the contrary, the value of the land depends on the expected value of its crops.

The present worth of any article is what buyers are willing to give for it and sellers are ready to take for it. In order that each man may logically decide what he is willing to give or take, he must have: (1) some idea of the value of the future benefits which that article will yield, and (2) some idea of the rate of interest by which these future values may be translated into present values by discounting.

10. COSTS, OR NEGATIVE INCOME

Cost of production of durable agents or capital goods has its influence included in the preceding formulation, since any cost is simply a negative item of income. Future negative items are to be discounted exactly as future positive items. It is to be remembered that at the given point of time when the value is being computed only *future* costs can enter into the valuation of any good. Past costs have no *direct* influence on value. Only indirectly do they enter to the extent that they have determined the existing supply of goods and have thus either raised or lowered the value of the services of these goods.

In this indirect way, past costs can determine present values temporarily and until the prices of goods available are brought into conformity with the present costs of production through the operation of supply and demand. For example, the cost of producing woollen cloth declined very sharply after the close of the [First] World War, but the price did not decline for many months because the new cloth made at less expense was not sufficient to meet the demand, hence the price remained above the new costs of production for a time. Again, the cost of making shoes advanced rapidly during the early years of the twentieth century, but the price of shoes did not advance *pari passu* with increased costs, because the supply of more cheaply made shoes was still large and for a time controlled the market price. In the same indirect way, many other influences affect the value of the services of any good, especially any alternative to those services. But none of these considerations affects the principle that the value of the good itself is the discounted value of the value (however determined) of its future services.

11. THE DISCOUNT PRINCIPLE APPLIED

The principles which have been explained for obtaining the present value of a future sum apply very definitely to many commercial transactions, such as to the valuation of bank assets, which indeed exist largely in the form of discount paper, or short time loans of some other kinds. The value of a note is always the discounted value of the future payment to which it entitles the holder.

Elaborate mathematical tables have been calculated and are used by brokers for informing their customers what price should be paid for a five per cent bond in order that the purchaser may realize 5 per cent, 4 per cent, or any other rate of interest on the prices to be paid. The price of the bond is calculated from two items, the rate of interest to be realized and the series of sums or other benefits which the bond is going to return to the investor. Aside from risk, there can never be any other factors in the calculation except these two. Of course, an investor may refuse to buy a bond at the market price because he has, as an alternative, the opportunity to buy another bond cheaper so that he can realize a higher rate on his purchase price. But that fact does not alter the principle that market prices represent discounted benefits. The only market effect of this man's refusal will be a slight tendency to lower the market price of the first bond and raise that of its rival, that is, to alter the rate of interest realized. Later we shall study more fully the effects of such alternative opportunities. Here we are concerned only to note that the price of the bond is dependent solely on two factors: (1) its benefits and (2) the interest rate by which these are discounted.

The principle is, of course, not confined to bonds. It applies in any market to all property and wealth—stocks, land (which has a discounted capital value just as truly as any other capital), buildings, machinery, or anything whatsoever. Risk aside, each has a market value dependent solely on the same two factors, the benefits,[1] or returns, expected by the investor and the market rate of interest by which those benefits are discounted.

The income which he expects may be a perpetual income (flowing uniformly or in recurring cycles) or it may be any one of innumerable other types. If we assume that five per cent is the rate of interest, any one of the following income streams will have a present value of $1,000: a perpetual annuity of $50 per year; or an annuity of $50 a year for ten

---

[1] Including, of course, all benefits or services whatever from the possession of the wealth such as the option to subscribe to stock, now often attached to bonds, or the privilege attaching to certain bonds which permits National Banks to use the bonds for the security of National Bank notes. Some of these benefits may be very indirect and related to whole groups. A man seeking voting control as a benefit who already possesses 49 per cent may pay a specially high price for a few more shares of stock for the benefit of raising his holdings to 51 per cent. Or, a man may include in the benefits of his wealth the fun of running the business, or the social standing he thinks it gives him, or political or other power and influence, or the mere miserly sense of possession or the satisfaction in the mere process of further accumulation. However indirect, unusual, or bizarre the benefit, the principle still holds that the value of any capital good or goods is derived solely from the prospect of future benefits.

years, together with $1,000 at the end of the period; or $100 a year for fourteen years, after which nothing at all; of $25 a year for ten years, followed by $187.50 a year for ten years, after which nothing at all.

12. DOUBLE-ENTRY BOOKKEEPING

We began this chapter with the enjoyment income received by a person and then travelled back, by way of real income, cost of living, and money income to capital value, which simply embodies the capitalization or anticipation of income. This was going upstream, as it were, from the enjoyer of income to its source. We may now reverse our point of view and look downstream. We then think of the income stream not so much as flowing *to* its enjoyers as flowing *from* its various sources.[1]

Capital value is income capitalized and nothing else. Income flows from, or is produced by, capital goods and human beings, so that the capital value is also the value of capital goods. The income is credited to (and outgo or cost debited to) these goods and (or including) human beings.

As every bookkeeper knows, most of the items of income (positive or negative) take the form of *money payments*. (These are not a *stock* of money, which is always capital, but a *flow* of money.) Some are operations paid for—events in the productive process, such as grinding, spinning, weaving, hoisting, hauling, ploughing; others are events of consumption, such as eating food, wearing clothes, hearing music, or seeing a play at the theatre; while still others are within the human mind, such as enjoyments or their opposite, labour effort or discomfort.

It might seem that in sorting and combining such a miscellany of income items we could never avoid confusion and double counting and that the sum total would far exceed the true psychic or enjoyment income. But the fact is that almost as many negative items as positive items are included here and that, *in fact, except for enjoyment income and labour pain,*

---

[1] Possibly it would help to adjust our mental attitudes to this changed point of view if we could change the name of income to outcome, or output. Income suggests coming *toward us* while outcome suggests coming *from the source*. Thus the outcome from a farm is the net value of its crops; the outcome from a railway company is its dividends, etc.

Under this new procedure, we credit each item of income as outcome from its source and debit every negative item. Negative items of income are outgo. If we could change this name also, we would call it ingo, or input.

It is a mere clerical matter of bookkeeping thus to credit to its source every service rendered as so much outcome (or income) and debit it with every disservice rendered, as so much ingo (or outgo).

Having suggested these new terms, however, so that the student may mentally, or literally by lead pencil, substitute them for the old, I shall hereafter, for simplicity, adhere uniformly to the original terminology, using the term income even when we are thinking merely of its coming *from its capital source* while the recipient is forgotten.

55

every positive item is also negative, according to its relation to the capital source. Thus when Smith pays Jones $100 (no matter where it came from), Jones receives an item of income of $100 while Smith suffers an item of outgo of the same amount; and when a coupon of $100 is cut from a bond and deposited, the bond is credited with yielding $100 and the bank account is debited with the same sum. The same principle is applicable to the final big coupon called the principal of the bond. The same item is thus entered twice, once on one side of somebody's books and the other time on the other side of somebody's books.

The bookkeeping implications of such couples of items were discovered by accountants long ago and are the basis of their double-entry bookkeeping, though its economic significance has been largely overlooked. One important significance is that this double entry prevents double counting; when we take the sum total of all income items for society, including psychic as well as physical items, this double entry results in cancelling out everything except the psychic items of enjoyment and labour pain.

Every operation of production, transportation, exchange, or consumption—every process, in fact, except final enjoyment—is double faced, or two items in one. I have called such an operation an 'interaction' because it is income to be credited to the capital which yields it, while it is outgo to be debited to the capital which receives it. Thus, in any complete bookkeeping, $100 worth of ploughing, on the one hand, is credited jointly to the plough, the ploughman, and the team, or motor, which do the ploughing; that is, which yield or bestow the service. On the other hand, it is debited to the land which is ploughed, that is, which receives the service.

If the plough is owned by one person and the land by another, the latter paying $100 to the former, then the service of ploughing, though a self-cancelling interaction for the two persons taken together, evidently cannot be ignored by either separately. If $100 is paid for this service of ploughing, the $100 item is an expense to the landowner to be subtracted from his gross income. It is no concern of his that this selfsame service of ploughing is counted as income by the plough-owner. So this item of $100 worth of ploughing affects our accounts quite differently according to the point of view. It may be a plus item from the point of view of one person and a minus item from that of another. When, however, the two accounts are combined and the plus and minus items are added, their algebraic sum is zero. For society as a whole, therefore, no postitive income results from ploughing until the land has yielded its crop and the crop has been finally consumed.

Thus, simply by the mechanical, clerical processes of making bookkeepers' entries, we reach again, in the opposite order, the various stages originally described in the opening pages of this chapter. That is, the sum total of income flowing from a group of capital sources is naturally different according to which capital sources are included. There are certain cancellations within any group of capital goods which have an uncancelled fringe, and this may itself in turn disappear by cancellation if the group is enlarged by including other capital items with interactions between the new and old members. Henry Ford's mines yield a net income, the difference between certain credits and debits. If we include the railway which transports the product to the factory, certain credits to the mines from turning their product over to the railroad now disappear, being debits to the railway. If the circle be still further enlarged, say to include the Ford factories, other items likewise disappear as parts of interactions withing the enlarged circle, and so on.

We must of course, include all services as income. A dwelling renders income to the owner who dwells in it himself just as truly as when he lets it to another. In the first case, his income is shelter; in the second, his income is rent payments in money. All wealth existing at any moment is capital and yields income in some form. As a business man said to me, his pleasure yacht is capital and gives him dividends every Saturday afternoon.

13. SIMPLICITY UNDERLYING COMPLICATIONS

In our present-day complicated economic life we are likely to be confused by the many industrial operations and money transactions. But net income still remains exactly what it was to primitive Robinson Crusoe on his island—the enjoyment from eating the berries we pick, so to speak, less the discomfort or the labour of picking them. The only difference is that today the picking is not so entirely hand-to-mouth, but is done by means of complicated apparatus and after the frequent exchange of money; that is, a long chain of middlemen, capital, and money transactions intervenes between the labour of picking at the start and the satisfaction of eating at the end. To continue the literal example of berry picking, we find today huckleberries picked by hired labourers on the Pocono Mountains, sorted, graded, shipped by rail and motor to New York City wholesalers, resold to retailers who sell and deliver them to the housewife in whose kitchen they are again sorted and prepared for their ultimate mission of giving enjoyment. The individual's total income when elaborately worked out, after cancelling, in pairs or couples, all such credits and debits, whether of money payments or the money value of services—in production or exchange—coincides necessarily with his enjoyment income, less the labour pain suffered in the same period, from which sort of income we started

57

our discussion in this chapter. This coincidence occurs necessarily and automatically, by virtue of these mathematical cancellations.

It is interesting to observe that a corporation as such can have no net income. Since a corporation is a fictitious, not a real, person, each of its items without exception is doubly entered. Its stockholders may get income from it, but the corporation itself, considered as a separate person apart from these stockholders, receives none.

The *total income* of a real person is his *enjoyment income* only provided we include the credits and debits of his own body. The physical music, or vibrations which pass from his piano to his ear are, strictly speaking, only interactions to be credited to his piano and debited to his bodily ear. The music in his consciousness comes at the other, or brain, end of the auditory nerve. The piano plays to his ear, his ear to his brain, and his brain to his consciousness. His whole body mechanism is a transmitter from the outer world to his inner life, through ear, eye, and its other sense organs.

Or if the body mechanism, with its debits and credits, be omitted the total result is not his enjoyment income, subjectively considered, but the real income as above set forth. If we measure this, his real income, in money units, we find it equal to the total valuation of his cost of living less the total valuation of his own labour pain.

How to place a money valuation on a labour pain is a difficult question. This question is important in accounting theory, especially in its relation to the problems of measuring human welfare. But fortunately for us the difficulties of this valuation do not disturb the theory of the rate of interest, since this theory is actually concerned only with *differences* in the income stream at different times, not in a meticulous measurement of the *total*. Moreover, practically the only point in interest theory where labour pain enters is the case of a worker who suffers present labour pain in order to secure future satisfactions for himself or his family. This case is that of a labourer's savings; and all we need do here is to take the labourer's own valuation. Presumably, if the rate of interest is 5 per cent, the labour he will exert this year for the sake of $100 next year has a valuation in his mind of about $95.

But a labourer's savings are practically a negligible element in determining the rate of interest. To others than labourers the only important way labour enters is through the payment of wages and salaries, and these are money expenses incurred for the sake of future money returns. A labourer building a railway does not work for the future dividends from the railway. He is paid for immediate living by his employer in expectation of those future dividends. Thus wages are a sort of measure of labour pain to the employer of labour, whether or not they be so regarded by the labourer.[1]

If we exclude labour pain and further exclude from the labourer's book-keeping the income items, positive and negative, flowing from his household effects—the use of furniture, clothing, food, and so on—the total income then turns out to be not his real income *but his money income*—assuming that, as is ordinarily true, all his income flows in through money payments and none in kind.

14. CAPITAL GAIN NOT INCOME

The most interesting and valuable result of applying these bookkeeping principles is that thereby we automatically separate capital from income, two things which are so often confused and in so many ways. It is not uncommon for economic students to make the mistake of including capital gains as income. Capital gains, as already implied, are merely capitalization of future income. They are never present income. Therefore a true meticulous accounting, item by item, of the income, or of the services and disservices, rendered by any specified group of capital items will infallibly grind out this truth. It will never confuse capital gain in that capital group with income realized from that group. This is true whether our capital group and its income are so extended as to include enjoyment income (positive and negative) as the final net income, or whether our specific group is so restricted as to leave ploughing or money payments as the uncancelled fringe.[2] We shall always find that only the income actually detached from, or given off for enjoyment by, that group, as in cutting coupons from a bond, will result from the summation of the accountant, who will never record as income the increase or decrease in the capital itself.

A bond price, for example, will grow with accrued interest *between* two coupon cuttings. That growth in its value is not income but increase of capital. Only when the coupon is detached does the bond render, or give off, a service, and so yield income. The income consists in the event of such off-giving, the yielding or separation, to use the language of the United States Supreme Court. If the coupon thus given off is reinvested in another bond, that event is outgo, and offsets the simultaneous income realized from the first bond. There is then *no* net income from the group but only growth of capital. If the final large payment of the principal is commonly

---

[1] They may be so regarded in cases where labour is paid by the piece and the labourer is free to stop work at any point.
[2] See *The Nature of Capital and Income*, chapters VII–X.

thought of not as income (which it is if not reinvested) but as capital it is because it is usually and normally so reinvested.

Likewise, if my savings bank account gains by compound interest, there is no income but only an accretion of capital. If we adopt the fiction that the bank teller hands over that accretion at any moment to me through his window, we must also adopt the fiction that it is simultaneously handed back by me through the same window. If the first event is income, the second is outgo. If it passes both ways, or does not pass at all, there can be no net income resulting. This is good bookkeeping and sound economics. There is no escape from such mathematical conclusions. By no hocus pocus can we have our cake and eat it too. This is as impossible as perpetual motion, and fundamentally as absurd. The absurdity is especially evident when the cause of an increase or decrease in the capital value of a bond or investment is not due to any change in the expected income at all but comes through a change in the *rate of interest*. Consols and *rentes* fluctuate in value every day with every change in the money market. Yet the income they actually yield flows on at the same rate. Merely the capital value is found sometimes on a 3 per cent basis and sometimes on a 4 per cent basis. A rise in the market is a capital gain, but it is not income. Income may be *invested* and thus transformed into capital; or capital may be *spent* and so transformed into income. In the first case, as we have seen, capital accumulates; in the second case, capital is diminished. In the first case the man is living inside his money income; in the second case he is living beyond his money income.

If Henry Ford receives $100,000,000 in dividends but reinvests all but $50,000, then his real income is only $50,000,[1] even if his money income is $100,000,000. And if, during the year of rebuilding his factories to make his new car, he received no dividends and yet spent $40,000 in that year for living expenses and all other satisfactions, then his *real* income was this $40,000 even if his money income that year was zero.

Thus the income enjoyed in any year is radically different from the ups and downs of one's capital value in that year—whether this is caused by savings or the opposite, or by changes in the rate of interest or by so-called chance.

We may in our bookkeeping add our savings to our real income and call the sum total gain. For my part, I prefer not to call it income. For the two parts of this total—enjoyed income and accumulation of capital or capitalized future enjoyments—are unlike. The only argument for adding

---

[1] Except as already stated in a previous footnote, he derives in addition to this obvious income other less tangible and more subtle income from the sense of possession, prestige, power, etc., which go with great wealth.

them together is that the recipient *could* use the savings as income and still keep his capital unchanged. Yes, he *could*, but he didn't, otherwise there would be no savings! One part is income, and the other is capital gain.

This distinction between the real income, actually enjoyed, and the accretion or accrual of capital value, that is, the capitalization of future enjoyments, is not only in general vital, but vital to the understanding of this book.[1]

We cannot understand the theory of interest so long as we play fast and loose with the concepts of capital and income. And enjoyment income, which plays the central role in interest theory, is never savings or increase of capital.

15. CAPITAL-INCOME RELATIONS

In conclusion we may say that the chief relations between capital and income are:

(1) Capital value is income capitalized or discounted.

(2) If the rate of interest falls, the capital value (capitalized value of expected income) rises, and vice versa.

(3) This rise or fall in capital value is relatively great for durable goods like land, and relatively small for transitory goods like clothes.

(4) Capital value is increased by savings, the income being decreased by the same amount that the capital is increased.

(5) These savings thus diverted from income and turned back into capital will, except for mischance, be the basis for real income later.

16. APPLICATION TO THIS BOOK

The problem of the rate of interest is entirely a problem of spending and investing, of deciding between various possible enjoyments constituting income, especially between relatively small but immediate enjoyments and relatively large but deferred enjoyments. There is an eternal conflict between the impulse to spend and the impulse to invest. The impulse of a man to spend is caused by his impatience to get enjoyments without delay, and his impulse to invest is caused by the opportunities to obtain by delay relatively more enjoyment either for himself or others.

For the study of interest from this point of view we need as our chief

[1] For fuller treatment of this subject the reader is referred to: 'The Nature of Capital and Income; Are Savings Income?' *Journal of American Economic Association*, third series, IX, no. I, 1–27; *The Income Concept in the Light of Experience*, privately printed as English translation of article in vol. III of the Wieser Festschrift, *Die Wirtschaftstheorie der Gegenwart* (Vienna, 1927), 29 pp.

subject matter a picture of a person's income stream. We may get this most clearly by plotting day by day, month by month, or year by year, the closest statistical measure of one's real income, namely, one's cost of living.

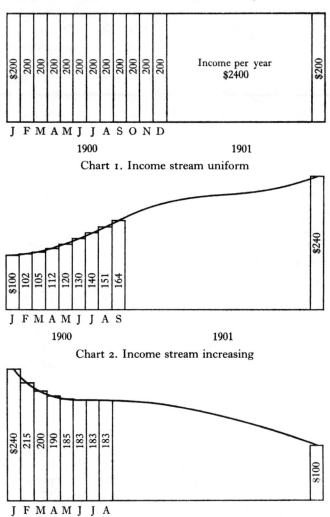

Chart 1. Income stream uniform

Chart 2. Income stream increasing

Chart 3. Income stream decreasing

If this income flows at a constant rate of $200 a month or $2400 a year, the picture of the income stream is as shown in Chart 1.

If the income stream flows at an increasing rate, the picture is as shown in Chart 2.

62

If it flows at a decreasing rate, the picture is as in Chart 3.[1]

Of course, these particular forms are only special types; numerous other types might be given.

In interest theory the income with which we deal are not statistical records of the past but those of the expected future. What is to be one's future income stream, chosen from among several income streams available, becomes of supreme importance.

17. CONFUSIONS TO BE AVOIDED

The very first effort of the beginner in this subject should be to rid his mind of all prepossessions as to the nature of income and capital. My grandchild of six recently asked the cashier of a savings bank, 'Show me the money I am going to get when I grow up'. The cashier gravely took him into a back room and held up a bag of coins. The vision of that bagful will doubtless persist into adult life as a picture of a savings bank account, even after he has learned in college that the total deposits of a bank far exceed the cash on hand, and that the depositor's capital is not actual cash but the right, measured in terms of cash, to the services or benefits flowing from the bank's assets, real estate, mortgages on real estate, stocks and bonds, and all the rest of its resources. Both capital and income *seem* to be simply money. We can always show a money sample, as did the cashier, and where one's capital is liquid so that it may readily be turned from one form to another via money—or rather credit—it is most simply and lazily pictured to the mind's eye as being itself money.

The student should also try to forget all former notions concerning the so-called supply and demand of capital as the causes of interest. Since capital is merely the translation of future expected income into present cash value, whatever supply and demand we have to deal with are rather the supply and demand of future income.

It will further help the student if he will, from the outset, divest himself of any preconception he may have acquired as to the role of the rate of interest in the distribution of income. It may be as well here to point out that interest is not, as traditional doctrine would have it, a separate branch of income in addition to rent, wages and profits.

[1] In all three examples, each month's income is represented by a rectangular column or bar. In the last two cases, the resultant row of bars makes a series of flat tops or steps. But by taking days instead of months, we come nearer to a sloping curve which is a better and simpler ideal picture. Hereafter we shall use such continuous curves. But they may always be thought of as made up approximately of a series of columns or bars. For fuller discussion of such charts, see *The Nature of Capital and Income*, pp. 204 ff.

Irving Fisher

The income stream is the most fundamental fact of economic life. It is the joint product of many agencies which may be classified under many heads, such as human beings, land, and (other) capital. The hire of human beings is wages; the hire of land is land rent. What, then, is the hire of (other) capital—houses, pianos, typewriters, and so forth? Is it interest? Certainly not. Their hire is obviously house rent, piano rent, typewriter rent, and so forth, just as the man in the street calls them. Rent is the ratio of the payment to the physical object—land, houses, pianos, typewriters, and so forth—so many dollars per piano, per acre, per room. Interest, on the other hand, is the ratio of payment to the money *value* of these things— so many dollars per hundred dollars (or per cent). It is, in each case, the ratio of the net rent to the capitalized value of that rent. It applies to all the categories—to land quite as truly as to houses, pianos, typewriters. The income from land is thus both rent and interest just as truly as the income from a typewriter or a bond. We can and do capitalize land rent just as truly as we do house rent. For example, land worth '20 years purchase' yields 5 per cent interest. All this is true quite irrespective of the question of distinctions between land rent, on the one hand, and house rent, piano rent, typewriter rent, and so forth on the other.[1] It is a question of that sort of price which links one point of time with another point of time in the markets of the world. And it is a question concerning every branch of economic theory in which the time element enters. The rate of interest is the most pervasive price in the whole price structure.

As to profits, I believe the most fruitful concept is also that of the man in the street. When risk attaches to any one of the aforementioned forms of capital—human beings, land, houses, pianos, typewriters and so forth— the man in the street calls the net income profits. And profits, likewise, may be measured either (as rent) in relation to the physical units producing them, or (as interest) in relation to the values of these profits; that is, either as dollars per acre, per room, per piano and so forth; or dollars per $100 worth of land (houses, pianos, and so forth); or as dollars per share of ownership in any of these; or dollars per $100 worth of such shares. To pretend that either interest or profits is the income solely from capital goods other than land and that these two concepts are inapplicable to land—to pretend, in short, that wages, rent, interest and profits are four mutually *exclusive* divisions of the income stream of society is to treat different classifications of one thing as if they were themselves different

[1] *See* Frank A. Fetter, 'Interest Theories Old and New', *American Economic Review* (March 1914), pp. 76 and 77; Fetter, *Principles of Economics*, pp. 122-7; H. J. Davenport 'Interest Theory and Theories', *American Economic Review* (December 1927), pp. 636, 639.

things. It is as if we should speak of a certain total space as consisting partly of acres of land, partly of tons of soil, and partly of bushels of ore. Or again, it is like classifying a pack of cards into aces, clubs and red suits and pretending that these three classes are mutually exclusive.

The simple fact is that any or all income may be capitalized, including that credited to human beings, thus giving the resultant economic value of a man. William Farr, J. Shield Nicholson, Louis I. Dublin and others have made such computations.[1] However, we so seldom capitalize wages that we have no practical need to call wages or any portion of them interest. Nor where risk is a dominant factor, as in profits, is there real need to call the income interest. For instance, hoped-for dividends, according as the hope varies, are daily and automatically capitalized in the stock market and need not themselves be called interest. Much less would it be worth while to call enterpriser's profits interest. No one ever attempted to capitalize them. But in meticulous theory, all may be capitalized and so become interest.

18. A WORKING CONCEPT OF THE RATE OF INTEREST

While any exact and practical definition of a pure rate of interest is impossible, we may say roughly that the pure rate is the rate on loans which are practically devoid of chance. In particular, there are two chances which should thus be eliminated. One tends to raise the rate, namely, the chance of default. The other tends to lower it, namely, the chance to use the security as a substitute for ready cash. In short, we thus rule out, on the one hand, all risky loans and, on the other, all bank deposits subject to withdrawal on demand, even if accorded some interest. We have left safe securities of fixed terms not likely to be transferred or transferred often before maturity. Such securities give us the nearest approach to pure interest both for short and long periods according to the time to maturity.

In this book, I shall usually confine the concept of the rate of interest to the rate in a (humanly speaking) safe loan, or other contract implying specific sums payable at one date or set of dates in consideration of repayment at another date or set of dates. The essentials in this concept are (1) definite and assured payments, and (2) definite and assured repayments, and (3) definite dates. The concept includes the concept of the rate realized on a safe security such as a bond purchased in the market. It is this that concerns us in this book. We are not primarily concerned with *total* interest, but with the *rate* of interest.

[1] For instance, Dr Dublin computes the total value of the 'human capital' of the United States to be 1,500 billion dollars, or about five times the value of all other capital.

2 The economics of accountancy

by Irving Fisher*

This book is neither a manual for the bookkeeper, nor a purely theoretical work on accountancy. It is best described as an exposition of accountancy theory in harmony with sound economic theory. The theme centres on *income*, which the author regards as the all-important concept in both economics and accountancy. The problem of the accountant is to value the inflows and outflows of payments incident to business enterprises.

Accountants take cognizance of the costs of durable instruments chiefly or solely as a means of evaluating the future services which these instruments may render. When the capacity of a capital good to render further services melts away, its value melts away no matter what its original cost. Accounting should be made, not solely for the benefit of the management, but for the benefit of individual shareholders and of the public who are potential investors in the corporation and purchasers of the services it renders.

The book points the way to a sounder science of economics and a better theory and practice of accountacy.

It would not seem an exaggeration to say that *The Economics of Accountancy: A Critical Analysis of Accounting Theory*,[1] by John B. Canning marks an epoch in the two branches of knowledge to which it relates—economics and accountancy—and none the less because it is a border-line study rather than strictly within the domain of either branch. It has come to be recognized as a good sign when any two sciences begin to encroach on each other so that the twilight zone becomes a new field for study. We all know that a new impulse was given to physics and chemistry when the traditional fence separating them was thrown down, and the new science of physico-chemistry established.

There is a fundamental reason why such studies as Canning's must be of value to economics. Any quantitative economic concept, to be of any use, should be capable of actual measurement. Accounts represent primarily those measures of business which are practical. They apply to business the acid test of practical workability—a test which might have saved much useless labour and disputation in economic literature. The 'wage fund' theory, for instance, could scarcely have been proposed in an atmosphere of actual accounts. No one ever has or ever could set up an account of a wage fund. And if he could set it up in a capital

* Professor of Political Economy, Yale University, 1898–1935.

[1] Published by Ronald Press, 1929. Reviewed in *American Economic Review*, March, 1930, p. 112.

account, he would see the inherent impossibility of transmuting it into wages in the income account. So also we might have been spared the wearisome discussions of the supposed important distinction between productive and unproductive labour. The illusory 'wage fund' concept and the illusory 'unproductive labour' concept each died a natural death, slowly and unobtrusively. Professor Canning's book will hasten the inevitable and unobtrusive death of many illusory concepts of capital and income such as the once popular formula, 'capital is wealth used to produce more wealth,' which is fully as futile as the notion of 'productive labour' (as distinct from 'unproductive labour') to which it is analogous.

Professor Canning keeps his feet on the ground. His work shows a painstaking effort to deal with many baffling problems of practice and theory. The book is not a manual for the bookkeeper nor is it primarily a purely theoretical study. It may perhaps best be described as an exposition of accounting procedure in harmony with sound economic theory. The author avoids, for the most part, inferences as to the intentions of accountants in their various procedures; for what accountants' intentions may have been must always be a matter of conjecture. Instead, he studies the statistical effects of these procedures and points out their economic significance. He complains that too little attention has been given to accounting in the colleges. Only in the last two decades have the university curricula given courses in accounting from the economic point of view, despite the fact that the practice of bookkeeping is centuries old.

The central theme of the work is the concept of *income*, which conforms to that which I have found essential in my own studies, namely, a series of services rendered. The author repeatedly calls attention to the importance of this income-concept, and criticises me for not emphasizing it enough. He says:

In a late article Fisher says: 'I believe that the concept of income is, without exception, the most vital central concept in economic science and that on fully grasping its nature and interrelations with other concepts largely depends the full fruition both of economic theory and of its applications to taxation and statistics.' If he had written instead that *income is, without exception, the simplest and most fundamental concept of economic science, that only by means of this concept can other economic concepts ever be fully developed and understood, and that upon beginning with this concept depends the full fruition of economic theory in economic statistics*, it would have been an equally true and a more significant statement (p. 175). (The italics are Canning's.)

Income may not consist entirely of money income, and even money income is not literally money.

Note that it is the *fruition* in money—not the money-fruit—that is gross income. When a grocer makes a cash sale, the money he receives is an asset—not income. It is the *bringing in* that is income, it is this *last conversion* in a long chain of events,

67

i.e., of establishing a place of business, of equipping the sales-rooms, of acquiring stock in trade, of preparing the wares for exhibit and delivery, and so on, that constitutes gross income. Many objects and persons within the establishment will have rendered non-monetary though valuable services to the grocer that are necessary antecedents to this final service of the object sold. It is this final service only, this service of bringing in money, that counts as income. To the extent that these antecedent services are applicable to future sales, future bringings-in of money, the grocer has assets—not income. In a 'cash' business the income cycle and the operation cycle are co-terminous. The cycle begins with money passing from the proprietor; it ends with the receipt of money that cannot be recovered by the person paying it (pp. 101–102). (Compare my *Nature of Capital and Income*, Part II.)

In an ordinary modern enterprise, the author points out, the whole problem of services is that of bringing in or paying out money and, since this money flows irregularly, the valuation of these flows fairly allocated to short periods can never be given any exact meaning. The accounting for all gains and losses can never be given completely and accurately until the business is wound up. For any interval between the date of founding, or first putting in of money, and the date of winding-up, or last taking out of money, only estimates or appraisals are possible. These intermediate year-by-year or month-by-month accounts can be only reports of progress. The income and outgo for a given week cannot consist merely of the money transactions which happen to occur within that particular week. There may be none; or there may be a whole quarter's disbursements. We must obviously include only the pro rata share for that week of any big items within it as well as the pro rata share of big items occurring before and after that week. It is this pro-rating, or spreading over time, of the irregular and unequally lumped receipts and expenditures which makes the chief trouble for accountants. These pro-ratings are necessarily estimates, not facts. The only actual facts of corporate income are the money receipts and expenditures in all their jagged irregularities; but unless there is some pro-rating the results of accounting are of little practical use.

It is possible, but not very useful, to prepare all income statistics of the past on the basis of realized income and cost valuations. This would be a cash receipts and disbursements accounting only. No accruals or earnings, positive or negative, would be included. That is to say, no depreciation and no appreciation could find a place, no costs of assets like manufactured inventories other than the cost of materials embodied in the goods and of direct labour services, could be shown. Such an accounting can show very little that is significant with respect either to a present financial and operating position or to performance during a period that is closed (pp. 320–321).

On the other hand, it is very difficult to define gross income under actual accounting. The concept includes two very unlike parts:

In a book of this kind the definition of gross income is of critical importance. But the writer has been unable to find anywhere in the literature either a simple definition, or a simple set of propositions amounting to a definition, that satisfactorily meets the tests just proposed. Nor has he ever been able to phrase a definition of his own that, tested upon good students, seemed to be a sufficiently apt one on the score of convenience (p. 100).

The gross income of a specified period is a mere summation. It is a measure only. *It is the summation of the amount of gross operating income plus the amount of gross financial income.* It is a summation only, both because the nature of the two classes of income have nothing in common that is peculiar to gross income, and because the *methods of measuring* (not the *unit of measure*) of the two kinds of income are different (p. 100).

When professional accountants speak of the gross operating income of a period they mean the *fruition in money* (or the equivalent of money), effected within the period of all those elementary services which are the components of enterprise operations (p. 101).

The gross financial income of a period consists of the hire earnings, effected within the period, arising from grants of moneyed funds made by one person (or persons) to another (or others) (p. 109). (Italics are the author's.)

Net income, however, is merely a difference; there are no separable series of services that can be ascribed to it. The separable series all belong to gross income.

No propositions that assign a qualitative nature to *net* income can be maintained (p. 126).

... Since what is true for each particular proprietor must be true for any succession of them, there can also be a final net income to an enterprise for the whole period of its existence. Just as with gross income, too, no measure of net income earned in an enterprise in a period shorter than a proprietor's tenure can ever be anything more than an index of progress (p. 127).

There seems to be no brief expression less general than 'net income is equal to gross income less deductions' that is wholly true; and this expression comes perilously near being meaningless. It is idle to attach any single term to the whole congeries of items that enter into the subtrahend summation unless some new term wholly free of alternative usages is invented (p. 127).

It would seem that the vagueness in the concept of gross income which troubles Mr Canning is of no great consequence because to whatever degree gross income is subject to fluctuation, in that same degree will the 'deductions' therefrom likewise be necessary. Just as in the complete accounting of the payment of 5 cents for a glass of soda water, it makes very little difference whether any attention is paid to 'making change.' If a customer first changes a dollar bill and then hands over a quarter, receiving back 20 cents in change, it might be difficult to decide whether a full accounting should state that a gross payment of 25 cents was made in exchange for 20 cents plus a glass of soda water, or that a gross payment of a dollar was made in exchange for 95 cents plus a glass of soda water, or even that $1.25 was paid for $1.20 and a glass of soda water. The only important fact is that the glass of soda water costs a net of 5 cents. So gross income and net deductions are important only as methods of computing net income. The only complication comes from the pro-rating process which must apply equally to gross income and its 'deductions' if double counting is to be avoided.

No treatise on the subject of income could avoid some discussion of the pitfalls of double counting. The accountant, like the economist, must ever be on the lookout for these pitfalls.

The accountant, in scheduling these adverse events, is extremely careful to avoid double counting. The spoiling of a partly manufactured product is an adverse event; so, too, are the payment for the materials that have gone into it, the wages paid for work done upon it, and the overhead charges incurred in its partial manufacture; but the loss of the article and the cost of the article lost have one, not several, adverse effects. If the damage due to spoilage were to be listed as a deduction item, then the items shown for wages, purchases, and a myriad of overhead accounts would have to be diminished below the corresponding account balances. The outlay for a new factory building is an adverse event just as the acquisition of the building is favourable. But the benefit from acquisition cannot be experienced in a period less than the entire tenure of it. The accountant parcels out the adverse element, the outlay, over the series of years in which the beneficial services are to be received. Just as he avoids counting both the receipt of the building and the receipt of the services of the building but counts only one, he avoids counting both the outlay and the expiration of service value. Depreciation expense is not an expense in and of itself; it is the oulay for the depreciating object that is the primary expense. By the end of the tenure of the building it makes no statistical difference in the balance sheet whether the outlay was treated as a single deduction from gross income when the outlay occurred or as a series of annual deduction items the summation of which is equal to the outlay. Obviously, the latter treatment is the more convenient for those who wish periodic information about net income. In the avoidance of double counting the accountant's statistical procedure is above reproach. Definitions of income, common in economic literature, that include both goods and services do not have this great statistical merit (pp. 128–129).

Professor Canning closely links the income concept of a series of services with the concept of assets. He points out that the essential idea of an asset is that it stands for a separable series of *future* services.

What is essential is that there must be some anticipated, identifiable, separate (or separable) services (or income) to be had by a proprietor as a matter of legal or equitable right, from some person or object, though not necessarily from an ascertainable person(s) or object(s). One speaks of a motor truck owned by a corporation and operated in its enterprise as an asset of the company. But neither the legal title in the object, nor the existence of the object, nor the two together, constitutes the asset. That which is fundamental is that certain anticipated services of the truck will inure to the benefit of the corporation. Note that it is not the whole of the

70

possible services of the truck, nor even all those services that could be rendered by it with maximum economy to society, but only those services which the company can *advantageously* obtain from it in the course of *its operation in their enterprise* (p. 14).

Thus, the idea of a series of future services is the essence of an asset rather than any specific source or means of those services like a motor truck or a person.

To distinguish between the source and the services from that source would be, for some items (indeed, for most), to split hairs, both practically and logically. But the source of the service to the holder of a negotiable note receivable, for example, may be either the person primarily liable, intermediate parties secondarily liable, or unascertained transferees, whether by full negotiation or by assignment 'without recourse' and/or 'without warranty,' or it may be some person who 'pays for honour.' Obviously some source must be anticipated; but no particular or ascertained source, nor even an unconditional source is requisite. It is not the *source* that is the note holder's asset; not is it the thing (or person) that will *prove to be* the source that is valued. It is the anticipated service, the payment of money at some future time, that is valued and that is fundamental to the existence of the asset (p. 15).

The idea is that as long as a group of future services can be wrapped up in a separate package, so to speak, bought or sold, or at any rate valued, under whatever label, the question of the physical or other means by which this package of services is secured is of no consequence.

The whole subject of accountancy, if not the whole essence of economics, lies in the study of series of services. Capital accounts, that is, accounts of assets and liabilities, merely represent the discounted valuation at a particular date of the series of services and disservices or 'outlays' which are expected to be rendered subsequent to that date.

It is worth noting that the author exonerates the accountants from the error of holding that past costs determine values. This will come as a surprise to many economists who have long complained that accountants deal solely, or principally, with past costs.

Economists and others have often made the gross mistake of attributing to accountants a confusion of cost and value, or of identifying cost and valuation. No such crude association can be shown from the facts of modern accounting procedure. Others, particularly the writers on accounts, have said that accountants adopt cost less depreciation as the measure of valuation. This is much nearer the mark. But even if depreciation be defined in the most refined and accurate sense, with respect to that which is found in practice, the statement is still wide of the mark. Modern accounting procedure abounds in instances that do not conform to this oversimplified description. To make this assertion about accountants' valuations would make the modern balance sheet assert things that the underlying procedures do not assert at all and would make it omit saying many things that it does assert. Cost is only one class of evidence considered; depreciation, however defined and measured, is only one class of evidence among many. In a multitude of cases, initial valuations greater than cost are recognized; in a like multitude, increases in value are exhibited (p. 186).

Accountants are properly sceptical of valuation bases other than original cost. But when the weight of evidence tends to show that some higher or lower basis is *really* more probable they are not unwilling to revises valuations (p. 254).

Past costs are utilized by accountants chiefly, if not solely, as a means of valuing future or anticipated services. No competent accountant would value any asset or liability except by valuing the anticipated future services and outlays. Just as soon as these anticipated future services melt away, the present value melts away too; and the valuation must be written off or reduced, however great the past cost may have been. One of the chief tasks of the accountants is, through 'valuation accounts,' or 'reserves,' to do this work of writing off or revising original valuations, whether these original valuations were taken from cost figures or not.

This attitude of the author, which is that of professional accountants, toward cost or expense as a valuation, though imperfect, of future services is shown in the discussion of 'organization expenses:'

The real meaning of the item, 'organization expenses,' is, therefore, 'this amount was paid to procure the adopted form of organization in the expectation that the services or assets to be utilized under it would be worth more to the proprietary interest (by at least the amount of the outlay) than they would otherwise be worth' (p. 32).

Professor Canning points out that where an asset and a liability are evenly matched by the substantial equivalence and simultaneity of a future series of services, on the one hand, and a corresponding future series of outlays or payments therefore, on the other, both are usually omitted in the accounts. For instance, if a man acquires a lease of a house and contracts to pay rent, the lease is not usually put down as an asset nor the obligation to pay rent as a liability, for the reason that the series of services, namely, the shelter of the house, and the series of outlays, namely the payments of rent, are supposed to match each other. But, if the two series are not substantially equivalent or not substantially simultaneous, the accountant may express the preponderance as an asset or as a liability or even set forth the present value of both. In the latter case it is better not to separate such pairs by placing one on one side of the balance sheet and the other on the other, but to set up the bigger one as an asset or liability, as the case may be, and the other as a deduction therefrom.

Some such procedure is called for not only in cases where, because of an increase, say, of shelter value over and above the rent contracted for, the lease has a saleable value, but also in cases where the rent is prepaid, in other words where the simultaneity has been materially interfered with. In such cases there is apt to be confusion in the economic interpretation if the interpreter does not realize what is really represented.

Thus one often sees in balance sheets items of 'prepaid wages,' 'prepaid rent,' etc. A *wage* cannot be an asset to the employer, nor a rent to a tenant. But the labour services and the services of the rented object still to be rendered are clearly assets within the meaning of the definition given in the preceding chapter; and supposedly, the services will be worth at least as much as they have cost (p. 24).

The author emphasizes the importance of taking more specific account of commitments. It occasionally happens that accounts conforming to the best criterion of accountants mislead purchasers of a business because of the omission of certain commitments, such as a long-time guarantee to replace a machine or else to refund its purchase price. Good accounting practice is moving toward a better procedure regarding commitments. Professor Canning intimates that it may shortly become the general practice to include all vital commitments in the balance sheet by giving more inclusive meanings to assets and liabilities:

That is to say, some accountants are beginning to list, as assets and as liabilities, the services to be had and the services to be performed under wholly unperformed contracts (p. 57).

Among the most interesting and penetrating of the author's observations are those on so-called 'good will.' He points out that, just as a pair of shoes is worth more than twice the value of a single shoe, since a single shoe is scarcely usable by itself, and just as an automobile is worth more than the sum of the values of its separate parts, so a business as a going concern may be worth more than the sum of the valuations of its separate parts (by 'sum' is meant, of course, the algebraic sum, including liabilities as negative assets). This difference between the value of the whole combination and the sum of the values of its constituent parts taken piecemeal, is, the author tells us, what accountants mean by 'good will.' From a dictionary point of view and still more from an etymological point of view, this interpretation might be accused of perverting the meaning of the term 'good will,' or of extending it to include patents, trade marks, franchises, and all other 'intangibles;' but that is a mere matter of words. It might be better, from a verbal point of view, to return to the original meaning of 'good will' as merely one of many kinds of intangibles, namely the valuation of the probability of continued patronage of satisfied customers—customers feeling literally a good will toward the concern—in which case there would still remain an excess of the total valuation of an enterprise and the sum of the valuations of its separable parts.

73

In practice, however, it is seldom, if ever, possible to separate 'good will' from other intangibles. Thus good will in the strict and original sense has very little useful meaning. It is the 'going-concern excess,' including other intangibles, which has the useful meaning—the excess of the total valuation over the sum of the valuations of the separable parts. If accountants call this entire sum 'good will,' there can be little objection either from the accountant or the economist. This excess, whether called good will or not, explains the excess of market value over book value. Of course the 'excess' may be negative.

In this connection the author raises the question as to whether good will, in the sense of going-concern excess, is properly to be regarded as an asset at all, or whether, as he inclines to think, the concept of 'assets' should be restricted to designate only the piecemeal parts.

In discussing this problem, Professor Canning helps us to see the justification for the reluctance of accountants to make their book values correspond more nearly to actual or market values by refusing, in general, fully to evaluate 'good will.' The accountant's proper business under the terms for which he is usually engaged is primarily confined to making a correct valuation of *the separable parts* and does not include making a valuation of the going concern *as a whole*.

Sometimes, therefore, the accountant puts down the so-called good will as worth 'one dollar'—not, of course, because he thinks that one dollar is its true worth, but merely as a memorandum that good will exists and that the accountant has not attempted to evaluate it. To evaluate it properly requires an entirely different sort of expert than an accountant, with a different sort of training.

Of course where the 'good will' has actually been sold in good faith for a definite sum or, for any other reason, has a specific measurable valuation, the accountant is justified in placing such valuation upon it and he can then do so by the same methods he uses in his ordinary professional work.

This problem of the discrepancy between the valuation of a concern as a whole and the valuation of its parts is at bottom the same as the much discussed problem of economists as to whether the sum of the marginal productivities of the agents of production will account for the whole product, or whether, instead, there emerges a residual element.

Another problem with which Professor Canning deals is the 'equation of proprietorship.' It has long been an aphorism of economists that the value of the assets is equal to the value of the liabilities plus the value of the proprietorship.

Is this 'equation of accounts' an identity or is it an equivalence between three independently measurable magnitudes? If it is an identity, which two of the three magnitudes are really the independent ones? The author answers these questions by concluding that the two independent items are assets and liabilities and that the derivative item is the net proprietorship. In a still more simplified way we may regard liabilities as a form of assets merely having a negative sign. The assets represent the series of services running to the proprietor and the liabilities represent the series running from the proprietor.

Arithmetically there are but two quantities exhibited: (1) the money valuation (importance to the proprietor) of the ultimate benefits to be received from the services proceeding from the several items to the proprietor; and (2) the money valuation of the services which the proprietor has bound himself to render to other persons. Statistically the equation of accounts is epitomized in the difference between the volume of benefits expected to flow in (with reference to the proprietor) and the volume of adverse elements to flow out.

In the matter of valuation, liabilities do not differ from assets except in characteristic direction of flow. Those writers who urge consideration of liabilities as negative assets express a view more fruitfully suggestive than do those who habitually associate liabilities and *net* proprietorship in their discussion. But the problems of revenue-getting are so vastly different from those of procuring funds for it and from those of dividing the fruits of enterprise that no degree of similarity of quantitative aspects of the single items can ever make the groups of assets and the groups of liabilities homogeneous with respect to the accountant's principal inquiries.

The association in speech and writing of liabilities and of net proprietorship as though these two quantities were coordinate and had an independent existence, cannot but be misleading to those not fully informed. That they usually appear in the same member of the balance sheet as though they were coordinate is a mere statistical convention (pp. 50–51).

He concludes:

Proprietorship consists of the entire beneficial interest of a holder of a set of assets in those assets. A liability is a service, valuable in money, which a proprietor is under an existing legal (or equitable) duty to render to a second person (or set of persons) and which is not unconditionally an agreed set-off to its full amount against specific services of equal or greater money value due from this second person to the proprietor.

Net proprietorship cannot be qualitatively defined except as a mere difference. It is the *difference found by subtracting the summation of the liabilities from the amount of the proprietorship* (pp. 55–56). (Italics are the author's.)

I think this statement, which the author offers not as his personal solution but as his interpretation of the best usage of accountants, does not fully clear up the difficulties and ambiguities involved in the concept of a 'proprietor.' In the old days, when accounting began, the proprietor was a very definite individual with specific liabilities; but today, with a multitude of investment forms and with contracts in which creditors share in profits and take explicit risks instead of enjoying returns which are theoretically guaranteed, the whole concept of a proprietor becomes more and more difficult, if indeed it does not vanish into thin air, while the concept of the corporation as a fictitious or artificial person which, for bookkeeping purposes, receives and dispenses all elements of the accounts becomes increasingly useful.

Today the essential differences, economically speaking, between investments such as common stocks of various types, preferred stocks of various types, and bonds of various types, are chiefly differences of risks. The problem cannot, it seems to me, be worked out from a merely legalistic point of view, though legal rights are of great importance and the author pays much attention to their bearing on the subject (*e.g.*, pp. 60–63). He is not at all convincing when he concludes that a debenture bond is not a bond at all and so is 'clearly *not a liability*.' And in this he clearly departs from his rule of interpreting accounting procedure.

That is to say, so long as there is any contract between the company and another person not wholly and completely performed on the company's part, and so long as any tort or criminal liability exists undischarged, no claim can be enforced (p. 62).

But a good debenture bond is ordinarily regarded by its owner as almost identical with a mortgage bond. It is merely a matter of the relative chances involved. In fact, a debenture bond of one company may be far safer than a mortgage bond of another. When there is no chance of insolvency, the distinct becomes a distinction without a difference. With our modern mixtures of bonds and stocks and with so many persons in many roles of stockholder and bondholder, with customer stock ownership and employee stock ownership, with profit-sharing and cooperation, the idea of 'the' residual ownership becomes too complicated to be covered by the share of any one 'responsible proprietor' or group of proprietors. The author himself seems to regard the owner of a debenture or of an 'income bond' as almost as purely a proprietor as the owner of preferred stock. Many bonds today are convertible into stock or have stock warrants attached so that the 'residual' claims include a part of the interests of 'creditors.'

In short, the old idea of a proprietor as one insider with specific and simple obligations to outsiders called creditors will no longer serve; for certain types of 'creditors' instead of being really outsiders are partly inside the business and partake of the nature of proprietors.

For this reason I venture to think that there is more value than the author seems to assign to it of the concept of a 'fictitious person,' such as a corporation considered as a bookkeeping entity. This 'person' is the sole proprietor and its liabilities include stocks as well as bonds. Thus, with respect to a corporation, the residual element in the balance sheet is a true liability, a liability to stockholders.

We could even imagine a company in which each of the parties at interest has precisely the same rights and obligations as every other, owing the same quota of bonds, preferred stock and common stock, etc. Who then is 'the proprietor?'

The valuation of some kinds of assets is far more *direct* than that of others. This leads Professor Canning to make a broad distinction between direct and indirect valuation although there are many imperceptible gradations between the two, according to how definitely one can estimate the contribution of the asset to the money making which is the supreme object of the enterprise. Among the assets capable of what he calls 'direct' valuation are cash and accounts receivable.

Cash involves no estimate. Accounts receivable involves an estimate of collectibility only. Merchandise involves likewise merely an estimate of funds to be collected as a result of sales, though, of course, a highly reliable estimate is not always possible. In the case of cash the enterprise services have all been rendered. In the case of the accounts receivable and the merchandise, only one service, the bringing in of money, is involved (p. 183).

As to 'indirect valuations,' he says:

But not all assets are of this kind. In a manufacturing establishment many kinds of machines are employed each of which renders a kind of service peculiar to itself. None of these services consists in the direct and immediate bringing in of money. And while no one will question the proposition that the value of a machine is derived from the value of its services and from the outlays incident to procuring its services, no one can make a direct money valuation of those services unless they are to be sold separately (pp. 183–184).

Professor Canning thinks that one of the improvements to which we may look forward in accounting procedure is the substitution of direct valuations in certain cases such as inventories, where indirect valuations are now employed because they are easier.

If any substantial increase in reliability can be had at reasonable expense by resorting to direct valuation, clearly it is worth getting, and, in any event, the direct valuation gives *additional* information. The inventory is almost always the biggest single current item in merchandising concerns. In mercantile establishments, too, it is often the largest item in the balance sheet. The present writer's belief is that, in proportion to the effort needed to accomplish it, improvement of inventory valuation offers a prospect for a greater gain in usefulness of accounting reports than does any other element of technique in accountancy (p. 227).

Sometimes—all too often in the writer's opinion—accountants employ indirect valuations when legitimate and reasonably reliable direct capital values can be found. This is the case with finished goods inventory (p. 246).

Irving Fisher

Professor Canning considers carefully the various formulas which have been proposed for correcting valuations of assets, especially in depreciation accounts. He discusses various types including the ordinary straight line formula by which an asset is supposed to depreciate evenly through a certain specific period until it vanishes, and also the 'sinking fund' formula in which interest is taken into account.

The writer has made a test of every formula proposed in the literature and has invented some hundreds of modifications upon these. But every one of these can be demonstrated to be inferior in the conditions that prevail in use to the modifications of the service unit rule proposed here (p. 284).

He concludes that a modification of the service unit formula is the best, since it possesses none of the demerits of the other formulas discussed and

possesses not only all of the merits of all of them but many more. If the postulates laid down for its support approximate the truth, the formula produces useful answers to the questions:

1. Of that which has been paid or must be paid for services of long-lived devices, how much expense was impliedly incurred on behalf of services already realized and how much for services that are still to be had?

2. Of those services paid for or to be paid for how much is applicable to the services used this year?

3. How much has been or will have to be paid out per unit of service realized (p. 294)?

The author believes in the judicious use of mathematics but does not wish to be too meticulous in this regard, as the cost of the mathematics may have to be taken into account as itself a material element in cost.

But any one who has the patience to find out for himself what accountants actually do and who will reflect upon what he finds, will discover that modern accounting practice is, on the whole, sounder than that which has been written about it (pp. 45–46).

Professor Canning impresses upon the reader that accounts are not prepared primarily for economists but for employers who are anxious to get the most practical valuations possible and who are interested in economic theory only to the extent that it leads to an improvement in such practical valuations.

Many economists are grieved to find that the balance sheet valuations of accountants are of mongrel origin (from the economist's point of view). They find that cash has been counted (a present valuation); that accounts, bills, and notes receivable have been valued at the number of dollars expected to come in (a future valuation); that interim receivable interest accruals are valued separately from the principals to which they attach (an earning); that inventories are valued at cost or market (a purely arbitrary index); that items like organization expense, purchased good will, etc., having no attributes in common with the assets grouped with them are included

78

(valuation account balances); that fixed assets are valued at an approximation to the cost of the future services expected to become available provided that cost does not exceed the cost of available substitute services (a division of costs into past and future charges). They find, moreover, that these diverse valuations of diverse things are added to find an asset total that, dollar for dollar, cannot possibly have a common significance.

In the other branch of the balance sheet they find a group of current liabilities valued at the amount to become payable (a future valuation); that fixed liabilities are valued to yield the effective rate implicit in their net issue price (a present valuation); and that a more or less arbitrary distribution of the difference between asset and liability totals is made among capital stock and elements of surplus or deficit (the total thus divided being merely the resultant of the diverse measures of assets and of liabilities). They find that this net proprietary interest figure bears no stable relation to the true capital value (if the latter could be found) of the enterprise as a whole.

No less are they distressed by the figures they find in the income statement for a specified period. They find a mixture of realized income positive and negative, of many negative earnings, of some positive earnings; and of a figure like that resulting from the difference between (1) the sum of purchase costs and beginning inventory valued at cost or market, and (2) the closing inventory valued at cost or market—a difference figure that is neither a realized (negative) income nor a (negative) earning.

The statistical state of affairs complained of does exist. No competent student of the joint field of economics and accounting can doubt that the measurements in accountants' reports are of diverse statistical orders. But that is a very different matter from charging professional accountants with responsibility for statistical absurdities. To such a charge the accountants could make the perfect rejoinder, 'Show us a better way of doing this work that is both practicable and that clients would pay to have done' (pp. 319–320).

The author suggests that, in view of the importance of the information given in the balance sheet, it would be well to supersede the single 'all purpose' balance sheet by various balance sheets constructed for various purposes. He hopes the day may come when public accountants will serve notice that a particular balance sheet was framed for a particular purpose and that he who uses it for any other purpose 'does so at his own risk' (p. 88).

In short, while the author is critical of the economists' criticism of accountants, he points out the need for better accounting and the necessity of providing the money to pay for it. He stresses the importance of having an accounting made, not simply by and for the interested management, but by and for those whom the management serves. Thus, the shareholders in an enterprise might well have their own accountants report to them on the state of the financial condition of the company from their point of view.

There can be no doubt of the too great apathy of the financially interested public in the past in procuring disinterested expert reviews of corporate affairs. There can be no doubt, however, that bankers, in the interest of their depositors and shareholders, that investment houses, in the interest of their customers, and that governing boards of the stock exchanges, in the interest of their members and their members' clients, have in recent years done much to press the protective services of public accountants upon corporate business. The comment excited both in the popular press and in financial and trade journals by Professor Ripley's 'Stop, Look, Listen' article,[1] in which among other measures, he urged an annual accounting by public accountants acting in the interests of shareholders other than directors and officers, could hardly have followed the publication of such an article fifteen years ago. Pressure for better service by those entitled to receive it can be counted on both to extend and to better the service (p. 327).

While the great bulk of the work done by public accountants still consists of 'balance sheet audits' and of 'detailed audits' covering the activities of a fiscal year, many more important and far-reaching investigations have been required of them in recent years. 'Financial and industrial surveys' are often asked for. In these, something more than the history of the concern under examination is brought in. The prospect for the industry as a whole, the form and magnitude of the enterprise most likely to succeed in the industry, the appropriate capital 'set-up,' the most advantageous mode of market development, and so on, are considered. Such tasks give scope for the best service of broadly trained, experienced professional men, men whose competence and vision go far beyond that requisite for the conventional procedures of account keeping (pp. 327–328).

The author points out that the profession of accounting, with its rules, associations, and training, has become increasingly ethical and therefore increasingly important to all concerned. While the accountant is almost universally paid by the employer, he will not, if in a reputable firm, falsify accounts for his own or his employers' benefit. He is in a semi-judicial position and under obligation to report correct valuations for the benefit of the creditors or others interested besides the proprietor who pays for his work. As interest in and understanding of the importance of accounting grow, the economist, the statisticians and the general public will demand that accountants furnish the information needed by investors and the consumers as well as that required by the proprietor. If some day our census taking, which has already grown vast in scope and complexity, should include an accounting survey, or if some future Rockefeller Foundation should make such a survey, presumably the accountants making the survey would find themselves seeking to reach such valuations as will serve the purposes of economists and statisticians rather than proprietors.

The most of the book is given up to accounts of money making enterprises. But to me, because of my own studies in this line, one of the most interesting portions of the book is that which gives an ideal accounting of a person's individual income (pp. 163–168).

[1] *Atlantic Monthly*, September, 1926.

The economics of accountancy

The shortcomings of economists who have neglected accounting studies are pointed out with much plain speaking. The author shows (p. 7) that the economist is prone to assume that those who are in the market possess and use certain information about cost which they have not and can never get. He also points out (p. 7) that much in economic theory is only quasi-quantitative; that, for instance, the notions of increasing or decreasing returns are 'too coarse for practical analysis.'

He criticises the often cited case of the telephone business as subject to decreasing returns or increasing cost, pointing out that when the cost *per subscriber* increases with the increasing size of a telephone business the cost *per unit of service* may be decreasing. And in general, a service unit suggested to replace the time unit which is a poor makeshift for a standard for measuring amounts and values of services.

It takes no great insight to see that one year's use of a truck may vastly differ from another year's uses in everything that is really significant. But if a ton-mile-under-useful-load has a stabler significance, and if the ratio of miles run to ton-miles-under-useful-load for periods as long as a year is relatively constant, then miles run is a better (that is, more convenient and, hence, more significant) measure than is a year of use (p. 281).

Any one who drives an automobile and watches his expenses knows that gasoline cost, tyre costs, valve grinding, greasing, bearing adjustments, reboring of cylinders, etc., are much more closely related to miles run, under given road and use conditions, than they are to months or years in service (p. 282).

The author does not claim to have covered the whole ground of the economics of accountancy; nor does he claim to have solved satisfactorily all the problems with which he does deal. The vitally important subject of cost accounting he has deliberately refrained from treating. It is to be hoped that he will deal with this subject in a future book.

Professor Canning has written a sound and penetrating book which should be highly serviceable to accountants and economists alike. Although he defends the accountants against the unjustified criticisms of statisticians and economists, he does not attempt to make out that accountants can do no wrong. His book points the way to a sounder science of economics as well as better theory and practice of accountancy.

3 The concept of income

by Erik Lindahl*

The main essentials of the concept of income have perhaps been most clearly laid down by Irving Fisher in his well-known definitions: 'A *stock of wealth* existing at a given *instant* of time is called *capital*; a *flow of benefits* from wealth through a *period* of time is called *income*.'[1] According to this, income consists of certain benefits accruing during a definite period of time, and further, these benefits arise from the employment of wealth; legacies, gifts, and the like are considered as falling outside the concept of income.

In order to give expression in one comprehensive measure to the size of these benefits, they are best considered as *amounts of exchange value*. It is simplest to base these calculations on the market prices during the period to which the estimation of income refers and subsequently to allow for changes in monetary purchasing power. Thus income is regarded as a concept of value; this applies also to the term 'real income', by which is simply meant income expressed in some unchanging monetary unit.

The following is designed to show that, starting from these premises, it is possible to arrive at alternative definitions of scientific importance which should be kept quite separate.

I. INCOME AS CONSUMPTION

This is Irving Fisher's own concept which he expounds in the following way. The benefits which constitute income consist of the *services* obtained from capital goods during a certain period, services from human beings included under this head. The problem of how to avoid double counting, when adding up those services which result in new capital goods and those services which flow from these goods, is solved in this manner: the capital-producing services are credited to the capital goods that deliver them, but at the same time they are debited to the resulting new capital goods; they are therefore excluded from the net income obtained from the total capital stock. The net income consists only of the services for the said period which are debited to various persons as consumers, that is to say, which enter into their consumption and thereby lead to the satisfaction of wants.

---

* Professor of Economics, Lund University, 1939–1958.
[1] Irving Fisher, *Elementary Principles of Economics* (New York, 1919), p. 38. Cf. his earlier fundamental work, *The Nature of Capital and Income* (New York, 1906).

Irving Fisher's analysis is carried out in masterly fashion, but all his attempts to demonstrate that his concept of income is the usual one and that is is the only logical one must be considered unsatisfactory. In neither popular nor scientific terminology are income and consumption equated; on the contrary, income is generally taken to include saving (either positive or negative), and the crux of the matter is to decide just what this term saving may be taken to cover. It should also be possible to construct quite logically a concept of income to include saving, starting from the same premises as Irving Fisher.

In that case, however, it is best to distinguish between *anticipated income*, which refers to a certain period forward, and *income obtained*, which is reckoned after the termination of the period in question. The first of the following concepts is of the former type, the two others of the latter.

2. INCOME AS INTEREST

This concept, reduced to theoretical simplicity, may be taken as referring to the continuous *appreciation* of capital goods owing to the time-factor, that is to say, the current interest on the capital value which the goods represent. Income in this sense stands in quite a different relation to the concept of capital as against income regarded as a stream of services. The expected future services of the capital goods are the basic factor in the estimation of capital value, for the latter can be considered equal to the sum of the anticipated value of these services, discounted at the current rate of interest, due reduction also having been made for the risk factor. Capital value must again be the starting-point for the estimation of income as interest, that is to say, as the appreciation which arises when the discounted future services come nearer and nearer—an increase in value which for a given period forward can be regarded as the product of the capital value and the rate of interest applying to the period. We thus arrive at a quite different and in a certain sense secondary concept of income. But the term income in this case is quite as justifiable as in the former, for the continuous appreciation due to the time-factor can fairly be regarded as a 'flow of benefits from wealth through a period of time'.[1]

[1] The above-given deduction of the concept of income from Fisher's own premises, Fisher himself has chosen to disregard. He lays it down emphatically that the term income should be reserved for the stream of services on which the estimation of capital value is based, and should not, therefore, be taken to cover the appreciation of capital goods: 'Clearly, then, increase of capital is not income in the sense that it can be discounted in addition to other items of income. If it is income at all, it is income in a peculiar sense, and nothing but confusion can result from having to consider two kinds of income so widely divergent that whereas one is discounted to obtain capital-value, the other is not' (*The Nature of Capital and Income*, p. 249). He thus lays himself open

83

Erik Lindahl

If services created by one group of capital goods are invested in another, a certain amount of value is thereby transferred. The total value of the capital stocks is not necessarily affected by such a procedure. If, on the other hand, the services created pass directly into personal consumption, a corresponding diminishing effect on the total capital value may be expected. During a given period of time, this reduction in value through consumption may be less or greater than the contemporaneous appreciation due to the time-factor. These differences between interest and consumption anticipated for a certain period can be regarded as the *saving*, positive or negative as the case may be, which takes place during the period. But it should be pointed out that the net increase in capital values, in which saving expresses itself, need not correspond to the actual change in value during the period for, through more or less unforeseen circumstances, the capital values may at the same time undergo other more discontinuous changes in the shape of gains or losses (see below).

Income as interest can thus be said to correspond to the total *sum of the consumption and the saving* expected to take place during a certain period, the element of saving being expressed in the increase in value of the capital, exclusive of gains and losses.

Here it is assumed that the concept of income as interest is to apply generally, that is to say, not only as regards produced capital instruments, but also as regards land and labour, analogically with the comprehensive concept of capital developed with such success by Fisher, Fetter, and others. Interest can, then, no longer be regarded as a special income-category side by side with rent and wages: on the contrary, all forms of income are to be taken as current interests on the corresponding capital values. If, in accordance with the traditional definitions, rent and wages are taken as the value of services supplied during a certain period, an addition should consequently be made for any increases in value which these factors of production have undergone by reason of a surplus of accumulated interest, and alternatively, deductions should be made for any decreases in value that may have arisen as a result of the value of the services supplied exceeding the interest.

to the charge of inconsistency in making the term capital include all increase of capital, even such increases as arise through the accumulation of interest: 'Daraus folgt, daß Ersparnisse und Wertvermehrung immer Kapital und nicht Einkommen sind' (*Der Einkommensbegriff im Lichte der Erfahrung*, in *Wirtschaftstheorie der Gegenwart*, III, Wien, 1928, p. 28). This obviously runs contrary to his fundamental postulate, according to which capital consists of value at a given *instant* of time. The interest which applies to a *period* of time is in the nature of a time stream and cannot, from this point of view, be dragged into the concept of capital; it is clearly income. It is, moreover, significant that Fisher himself employs the terms 'earned income' and 'standard income' for this concept, which he contrasts with his own concept of income, 'the realized income'. The conflict is to be solved in this way: that we clearly distinguish two different categories of income—income as a 'flow of services' and income as a 'flow of capital value'.

If it is considered desirable to adhere more closely to the conventional concepts, the most satisfactory compromise would be wholly to disregard changes in the capital value of labour. By way of justification, it may readily be urged that since the abolition of slavery it has not been necessary to set a capital value on human labour-power, except in the way one estimates the solvency of an individual when advancing him credit. In this case the total income emerges as the sum of the current interest on all capital, exclusive of human capital, and the value of the labour-services during the period. But from this sum a deduction must be made for expenses incurred in bringing the workers up to the requisite standard of efficiency (provided that these expenses do not at the same time conduce to personal satisfactions). Otherwise double counting will arise, as in the calculation of wages no deduction corresponding to the amortization of these expenses is made. Consequently the saving included in the calculation of income only corresponds to external capital goods; capital in a personal form is left out of account.

It does not matter so much which of these constructions one chooses, provided only that it is carried to its logical conclusion. In both cases a concept of income emerges of great value from the point of view of theoretical analysis; for, referring to a certain period forward, it allows a quite consistent determination of the much debated concept of saving as one of the price-determining factors for the said period. For statistical purposes, on the other hand, this concept of income is less useful, as it is based to such a great extent on subjective factors, not statistically computable.[1]

The question arises, therefore, how may we widen the usefulness of the concept of income for statistical purposes, without too big a sacrifice of its theoretical preciseness.

---

[1] It should be understood that this calculation of interest is undertaken by the owners of the capital and is, accordingly, based upon their own individual anticipation of yields and their own judgment and valuation of the risk factor. Also the rates of interest at which the estimated yields of future periods are discounted, and the rate at which the current interest on capital is estimated, are not the same for all persons, as the conditions of making and receiving loans are fixed in different ways. Further, it should be borne in mind that both the capital values and the rates of interest may change as time goes on; so that the total current interest for so long a period of time as a year should be calculated as a sum of the interests during the shorter periods of time during which the capital value, no less than the rate of interest, can be assumed to remain unchanged. (As regards the calculation of current income from work, this presents no difficulties as far as it is contractual in character. A calculation of other kinds of income from work must again be based upon an anticipation of unascertained items, that is to say, upon subjective factors as in the case just considered.)

Erik Lindahl

3. INCOME AS EARNINGS

The simplest procedure would perhaps be to add together income as interest and the gains and losses which arise during the period to which the calculation of income applies. Income in this very wide sense would thus be calculated as the sum of the actual consumption and the increase of both capital value which has taken place during a certain period. Both these items could be treated statistically, especially if human beings are excluded from capital stock. For this concept of income, the term used in this paper is 'earnings'.

The conept 'earnings', understood in this sense, has the great merit that its compass can be determined in a quite obvious way. It has therefore proved of great use in business economics, and in certain cases it has been used (though in a somewhat modified form) as a basis for assessing the taxation of income, e.g. in the case of the federal income tax of the United States of America. It is, accordingly, of interest to investigate the theoretical significance of the points of divergence between this concept of income and the one discussed just above, i.e. the nature of the before-mentioned gains and losses.

If the future could be completely foreseen, so that future streams of services and the rates of interest at which they should be capitalized were known beforehand, the total value of the capital stock could only be changed by the element of saving as defined above, that is to say, the difference between the interest income and the consumption. On this supposition, income as earnings (actual consumption plus appreciation of capital stock) would correspond to income as interest (anticipated consumption plus saving).

Actually, however, as the future is only anticipated as a series of more or less probable alternatives, the determination of capital values becomes dependent on a number of factors which change as time goes on. Thus the expectations of future services clearly change their character the nearer the time comes for these services to fall due. At the same time the estimation of the risk factor will undergo modification. The result of this will not necessarily be a change in capital value, as these changes in effect may neutralize each other. But, as a general rule, it may be assumed that changes in the factors of capitalization will be accompanied by greater or smaller changes in the capital values themselves. These discontinuous changes in the value of capital stock, dependent as they are on the fact that individuals, through unforeseen circumstances, find themselves obliged to modify their capitaliz ations, are what have here been termed 'gains and losses'.[1]

---

[1] Cf. Gunnar Myrdal, *Prisbildningsproblemet och föränderligheten* [The Pricing Problem and the Change Factor] (Uppsala, 1927), where the distinction between incomes and costs on the one side and gains and losses on the other is considered fundamental in the treatment of the problem of profits.

From the above it follows that, for the reasons given, the classification of gains and losses as positive or negative items of income for the period in which they occur is hardly satisfactory. For here it is not a question of a flow of benefits through a *period* of time, but of changes which occur at certain *instants* of time (that is to say, when the owner of capital goods changes his estimation of its value) and thus, strictly speaking, have no time dimension. Consequently these instantaneous changes should not be reckoned in with the saving which occurs during a certain period either, as the term saving should really be kept for the refraining to consume income. Instead, we may assert that the gains and losses constitute *adjustments* of the estimation of savings which have been realized during *preceding* periods, because the anticipation of the future, upon which every attempt to estimate the savings must be based, changes in nature with the passing of time. These adjustments of the existing capital values have of course a quite different economic meaning from an increase or reduction in capital value through an excess or deficit of current interest in relation to consumption.

The conclusion must be, then, that the concept 'earnings', understood in the above-determined sense, is inclusive of elements which must be kept separate in a theoretical analysis. This concept, therefore, hardly provides an ideal solution of the problem of how to arrive at a concept of income that will be both tenable theoretically and practically useful at the same time.

4. INCOME AS PRODUCE

In this case, income is defined analogously to the concept of production. Net income becomes identifiable with the net value which the owners of the factors of production receive as remuneration for their contributions to the productive process. This net value is usually defined as the difference between the value of the product realized during the period and certain items which have been reckoned as products of previous periods and therefore must be deducted to avoid double counting.

In the majority of cases, income in the practical sense is understood in this way. In business economics and tax law this concept of income, the 'income produced', is more favoured than the concept of income we have just discussed, the earned income. It lies at the base of most computations of the national income, and corresponds roughly to what, in the language of daily life, usually goes under the name of income.

It is to be regretted, therefore, that this concept of income cannot be defined in such unambiguous terms as the concepts which have already

Erik Lindahl

been dealt with. In determining the plus and minus items which are included in the income calculation for a certain period, different principles are often applied, so that the content of the concept is apt to vary within rather wide limits. These variations can be brought into line with each one of the three concepts of income dealt with above: in determining the positive items the choice lies between the consumption concept on the one hand and the interest and earnings concepts on the other; as far as the negative items are concerned, one has to choose between the two latter concepts.

As regards the calculating of the positive items, an approach is made to the first alternative—income as *consumption*—according as to whether we insist that only finished products should be reckoned in the value of production. The more it is insisted that the reckoned products should be considered as marking the climax of the productive process, the more will the income calculus for these products tend to be postponed to the consumption period. The agreement between income as consumption and income as produce would clearly be complete if only the products consumed were reckoned as positive items, in which case there would of course be no negative items.

If, again, the positive items are not limited to finished products in the technical or economic sense, but are taken to cover all services rendered during the period, the net value of the production will be equal to the whole increase in value of the capital stock, which results from the productive process. In this case we come nearer the two other concepts of income (interest and earnings).

The minus items are, in the produce concept of income, calculated in a different way from that of Fisher. He, as mentioned above, subtracts all capital-producing services during the period when they are furnished. Here, on the contrary, they are not deducted until the periods during which the capital goods concerned are utilized. Thus income as produce will cover not only consumption but also the amount by which the production of capital goods exceeds the capital consumed. The capital consumed can, however, be calculated in different ways. Approach may be made in this connexion either to the concept of income as earnings or to the concept of income as interest.

The concept of *earnings* we approach, according as the deductions for raw materials and the depreciation of capital instruments are based on the original costs of production. If (owing to unforeseen circumstances) the value of these goods subsequently rises or falls, the gain or loss which this change in value implies is, by this method of calculating, partly reckoned in with the net income. The gains and losses, however, cannot be so fully

88

accounted for as in the concept earnings as above defined. In the first place, as regards the durable capital instruments, the gains and losses are not reckoned in the income for the period during which they take place. They are, on the contrary, spread out over all the periods during which the capital is used, since the amounts written off, which have been determined by the original costs, are too high or too low in relation to the later values. It is to be noted, further, that gains and losses referring to land and capital instruments which are not being used up and for which, therefore, no deduction is made, do not enter into the calculation of income at all.

In so far as these deductions, on the other hand, are calculated according to the prices for the current period and are thus based not on the original but on the actual cost of production, income as produce will tend to correspond to income as *interest*. In this case capital gains and losses will not be included in the income: the income will correspond to the net value earned during the period, due deduction having been made for the actual diminution in value of the capital instruments caused by the productive process. This diminution can, for a durable capital instrument, be defined as the amount by which the value of the services rendered exceeds the accumulated interest on the capital value during the same period. If this amount is written off, that is to say, deducted from the positive item, i.e. the value of the services rendered, the accumulated interest emerges as the net income.

Even so, this correspondence to the income as interest concept can never be regarded as complete. Firstly, all appreciation due to the time-factor is not counted as produce. In so far as this appreciation does not apply to the product but to the factors of production, it can only be included in a somewhat incomplete way by fixing the deductions for the using up of capital. Further, the calculation of income as produce is made after the termination of the period concerned, whilst income as interest applies to a certain period forward. Consequently gains and losses referring to the interest realized during a certain period (not the capital proper) are included in the latter but not in the former concept.

For various practical purposes it is perhaps possible to defend different variants of the produced income concept. But from the point of view of theoretical analysis there can be no doubt as to which of the variants is most satisfactory. An approach to the consumption or the earning concept leads to mere compromise which should be abandoned in favour of the fundamental concepts, consumption and earnings. These concepts, moreover, could be turned to good statistical use. An approach to the interest concept—which implies that all services rendered during the period are reckoned as positive items and that the negative items, referring to services

Erik Lindahl

furnished during previous periods, are reckoned according to, not the original, but the actual costs of production—has, on the other hand, a more definite theoretical content: that the produced income is the interest which is realized during a given period.

The result of this investigation is, then, that for a certain period forward the anticipated interest, and for a period reckoned backward the produce in the sense of realized interest, is the most adequate expression of the income idea. According to this, saving can be defined as the difference between the anticipations of interest and those of consumption, and realized savings as the difference between realized interest and actual consumption during a given period.

4 The definition of income

by H. C. Simons[*]

The development of income taxes may be viewed as a response to increasingly insistent and articulate demand for a more equitable apportionment of tax burdens.[1] These taxes are the outstanding contribution of popular government and liberal political philosophy to modern fiscal practice. Thus they may properly be studied in the light of considerations raised in the preceding chapter. Income taxation is broadly an instrument of economic control, a means of mitigating economic inequality. In what follows we shall assume that moderation of inequality is an important objective of policy and proceed to consider income taxes as devices for effecting it. We shall be concerned, that is to say, largely with problems centring around that elusive something which we call 'discrimination'. Income taxes, in general, may seem peculiarly equitable; but serious problems arise when one proceeds to the task of describing, delimiting, and defining closely the actual tax base. Here, too, the problems may be dealt with largely in the light of considerations of justice.

We must face now the task of defining 'income'. Many writers have undertaken to formulate definitions, and with the most curious results. Whereas the word is widely used in discussions of justice in taxation and without evident confusion, the greatest variety and dissimilarity appear, as to both content and phraseology, in the actual definitions proposed by particular writers. The consistent recourse to definition in terms which are themselves undefinable (or undefined or equally ambiguous) testifies eloquently to the underlying confusion.

The fact that the term is widely used without serious misunderstanding in certain ranges of discourse, however, is significant. Since it is widely agreed that income is a good tax base, its meaning may be sought by inquiring what definition would provide the basis for most nearly equitable levies. At the same time we may seek to point out conflicts and contradictions in established usage and to discover the connotations of income which are essential and relevant for present purposes. Thus we may find those

---

[*] Professor of Economics, University of Chicago, 1927–1946.
[1] For stimulating development of this thesis see W. Moll, *Über Steuern* (Berlin, 1911), pp. 3–46. See also Bruno Moll, *Probleme der Finanzwissenschaft* (Leipzig, 1924), *passim*. The latter writer remarks (p. 99): 'Vermögens- und Einkommensbegriff entspringen der gleichen Wurzel, dem Begriff des wirtschaftlichen Könnens, dem Vermögensbegriff im weitesten Sinne.'

denotations which may best be accepted, to avoid ambiguity, and to minimize disturbance of terminological tradition.

What is requisite to satisfactory definition of income will appear clearly only as we come to grips with various problems. It may help, however, to indicate some general requirements—if only because their neglect has been responsible for so much careless writing in the past. Income must be conceived as something quantitative and objective. It must be measurable; indeed, definition must indicate or clearly imply an actual procedure of measuring.[1] Moreover, the arbitrary distinctions implicit in one's definition must be reduced to a minimum. That it should be possible to delimit the concept precisely in every direction is hardly to be expected.[2] The task rather is that of making the best of available materials; for no very useful conception in 'social science' or in 'welfare economics' will entirely satisfy the tough-minded; nor can available materials so be put together as to provide an ideal tax base. But one devises tools of analysis which are useful, if crude; and a tax base may be defined in such manner as to minimize obvious inequities and ambiguities. Such at least is the present task.

The noun 'income' denotes, broadly, that which comes in. Thus, it may be used with almost any referent.[3] Even in the current usage of economics and business the term is commonly used in different contexts to denote several different things. It will suffice here to note three or four distinct senses in which the term is employed.

There is, first, and most common in economic theory, the conception of what may be called *income from things*.[4] In this sense, income may be conceived in terms of services derived from things or, quantitatively, in terms of the market value of uses. Thus, we speak commonly of income from land, from produced instruments, or from consumers' capital. When

---

[1] The importance of this requirement may be suggested by the following definition: 'Net individual income is the flow of commodities and services accruing to an individual through a period of time and available for disposition after deducting the necessary costs of acquisition' (W. W. Hewett, *The Definition of Income*, Philadelphia, 1925, pp. 22–3). The author never undertakes to specify how this conception might be reduced to quantitative expression; he simply leaves the reader to guess how 'the necessary costs of acquisition' might be deducted from 'the flow of commodities and services accruing', or how either of these 'quantities' might be arrived at separately.

[2] Kleinwächter, notably, endeavours to discredit the whole concept of income by pointing out that some arbitrary delimitations are unavoidable (*Das Einkommen und seine Verteilung*, Leipzig, 1896, pp. 1–16). He confounds himself and his reader with interesting conundrums having to do mainly with income in kind.

[3] For discussion of the development of the income concept see Kleinwächter, *op. cit.* introduction; also Bruno Moll, *op. cit.* esp. chapter XII; also Bücher, *Zwei mittelalterische Steuerordnungen (Fests. z. Leipziger Hist.* 1894), pp. 138–9 (cited in B. Moll, *op. cit.* p. 96).

[4] This is nicely covered by the German *Ertrag*—which most writers distinguish (some, carefully and consistently) from *Einkommen*. The *Ertrag* conception is that commonly employed (e.g. by Irving Fisher) in analysis of the discounting process.

used in this way, the term may have a merely acquisitive implication; for any property right, any mortgage against the community, has its yield.

The term is also frequently used to denote, second, *gain from transactions* or trading profit. If a share of stock is purchased for $100 and later sold for $150, it is customary to say that the venture has yielded an income of $50. The distinguishing feature of this conception is that it presupposes no allocation of income to assigned periods of time—that it does not raise the often crucial question as to when 'income' accrues.[1] The period is merely the time between the first and last transactions in a complete and mutually related series. 'Income' is imputed neither to preassigned time intervals nor to persons but merely to certain ventures, certain market operations.

There is, third, the familiar conception of *social or national income*—which appears frequently in the literature and is often defined after a fashion.[2] Social income denotes, broadly, a measure of the net results of economic activity in a community during a specified period of time. This, of course, is no definition; indeed, it is perhaps impossible to do more than indicate some roughly synonymous, and equally ambiguous, expressions. While commonly employed as though it denoted something quantitative, social income cannot be defined to any advantage in strictly quantitative terms. Economics deals with economy; economy implies valuation; and valuation is peculiarly and essentially relative. The prices with which rigorous economics deals are pure relations; and relatives cannot be summated into meaningful totals. Market prices afford only the most meagre clues (or none at all) to the 'value' of *all* goods produced and services rendered.

The concept of production, moreover, has itself a strong ethical or welfare flavour. The social income might be conceived in terms either of the value of goods and services produced or of the value of the productive services utilized during the period (after deduction for depreciation and depletion).[3] On neither basis, however, is it possible to avoid the question as to whether all economic (acquisitive) activity may be deemed productive. The use of resources to establish monopoly control can hardly be thought of as adding to the income of the community as a whole; nor is it easy

---

[1] Actually, it is always misleading to talk about the accrual of income.

[2] 'The aggregate money income of a country...must equal the aggregate money value of all goods produced and services rendered during the year' (R. T. Ely, *Outlines of Economics*, 4th ed. New York, 1923, pp. 100 and 105). One may remark upon the failure to introduce depreciation or depletion into the calculation. The necessity of such deduction is recognized in Alfred Marshall, *Principles of Economics* (8th ed.), p. 81; but Marshall's conception of social income is nowhere made explicit.

[3] This view is developed especially in Cassel, *The Theory of Social Economy*, trans. Barron (New York, 1932), chapters I and II. See also the same author's *Fundamental Thoughts on Economics* (New York, 1925).

to include the cost of the more egregious frauds perpetrated upon consumers. The tough-minded economist may argue that advertising is merely a service demanded by consumers—that an advertized product is simply a different commodity from a physically identical article with no distinctive label on the container; and this may solve the difficulty for one interested in the mechanics of the pricing process. But even a person of such interests will hesitate to maintain that all selling devices, truthful, false, and ludicrous, contribute to the social income. Large amounts of resources are employed to conceal issues in elections and to secure favour with actual and prospective government officials. But the point need not be laboured. Surely it is impossible to distinguish sharply between uses of resources which involve production, predation, and mere waste. Such distinctions, however, are implicit in the idea of social income.

In short, social income is merely a welfare conception. To say that it has increased is to say that things which must be economized are more abundant (or, perhaps, are utilized with greater 'efficiency'). This manifests an ethical or aesthetic judgment. Increase in the social income suggests progress toward 'the good life', toward a world better in its economic aspect, whatever that may be; and it is precisely as definite and measurable as is such progress.

If it be true that social income belongs far outside the realm of rigorous, quantitative concepts, the conclusion is important for the definition of *personal income*—a fourth sense in which the term is commonly used. Many writers imply or assert explicitly that personal income is merely a derivative, subordinate concept in the hierarchy of economic terminology. The view that personal income is merely a share in the total income of society is to be found in almost every treatise on economics; and some writers, forgetting even the distinction between a real and a personal tax (and that between *base* and *source*), insist that income taxes must bear—presumably by definition!—only on the net social income as it accrues to individuals.[1] On this view, gifts, capital gains, and other items must be excluded from the base of a personal tax because such items cannot be counted in the income of society as a whole!

Such notions derive, perhaps, from the central emphasis placed upon national income by Adam Smith and the mercantilists and from the central place of so-called distribution theory in classical economics. Economists have discussed the influence of trade policy upon the size of the national income; they have broken up that income curiously into functional elements; indeed, they have done almost everything with the income concept except to give it such definition as would make it eligible to a place among our

---

[1] E.g. Walther Lotz, *Finanzwissenschaft* (1st ed. Tübingen, 1917), pp. 444–50.

94

analytical tools. As a matter of fact, traditional theory is concerned primarily not with *Einkommen* but with *Ertrag*—with the pricing of goods and productive services. Its acquaintance with *Einkommen* is tenuous, implicit, and largely incidental.[1] Social income is neither an indispensable analytical tool for relative-price theory nor a concept whose content must be specified implicitly by a sound system of theory. At all events no writer, to our knowledge, has succeeded in giving any real meaning to the idea that personal income is merely a share in some undistributed whole. The essential point has been most happily phrased by Schmoller, who says in an early work, 'Nach unserer Ansicht gehört der Einkommensbegriff aber überhaupt streng genommen nur der Einzelwirtschaft an, der Volkswirtschaft nur in bildlich analoger Ausdehnung'.[2] Certainly much should be gained by cutting loose from a terminology ambiguous at best and inherited from the discussion of problems largely, even totally, irrelevant to those with which we are here concerned.[3]

Although personal income is not amenable to precise definition, it has, by comparison with the concept of social income, a much smaller degree of ambiguity. Its measurement implies estimating merely the *relative* results of individual economic activity during a period of time. Moreover, there arises no question of distinction between production and predation. Social income implies valuation of a total product of goods and services; while personal income is a purely acquisitive concept having to do with the possession and exercise of rights.

[1] For discussion of this point see A. Ammon, 'Die Begriffe "Volkseinkommen" und "Volksvermögen" und ihre Bedeutung für die Volkswirtschaftslehre', *Schr. d. Verein für Sozialpolitik*, CLXXIII, 19–26.

[2] G. Schmoller, 'Die Lehre vom Einkommen...', *Zeitschrift für di gesamte Staatswissenschaft*, XIX (1863), 78. Schmoller himself actually defines national income as the sum of all individual incomes (*ibid.* p. 20) but in such context that one may hardly charge inconsistency.

[3] Most of the innumerable German discussions of the meaning of income start with, and pretend to lean upon, Hermann, who was concerned primarily with the concept of social income, and who certainly did not write from the point of view of taxation (as do his 'followers'). See Hermann, *Staatswissenschaftliche Untersuchungen* (2nd (posthumous) ed., München, 1870), esp. chapter IX.

In Germany the 'correction' of Adam Smith's overemphasis upon the 'accounting' conception of social income ('ausschliesslich in dem von Standpunkte des capitalistischen Unternehmers Überechneten berschusse das reine Einkommen zu erblicken', is Robert Meyer's characterization of Smith's 'narrow' conception (*Das Wesen des Einkommens*, Berlin, 1887, p. 3) is regarded as a major contribution of German economics. Schmoller and most writers after him give credit to Hermann for this contribution. Meyer (*ibid.* chapter I) insists, however, that Schmoller has found in Hermann the opposite emphasis from what is really there and that credit for the contribution belongs really to Schmoller (and to Rodbertus). The controversy is hardly important for present purposes in any event, for the present writer's position implies, so far as concerns the definition of personal income, that Schmoller to some extent, and his followers especially, erred simply in getting away from Smith.

H. C. Simons

Personal income connotes, broadly, the exercise of control over the use of society's scarce resources. It has to do not with sensations, services, or goods but rather with rights which command prices (or to which prices may be imputed). Its calculation implies estimate (*a*) of the amount by which the value of a person's store of property rights would have increased, as between the beginning and end of the period, if he had consumed (destroyed) nothing, or (*b*) of the value of rights which he might have in exercised in consumption without altering the value of his store of rights. In other words, it implies estimate of consumption and accumulation. Consumption as a quantity denotes the value of rights exercised in a certain way (in destruction of economic goods); accumulation denotes the the change in ownership of valuable rights as between the beginning and end of a period.

The relation of the income concept to the specified time interval is fundamental—and neglect of this crucial relation has been responsible for much confusion in the relevant literature. The measurement of income implies allocation of consumption and accumulation to specified periods. In a sense, it implies the possibility of measuring the results of individual participation in economic relations *for an assigned interval* and without regard for anything which happened before the beginning of that (before the end of the previous) interval or for what may happen in subsequent periods. All data for the measurement would be found, ideally, within the period analysed.

Personal income may be defined as the alaebraic sum of (1) the market value of rights exercised in consumption and (2) the change in the value of the store of property rights between the beginning and end of the period in question. In other words, it is merely the result obtained by adding consumption during the period to 'wealth' at the end of the period and then subtracting 'wealth' at the beginning. The *sine qua non* of income is *gain*, as our courts have recognized in their more lucid moments—and gain *to* someone during a specified time interval. Moreover, this gain may be measured and defined most easily by positing a dual objective or purpose, consumption and accumulation, each of which may be estimated in a common unit by appeal to market prices.

This position, if tenable, must suggest the folly of describing income as a flow and, more emphatically, of regarding it as a quantity of goods, services, receipts, fruits, etc. As Schäffle has said so pointedly, 'Das Einkommen hat nur buchhalterische Existenz'.[1] It is indeed merely an arithmetic answer and exists only as the end result of appropriate calculations. To conceive of income in terms of things is to invite all the confusion

---

[1] Quoted by Schmoller (*op. cit.* p. 54) from Schäffle, 'Mensch und Gut in der Volkswirtschaft', *Deutsche Vierteljahrschrift* (1861).

of the elementary student in accounting who insists upon identifying 'surplus' and 'cash'.[1] If one views society as a kind of giant partnership, one may conceive of a person's income as the sum of his withdrawals (consumption) and the change in the value of his equity or interest in the enterprise. The essential connotation of income, to repeat, is *gain*—gain *to* someone during a specified period and measured according to objective market standards. Let us now note some of the more obvious limitations and ambiguities of this conception of income.

In the first place, it raises the unanswerable question as to where or how a line may be drawn between what is and what is not economic activity. If a man raises vegetables in his garden, it seems clearly appropriate to include the value of the product in measuring his income. If he raises flowers and shrubs, the case is less clear. If he shaves himself, it is difficult to argue that the value of the shaves must also be accounted for. Most economists recognize housewives' services as an important item of income. So they are, perhaps; but what becomes of this view as one proceeds to extreme cases? Do families have larger incomes because parents give competent instruction to children instead of paying for institutional training? Does a doctor or an apothecary have relatively large income in years when his family requires and receives an extraordinary amount of his own professional services? Kleinwächter suggests[2] that the poorest families might be shown to have substantial incomes if one went far in accounting for instruction, nursing, cooking, maid service, and other things which the upper classes obtain by purchase.

A little reflection along these lines suggests that leisure is itself a major item of consumption; that income per hour of leisure, beyond a certain minimum, might well be imputed to persons according to what they might earn per hour if otherwise engaged. Of course, it is one thing to note that such procedure is appropriate in principle and quite another to propose that it be applied. Such considerations do suggest, however, that the neglect of 'earned income in kind' may be substantially offset, for comparative purposes (for measurement of relative incomes), if leisure income is also neglected. For income taxation it is important that these elements of income vary with considerable regularity, from one income class to the next, along the income scale.

---

[1] This point, with all its triteness, can hardly be overemphasized, for it implies a decisive criticism of most of the extant definitions of income. Professor Hewett, e.g. asserts and implies consistently that income is merely a collection of goods and services which may, so to speak, be thrown off into a separate pile and then measured in terms of money. He and others too, no doubt, know better; but, when one undertakes the task of definition, one may expect to be held accountable for what he literally says.

[2] *Das Einkommen und seine Verteilung*, Introduction. We have drawn heavily, in this and other passages, on Kleinwächter's conundrums.

A similar difficulty arises with reference to receipts in the form of compensation in kind. Let us consider here another of Kleinwächter's conundrums. We are asked to measure the relative incomes of an ordinary officer serving with his troops and a *Flügeladjutant* to the sovereign. Both receive the same nominal pay; but the latter receives quarters in the palace, food at the royal table, servants, and horses for sport. He accompanies the prince to theatre and opera and, in general, lives royally at no expense to himself and is able to save generously from his salary. But suppose, as one possible complication, that the *Flügeladjutant* detests opera and hunting.

The problem is clearly hopeless. To neglect all compensation in kind is obviously inappropriate. On the other hand, to include the perquisites as a major addition to the salary implies that all income should be measured with regard for the relative pleasurableness of different activities—which would be the negation of measurement. There is hardly more reason for imputing additional income to the *Flügeladjutant* on account of his luxurious wardrobe than for bringing into account the prestige and social distinction of a (German) university professor. Fortunately, however, such difficulties in satisfactory measurement of relative incomes do not bulk large in modern times; and, again, these elements of unmeasurable psychic income may be presumed to vary in a somewhat continuous manner along the income scale.

If difficulties arise in determining what positive items shall be included in calculations of income (in measuring consumption), they are hardly less serious than those involved in determining and defining appropriate deductions. At the outset there appears the necessity of distinguishing between consumption and expense; and here one finds inescapable the unwelcome criterion of intention. A thoroughly precise and objective distinction is inconceivable. Given items will represent business expense in one instance and merely consumption in another, and often the motives will be quite mixed. A commercial artist buys paints and brushes to use in making his living. Another person may buy the same articles as playthings for his children, or to cultivate a hobby of his own. Even the professional artist may use some of his materials for things he intends or hopes to sell, and some on work done purely for his own pleasure. In another instance, moreover, the same items may represent investment in training for earning activity later on.

The latter instance suggests that there is something quite arbitrary even about the distinction between consumption and accumulation. On the face of it, this is not important for the definition of income; but it must be remembered that accumulation or investment provides a basis for expense deductions in the future, while consumption does not. The distinction in

98

question can be made somewhat definite if one adopts the drastic expedient of treating all outlays for augmenting personal earning capacity as consumption. This expedient has little more than empty, formal, legalistic justification. On the other hand, one does well to accept, here as elsewhere, a loss of relevance of adequacy as the necessary cost of an essential definiteness. It would require some temerity to propose recognition of depreciation or depletion in the measurement of personal-service incomes—if only because the determination of the base, upon which to apply depreciation rates, presents a simply fantastic problem. It is better simply to recognize the limitations of measurable personal income for purposes of certain comparisons (e.g. by granting special credits to personal-service incomes under income taxes).

Our definition of income may also be criticized on the ground that it ignores the patent instability of the monetary *numéraire*;[1] and it may also be maintained that there is no rigorous, objective method either of measuring or of allowing for this instability. No serious difficulty is involved here for the measurement of consumption—which presumably must be measured in terms of prices at the time goods and services are actually acquired or consumed.[2] In periods of changing price levels, comparisons of incomes would be partially vitiated as between persons who distributed consumption outlays differently over the year. Such difficulties are negligible, however, as against those involved in the measurement of accumulation. This element of annual income would be grossly misrepresented if the price level changed markedly during the year. These limitations of the income concept are real and inescapable; but it must suffice here merely to point them out. (Their significance for income taxation will be considered later on.)

Another difficulty with the income concept has to do with the whole problem of valuation. The precise, objective measurement of income implies the existence of perfect markets from which one, after ascertaining quantities, may obtain the prices necessary for routine valuation of all possible inventories of commodities, services, and property rights. In actuality there are few approximately perfect markets and few collections of goods or properties which can be valued accurately by recourse to market prices. Thus, every calculation of income depends upon 'constructive valuation', i.e. upon highly conjectural estimates made, at best, by persons of wide information and sound judgment; and the results of

---

[1] See Jacob Viner, 'Taxation and Changes in Price Levels', *Journal of Political Economy*, XXXI (1923), esp. pp. 494–504.

[2] In a sense relevant to income measurement, two persons' consumption of, say, strawberries might be very unequal for a period, though the physical quantities involved were identical, provided one consumed them largely in season and the other largely out of season.

such calculations have objective validity only in so far as the meagre objective market data provide limits beyond which errors of estimate are palpable. One touches here upon familiar problems of accounting and, with reference to actual estimates of income, especially upon problems centring around the 'realization criterion'.

Our definition of income perhaps does violence to traditional usage in specifying impliedly a calculation which would include gratuitous receipts. To exclude gifts, inheritances, and bequests, however, would be to introduce additional arbitrary distinctions;[1] it would be necessary to distinguish among individual's receipts according to the intentions of second parties. Gratuities denote transfers not in the form of exchange—receipts not in the form of 'consideration' for something 'paid' by the recipient. Here, again, no objective test would be available; and, if the distinctions may be avoided, the income concept will thus be left more precise and more definite.[2]

It has been argued that the inclusion of gratuities introduces an objectionable sort of double counting. The practice of giving seems a perhaps too simple means for increasing average personal income in the community. But philosophers have long discoursed upon the blessings of social consciousness and upon the possibilities of improving society by transforming narrow, acquisitive desires into desire for the welfare of our fellows. If it is not more pleasant to give than to receive, one may still hesitate to assert that giving is not a form of consumption for the giver. The proposition that everyone tries to allocate his consumption expenditure among different goods in such manner as to equalize the utility of dollars-worths may not be highly illuminating; but there is no apparent reason for treating gifts as an exception. And certainly it is difficult to see why gifts should not be regarded as income to the recipient.

The very notion of double counting implies, indeed, the familiar and disastrous misconception that personal income is merely a share in some

[1] The greater part of the enormous German literature on *Einkommensbegriff* may be regarded as the product of effort to manipulate verbal symbols into some arrangement which would capture the essential connotations of *Einkommen* (as something distinct from *Ertrag, Einnahme, Einkünfte*, etc.), provide a not too arbitrarily delimited conception, and yet decisively exclude gifts and bequests. It is as though an army of scholars had joined together in the search for a definition which, perfected and established in usage, would provide a sort of 'linguistic-constitutional' prohibition of an (to them) objectionable tax practice. For summary of this literature see Bauckner, *Der privatwirtschaftliche Einkommensbegriff* (München, 1921).

Of course, we must avoid the implication that our definition establishes any decisive presumption regarding policy in income taxation. The case for or against taxation of gratuitous receipts as income ought not to be hidden in a definition.

[2] The force of the foregoing argument is perhaps diminished when one remembers that the distinction creeps in unavoidably on the other side of the transaction—i.e. in the distinction between consumption and expense in the case of the donor. But there remains a presumption against introducing the distinction twice over if once will do.

undistributed, separately measurable whole.[1] Certainly it is a curious presumption that a good method for measuring the relative incomes of individuals must yield quantitites which, summated, will in turn afford a satisfactory measure of that ambiguous something which we call social income. This double-counting criticism, in the case of some writers (notably Irving Fisher), carries with it the implied contention that all possible referents of the word 'income', in different usages, must be definable or expressible in terms of one another. We have pointed out several different usages of the term in order to show that they represent distinct, and relatively unrelated, conceptions—conceptions which only poverty of language and vocabulary justifies calling by the same name.

[1] Some writers explicitly avoid the implication that social income should be definable in terms of individual incomes or vice versa: Held, *Die Einkommensteuer* (Bonn, 1872), chapter IV, esp. pp. 92 ff.; F. J. Neumann, *Grundlagen der Volkswirtschaft* (Tübingen, 1899), pp. 220–1; Schmoller, *op. cit.* p. 78; Ammon, *op. cit.* pp. 21–6; Meyer, *op. cit.* chapter XII.

5 Income

by J. R. Hicks*

I

We have now concluded our discussion of interest; and, by so doing, we have also concluded all that it is absolutely necessary to say about the foundations of dynamic economics. If we chose, we could thus proceed at once to analyse the working of the dynamic system, proceeding on parallel lines to those on which we analysed the working of a static system in Part II. That is what we shall do, ultimately; but meanwhile the reader has the right to raise an objection. Nothing has been said in the foregoing about any of a series of concepts which have usually been regarded in the past as fundamental for dynamic theory. Nothing has been said about Income, about Saving, about Depreciation, or about Investment (with a capital I). These are the terms in which one has been used to think; how do they fit here?

My decision to abstain from using these concepts in the last five chapters was, of course, quite deliberate. In spite of their familiarity, I do not believe that they are suitable tools for any analysis which aims at logical precision. There is far too much equivocation in their meaning, equivocation which cannot be removed by the most painstaking effort. At bottom, they are not logical categories at all; they are rough approximations, used by the business man to steer himself through the bewildering changes of situation which confront him. For this purpose, strict logical categories are not what is needed; something rougher is actually better. But if we try to work with terms of this sort in the investigations we are here concerned with, we are putting upon them a weight of refinement they, cannot bear.

I do not think that anyone who has followed the theoretical controversies of recent years will be very surprised at my putting foward this view. We have seen eminent authorities confusing each other and even themselves by adopting different definitions of saving and income, none quite consistent, none quite satisfactory. When this sort of thing happens, there is usually some reason for the confusion; and that reason needs to be brought out before any further progress can be made.

* Drummond Professor of Political Economy, University of Oxford, 1952–65. Fellow of All Souls. Nobel Prize for Economics, 1972.

Although we have refrained from using the term income in our dynamic theory, the reader will remember that we had no such inhibition when we were concerned with statics. In statics the difficulty about income does not arise. A person's income can be taken without qualification as equal to his receipts (earnings of labour, or rent from property). Sleeping dogs can be left to lie. The same is true in the economics of the stationary state, a branch of dynamic economics, but one which (as we have seen) blacks out some of the most important of dynamic problems. If a person expects no change in economic conditions, and expects to receive a constant flow of receipts, the same amount in every future week as he receives this week, it is reasonable to say that that amount is his income. But suppose he expects to receive a smaller amount in future weeks than this week (this week's receipts may include wages for several weeks' work, or perhaps a bonus on shares), then we should not regard the whole of his current receipts as income; some part would be reckoned to capital account. Similarly, if it so happened that he was entirely dependent on a salary paid every fourth week, and the present week was one in which his salary was not paid, we should not regard his income this week as being zero. How much would it be? We cannot give an exact answer without having a clear idea about the nature of income in general.

The purpose of income calculations in practical affairs is to give people an indication of the amount which they can consume without impoverishing themselves. Following out this idea, it would seem that we ought to define a man's income as the maximum value which he can consume during a week, and still expect to be as well off at the end of the week as he was at the beginning. Thus, when a person saves, he plans to be better off in the future; when he lives beyond his income, he plans to be worse off. Remembering that the practical purpose of income is to serve as a guide for prudent conduct, I think it is fairly clear that this is what the central meaning must be.

However, business men and economists alike are usually content to employ one or other of a series of approximations to the central meaning. Let us consider some of these approximations in turn.

3

The first approximation would make everything depend on the capitalized money value of the individual's prospective receipts. Suppose that the stream of receipts expected by an individual at the beginning of the week is the same as that which would be yielded by investing in securities a sum of £M. Then, if he spends nothing in the current week, reinvesting any receipts which he gets, and leaving to accumulate those that have not yet fallen due, he can expect that the stream which will be in prospect at the end of the week will be £M plus a week's interest on £M. But if he spends something, the expected value of his prospect at the end of the week will be less than this. There will be a certain particular amount of expenditure which will reduce the expected value of his prospect to exactly £M. On this interpretation, that amount is his income.

This definition is obviously sensible in the case when receipts are derived entirely from property—securities, land, buildings, and so on. Suppose that at the beginning of the week our individual possesses property worth £10,010, and no other source of income. Then if the rate of interest were $\frac{1}{10}$ per cent per week, income would be £10 for the week. For if £10 were spent, £10,000 would be left to be reinvested; and in one week this would have accumulated to £10,010—the original sum.

In the case of incomes from work, the definition is less obviously sensible, but it is still quite consistent with ordinary practice. Not having to do with a slave market, we are not in the habit of capitalizing incomes from work; but in the sorts of cases which generally arise this makes no difference. Fluctuations in receipts from work are not usually easy to foresee in advance; and any one who expects a constant stream of receipts (and does not expect any change in interest rates) will reckon that constant amount as his income, on this definition. If fluctuations are foreseen, they are nearly always so near ahead that interest on the variations is negligible. With interest neglected, calculation by capitalization reduces to mere arithmetical division over time. £20 per month of four weeks can be taken as equivalent to £5 per week.

Income No. 1 is thus the maximum amount which can be spent during a period if there is to be an expectation of maintaining intact the capital value of prospective receipts (in money terms). This is probably the definition which most people do implicitly use in their private affairs; but it is far from being in all circumstances a good approximation to the central concept.

4

For consider what happens, first, if interest rates are expected to change. If the rate of interest for a week's loan which is expected to rule in one future week is not the same as that which is expected to rule in another future week, then a definition based upon constancy of money capital becomes unsatisfactory. For (reverting to the numerical example we used above), suppose that the rate of interest per week for a loan of one week is $\frac{1}{10}$ per cent, but that the corresponding rate expected to rule in the second week from now is $\frac{1}{5}$ per cent, and that this higher rate is expected to continue indefinitely afterwards. Then the individual is bound to spend no more than £10 in the current week, if he is to expect to have £10,010 again at his disposal at the end of the week; but if he desires to have the same sum available at the end of the second week, he will be able to spend nearly £20 in the second week, not £10 only. The same sum (£10,010) available at the beginning of the first week makes possible a stream of expenditures

$$£10, \; £20, \; £20, \; £20, \ldots,$$

while if it is available at the beginning of the second week it makes possible a stream

$$£20, \; £20, \; £20, \; £20, \ldots$$

It will ordinarily be reasonable to say that a person with the latter prospect is better off than one with the former.

This leads us to the definition of Income No. 2. We now define income as the maximum amount the individual can spend this week, and still expect to be able to spend the same amount in each ensuing week. So long as the rate of interest is not expected to change, this definition comes to the same thing as the first; but when the rate of interest is expected to change, they cease to be identical. Income No. 2 is then a closer approximation to the central concept than Income No. 1 is.

5

Now what happens if prices are expected to change? The correction which must be introduced suggests itself almost immediately. Income No. 3 must be defined as the maximum amount of money which the individual can spend this week, and still expect to be able to spend the same amount *in real terms* in each ensuing week. If prices are expected to rise, then an individual who plans to spend £10 in the present and each ensuing week must expect to be less well off at the end of the week than he is at the beginning. At each date he can look forward to the opportunity of spending £10 in each future week; but at the first date one of the £10s will be spent in a week when prices are relatively low. An opportunity of spending on favourable terms is present in the first case, but absent in the second.

Thus, if £10 is to be his income for this week, according to definition No. 3 he will have to expect to be able to spend in each future week not £10, but a sum greater or less than £10 by the extent to which prices have risen or fallen in that week above or below their level in the first week.

Some correction of this sort is obviously desirable. But what do we mean by 'in real terms'? What is the appropriate index-number of prices to take? To this question there is, I believe, no completely satisfactory answer.

Even when prices are expected to change there is, indeed, still available a very laborious criterion which would enable us to say, for any given set of planned expenditures, whether it is such that the planner is living within his income or not.[1] If the application of this test were to show that the individual's expenditure equalled his income, then of course it would determine his income; but in all other cases it does not suffice to show by how much he is living within his income, that is to say, exactly how much his income is.

Income No. 3 is thus already subject to some indeterminateness; but that is not the end of the difficulty. For Income No. 3 is still only an approximation to the central meaning of the concept of income; it is not that central meaning itself. One point is still left out of consideration; by its failure to consider this even Income No. 3 falls short of being a perfect definition.

This is the matter of durable consumption goods. Strictly speaking, saving is not the difference between income and expenditure, it is the difference between income and consumption. Income is not the maximum amount the individual can *spend* while expecting to be as well off as before at the end of the week; it is the maximum amount he can *consume*. If some part of his expenditure goes on durable consumption goods, that will tend to make his expenditure exceed his consumption; if some part of his consumption is consumption of durable consumption goods, already bought in the past, that tends to make consumption exceed expenditure. It is only if these two things match, if the acquisition of new consumption goods just matches the using up of old ones, that we can equate consumption to spending and proceed as before.

But what is to be done if these things do not match? And worse, how are we to tell if they do match? If there is a perfect secondhand market for the goods in question, so that a market value can be assessed for them with precision, corresponding to each particular degree of wear, then the value-loss due to consumption can be exactly measured; but if not there is

---

[1] If his is living within his income he must be able to plan for the second Monday the same stream of purchases as for the first, and still have something left over. Suppose he plans to purchase of commodity X quantities X_0, X_1, X_2,...in successive weeks; of commodity Y quantities Y_0, Y_1, Y_2,...; and so on. The condition for him to live within his income in the first week is that the stream of purchases actually planned for later weeks,

$$X_1 Y_1 Z_1 \ldots, \qquad X_2 Y_2 Z_2 \ldots, \qquad X_3 Y_3 Z_3 \ldots,$$

valued at the prices at which each is actually expected to be made (those of the 2nd, 3rd, 4th,...weeks respectively), should have a greater value than the original stream

$$X_0 Y_0 Z_0 \ldots, \qquad X_1 Y_1 Z_1 \ldots, \qquad X_2 Y_2 Z_2 \ldots,$$

valued, not at the first but at the second Monday, and valued at the same prices as that of the other stream (those of the 2nd, 3rd, 4th weeks, &c.), that is to say, valued at prices expected to rule one week later in each case than the dates at which these purchases are expected to be made in fact.

nothing for it but to revert to the central concept itself. If the individual is using up his existing stock of durable consumption goods, and not acquiring new ones, he will be worse off at the end of the week if he can then only plan the same stream of purchases as he could at the beginning. If he is to live within his income, he must in this case take steps to be able to plan a larger stream at the end of the week; but how much larger can be told from nothing else but the central criterion itself.

6

We are thus forced back on the central criterion, that a person's income is what he can consume during the week and still expect to be as well off at the end of the week as he was at the beginning. By considering the approximations to this criterion, we have come to see how very complex it is, how unattractive it looks when subjected to detailed analysis. We may now allow a doubt to escape us whether it does, in the last resort, stand up to analysis at all, whether we have not been chasing a will-o'-the-wisp.

At the beginning of the week the individual possesses a stock of consumption goods, and expects a stream of receipts which will enable him to acquire in the future other consumption goods, perishable or durable. Call this Prospect I. At the end of the week he knows that one week out of that prospect will have disappeared; the new prospect which he expects to emerge will have a new first week which is the old second week, a new second week which is the old third week, and so on. Call this Prospect II. Now if Prospect II were available on the first Monday, we may assume that the individual would know whether he preferred I to II at that date; similarly, if Prospect I were available on the second Monday, he would know if he preferred I to II then. But to inquire whether I on the first Monday is preferred to II on the second Monday is a nonsense question; the choice between them could never be actual at all; the terms of comparison are not *in pari materia*.

This point is of course exceedingly academic; yet it has the same sort of significance as the point we made at a much earlier stage of our investigations, about the immeasurability of utility. In order to get clear-cut results in economic theory, we must work with concepts which are directly dependent on the individual's scale of preferences, not on any vaguer properties of his psychology. By eschewing *utility* we were able to sharpen the edge of our conclusions in economic statics; for the same reason, we shall be well advised to eschew *income* and *saving* in economic dynamics. They are bad tools, which break in our hands.

7

These considerations are much fortified by another, which emerges when we pass from the consideration of individual income (with which we have been wholly concerned hitherto) to the consideration of social income. Even if we content ourselves with one of the approximations to the concept of individual income (say Income No. 1, which is good enough for most purposes), it remains true that income is a subjective concept, dependent on the particular expectations of the individual in question. Now, as we have seen, there is no reason why the expectations of different individuals should be consistent; one of the main causes of disequilibrium in the economic system is a lack of consistency in expectations and plans. If *A*s income is based on *A*s expectations, and *B*s income upon *B*s expectations, and these expectations are inconsistent (because they expect different prices for the same commodity at particular future dates, or plan supplies and demands that will not match on the market), then an aggregate of their incomes has little meaning. It has no more to its credit than its obedience to the laws of arithmetic.

This conclusion seems unavoidable, but it is very upsetting, perhaps even more upsetting than our doubts about the ultimate intelligibility of the concept of individual income itself. Social income plays so large a part in modern economics, not only in the dynamic and monetary theory with which we are here concerned but also in the economics of welfare, that it is hard to imagine ourselves doing without it. It is hard to believe that the social income which economists discuss so much can be nothing else but a mere aggregate of possibly inconsistent expectations. But if it is not that, what is it?

In order to answer this question, we must begin by making a further distinction within the field of individual income. All the definitions of income we have hitherto discussed are *ex ante* definitions[1]—they are concerned with what a person can consume during a week and still *expect* to be as well off as he was. Nothing is said about the realization of this expectation. If it is not realized exactly, the value of his prospect at the end of the week will be greater or less than it was expected to be, so that he makes a 'windfall' profit or loss.[2] If we add this windfall gain to any of our preceding definitions of income (or subtract the loss), we get a new set of definitions, definitions of 'income including windfalls' or 'income *ex post*'. There is a definition of income *ex post* corresponding to each of our previous definitions of income *ex ante*; but for most purposes it is that corresponding to Income No. 1 which is the most important. Income

---

[1] To use a term invented by Professor Myrdal, and exported by other Swedish economists.
[2] To use a term of Mr Keynes.

No. 1 *ex post* equals the value of the individual's consumption *plus* the increment in the money value of his prospect which has accrued during the week; it equals consumption *plus* capital accumulation.

This last very special sort of 'income' has one supremely important property. So long as we confine our attention to income from property, and leave out of account any increment or decrement in the value of prospects due to changes in people's own earning power (accumulation or decumulation of 'human capital'), Income No. 1 *ex post* is not a subjective affair, like other kinds of income; it is almost completely objective. The capital value of the individual's property at the beginning of the week is an assessable figure; so is the capital value of his property at the end of the week; thus, if we assume that we can measure his consumption, his income *ex post* can be directly calculated. Since the income *ex post* of any individual is thus an objective magnitude, the incomes *ex post* of all individuals composing the community can be aggregated without difficulty; and the same rule, that Income No. 1 *ex post* equals consumption *plus* capital accumulation, will hold for the community as a whole.

This is a very convenient property, but unfortunately it does not justify an extensive use of the concept in economic theory. *Ex post* calculations of capital accumulation have their place in economic and statistical *history*; they are a useful measuring-rod for economic progress; but they are of no use to theoretical economists, who are trying to find out how the economic system works, because they have no significance for conduct. The income *ex post* of any particular week cannot be calculated until the end of the week, and then it involves a comparison between present values and values which belong wholly to the past. On the general principle of 'bygones are bygones', it can have no relevance to present decisions. The income which is relevant to conduct must always exclude windfall gains; if they occur, they have to be thought of as rasing income for future weeks (by the interest on them) rather than as entering into any effective sort of income for the current week. Theoretical confusion between income *ex post* and *ex ante* corresponds to practical confusion between income and capital.

8

It seems to follow that anyone who seeks to make a statistical calculation of social income is confronted with a dilemma. The income he can calculate is not the true income he seeks; the income he seeks cannot be calculated. From this dilemma there is only one way out; it is of course the way that has to be taken in practice. He must take his objective magnitude, the social income *ex post*, and proceed to adjust it, in some way that seems plausible or reasonable, for those changes in capital values which look as if they have had the character of windfalls. This sort of estimation is normal statistical procedure, and on its own ground it is wholly justified. But it can only result in a statistical estimate; by its very nature, it is not the measurement of an economic quantity.[1]

For purposes of welfare economics it is generally the *real* social income which we desire to measure; this means that an estimate has to be made which will correspond to Income No. 3 in the same way as the above estimate corresponds to Income No. 1. Here we have the additional difficulty that it is impossible to get an objective measurement of Income No. 3, even *ex post*; since Income No. 3 always depends upon expectations of prices of consumption goods. But something with the same sort of correspondence can be constructed. Variations in prices can be excluded from the calculation of capital values, in one way or another; one of the best ways theoretically conceivable would be to take the actual capital goods existing at the end of the period, and to value them at the prices which any similar goods would have had at the beginning; any accumulation of capital which survives this test will be an accumulation in *real* terms. By adding the amount of consumption during the period, we get at least one sense of real income *ex post*; by then correcting for windfalls, we get a useful measure of real social income.[2] But is is just the same sort of estimate as the measure of social money income.

I hope that this chapter will have made it clear how it is possible for individual income calculations to have an important influence on individual economic conduct; for calculations of social income to play such an important part in social statistics, and in welfare economics; and yet, at the same time, for the concept of income to be one which the positive theoretical economist only employs in his arguments at his peril. For him, income is a very dangerous term, and it can be avoided; as we shall see, a whole general theory of economic dynamics can be worked out without using it. Or rather, it only becomes necessary to use it at a very late stage in our investigations, when we shall wish to examine the effect of the practical precept of 'living within one's income' upon the course of economic development. For that purpose, it is not necessary to have an exact definition of income; something quite rough, suitable to a rough practical precept, will do quite well.

[1] Since the statistician must adopt this line, it is not surprising to find him turning for assistance to those other seekers after objective income—the Commissioners for Inland Revenue. The best thing he can do is to follow the practice of the Income Tax authorities. But it is the business of the theoretical economist to be able to criticize the practice of such authorities; he has no right to be found in their company himself!

[2] The process of correcting for windfalls will usually be less important in this case of real income, since all windfalls due to mere changes in money values have already been excluded; only such things as windfall losses due to natural catastrophes and wars are left to be allowed for.

6 The concept of income in economic theory

by N. Kaldor*

Income, unlike some other notions which have been taken over into economics from everyday usage, is not generally subjected to any searching or systematic analysis in economic textbooks. Moreover, such discussion as there is usually proceeds from the standpoint of production and distribution theory and has no direct application to the problem of individual income that is relevant from the point of view of the measurement of taxable capacity. In the chapters dealing with taxation, on the other hand, the definition of income is generally taken for granted as something settled by the more fundamental notions of general economic theory. Even the orthodox textbooks on public finance, while they devote much space and argument to the question of how progressive taxation ought to be—to the problem of the 'ideal' scale of progression—tend to slur over the more fundamental question of how the base of progressive taxation should be determined.[1]

Thus Marshall in the *Principles* contented himself with the enumeration of a number of special issues in connexion with the notion of income and in effect, as Keynes said, 'decided to take refuge in the practices of the Income Tax Commissioners and, broadly speaking, to regard as income whatever they, with their experience, choose to treat as such. For the fabric of their decisions can be regarded as the result of the most careful and extensive investigation which is available, to interpret what, in practice, it is usual to treat as net income.'[2]

This empiricism may be justified if one, in the words of Marshall, 'deliberately adopts the *social*, in contrast with the individual point of view' and therefore thinks of income primarily as a measure of the 'pro-

* Emeritus Professor of Economics, University of Cambridge, 1966–1975.

[1] This is true of the English literature, though the question has received far more attention in American literature; there was also an extended discussion among German writers on public finance from 1832 onwards and Italian writers in the first two decades of this century. The protracted controversy among German economists abated in liveliness after the publication of the famous paper by Georg Schanz, 'Der Einkommensbegriff und die Einkommensteuergesetze', *Finanz-Archiv*, XIII (1896), 23. Schanz's position was substantially that of later American proponents of the comprehensive concept of income (such as Haig and Simons), and his devastating criticism of narrower concepts evidently discouraged their academic protagonists.

[2] *General Theory*, p. 59.

duction of the community as a whole'.[1] For, as will be argued below, the business concept of income which was gradually evolved with the progress of accountancy and which aims at isolating the net results of the ordinary activities of businesses, broadly aims at excluding much the same kind of things as an economist or social accountant would wish to exclude from 'income' in measuring the national dividend. The Income Tax Commissioners of the nineteenth century who looked upon the income tax not as a personal tax but as a tax on the revenue yielded by certain sources— an attitude that was probably justified when income tax was a proportional tax—were chiefly concerned with discovering what is the everyday business meaning of the notion in order to decide what is to be taxable and what is not. But with a system of progressive taxation which aims at taxing individuals according to their respective taxable capacities, this procedure is clearly question-begging from the point of view of taxation. Equally, from the point of view of economic theory, Marshall's empiricism can only be accepted 'for want of something better'—the aim of theory is to lay down clear and consistent general principles from which theoretically correct definitions can be drawn and on the basis of which the popular use of concepts can be criticized.

The fundamental theoretical work concerning the notion of income is of more recent origin. Apart from the brilliant but rather isolated work of Irving Fisher—who tried to gain acceptance for a concept of income that is free of ambiguity and capable of measurement, but which plainly does *not* correspond with the sense of the everyday use of the term—the main work was done by the writers of the Swedish School in the 1920s and 1930s, only very little of which is available in the English language.

In this appendix we shall review the various alternative theoretical approaches to income. We shall attempt to show that the meaning of income with which the Swedish approach is concerned is not the one which would provide a yardstick of taxable capacity; since the former is concerned with isolating accruals from revaluations, whereas the latter should be concerned with isolating the *real* increment of 'economic power' or 'spending power'—i.e. of a person's command over economic goods and services. We shall show that neither of these notions is capable of objective measurement; whilst the conventional notions of income provide a more reasonable approximation to the meaning of income that is relevant to accounting purposes or to national income estimates than to the one relevant to the measurement of taxable capacity.

[1] *Principles* (8th ed.), p. 76.

The concept of income in economic theory

I. INCOME AS CONSUMPTION

Fisher's main work on the subject is contained in his *Nature of Capital and Income*, published in 1906. Fisher regarded the notions of income and capital as essentially correlative; 'a *stock of wealth* existing at a given *instant* of time is called capital, a *flow of benefits* from wealth through a *period* of time is called income'. If we include human beings, as well as all forms of material wealth, under capital (since they are equally a source of income—the difference is simply that the capitalized value of human earning power is not valued in the market as, in a non-slave state, it cannot be bought and sold), income is simply the net benefit obtained from capital goods over a period; and the term 'net' is to be interpreted as what remains *after all double counting is eliminated*. This means, according to Fisher, the elimination of all such services (benefits flowing from capital goods) as serve the maintenance or the creation of other capital goods, and which are debited to the capital goods which received them, as well as being credited to the capital goods which yielded them. Hence the *net* yield of all capital consists of the total of goods and services received over a period by individuals in their capacity as consumers. On this definition income is simply consumption; saving is not part of income, since it is not part of the net yield of *all* capital goods taken together. By saving the stock of capital is enlarged and thereby the future yield of capital is enlarged, at the cost of reducing its current yield. But the increase in capital over the period is not part of its current yield, since it is merely a reflection of an increase in future yield; to regard it as part of the current yield means counting the same thing twice over—an element of the discounted value of future income is added to the undiscounted present income. (This point—that any notion of income which is *not* consumption implies adding together undiscounted values and discounted values—is really Fisher's main contention.)

If the expected income stream, for whatever reason, is rising, the value of the stock of capital will be rising too; but for any particular period of time the increase in the latter should not be added to the former, since this involves, in Fisher's view, circular reasoning in the sense of both the tree and the fruit being regarded as part of the same thing, instead of being treated as two different things. Similarly an expected fall in future income would be reflected in a decrease in capital value; but this decrease should not be treated as a *deduction* for arriving at current income; it is future income, not current income, which has fallen.

Fisher's approach has the virtue of yielding a simple and unambiguous result, but it does not accord with everyday notions on the subject; and in a sense, it only solves the problem by eliminating it. Keeping to Fisher's

113

approach and terminology, the problem might be posed in this way. De-fining for the moment the 'net yield' of all capital as consumption, this 'net yield' will depend not only on the quantities and the productivity of different kinds of resources in existence, but also on the dispositions of their owners as between using these resources for purposes of current consumption and using them for future consumption. It is desirable to have a concept which is *not* dependent on this latter factor; and which shows, not the actual yield, but the 'potential net yield' of capital: the yield that would obtain if individuals neither saved nor dis-saved—or, in other words, that potential yield which, *in any given situation*, could be permanently maintained.[1] If we defined income as consumption, we should still re-quire another term to denote as potential income the consumption that would obtain if net savings were zero. Hence, apart from the trivial question of which is the right use of words, it is evident that income and consumption (as ordinarily understood) do not refer to the same thing, but to two different things; and if we reserved the term income for consumption we should still need another term for what would otherwise be called income; and we should still be left with the problem of how to define the latter.[2]

Returning then to the ordinary terminology, income is consumption plus net saving; the problem of defining income is really identical with the problem of defining net saving, which in turn is merely a different aspect of the problem of what is meant by 'maintaining capital intact'. A solution of any one of these three problems should therefore automatically carry with it the solution of the other two.

2. INCOME AS INTEREST

Starting from Fisher's basic premise, that income is a *flow* of wealth through a period of time, whereas capital is a stock of wealth existing at an instant of time, it is possible, as Lindahl has shown,[3] to look upon income not as the actual net yield of capital goods (i.e. the stream of services derived from them) but as the continuous appreciation in the value of capital goods due to the time factor.[4] For any given period, income in this sense can be regarded as the product of the capital value existing at the beginning of

---

[1] The qualification 'in any given situation' is important—as we shall see later when discussing other notions of Income [see p. 121 below].

[2] Fisher himself uses the term 'earnings' or 'standard income' to cover the meaning of the concept in this sense, as against 'realized income' which he defines as consumption.

[3] 'The Concept of Income', *Essays in Honour of Gustav Cassel* (London, 1933), pp. 399–407. [Reprinted as chapter 3 of this book.]

[4] This continuous appreciation, or augmentation, is of course merely another aspect of the net value created by production—or net excess of the things produced in a given period over the value of the things consumed in producing them.

the period and the rate of interest ruling in that period. This measures the appreciation in capital value that arises because the discounted future services (which make up the value) come nearer and nearer in time; in other words it measures the rate at which the value of capital goods increases through time (or rather would so increase if none of the value were withdrawn from it, for purposes of consumption).

In a world in which future events were accurately foreseen and there was no uncertainty, income thus defined[1] would be a measurable concept; it could be inferred from market prices. For in that world (i) there would be a single rate of interest, applicable to the discounting of future streams of net receipts accruing from all kinds of capital goods; (ii) the value of capital goods, at any point of time, would represent the discounted sum of these receipts; (iii) the difference in the value of capital goods between two points of time would be necessarily equal to the discounting factor (after appropriate adjustment for any 'withdrawal' of value into consumption during the interval); (iv) the rate of interest would measure the rate at which the *stock* of capital goods of all kinds would increase in time if none of the benefits accruing from capital goods were utilized for personal consumption.

But as soon as we step out of this textbook world this concept of income ceases to be objectively measurable, for several reasons.

1. In the first place, there is no longer a *single* rate of interest, applicable to the discounting of future returns of different types of assets. The so-called 'pure interest rates' applicable to loans of different duration themselves differ, both owing to the expectation of changing interest rates in the future, and the mere uncertainty of future rates. In addition, the rate of discount applicable to particular assets differs owing to various kinds of risks—lenders' risks and borrowers' risks. Hence each different kind of asset will appear to have a different *market* rate of interest attached to it—I use the word 'appear' advisedly, since the market value of assets, being the product of expected future returns and the rate of discount, does not enable us to conclude what the rate of discount is, without knowing the expected stream of returns which underlie this market value. (If a particular share A yields 5 per cent, while a share B yields 10 per cent, it is not possible to say how far the difference is due to the expectation

[1] This concept of income could be applied quite generally, to cover the income from land and labour, as well as the income from capital in the narrower sense; except that in a non-slave state, the capitalized value of personal earning power is a matter of subjective estimation only, since personal earning power cannot as such be bought or sold, and has no market price. Since there is in fact no *objective* measure of income derived from personal earning power other than actual earnings—with possibly some over-all allowance for the element of negative appreciation involved in the age factor—the particular question of income from work will not as such be further considered in this appendix.

of future returns being lower in the one case than in the other, and how far it is due to differences in the rates at which those returns are discounted, owing to their varying risk of uncertainty; it is doubtful even whether this is a legitimate question to ask.)[1] And even if we assumed that the correct *market* rate of interest applicable to each type of asset could somehow be elicited, the income thus obtained as the product of the particular rate of interest of each asset and its market value would no longer be an adequate measure of the psychic 'income' their owners derive from their possessing them. For assets which earn a low interest, owing to their safety, are productive of a higher psychic income to their owners, relative to their money-return, than other assets which owing to their riskiness have a high yield— the limiting case being cash, the money-return on which is zero. (The theoretically correct interest rates therefore, as Lindahl pointed out,[2] are not the objective (market) rates, but each individual owner's subjective estimation of these rates, based upon his own valuation of the risk factor.)

2. The income which is thus derived as the interest over a period on the capital value at a particular instant of time, is a forward-looking concept; it is the income *expected* for the coming 'period', or income *ex ante*. The income actually realized over a period can differ from this (i) if the stream of returns for the period in question (let us call it the 'first period') turns out differently from what was expected; (ii) if the expectations concerning returns in future periods (i.e. the returns expected for the second, third, etc., periods) were different at the end of the first period from what they were at the beginning; (iii) if the rate of interest changed during the first period; (iv) if the expectations concerning the interest rates in the second, etc., period are different at the end of the first period from what they were at the beginning.

These four types of differences between expectations and realizations, though analytically distinct, are not of course entirely independent of each other. Expectations are normally revised in the light of current experience (though they may be revised for other reasons as well—e.g. if some future event becomes expected that was previously unexpected) so that the differences between expectations and realizations in the first period normally involve changes in expectations concerning future periods, though there need be no correspondence between the two in magnitude, and it is even possible that positive changes in the one should involve negative changes in the other. Again it might be supposed that the difference between the actual and expected return of an asset over a period must be the same thing as the difference between the actual and expected interest over that period; yet the two are not the same, since the former might simply represent a change in the time-shape of receipts—as e.g. when certain particular receipts expected for the second period are actually realized in the first period, or vice versa.

The income that can actually be measured or observed from market data is the actual change in the value of assets over a period (adding back, for the purpose of this calculation, any value which was separated off during the period in the shape of dividend payments, etc.); in other words income defined as consumption plus *actual* capital accumulation. This is the meaning of income which was referred to as accrued income earlier in this chapter. But it automatically absorbs into the concepts of income all changes which have resulted from changes in expectations (relating to future periods) between the beginning and the end of our income-period— whether they relate to the expectation of yields, or to interest rates. It therefore includes not only the differences between actual and anticipated accrual relating to the period in question but revisions of capitalizations due to changes in expectations (or in uncertainty) relating to the further future. It is generally accepted by both economists and accountants (for reasons that will be discussed presently) that the element of capital appreciation which is due to this change in expectations ought to be separated off from the element of capital appreciation which represents accrual—that part of capital appreciation, in other words, which would still have taken place if both the events and the states of mind over the period had been correctly anticipated at the beginning. It is only the latter which is a continuous *flow* in time (so much per week, or per month); the former is the result of a revaluation occurring in an instant of time.[1]

Income *ex post* is therefore not consumption plus actual capital accumulation but consumption plus actual capital accumulation excluding windfalls.[2][3] This latter concept cannot be inferred from observed phenomena

[1] This distinction between gains and losses on the one hand which occur at particular *moments* in time, and incomes and costs on the other which represent regular *processes* in time was first elaborated by Myrdal (*Prisbildningsproblemet och föränderligheten*, Uppsala, 1927).

[2] Professor Hicks in *Value and Capital* [see pp. 102–110 above] and, I believe, some other writers, use the terms 'income ex-post' to denote what we called, following American writers, *accrued income*—i.e. consumption plus *actual* capital accumulation. Yet this is not the proper interpretation of the Swedish *ex-ante–ex-post* approach. The distinction is used to denote the difference between anticipated and realized *interest* but it does not include in interest the change in capital value due to the reassessment of future prospects.

[3] The distinction can best be elucidated by an example. If a piece of land which is expected to yield £x in the year, and has a capital value (based on that expectation) of £k, actually yields £y, its capital value may have changed in consequence to £l. If we call £x the *ex ante* income from land, the *ex post* income is £y, and not £$y+(l-k)$; or else, if we call £$y+(l-k)$ the income *ex post* we still need another term for £y. So long as x and y are *money rents*, the situation is simple and obvious. The difficulties

any more than income *ex ante*. For to estimate it it is necessary to know what the value of assets would have been at the beginning of the period if the events of that period had been correctly foreseen; and if the states of mind relating to the second, etc., periods had been the same at the beginning of the period as at the end. Income then emerges as the difference between this hypothetical capital value at the beginning of the period and its actual value at the end.[1] It may be suggested that on this definition income is the product of the capital value ruling at the *end* of the period multiplied by the rate of interest that *has obtained* during that period (looking backwards); but this way of looking at the matter does not really get us any further, since interest *ex post* can no more be inferred from market price than interest *ex ante*; in both cases the concept depends on a hypothetical valuation: the expected value of assets at the end of the period in the case of the latter, and what may be termed their 'revised value', relating to the beginning of the period, in the case of the former.

3. INCOME 'EX ANTE' AND 'EX POST'

These relationships may be set out more clearly as follows. Let K_1 and K_2 be the *actual* values of assets at the beginning and the end of the period in question respectively (K_2 being calculated by adding back any value that was separated off during the period such as a formal interest or dividend payments). Let K_2' represent the value which the assets are *expected* to have at the end of the period, at the beginning of the period; and K_1' the *revised* value of the assets relating to the beginning of the period, as estimated at the end of the period (i.e., the value the assets would have possessed if the structure of expectations at the end of the period had been the same as at the beginning; and if the events occurring during the period had been correctly foreseen at the beginning). Let i represent the rate of interest for the period *ex ante*, and i' the rate of interest *ex post*. Then income *ex ante* is $K_2' - K_1$; income *ex post* is $K_2 - K_1'$;

$$i = \frac{K_2' - K_1}{K_1}; \quad i' = \frac{K_2 - K_1'}{K_1'}.$$

arise because x and y need not take the form of rents only but may consist, in varying degrees, of improvements in the land itself, etc., with the consequent need of separating that part of the actual capital appreciation which is part of y from that part which represents $l - k$.

[1] Something akin to this was the notion of income (as far as I understand it) that Keynes was after in chapter 6 of the *General Theory*: though he was mistaken, I believe, in thinking that the ambiguities due to changes in capital values only affect the notion of *net income* (i.e. net after deducting depreciation) and not of gross income (or what he called income *simpliciter*). As we shall argue below, the latter proposition is true as regards social income (or the income of enterprises which can be defined in an analogous way to social income) but not as regards individual income.

The concept of income in economic theory

Under the postulate of perfect foresight, $K_2 = K_2'$ and $K_1 = K_1'$ hence $i = i'$, income *ex ante*, $K_1 i$, is identical with income *ex post*, $K_2[i'/(1 + i')]$ and both can be written $K_2 - K_1$, in other words, the actual appreciation in capital, as measured by market values.

In all other cases, however, neither *ex ante* nor *ex post* income can be objectively measured, or inferred from market prices, for either concept depends on a hypothetical value, K_2' or K_1', which has not even any definite meaning if the different individuals' expectations or estimates are not unanimous.[1] The exception is the case of short term loans of perfect security made for the standard income-period, e.g. one-year Treasury bonds (assuming a year to be the standard period) where K_2' is independently given by the redemption value and therefore i or i' can be inferred from their actual purchase price, K_1.[2] If we could apply this particular rate of interest to all other assets, we could infer therefore K_2' and K_1' from our formulae—in other words, define and measure both *ex ante* and *ex post* income as $K_1 i$ and $K_2[i'/(1 + i')]$ respectively. But this, as we have seen, is not the case; different assets earn different rates of interest, and there is no analogous method at hand for finding out what these are.[3] Thus if two-year bonds earn a different interest from one-year bonds, the calculation of interest by the method of the redemption-yield only gives the *average interest* for two years; the interest for the first year (*ex ante*) could only be determined if the expected value of one-year bonds a year hence were known. (Since a two-year bond half-way through its life is identical

---

[1] Since K_1 and K_2 are market values, K_2' and K_1' must also refer to expectations or estimates by the *market*—which can only be conceived of as representing some kind of average of different individuals' estimates and expectations; there is however no unique way of defining such an average. On the other hand if the expectation or estimates are taken to relate to each individual owner of assets separately, K_1 and K_2 must also be taken as the subjective value to the owner, which need not correspond to market values except in so far as the owner happens to be at the margin of indifference as a buyer or seller. This procedure avoids the major pitfalls but only at the cost of reducing income to a purely psychic concept which can neither be inferred from behaviour nor compared as between different individuals. (It would mean, for example, that two individuals could enjoy two different incomes from the ownership of two identical assets; but for that very reason, the one is not *in pari materia* with the other.)

[2] In the case of such one-year bonds i and i' can only differ for periods shorter than a year when, of course, the same difficulties emerge. But income itself is meaningful only when defined in relation to a standard period (which may be a year or only a week, but cannot be *both*) which means that we can ignore variations in interest (actual or expected) *within* that period (a year can begin, of course, every day of a calendar year).

[3] Since they cannot be inferred from market prices there is no way of *proving* that they are different either; all that one can say is that to assume them to be identical would require highly peculiar assumptions about the state of expectations which persisted in the light of continued conflict between anticipations and actual experience. Thus if a particular asset had a constant yield in time and its value (excluding the yield) was also constant, it would be difficult to contend that the excess of the yield over the 'standard' interest on the capital value was a recurrent windfall gain.

with a one-year bond.) Similarly the current price of one-year-old two-year bonds gives no clue to the 'pure interest' they earned in the past year, since the difference between this and their original value may include an element of windfall.[1] In the case of two-year bonds the accrued interest in the first year can only be inferred on the assumption that no change in the rate of interest is expected during its lifetime. The same holds for all other bonds (including perpetual annuities); while in the case of other assets, the rate of interest cannot be inferred, even on the assumption that no change in that interest is foreseen for the future.

4. INCOME AS 'STANDARD STREAM'

In his chapter on income in *Value and Capital* [reprinted as chapter 5 of this book] Professor Hicks suggests that the 'central meaning' of the income concept is to serve as a guide to 'prudent conduct'—to give people an indication of the amount which they can consume without impoverishing themselves. Following out this idea, he defines a man's income as 'the maximum amount which he can consume during a week, and still expect to be as well off at the end of the week as he was at the beginning.[2] He then finds that income is equal to the interest on the capitalized value of prospective receipts, if the rate of interest is constant; but if the rate of interest is not *expected* to remain constant, it is no longer equal to that (or to the amount which is left over after maintaining the capitalized value of the prospect constant); nor can it be described what it is, except in terms of the 'central criterion' itself. Hence, Professor Hicks concludes, 'we shall be well advised to eschew *income* and *saving* in economic dynamics. They are bad tools which break in our hands.'[3]

The novelty of this approach to the income concept is that it eschews any connexion between the notion of income and the notion of capital. Fisher, Lindahl, and the other writers on the subject invariably looked upon income as the yield derived from some *given source*: in the case of Fisher, it is the *net* yield of capital goods after elimination of all 'double counting'; for the others, it is *net* yield after deducting (or adding as the case may be) whatever is necessary to maintain the 'source' or the 'corpus' constant. In Hicks's approach the source or corpus from which the income is derived disappears altogether as a separate entity—capital appears only as the capitalized value of a certain future propsect and income as the

---

[1] The difference in the current price of *new* two-year-old bonds and two-year bonds issued a year ago, measures the difference between the *ex ante* interest of one-year bonds for the coming year and the average *ex ante* interest of two-year bonds for the coming two years: not the rate applicable for two-year bonds for the coming year.

[2] p. 103 above. [3] p. 107 above.

'standard stream equivalent' of that prospect. Capital and income are thus two different ways of expressing the same thing, not two different things.

It is easily seen that the conditions under which this 'standard-stream equivalent' has no explicitly definable meaning are the conditions under which the income (in the more usual sense) derived from a given capital (in the more usual sense) is expected to change over time.[1] 'The maximum amount the individual can spend this week and still expect to be able to spend the same amount in each ensuing week' is thus not necessarily identical with 'the maximum amount the individual can spend this week after maintaining his capital resouces intact'; and when the two differ, the former notion ceases to have any operationally definable meaning.[2] The reason for this is that income and capital are separate but correlative notions; and neither could be endowed with a definite meaning in entire abstraction from the other.

This is not meant to imply that the notion of 'maintaining capital intact' is free from difficulties. From the point of view of the individual owner of resources *expected* diminutions in the market value of resources have the same significance whether they are due to physical depreciation or depletion, technical obsolesence or foreseen changes in demand. But this does not mean that *any* expected change in earnings could be allowed for in the depreciation provision, irrespective of whether it is reflected or not

---

[1] On Hicks's terminology an expectation of a change in income in the future is itself a contradiction in terms. Income is that magnitude which cannot be *expected* to change under any circumstances whatsoever, since all such changes are implicitly absorbed in the conversion into the standard-stream equivalent. This conversion however cannot really be accomplished when the change in income over time has other causes than the accumulation or decumulation of capital. Thus (taking the economy as a whole) a future increase in the yield of resources (due to greater productivity or prosperity) means the expectation of a rising income. It is not possible to express that future improvement in terms of a constant perpetual stream—since the 'interest rates' themselves are reflections of these yields, there is no method by which such a conversion could be accomplished.

Nor is it self-evident why, for example, an individual who expects to receive an inheritance in the future should, as a matter of 'prudent conduct', treat as part of his current income and saving the interest on the present value of that prospect. To say that 'when a person saves, he plans to be better off in the future' is not of course the same as saying that a person is saving *whenever* he plans or expects to be better off.

[2] It is not clear from Hicks's treatment either, how he would regard the case of a change in actual receipts relative to expected receipts (as against a change in future receipt-expectations). Assume that a man receives an unexpected sum in a particular week, which does not affect his expectations for the future. According as we regard his state of wealth before or after the accrual of these receipts the extra amount which he can spend during the week 'without impoverishing himself' is either equal to the whole of that sum, or to the interest on that sum. Clearly the man could spend the whole of that amount and still be 'as well off at the end of the week as he was at the beginning', but if he does he cannot 'expect to be able to spend the same amount in each succeeding week' as in that particular week.

either in the physical productivity or in the market value of capital resources. The difficulties surrounding the notion of capital and of 'maintaining capital intact' must imply a corresponding limitation in the income
concept,[1] but these difficulties cannot be disposed of in the simple manner
suggested by Professor Hayek[2] (and implied in Hicks's approach) of *defining*
the maintenance of capital simply in terms of the maintenance of income.
We cannot first define income as what is left after maintaining capital intact
and then define the latter as what is required to maintain income intact,
without getting involved in circular reasoning.

The Hayek–Hicks approach to income and capital does however focus
attention on another basic difficulty. Suppose people *expect* a general fall
in interest rates, is the resulting *expected* appreciation in capital value part
of income? The textbook answer would be that in the textbook world a
fall in interest rates means a fall in the expected yield of resources—since
interest measures the productivity of capital, it is simply a reflection of the
yield of resources in *general*. Hence a fall in interest could not lead to a
general increase in capital values since *ex hypothesi* it is just sufficient to
offset that fall in the market value of capital that would otherwise have
occurred on account of the fall in the general yield of capital.[3] In the real
world, however, the market value of all assets can rise and fall together
with a change in the level of interest rates which is a bogus change, since
it does not reflect any real change in the income derived from capital
resources. To the extent, therefore, that people *expect* a general change in
interest rates, the *ex ante–ex post* method of calculating true income does
not succeed in excluding elements which represent revaluations and not
accruals.

An analogous difficulty arises out of *expected* changes in the value of
money. When prices, in general, are expected to rise, this is reflected in
an expected appreciation of capital values. In other words, the interest on

---

[1] A useful guide-post to one's thinking on these matters is to remember that 'maintaining capital intact' has a fairly definite meaning (the word 'fairly' will be further
explained later) when applied to the stock of resources of the community as a whole.
This means that in making provision for 'depreciation' of particular assets all such
expected value-changes can be allowed for as cancel out when the resulting net change
in capital values is added together, but not those which would make the value of the
net change in the total stock of capital something different from what it, in fact, is.
But unfortunately this is no more than a guide-post: it does not enable us to lay down
any definite or precise rules, for the use of accountants or others, as to how the depreciation provision should be calculated.

[2] 'The Maintenance of Capital', *Economica* (August 1935), p. 241.

[3] The owners of bonds would still make a capital gain in this case, but it would represent
a genuine redistribution of income in their favour; since it would mean that *their* income
from capital was maintained, while the income from other resources had fallen; and
it would be offset, from the point of view of society as a whole, by the *fall* in the market
value of other resources, i.e. that of their debtors.

capital—whether measured *ex ante* or *ex post*—goes up.[1] But this again introduces a bogus element in the calculation of income, since the resulting estimate of income (as measured in *current* prices) will exceed the true figure of accruals by the amount by which the expected increase in the value of assets exceeds the value of the increase in assets.

The general conclusion must therefore be that even if the windfall element in capital appreciation could be exluded—even, in other words, if we could discover by some objective test the values of K_2' and K_1' in the above denotation—the expectational approach would not really solve the problem of finding a measure of 'net saving' that corresponds to the real increase in 'resources'. It would only do so if the general level of prices was expected to remain constant; and if expectations concerning changes in the level of interest rates were consistent with, and reflected nothing else but, the expectations concerning the change in the yield of resources in general.

5. INCOME AS A MEASURE OF TAXABLE CAPACITY

We have left over until now the question whether the whole search for a concept of income which excludes the 'windfall element' is relevant from the point of view of a definition of income designed to measure the taxable capacity of individuals. The idea of excluding from income the casual or windfall element serves a clear and definite purpose in accountancy. For the main purpose of accounting is to exhibit, for the proprietors of the business, the actual results in terms as nearly comparable as can be to the expected results; in terms, in other words, which make it possible for the proprietors to judge whether the business is a 'success' and fulfils those expectations in the light of which they invested their capital, and which they alone are ultimately capable of deciding. The accountant is rightly in search therefore of a concept of income *ex post* which is as near a counterpart as can be found to the investor's income *ex ante*. In the light of the foregoing analysis, it is not surprising that the accountant's definition of income *ex post* is based, as it can only be based, on a series of admittedly arbitrary conventions whose value depends, to a large extent, on their status as time-honoured conventions—i.e. on their steady and consistent application.[2]

---

[1] This of course is Fisher's old proposition about the money rate of interest deviating from the real rate on account of changing prices; the difference is that only *expected* changes in the value of money enter into it.

[2] The nature of these conventions cannot be discussed here, but their net result (in accordance with the general accounting principle that it is better to err on the conservative side) is to bring more of the gains and less of the losses into the windfall category than

Similarly the economist who is mainly interested in a notion of income which corresponds to the value generated in the process of production (and from a social rather than an individual point of view) is in search of criteria by means of which the saving which reflects productive activity devoted to investment can be separated off from the saving which merely reflects the revaluation of future prospects. To a considerable extent therefore—though by no means the whole extent—the interests of the economist and the accountant run parallel, and income definitions based on accountancy notions can be adapted, with a number of adjustments, to serve the purposes of national income calculations.

From the point of view of the measurement of the individual taxable capacity, however, the problems that beset both accountants and economists are largely irrelevant and others take their place. For here the problem is to find a yardstick in terms of which the tax burden can fairly be apportioned among individuals; and whether an individual's taxable capacity is regarded as consisting in his personal spending power, or the 'net accretion of his economic power', the windfall character of gains (or losses) does not make the slightest difference. From the point of view of a man's ability to afford consumption goods or pay taxes it is a matter of indifference whether he makes his money at Monte Carlo or by selling shoestrings; and it may even be argued that unexpected gains possess a greater taxable capacity per £ than expected gains or returns since *ex hypothesi* they cannot have any effect on conduct. Windfalls, as Professor Pigou said, are the 'ideal objects of taxation in their announcement aspect'.[1]

The proper distinction for the purpose of the measurement of taxable capacity therefore is not between accruals and windfalls, or between expected and unexpected gains, but between genuine and fictitious gains. The exclusion of 'windfalls' from taxable income could in fact only be justified if it could be shown that the gains in the windfall category are of the fictitious kind, and not the genuine kind. But there is no such presumption. Fortuitous gains can be genuine; and as we have seen, expected gains can also be fictitious.

Capital appreciation represents a genuine gain whenever it secures for the recipient an increased command over both consumption goods and income-yielding resources—i.e. an increase in the purchasing power of his wealth in terms of commodities whether viewed as a *stock* or as a *flow*. In the normal case a gain which represents increased command in terms

could properly be regarded as belonging there. Thus the conventions for writing *down* assets are far more liberal than for writing them *up*. Occasionally, however, the conventions have the opposite results—as, for example, the depreciation of fixed assets on the basis of historical costs, in times of inflation.

[1] A. C. Pigou, *A Study in Public Finance* (3rd ed. revised, London, 1949), p. 156.

of the one also implies increased command in terms of the other. But it is possible to think of cases where this is not so. Thus when there is a general rise in capital values due to a general fall in interest rates, the purchasing power of capital resources in terms of consumption goods is higher than before. But the resulting capital appreciation does not (or at any rate need not) make any one capitalist better off relatively to others; it does not secure him an increased command over capital assets. Whilst the aggregate purchasing power (in terms of consumption goods) of his capital resources has gone up, the flow of real income that he expects to derive from his capital has not; so that his 'spending power' is not higher— or at any rate not appreciably higher—than before.[1] Similarly if in times of inflation there is a rise of ordinary shares, the gain of the shareholders is genuine enough in relation to other capitalists (whose capital values have not increased); yet, it would be wrong to treat such an appreciation as income in the same way as one which implied a corresponding increased command over consumption goods.

It follows from this that the ideal definition of income, as a measure of taxable capacity, is to be thought of, not as consumption plus *actual* capital accumulation (*à la* Haig) nor as consumption plus capital accumulation excluding windfalls (the accountancy ideal) but as consumption plus *real* capital accumulation, where the term '*real* capital accumulation' is to be understood as actual capital accumulation subjected to a double series of corrections: first, for the change in the general level of prices (of consumers' goods), and second, for the change in the general level of interest rates.

The correction for the change in the general level of prices could be regarded as an 'index-number problem'—i.e. a problem that is in principle capable of being dealt with in terms of approximative solutions though not of exact solutions.[2] But the correction for the general level of interest rates is not just an index-number problem: for the true change in interest rates,

---

[1] As we have seen earlier, an increase in the value of capital resources *in relation to income* does represent an increase in spending power, but this increase is not of the same order as one which secures for the recipient an equivalent appreciation of capital values and a correspondingly larger command over future income. Hence capital appreciation of the former type cannot be regarded as part of income in the same way as the latter type; and it may be considered that a more appropriate method of taxing benefits from capital appreciation which merely represent a fall in interest rates is through an annual tax on capital, rather than through a tax on capital gains.

[2] It must be borne in mind however that what needs to be corrected for price changes is not the saving, or the capital appreciation for the year, but the total value of assets at the end of the year by the change in prices in the course of the year. Such a correction is therefore only feasible for accrued income (which reckons unrealized capital appreciation, and not only realized) and not for realized income. Even if net realized capital gains were assumed to correspond to total net gains, realized and unrealized, it would not be possible to make the correction without knowing the total capital value at the beginning of the year.

125

as we have attempted to demonstrate above, is not something that can be inferred from market data. When the general level of share values goes up it is not possible to say how far the rise represents increased expectations of profits and how far it represents increased confidence resulting in a lower rate at which the expected profits are discounted. Thus the problem of *defining* individual income, quite apart from any problem of practical measurement, appears in principle insoluble.

6. SOCIAL INCOME AND INDIVIDUAL INCOME

Contrary to what is often supposed, the concept of social income does not suffer from quite the same ambiguity and vagueness as that of individual income; at any rate the arbitrariness in the former is of a different character, and raises less intractable problems than in the latter. The reason for this is that social income consists of the value of consumption plus the *value of the increase* in the stock of goods in existence (and not the *real increase in the value* of capital assets); and the measurement of a change in the stock of goods raises lesser problems than the measurement of the *real* change in their individual value. The change in the quantity of social capital, between any two dates, could in principle be measured by making an inventory of goods at each of the two dates and valuing the different kinds of goods at each at the same set of prices. To the extent that the actual goods in the two series are identical in character and only differ in the relative quantities in which they are available, the problem is the usual one of index numbers, of whether to take the prices ruling at the base date, and apply them to the end date, or vice versa.[1] It is only to the extent that the types of goods at the two dates are not identical—that new *kinds* of goods have appeared, and others have disappeared—that the problem of valuation emerges in the more acute form: since we have nothing to go on to show what the prices of the new goods would have been, had they been available on date 1, or what the prices of the vanished goods would have been had their kind still existed at date 2. To that extent the measurement of the change in capital must necessarily remain arbitrary.[2]

---

[1] Each particular piece of equipment will of course have changed its character: a two-year-old machine will have become a three-year-old machine, and so on. But so long as the two-year-old machine at date 1 can be taken as identical in character with the two-year-old machines at date 2, the values applied to two-year-old machines in *relation* to three-year-old machines do not present a problem, as the same price relatives are applied at both dates.

[2] All this is not to suggest that existing estimates of the national income are in conformity with these principles of measurement. But the point is that in the case of the national income there is a reasonably clear standard or 'ideal' to which existing techniques of estimation can, in greater or lesser degree, approximate.

From the point of view of national income estimates, moreover, the problem of depreciation can be ignored altogether for certain purposes, and the estimates confined to a measurement of the output of final goods realized during a period plus the net change in the stock of intermediate products. This corresponds to the gross income of enterprises (sales-proceeds less fuel and materials consumed) with a correction only for the element of price-change in the valuation of stocks.

But whilst the changes in capital values can thus be ignored when social income is taken in the aggregate, they cannot be ignored when it is a question of determining how command over wealth is divided among the different individuals. From the point of view of the individual increased command over resources due to owning 'more things' is logically indistinguishable from increased command due to the possession of things which have gone up in price relatively to other things. The 'things' moreover are not the same *kind* of things in the two cases. Whereas the social capital relates to physical objects, buildings, plant and machinery and so on, the individual's assets consist mainly of titles—loans and shares in businesses valued not as collections of physical objects but as going concerns whose earning power depends on the efficiency with which the use of physical resources is organized, and not just on the physical resources they command. The methods that can be applied for separating quantitative from value changes, or the rules that can be adopted for measuring depreciation in the one case have no application (or meaning) in the other case. When the capital in question is the value of a whole enterprise it is meaningless to distinguish between increases which represent a greater quantity of 'real capital' and others which merely reflect a higher valuation put on 'goodwill'. The problem of measuring the 'real savings' of individuals raises therefore quite different issues from those involved in the question of the 'real savings' of business enterprises or of society as a whole.

7. INCOME AS DIVIDEND

Before we leave the subject we ought to introduce yet another concept of income, which differs from income as interest in that it confines itself to that part of interest which 'gets separated off' from the principal, in the shape of formal interest or dividend payments. Here the fact of *separation* is taken as the principal criterion of what constitutes income; and to distinguish it from what, in obedience to accepted terminology, we have here called income as interest, this conception might perhaps be designated as income as dividend. Income as dividend has the merit of coming nearest to conventional ideas of income; it is perhaps on that account one of the

127

basic notions underlying our income tax legislation,[1] but logically there is nothing to be said for it, even as a kind of half-way house between income as consumption and income as interest. It falls short of income as interest, or, more accurately, of the measurable concept of accrued income, by the net amount of gains due to capital appreciation. It differs from income as consumption to the extent that the consumption of individuals exceeds or falls short of that part of their earnings which is formally distributed. Arguments which have been advanced (apart from administrative ones) for preferring it to income as interest as a tax base, are in fact identical with the arguments for preferring consumption to income as a tax base and are perhaps be shown in the following passage by Professor Pigou:

Thus consider two men of equal wealth one of whom buys with £10,000 a property reckoned to yield a permanent income of £500 a year, and the other buys for the same sum a property of equal present value reckoned to yield...an income which begins at a low figure and is destined, and known to be destined, to grow progressively larger; that, for example, there is to be no income at all for ten years, and thereafter, a perpetual income of a large amount. A property tax in this case is not merely inconvenient, in that it forces a man to make payments (possibly by borrowing) before he has any income to pay with. It is also guilty of an inequity, for since the two series of incomes have *ex hypothesi* the same present value, they ought to be subject to taxes of the same present value. But whereas a permanent 10 per cent income tax on the first series beginning now will have the same present value as a permanent 10 per cent income tax on the second series, a permanent ½ per cent property tax beginning now on the property yielding the second series will have a substantially larger value than a permanent ½ per cent property tax beginning now on the property yielding the first series. What happens in effect is that the incomes which are to begin ten years hence are, under property taxes, assessed both when they arrive and also in anticipation of their arrival. There is here, clearly, a 'distributional evil'.[2]

The reader will note the complete analogy between this argument and the one used by Irving Fisher to justify his own definition of income as consumption. Indeed if one could be certain that individuals consumed the same amount, no more and no less, than that part of their income which is in fact distributed, income as consumption and income as dividend would amount to the same thing.

[1] This is true, even though the taxation of the undistributed profits of companies may be regarded as a tax on the potential capital appreciation of shares. But it is an indirect tax on the capital gains of shareholders as a class, not a tax on the capital appreciation of the individual owner of shares. It is not, therefore, even notionally a tax on 'income as interest'.

[2] *Op. cit.* pp. 135–6. Pigou is discussing here the relative merits of an annual tax on property and that of a tax on investment income. But since he is not concerned with differences in the rates of interest applicable to different assets, the argument is equally applicable to a comparison between using income as interest and income as dividend (in our sense) as the tax base. Hence for 'property tax' we can read a 'tax on income as interest' and for 'income tax' a 'tax on income as dividend'.

The concept of income in economic theory

This, however, cannot be assumed—the man who receives no income from his property for ten years presumably will not live on air—so that the only argument in favour of income as dividend, as against income as interest, on the above lines, would be if it could be shown that the former is in fact *more closely related* to consumption than the latter. This, however, cannot be shown either; indeed the general presumption is the opposite. Two men of equal wealth will tend to live on an identical scale, and consume equal amounts if they have the same 'tastes and temperaments', quite irrespective of the forms in which they choose to invest their property. If they have different 'tastes and temperaments', and in consequence, consume unequal amounts again there is no presumption that the man who consumes more will invest in forms which yield more money income, and a smaller degree of capital appreciation, than the other—with the limited qualification that in so far as he is concerned to maximize the amount of his annual income readily available for spending he will avoid investing in property which is indivisible, and cannot be realized in small batches.[1] To the extent that the one form of income is taxed and the other is not, they both have the same incentive to invest their property in forms which reduce the tax liability; in fact the man who saves less, and spends more, may even have a stronger incentive than the other, since being more of a spendthrift, he is in greater need to save taxes.

Income as dividend comes off very poorly, therefore, as a tax base; it is neither a good income tax nor a good consumption tax; it does not manage to tax savings (as an income tax is supposed to do) since net savings are left untaxed if they take the form of capital appreciation; nor does it manage to tax consumption (as an expenditure tax does) since consumption is left untaxed if it is made at the expense of capital appreciation or out of capital; it is not a true 'half-way house' between the two—as for example a tax would be which taxed genuine consumption at one rate and genuine savings at some other.[2]

[1] Professor Pigou's argument that the man who receives no money income in his example would suffer in paying tax since he would have 'to make payments (possibly by borrowing before he has any income to pay with' assumes in effect that the property is indivisible.

[2] Professor Pigou cannot be found guilty of inconsistency in this matter, in as much as in an earlier chapter of the same book he strongly argued in favour of expenditure, as against income, as the base for taxation. But he was clearly mistaken in thinking that in the absence of an expenditure tax, a tax on investment income is a kind of second best, and preferable *on distributional grounds*, to an annual tax on property. This is not so. His conclusions only follow if the consumption of the two men is more nearly related to their money incomes than to their properties—and this clearly cannot be assumed. If taxable capacity is conceived as spending power, and not actual spending, property provides a more reliable guide to taxable capacity than investment income; though as we have seen not an adequate guide except in the case where all property has the same interest (i.e. is expected to have the same net yield in time, in the form of both dividends and appreciation).

The conception of income as dividend is sometimes defended—apart from defence on the administrative consideration that it is more convenient to assess and to collect than any alternative—on the ground that any broadening of the conception of income would create more inequities than it would remedy. This of course is an admission that any conception of income, or at any rate any practicable conception, is bound to be inequitable as a tax base. But in point of fact it is a very questionable argument. The fact that fictitious gains and losses escape hardly makes up in equity for the exclusion of genuine gains and losses; and the argument entirely ignores the point that the division between income which takes the form of dividend and income which takes the form of capital appreciation is not fixed by nature but is subject to manipulation by the taxpayer. There are innumerable ways of converting income into capital appreciation against which specific provisions designed to prevent tax avoidance are quite ineffective.

In the foregoing chapter [not reproduced here] I carefully refrained from advocating expenditure as the basis of progressive taxation on the 'Fisherian' argument that income is really consumption, and consumption plus net saving. If income could be satisfactorily defined—in other words if true net saving could be ascertained and brought into charge, and the benefit derived from ownership as such brought into charge by an annual tax on property—then at least on a narrow view of equity which considers taxation in its immediate distributional aspects there would be something to say in favour of income. But income cannot be satisfactorily defined. Hence even if consumption plus net saving (and not consumption as such) is taken as the ideal criterion of taxable capacity, there is no presumption that any definition of income that is objectively measurable could provide a better, or even as good an index of that taxable capacity as expenditure.

There is therefore a case for taking expenditure as the tax base even on this particular view of equity. There is, however, as we suggested at the end of the last chapter, a wider conception of equity, which takes into account the social consequences of individual behaviour and on the basis of which consumption *is* the ideal criterion not consumption plus net saving. On the latter view expenditure is a superior tax base to income, quite apart from the problem of definition and measurement.

8. EXPENDITURE AND CONSUMPTION

It may be objected on the other hand that expenditure is not the same thing as consumption; what a man spends in a given period will differ from the value of his true consumption during that period on account of

(*a*) the net accumulation of decumulation of his stock of consumable goods;
(*b*) the notional income, or 'flow of benefits in kind' derived from that stock. A proper tax on consumption, it may be thought, ought to make adjustments both for (*a*) and for (*b*); and the question may be asked whether the need for these adjustments does not reintroduce by the back door, so to speak, the same problems with regard to the definition of consumption as were found with the notion of income. Indeed, Professor Hicks came near to suggesting in one place that the concept of consumption suffers from the same ambiguity or vagueness as the concept of income.[1]

Before considering the nature of the problems involved in making the necessary adjustments for the differences between expenditure and consumption it is important to be clear that the problem created by consumers' 'capital goods' is not the same problem when the objective is to measure consumption, and not income. Discrimination between taxpayers results under an income tax when, because of the problems of valuation involved, the income derived from consumers' capital goods—whether in the form of a flow of benefits, or of capital appreciation—is ignored. On the principle that an income tax taxes both savings and the fruit of savings, such income from consumers' capital ought to be charged, regardless of the fact that the initial purchase was made out of taxed income. From the point of view of a tax on consumption, on the other hand, either the expenditure itself (or its annual equivalent), or the annual benefit derived from the possession of goods, ought to be subjected to charge, but not both.

Hence the problem of assessing the 'notional income' derived from consumers' capital only arises in those cases where the acquisition of an item is regarded as partaking primarily the character of investment and in consequence the expenditure on that item is treated as part of savings rather than of spendings. The most obvious example of this is the dwelling house which requires a valuation of the annual use-benfit, in much the same way as under our present conception of taxable income. The same notion could be extended to other items (such as diamonds or valuable works of art), the purchase of which could be excluded from chargeable expenditure, provided an annual charge were imposed[2] and the sales-proceeds brought into charge when the asset is sold, in so far as they were spent. In this latter case the purchaser of a piece of consumers' capital is treated in the same way as the man who saves a sum, consumes, and is

---

[1] p. 106 above.

[2] It is true that, apart from the case of the dwelling house, the proper amount of this annual charge could not usually be determined by any market price (since diamonds, Old Masters, etc. are not customarily hired out on an annual basis), and would have to be assessed on the basis of an arbitrary percentage of the purchase price.

therefore taxed on, the income derived from his savings, and is also taxed on the principal if and when he spends his savings.

The real question is whether the difference between expenditure and consumption gives rise to conceptual difficulties analogous to those involved in the difference between income and consumption. This difference is the net saving in the form of consumers' goods; and it may appear at first sight that it raises the same problems of valuation (though on a smaller scale) as the net saving that is associated with income.

But the two kinds of 'savings' are not only quantitatively but *conceptually* different—and this is the basic reason why the one notion does not suffer from the same kind of ambiguity as the other. The net saving that constitutes the difference between expenditure and consumption is the *value of the change in the stock* of durable consumers' goods in the individual's possession; the net saving that constitutes the difference between income and consumption is the (real) *change in the value of the stock* of both consumers' goods and other forms of property. As we have seen above, the evaluation of the latter kind of change raises quite different problems from the former. The difference between expenditure and consumption raises the same problems (on a smaller scale) as are involved in measuring the net saving of enterprises or the net change in the stock of social capital. Ideally, if there is a secondhand market for each kind of durable commodity of each particular degree of wear, the change in the stock between two dates can be measured by the inventory method described above. Failing that the adjustment involves some estimate of depreciation—with the usual choice between historical or replacement cost, the straight-line method, the reducing-balance method, and so on. But there is no need to take account of the rise in the *value* of possessions as such—the rise in the price of old furniture or jewellery, the question whether this rise is a real rise or only a rise in money terms, whether it represents higher future returns or a fall in the rate of discount: all these problems would only become relevant in evaluating real capital accumulation which enters into income; they do not affect the evaluation of consumption in relation to expenditure.

In other words the theoretical problem here is not one of measuring net savings in the sense of *real* capital appreciation at all, but only of making the correct provision for depreciation. I am not suggesting that there are no conceptual difficulties about depreciation. But I hope the above analysis has convinced the reader that the problem of individual income is not *just* a problem of depreciation; it raises far more complex issues which, unlike the problem of depreciation, do not lend themselves to approximative solutions in relation to a standard of reference.

PART II

INCOME AND THE MAINTENANCE OF CAPITAL INTACT

7 Maintaining capital intact

by A. C. Pigou[*]

In a rough general way the concept 'maintaining capital intact' is easy to grasp. Capital consists at any given moment of a definite inventory of physical things. What these are depends in part on how the general interplay of demand and supply has worked in the past. But at any given moment they are constituted by an unambiguous physical collection. In order that capital may be kept intact, if any object embraced in this collection becomes worn out or is thrown out (scrapped), it must be replaced by 'equivalent' objects. When we have got hold of this notion we are able to develop a correlative notion, net real income. From the joint work of the whole mass of productive factors there comes an (annual) in-flowing stream of output.[1] This is gross real income. When what is required to maintain capital intact is subtracted from this there is left net real income. This is Marshall's way of approach.

In his book on *The Pure Theory of Capital*[2] Professor Hayek proposes to throw over the concept of maintaining capital intact and—necessarily—with it the concept of net real income, and to use only the concept gross real income. When he speaks of 'the really relevant magnitude, income' (p. 298), it is gross real income that he has in mind. His reasons for this attitude are twofold. On the one hand, except in a stationary state the notion of maintaining capital intact has no 'strict meaning'; on the other hand, it is a concept of which the economist has no need. Thus, whereas I like to set out three identities: (1) net income = net investment plus consumption, (2) net income = gross income minus depreciation, (3) net investment = gross investment minus depreciation, Professor Hayek only cares to set out one, namely gross income = gross investment plus consumption. My identities, of course, imply Professor Hayek's, but his identities do not imply mine. He is satisfied with a part only of what I require. I shall begin with the first of his two reasons.

The gist of it, if I have not misunderstood, is as follows. If capital were perfectly homogeneous, consisting of a single type of article only, the quantity of capital would be something perfectly self-contained and un-

[*] Professor of Political Economy, University of Cambridge, 1908–43.

[1] There are, of course, depletions of capital other than those due to wear and tear and obsolescence, e.g. capital losses due to earthquake or war, which it is *not* customary to offset before reckoning net income. In what follows these will be ignored. They are discussed in my article on 'Net Income and Capital Depletion' in the *Economic Journal* of June 1935.　　　　　　　　　[2] London, 1940.

ambiguous. What this quantity amounted to at any time would, of course, be a consequence of the interplay of demand and supply in the past. But at any given moment it would be a physical datum, independent of, prior to, affecting, not affected by, the equilibrating process. But in actual life capital is not homogeneous; it is heterogeneous, consisting of a great number of different sorts of things. It is still true that at any given moment the quantities of the several items included in it constitute an independent physical datum. But how exactly is an inventory of diverse items to be conceived as a 'physical magnitude'? Clearly it can only be so conceived if we treat the given quantities of its several items as all *equivalent to* so many units of one item; and the only plausible way of doing this is to equate a unit of *B* to a unit of *A* when it is *worth* a unit of *A*. But the relative values of *A* and *B* and of all other things, so far from being independent of the equilibrating process, are determined through that process. For example, the relative current values of different types of machines are affected by the rate of interest, those promising a given yield in the distant future being more valuable relatively to those promising the same yield in the near future, the lower is the rate of interest.[1] Hence the quantity of capital expressed in the only way in which it is practicable to express it is not an unambiguous physical datum, as it would be if capital were an homogeneous entity. On the contrary, the quantity expressed in terms of any given component will be different at two times if the relative values of the components have changed, even though the physical constituents of the capital stock are identical at both times. It follows that the maintenance of these physical constituents unaltered need not entail that capital is maintained intact. That concept has no clear or sensible meaning.

The whole of this reasoning apart from the two last sentences I accept. I accept too the view that, if maintaining capital intact has to be defined in such a way that capital need not be maintained intact even though every item in its physical inventory is unaltered, the concept is worthless. But the inference I draw is, not that we should abandon the concept; rather that we should try to define it in such a way that, when the physical inventory of goods in the capital stock is unaltered, capital *is* maintained intact; more generally, in such a way that, not indeed the quantity of capital—which, with heterogeneous items, can only be a conventionalized number—is independent of the equilibrating process, but changes in its quantity are independent of changes in that process. Let us enquire whether and how this can be done.

[1] For, if machine *A* promises a yield *x* n years hence and machine *B* an equal yield *m* years hence (*m* being greater than *n*) the value of *B* = the value of A multipled by $(1/1+r)^{m-n}$ where *r* is the annual rate of interest.

Suppose that capital consists of two sorts of goods only, A and B, that at date 1 there are 500 units of each, and that one unit of A is worth 2 units of B. Then the stock of capital as a whole is 'equivalent' either to 750 units of A or to 1,500 units of B. At date 2 one unit of A has become worth 4 units of B, so that at that date 500 units of A plus 500 units of B are equivalent to either 625 units of A or to 2,500 units of B. As between the two dates one unit of A has become worn out or has been discarded out of the capital stock (e.g. scrapped on account of obsolescence). How many additional units of B must have been created in order that capital as a whole may have remained intact between the two dates? *Prima facie* it seems that there is nothing to choose between two answers, first, 2 units (in accordance with the valuation of the first date), secondly, 4 units (in accordance with that of the second date). But let us seek guidance from the special case of homogeneous capital. The quantity of this is a physically given magnitude, and nothing that happens either to people's desire attitude towards capital or to the cost (in any sense of cost) of producing new units can affect it in any way. By analogy, with heterogeneous capital also it is proper so to define quantity change that, the physical constituents of the capital stock being given, no such change can be brought about by anything that happens either to desire attitudes or to cost of production. Hence, if between dates 1 and 2 a unit of A disappears, capital will be maintained intact provided that a new unit of A is introduced irrespective of what the relative values of A and B have become and irrespective of the cost of production of A. If it is decided for any reason not to provide a new unit of A, but to provide instead some units of B, the number of units of B required to make up for the loss of the unit of A must then clearly be the number that at date 2 is worth—which is equivalent to saying is expected to yield the same income as—one unit of A.[1]

This way of defining maintenance of capital intact is readily generalized when capital consists, not of two, but of many kinds of goods. Moreover, if we suppose wearing out or discarding on the one side and replacement on the other to be a continuous balanced process, it is unambiguous. In practice, indeed, we have to do with finite time-intervals. That being so, the quantity of B that is deemed equivalent to a given quantity of A over any period may be different if replacement of decayed or discarded capital takes place once a week, once a month, once a quarter or once a year; for the relative values of A and B may undergo frequent variations. Hence the precise meaning of maintaining capital intact is relative to the length of

[1] We must not say 'which has the same cost of production as one unit of A would have', for that would give absurd results if A had become impossible to produce, i.e. had come to have infinite cost of production.

137

the accounting period with which we are accustomed to work. It will be agreed, however, I think, that in normal conditions this is not an important matter. In a rough general way then this definition will serve. It is not necessary to my purpose, nor do I wish, to claim that it is the best possible one. The possibility or, if we will, the high probability, that a better one could be found only strengthens my case.

Turn then to Professor Hayek's second reason for proposing to abandon the concept maintaining capital intact, namely that it is not needed. Against this I have two considerations to offer. First, as we have seen, and as is indeed obvious, to abandon this concept entails abandoning also that of net real income. In spite, however, of Professor Hayek's claim (p. 336) that the distinction between gross and net investment—which is, of course, the same as that between gross and net income—'has no relationship to anything in the real world', it cannot be denied that both business men and the income tax authorities seek after and make practical use of this distinction—or the best approach to it that they can find. It is net income, not gross income, upon which income tax is assessed. If a Chancellor of the Exchequer were to attempt to assess it upon gross income, what an outcry there would be! Surely it is proper for economists to take cognizance of this fact and, while admitting that perfect definitions cannot be found, to try to make them as little imperfect as they can.

Secondly, real income is of interest to economists largely because of its relevance to what Professor Irving Fisher calls psychic income—income of satisfaction or utility. Of course the relationship between these things is highly intricate—a matter not to be discussed here. But gross and net income are not on a par. We can easily imagine two situations in one of which the production of a given gross real income entails the wearing out or using up of a much larger mass of capital elements than it does in the other. Hence net real income is, or at all events may be, a great deal more relevant to psychic income than gross real income. This is, so far as it goes, a second good reason for economists to try to disentangle it.

No doubt, if it could be shown that the disentanglement is, from the nature of the case, utterly and for ever impossible, it would be the part of wisdom to abandon the attempt. We do not want to spend our lives in squaring the circle or inventing perpetual-motion machines. But that is not the situation with which we are faced. We cannot, indeed, in this field evolve concepts which are perfectly clean cut. There are bound to be rough edges. Some of us, myself among the number, have tried our hand at smoothing these down. No doubt we have in some degree failed. But we have not, I suggest, failed so grievously that others, instead of giving our baby another wash, should empty both it and the bath away.

138

8 Maintaining capital intact: a reply

by F. A. von Hayek*

Professor Pigou's defence of the conception of 'maintaining capital intact' consists essentially of two parts. The first is a restatement of his own attempt to define its meaning. The second is a plea that, even if this particular attempt should not be regarded as successful, economists ought still to continue to seek for the definite and unique sense which he believes must be behind the admittedly vague meaning that this concept has in practice. I shall try briefly to answer each point in turn.

I

Professor Pigou's answer to the question of what is meant by 'maintaining capital intact' consists in effect of the suggestion that for this purpose we should disregard obsolescence and require merely that such losses of value of the existing stock of capital goods be made good as are due to physical wear and tear. Once this proposition is accepted and the concept is defined so that in all instances 'when the physical inventory of goods in the capital stock is unaltered, capital *is* maintained intact', the rest of his argument necessarily follows. I am unable to accept this basis of his solution.

If Professor Pigou's criterion is to be of any help, it would have to mean that we have to disregard *all* obsolescence, whether it is due to foreseen or foreseeable causes, or whether it is brought about by entirely unpredictable causes, such as the 'acts of God or the King's enemy', which alone he wanted to exclude in an earlier discussion of this problem.[1] Now this seems to me to be neither useful for theoretical purposes nor in conformity with actual practice. The consequences of using this concept of 'maintaining capital intact' can best be shown by considering an imaginary case. Assume three entrepreneurs, X, Y, and Z, to invest at the same time in equipment of different kinds but of the same cost and the same potential physical duration, say ten years. X expects to be able to use his machine continuously throughout the period of its physical 'life'. Y, who produces some fashion article, knows that at the end of one year his machine will have no more than its scrap value. Z undertakes a very risky venture in which the chances

---

* Emeritus Professor of Economics, University of Freiburg i. B.

[1] See *Economics of Welfare* (4th ed. 1932), p. 46, and my discussion of the various stages in the evolution of Professor Pigou's theory of 'maintaining capital intact' in *Economica* (August 1935), particularly pp. 245–8.

of employing the machine continuously so long as it lasts and having to scrap it almost as soon as it starts to produce are about even. According to Professor Pigou the three entrepreneurs will have to order their investments in such a way that during the first year they can expect to earn the same gross receipts: since the wear and tear of their respective machines during the first year will be the same, the amount they will have to put aside during the first year to 'maintain their capital intact' will also be the same, and this procedure will therefore lead to their earning during that year the same 'net' income from the same amount of capital.[1] Yet it is clear that the foreseen result of such dispositions would be that at the end of the year X would still possess the original capital, Y one-tenth of it, while Z would have an even chance of either having lost it all or just having preserved it.

I find it difficult to conceive that this procedure could have any practical value or any theoretical significance. That entrepreneur Y, acting in this manner, would to all intents and purposes throw his capital away, i.e. would plan to lose it, hardly needs pointing out. But take the case where a clear concept of net income is most wanted, namely, direct taxation. To treat all receipts except what is required to make good physical wear and tear as net income for income tax purposes would evidently discriminate heavily against industries where the rate of obsolescence is high and reduce investment in these industries below what is desirable. The manufacturer of wireless sets, for example, who expects this year's model to be superseded in a year's time by technical improvements, would certainly have to restrict investment and output so as to keep prices high enough to enable him to write off obsolescing equipment in the course of the year. But if his allowance for obsolescence were treated as income, this would in effect amount to a special capital turnover tax and force him further to reduce his investment. Such a system would therefore discriminate heavily against all industries with rapid technological progress (or new and experimental industries) and thus slow down technological advance.

Analytically the use of this concept of 'maintaining capital intact' would be no less misleading. One of the purposes for which we want a definition of net income is to know what are the long run costs on which an adequate profit must be made in order that investment in that particular industry should appear profitable. It is immediately clear that all foreseeable obsolescence (whether it can be predicted with certainty or only with a certain degree of probability) must here be taken into account. No entrepreneur would regard the three alternatives mentioned before as equally

---

[1] For our present purposes we can disregard any differences in the cost of operating the three machines.

profitable, if the gross returns to be expected were the same—although if he accepted Professor Pigou's conception of 'maintaining capital intact' he would have to do so. But in that case he would not long remain an entrepreneur.

But while I feel that it is impossible simply to disregard obsolescence in this connexion, it is not difficult to see why Professor Pigou is reluctant to admit it among the factors which have to be taken into account in 'maintaining capital intact': because, once one admits it, one is on the path which leads inevitably to complete scepticism concerning the possibility of any objective criterion of what 'maintaining capital intact' means. Most people will agree with Professor Pigou that not *all* obsolescence has to be made good before we can consider any income as being 'net'. To demand that all capital losses due to unforeseen and unforeseeable changes should be made good before any income can be described as net income might mean that not only certain individuals but, in certain circumstances, even whole communities, might have no net income for years on end—although they might be in a position permanently to maintain their consumption at their accustomed level or even to raise it. I entirely agree with Professor Pigou's implied contention that in many such cases the making good of past losses should be regarded as new saving rather than as mere maintenance of capital. But this applies only to losses due to causes which had not been foreseen. And the real problem of maintaining capital intact arises not after such losses have been made, but when the entrepreneur plans his investment. The question is what allowance for amortization he ought to make in his calculations so that, in view of all the circumstances known to him, he can expect to be able to earn the same income in the future. But the knowledge on the basis of which he has to make this decision will necessarily change as time goes on, and with it will change the provision he has to make in order to achieve his aim. No watching of the 'quantity' of his capital from the outside, that is, without knowing all the information he possesses at different dates, can tell us whether he has done his best to avoid involuntary encroachments upon his sources of income or the opposite. And if we know what information he commands at the different successive dates, the action which we should think most appropriate on his part is not likely to be one which would keep any measurement of his capital constant. In a changing world, where different people, and even the same people at different times, will possess different knowledge, there can be no objective standards by which we can measure whether a person has done as well in this effort as he might have done. In such a world there is no reason to expect that the quantity of capital, in whatever sense this term be meant, will ever be kept constant, even though every individual owner

141

of capital might do all in his power to avoid that involuntary 'splashing' or 'stinting' which capital accounting seeks to prevent. This is a conclusion of some importance, since much of present economic theory is based on the contrary assumption, so well expressed by Professor Pigou when he wrote of 'the concept of capital as an entity capable of maintaining its quantity while altering its form and by its nature always drawn to those forms on which, so to speak, the sun of profit is at the time shining'.[1]

There is one more point in this connexion where I am anxious to correct a wrong impression which seems to have been left by what I said on this question. I hope I nowhere did say, and I certainly ought not to have said, that with the concept of 'maintaining capital intact' the concept of net income should also disappear. All that I meant to argue was that we cannot hope to define the latter by any reference to the 'quantity' of capital and its changes. For an explanation of the alternative procedure I must refer to my *Pure Theory of Capital*, particularly pp. 336 ff.

2

It is unlikely that Professor Pigou would have been led to advocate a solution of the puzzle which is so obviously imperfect if it were not for the fact that among the various solutions yet suggested it seemed to be the least imperfect, and if he had not been convinced that there must be a solution. His argument is that business men and legislators constantly use the concept of maintaining capital intact and seek after a clear distinction, and that the economist ought to help them to approach as closely as possible to the ideal solution which has not yet been found. Nobody denies, of course, that the practices actually followed in this connexion are of the greatest importance for the economist and that he ought to know as much about them as possible. Nor do I want to deny that these practices aim at some purpose and that the economist ought to try to help as much as he can in achieving it. The question is, however, whether this ultimate purpose of the practices ostensibly aiming at 'maintaining capital intact' is adequately defined by these words. I personally have come to the conclusion that while the ordinary practice of trying to keep the money value of capital constant is in most circumstances a fairly good approximation to the real purpose of capital accounting, this is not true in all circumstances. I have tried to show that this ultimate purpose has no direct or necessary connexion with changes in the quantity of capital, however measured, and that therefore no policy which aims at maintaining a particular measurement of capital constant can fully achieve that purpose in all circumstances. If this conclusion is essentially negative, it need for that reason be no less

[1] *Economic Journal* (June 1935), p. 239.

useful. If the usefulness of the practices aiming at 'maintaining capital intact' have definite limitations, the important thing is that these limitations be recognized. The fact that practical men try to apply to all cases a formula which has served them well in a great many cases does not prove that in these attempts the formula must necessarily have any meaning at all. The problem which the accountant and the income tax inspector face is not what constitutes in any real sense 'maintaining capital intact' in these cases—although they may have to interpret provisions which use such or similar phrases—but what are the most appropriate practices which will achieve the same end, which in the more ordinary situations is adequately achieved by keeping the money value of capital constant.

9 Maintaining capital intact: a further suggestion

by J. R. Hicks*

I

To intrude upon a controversy being waged by such paladins as Professor Pigou and Professor Hayek seems an act bold even unto rashness; but the question of maintaining capital intact just cannot be left where they left it last summer. The present note will have justified itself if it serves to provoke them to another round.

At the point which has now been reached, Professor Pigou has offered us a carefully constructed method of measuring capital; it is based upon a comparison of physical units *in use* at the two dates which are being compared, the different sorts of capital goods being reduced to a common measure by using their relative values at the *latter* of the two dates. This principle of Professor Pigou's stands up very well to most sorts of criticism, but it has (I think) been torpedoed by Professor Hayek. His example of the firm which produces fashion goods, installs machinery which it plans to use for a limited period and then to scrap before the machinery is physically worn out, establishes conclusively that there are instances where the physical maintenance of capital would not suffice to ensure the maintenance of capital in an economic sense. If the second of our two dates was taken just previous to the time when the specialized machinery is discarded, the fact that the equipment would still be there, technically almost as good as new, would not prevent the firm from needing to have set aside amortization allowances for almost the whole original value of the machinery, if it was to have maintained capital intact in any significant sense. A satisfactory definition of maintaining capital intact has got to be able to deal with this case, and it seems clear that Professor Pigou's cannot do so.

Professor Hayek, on the other hand, having demolished the rival construction, fails (in my view) to provide anything solid to put in its place. His definition of net income (constructed so as to avoid the necessity of defining the maintenance of capital *en route* for the definition of net income) contains far too many subjective elements to be usable in practice,

* Drummond Professor of Political Economy, University of Oxford 1952–65. Fellow of All Souls. Nobel Prize for Economics, 1972.

and is much more at home in those simplified models beloved of economic theorists than it is when it seeks to put on flesh and blood. As we widen our assumptions to bring them nearer reality, the more tenuous does a definition by 'constant income stream' become. In a world in which expectations were *certain* (by *certain* I do not mean necessarily *correct*) the definition by constant income stream would be eminently reasonable; but when we allow for uncertainty of expectations it soon becomes unrealistic, or rather it has to be metamorphosed into something else.[1]

In what follows I shall try to suggest what that something else is. For certain purposes, at any rate, it turns out to be something not very far removed from Professor Pigou's definition, though it is inevitably not the same as Professor Pigou's definition. But it is near enough for me to have some hope that he may be willing to accept it as a possible modification.

I must emphasize the qualification 'for certain purposes'. I feel rather strongly nowadays that most economic controversies about definition arise from a failure to keep in mind the relation of every definition to the purpose for which it is to be used. We have to be prepared to use different definitions for different purposes; and although we can often save ourselves trouble by adopting compromises, which will do well enough for more than one purpose, we must always remember that compromises have the defects of compromises, and in fine analysis they will need qualification. It is not profitable to embark on the fine analysis of a definition unless we have decided on the purpose for which the definition is wanted.

The purpose I have in mind is the measurement of the net social income. It seems clear that this is the problem which is in Professor Pigou's mind too. I am not sure about Professor Hayek; it may be that he is thinking of a different problem and that the argument is thus proceeding to some extent at cross-purposes. In any case, I shall do no more than suggest a definition which I consider to be appropriate for defining the ideal measurement of the net social income; it needs a separate investigation to determine whether it is suitable for other purposes as well.

2

The way in which the problem is conceived by Professor Pigou is (I think) this. His ultimate object is the measurement of the net social income in real terms; all the magnitudes in his fundamental identities are to be taken

---

[1] When I wrote *Value and Capital*, chapter XIV [reproduced as chapter 5 above], I was myself an adherent of the Hayekian school on this matter, so I can appreciate the qualities of Professor Hayek's definition. I can also appreciate what Professor Hayek must feel about the quite unfounded accusation by Professor Pigou that the definition by constant income stream is a definition of gross income.

in such senses that they can be converted into real terms by a suitable multiplier. When he writes

$$\text{net income} = \text{consumption} + \text{net investment}$$

the various terms in the equation may be measured in terms of money, but we have only got to choose our units properly, and they would be capable of being understood in real terms. The definitions have got to be chosen so as to make this transformation possible. At once we run into the difficulty that if net investment is interpreted as the difference between the value of the capital stock at the beginning and end of the year, the transformation would not be possible. It is only in the special case when the prices of all sorts of capital instruments are the same (if their condition is the same) at the end of the year as at the beginning, that we should be able to measure the money value of real net investment by the increase in the money value of the capital stock. In all probability these prices will have changed during the year, so that we have a kind of index-number problem, parallel to the index-number problem of comparing real income in different years. The characteristics of that other problem are generally appreciated; what is not so generally appreciated is the fact that before we can begin to compare real income in different years, we have to solve a similar problem within the single year—we have to reduce the capital stock at the beginning and end of the year into comparable real terms.

This, I think, is how the problem has appeared to Professor Pigou; Professor Hayek's substantial reply is to deny that the problem of comparing *capital* at different dates is an index-number problem. The comparison of capital values at the beginning and end of the year is not the same kind of thing as the comparison of the prices of consumable goods in different years; for the price of a durable good at one date is related to its price at another date in a way in which the prices of different (albeit similar) consumable goods at different dates are not. The price of a house in January 1941 is largely based upon an estimate of what its price will be in January 1942; but the price of a loaf of bread in one year is influenced by expectations about the price of bread in another year to a usually negligible extent.

The value of a capital good at any particular time is based upon the anticipated quasi-rents which it will earn during its future 'life'. (This 'life', it should be noticed, does not only depend upon the physical durability of the good; it also depends upon the length of time for which it is expected to be useful.) Since it will be implicit in such expectations that the article will have some capital value at each date during its life, we may say that the capital value at the beginning of the year depends upon the quasi-rents the article is expected to earn during the year, and the capital value it is expected to have at the end. In practice, these expectations must be interpreted in a sense which allows for risk; but however we allow for risk, the proposition that capital values at the beginning and end of the year are intimately related magnitudes still holds.

The suggestion I desire to make here is that we can allow for this intimate relationship without sacrifiing the general approach which Professor Pigou is naturally determined to preserve. A way of doing so has been indicated by the Swedish economists, particularly Professor Lindahl.[1] In their presentation it has been mixed up with other elements which are perhaps less acceptable. My contention is that we can use Professor Lindahl's solution of this problem without at the same time swallowing more than we like of his *ex ante–ex post* constructions for use in our theory of the trade cycle.

3

The changes which may have taken place in the price-level of capital goods are not the only reason why the difference between the money value of an article at the beginning of the year and its money value at the end will not do as a measure of depreciation; the underlying reason why this measure will not do is that the beginning-value and end-value were arrived at on a different basis of knowledge. When a particular article from the capital stock was valued in January, there was implicit in that valuation an estimate of what the value would be in December; but the December value which is used for calculating the year's depreciation is not an estimate in the same sense—December is now past, so we *know*. If C_0 is the value of the capital stock at the beginning of the year, C_1 the value of these same goods at the end, then to measure depreciation by $C_0 - C_1$, and net income by

$$\text{consumption} + \text{gross investment} + C_1 - C_0$$

is internally inconsistent. The figures for consumption and gross investment will be based upon the actual historical events of the year; the figure for C_1 also takes into account the actual events of the year, though it is still influenced by uncertainty about what will happen when the year is over; but the figure of C_0 was arrived at when the events of the year were still in the future. As far as the events of the year in question are concerned, consumption, gross investment and C_1 all shine in the light of history; but what is history for them is shrouded for C_0 in the mists of futurity. In order to get a true measure for depreciation, hence for net investment, and hence for net income, C_0 must be brought out into the light too.

[1] *Theory of Money and Credit*, part I, 'Algebraic Discussion'.

Let us then define the depreciation of the original stock of capital as the difference between the total value of the goods comprising that original stock as it is at the end of the year (C_1) and the value (C_1') *which would have been put upon the initial stock at the beginning of the year if the events of the year had been correctly foreseen, including among those events the capital value C_1 at the end of the year.*[1] Net income is then

$$\text{consumption} + \text{gross investment} + C_1 - C_1'.$$

This I think, is the Swedish definition of *ex post* income; unlike their definition of *ex ante* income, which presents difficulties of interpretation in a world of uncertainty, the definition of *ex post* income is no harder to apply in a practical case than any other method which has been suggested for dealing with the problem of depreciation.

The corrected value for the initial capital stock is of course not easy to arrive at; but what we need is not this corrected value, but the consequential figure for depreciation ($C_1' - C_1$). We can proceed to estimate this by distinguishing, of the various experiences which the initial capital goods will have had during the year, which sorts will cause a divergence between C_1' and C_1. These are the things which will cause true depreciation. By applying the rule to each case as it comes up we ought to be able to discover them.

4

In nearly all the cases where I have been able to try it out, the Swedish definition gives eminently sensible results. They are not always the results which might have been expected beforehand, but they are always intelligible, and they stand looking at from several points of view. Let us check over a few of them.

Normal wear and tear in the course of production is clearly a reason why the value of a capital instrument should be greater at the beginning of a year than at the end, even if the final value was foreseen accurately. Normal wear and tear is therefore an element in true depreciation. So is exceptional wear and tear, due to exceptionally heavy usage; if the exceptionally heavy usage had been foreseen, the gap between the beginning-value and the end-value would have been larger. On the other hand, any deterioration which the machine undergoes outside its utilization does *not* give rise to true depreciation; if such deterioration had been foreseen, the initial capital value would have been written down in consequence; the deterioration is therefore not depreciation, but a capital loss. If a machine remains

---

[1] It should be noticed that this supposed foresight only extends to the events of the year under discussion; later events are still in the dark at the end of the year, so they must be left in the dark when we are constructing our corrected figure for the initial capital.

idle throughout the year, any deterioration which it undergoes is therefore not depreciation, but capital loss; and the use of productive resources to maintain the idle machine in good condition is net investment. This last result may appear surprising at first sight, but it is only reasonable when one thinks it over; the fact that the machine may have produced some output in the past is irrelevant; the 'maintenance' work done in the present is not a contribution to current final output, but to the final output of future years.

Obsolescence of the kind described in Professor Hayek's example is true depreciation on our test; the fashion firm scraps its machinery in accordance with anticipations; it is not failure of foresight which makes the end-values less than the beginning-value. But most problems of obsolescence do arise from imperfect foresight. The allowance for obsolescence which firms reckon among their costs is for the most part a reflection of their uncertainty about the value of their equipment at the end of the year; once this value is assumed known, the necessity for such obsolescence allowances disappears.

5

The definition of net income which I have been describing is, I think, in complete accordance with that proposed by Professor Hayek; in all cases where they can both be employed they would give the same results. There are certain instances, however, where the difference between the consequences of the Swedish definition and those of Professor Pigou's definition and those of Professor Pigou's definition become striking. One of these is the obsolescence case, which has been referred to; another is the case of a capital instrument, which is not used during the year, but also suffers no physical deterioration or technical supersession. Professor Pigou would (I think) say that in such a case capital is maintained intact; on the Swedish definition (and also on Professor Hayek's) there is accumulation of capital. For, assuming the end-value to be known, the beginning-value would be the discounted value of the end-value, that is, less than the end-value. Although it remains idle, nevertheless the instrument yields a net income. This looks absurd, particularly in the case of involuntary idleness (if the instrument is deliberately held over, it is more intelligible that it should earn an income by being deliberately devoted to the satisfaction of future wants). The involuntary case becomes a little more intelligible when we notice that it is almost inevitable for involuntary unemployment of a capital instrument to be attended by a capital loss during the year considerably in excess of the income earned. ($C_1' < C_1$ but $C_0 > C_1$.) It is thus not surprising that the business man should pay little attention to such 'income', but it does not follow that the economist should not pay more attention.

J. R. Hicks

I have a strong feeling that the reason why Professor Pigou answers these borderline questions in a different way from that in which they would be answered by Professor Hayek, Professor Lindahl, or myself, is because he is primarily thinking of the measurement of real national income as a means of comparing economic welfare in different periods. As I have shown elsewhere,[1] such comparison is only possible if one is prepared to assume that the wants of the community (their utility of indifference functions) are the same in each of the periods; nor does it seem possible to make much allowance when making these comparisons for the hopes and fears of different future conditions which exist in each of the periods. So long as one sticks to the welfare problem, Professor Pigou's definition of maintaining capital intact will do very well; the borderline cases will not come up. But comparing economic welfare is not the only purpose (nowadays, alas! it is not even the main purpose) of measuring the national income.

---

[1] 'The Valuation of the Social Income', *Economica* (1940), pp. 107 ff.

PART III

MEASUREMENT OF BUSINESS INCOME

10 Economic and accounting concepts of income[1]

by David Solomons*

In recent years, discussion of the measurement of income has been largely coloured and dominated by problems created by changes in the value of money. Serious as these problems are, they are really secondary ones, for they presuppose some basic agreement about the nature and measurement of income during a period of stable prices. Between accountants and economists, it need hardly be said, no such agreement exists. My purpose in this paper is first to examine these differences—a task which has been performed, with greater or less thoroughness, many times before—and then to consider the only attempt known to me to work out a concept of income which would, like the accountant's, be capable of practical use and yet would stay close to the fundamental definition of income with which we begin. The attempt at reconciliation to which I refer is Sidney Alexander's concept of variable income, put forward in his monograph, *Income Measurement in a Dynamic Economy*.[2] Alexander's suggestion deserves more discussion than it has received hitherto, whether we finally judge it to be a workable concept or not. It is for that reason that I shall have something to say about it here. My conclusion about the practical utility of the concept, as a matter of fact, will be adverse; and from that disappointing conclusion I am led on to the view that the time has come to develop other and more effective tools to do the jobs which periodic income so signally fails to do in the field of financial planning and control. As I shall suggest, there are signs that the central position which income occupies in accounting is already being usurped.

* Professor of Accounting, Wharton School of Finance and Commerce, University of Pennsylvania.

[1] This paper was presented at the Northeast Regional Meeting of the American Accounting Association at the Massachusetts Institute of Technology on 28–9 October 1960.
[2] Published as the first of *Five Monographs on Business Income* by the Study Group on Business Income, 1950. Alexander's work in a slightly revised version has been re-published in W. T. Baxter and Sidney Davidson (editors), *Studies in Accounting Theory* (London, 1962).

D. Solomons

Any discussion of competing ideas of income ought, I think, to start with the question: 'Do we really need an income concept, and if so, what for?' Only when we have asked and answered this question can we say whether there is anything we need to define, and whether one or more than one concept of income is necessary.

Let us consider income for taxation purposes first. It is really rather remarkable that income has become so universally accepted as a good measure of taxable capacity, for on closer inspection it seems to have grave defects. Command over capital resources would seem to be a much fairer guide to the subject's ability to pay taxes, and also to the demand made by the individual on various governmental services such as defence and law and order. Alternatively, as suggested by Mr Kaldor, it might be more sensible to tax people according to what they spend rather than on what they earn. This is not a plea for the substitution of indirect for direct taxation, of course, but for the use of a computation of expenditure rather then of income as the basis of taxation. It is not necessary to go into this matter here. For my purpose, it is enough to note that our system of direct taxation could get along quite well, and, indeed, perhaps better, if we did not have a concept of income at all.

A second important purpose which the concept of income is said to serve is in the determination of corporate dividend policy. So long as dividends are paid out of income and not otherwise, it is asserted, the right of creditors will not be prejudiced by the return of capital to stockholders. If this means, as it does in certain jurisdictions, that currently or recently earned net profits may be distributed without making good earlier losses of capital, it is clear that the rights of creditors are being very imperfectly protected. The payment of a legal dividend by no means implies, in such circumstances, that the stockholders' capital is intact. Moreover, a corporation may earn a profit and yet be too short of cash to be able to pay a dividend without endangering its short-term solvency. The existence of current net income, therefore, may tell directors nothing about the dividend policy they ought to follow. It makes much more sense for the law to require, as it sometimes does, either that stockholders' capital should be intact before a dividend is paid out of any excess, or to require some defined margin of assets over and above those necessary to pay creditors' claims, before allowing the payment of dividends to stockholders. Either type of restriction is more effective in protecting the rights of creditors than one based on an income concept, while at the same time being free of the difficulties of defining and measuring net income.

154

A third major need served, or said to be served by the concept of income, is as a guide to investment policy. Prospective investors seek to maximize their return on investment, and their search will be guided by the income earned on existing investments. This is related to another argument—that income provides the best measure we have of success in the management of business enterprise in a competitive economy. These are important needs, and they both point in the same direction. That investment is most attractive which offers us the greatest present value of future receipts per dollar invested, when discounted at the going rate of interest, and in so far as historical data can help us in the choice of investments, it will be data about the growth in present value of existing investments. Again, that manager is most successful who, during a given period, increases the present value of the enterprise entrusted to him proportionately the most. In both of these cases, it is growth in present value which alone appears to be significant; and since it seems to carry out the function generally attributed to income, growth in present value must be what we had better understand income to mean.

ECONOMIC INCOME

The concept of income to which we have been led corresponds, of course, to Hicks's definition of income. For an individual, he defines income as the maximum amount a man can consume in a period and still be as well off at the end of the period as he was at the beginning. There is no doubt that when, as individual salary-earners and investors, we think of our personal income for a year, we commonly do not think of it in this way, but rather as a stream of prorated receipts, unaffected by any changes in the value of the tangible assets with which we started the year and certainly as having nothing to do with any change in our future prospects—in our 'goodwill', in other words—which may take place during the year. But this does not lead me to conclude that 'the income of a person or other entity is what he believes to be his income...'[1] for we can be mistaken about the nature of income just as men were once mistaken about the nature of combustion when they attributed it to phlogiston. Rather, I would say 'Income is as income does.'

If we take Hicks's definition of income as applied even to an individual, it is easy to see, however we define our terms, that income in Hicks's sense and income as the accountant measures it will only by accident ever be the same thing. As Hicks points out, the difficulty about his definition is

---

[1] Myron J. Gordon, 'Scope and method of theory and research in the measurement of income and wealth', *Accounting Review* (October 1960), p. 608.

in saying what we mean by 'being as well off' at one date as at another. He offers us three different measures of well-offness which, however, come together, if we abstract from changes in the value of money and from changes in the rate of interest, to give us a single measure of well-offness command over money capital. If we accept constancy of money capital as representing constancy of well-offness, then income in Hicks's sense becomes the amount by which the individual's net worth has increased during the period, due allowance being made for the value of what he has consumed or given away during that time.

To use Hicks's definition for the income of a business entity rather than for that of an individual, we need only modify it slightly; the income of the business, whether it is incorporated as a separate legal entity or not, is the amount by which its net worth has increased during the period, due allowance being made for any new capital contributed by its owners or for any distributions made by the business to its owners. This form of words would also serve to define accounting income, in so far as net accounting income is the figure which links the net worth of the business as shown by its balance-sheet at the beginning of the accounting period with its net worth as shown by its balance-sheet at the end of the period. The correspondence between the two ideas of increased net worth is, however, a purely verbal one: for Hicksian income demands that in evaluating net worth we capitalize expected future net receipts, while accounting income only requires that we evaluate net assets on the basis of their unexpired cost.

It is hardly open to question that you cannot really assess the well-offness of an enterprise by aggregating the costs, or the unexpired costs, of its assets and deducting its liabilities. Any differences between the current value of its tangible assets and their book value based on cost will be excluded; and any value which the enterprise may have over and above the value of its tangible assets will also be excluded. We may sum up the relationship between these two different concepts of increase in net worth, economic income and accounting income, by starting with accounting income and arriving at economic income thus:

Accounting income

+ Unrealized changes in the value of tangible assets which took place during the period, over and above value changes recognized as depreciation of fixed assets and inventory mark-downs,

− Amounts realized this period in respect of value changes in tangible assets which took place in previous periods and were not recognized in those periods,

156

+ Changes in the value of intangible assets during the period, hereafter to be referred to as changes in the value of goodwill

= Economic income.

THE REALIZATION PRINCIPLE

Obviously the main difference between these two income concepts lies in the accountant's attachment to realization as the test of the emergence of income. The Study Group on Business Income, in its 1952 report, rather surprisingly suggested that 'the realization postulate was not accepted prior to the First World War',[1] and supported this with quotations from both American and British sources. It seems to me, on the contrary, that the trend has, for a long time now, been away from, rather than towards, placing emphasis on the importance of realization. For a long time the relationship of income to capital was likened to the relation of the fruit to the tree. Just as there was no difficulty in separating the crop from the tree, so there need be no difficulty in distinguishing income from the capital which produced it. It was in line with this thinking that, for the first thirty-six years after Peel had re-introduced the income tax in Britain in 1842, no relief was given by the British tax code for the using up of fixed assets in the course of carrying on a business. The introduction of income tax depreciation allowances in Britain in 1878, and their growth in importance there and here since then, constitute a movement away from the idea that you can evaluate the fruit without giving thought to the value of the tree—that realized profits can be measured in disregard of what have sometimes been called 'mere value changes' in the assets of the business. Another earlier step away from the pure realization principle was the 'cost or market-price' rule for valuing inventory. You will not find this in accounting literature before the mid-nineteenth century, for before that time consistent valuation at cost seems to have been the rule. The recognition of unrealized losses on inventory is a clear recognition of 'mere value changes', if only in one direction, as being relevant to the determination of income. As final evidence of the same tendency, I suppose we might cite the development of cash accounting into accrual accounting as itself a de-emphasizing of the importance of realization. For what it is worth, we can perhaps say that over the years accounting income and economic income have moved a little closer together. Yet of course, when everything has been said, accounting income is still substantially realized income.

The tableau set out above may make it easier for us to evaluate the two income concepts in terms of the two qualities which outweigh all others

[1] *Changing Concepts of Business Income* (New York, 1952), p. 23.

in importance, their usefulness and their practicality. It is because the results of this evaluation are what they are that it is natural to hanker after a compromise income concept which has a greater share of these qualities combined than either accounting or economic income has, taken by itself.

THE CASE FOR AND AGAINST ACCOUNTING INCOME AND ECONOMIC INCOME

Whether we use one concept of income or another, or indeed whether we use any concept of income at all, clearly should depend, as I have already said, on the purpose we want to serve and the income concept which will best serve it. In what follows I shall concentrate my attention on one aspect of this matter only, namely, the measurement of business income for the purpose of assessing entrepreneurial success of failure in the profit-making sector of the economy. From this point of view it must be said that accounting income is seriously defective. By focusing attention on the result of current realization of assets and ignoring all other value changes except such as are covered by the 'cost or market' rule, and by depreciation, it can lead to some rather ridiculous results. One such result is that described by Kenneth MacNeal.[1] Two investors each have $1,000 to invest. One buys $1,000 worth of stock A, the other buys $1,000 worth of stock B. By the end of the year both stocks have doubled in price. The first investor sells out just before 31 December, and reinvests the $2,000 he gets from the sale in stock B. The second investor continues to hold his block of of stock, which is also worth $2,000 at the end of the year. Thus both start equal, with $1,000 each in cash; they also finish equal, both holding equal quantities of stock B worth $2,000. It is impossible to say that one investor has been more successful than the other. Yet one of them shows an accounting profit of $1,000 as the result of his realization, while the other shows no accounting profit at all.

Another absurd result is cited by Sidney Alexander, that of the manager of a large corporation who is considering a deal which will increase his accounting profit by a million dollars but which will result in the destruction of the firm's goodwill by forcing it out of business. By looking only at changes in tangible equity (and only at a part of that), while ignoring changes in goodwill, accounting income provides us with a very unsatisfactory measure of managerial success. Another way of putting this is to say that if maximizing profit is ever a rational business goal, it is rational only if profit means economic profit, not accounting profit.

[1] In his article 'What's Wrong with Accounting', *The Nation* (7–14 October 1939), and reprinted in *Studies in Accounting*, ed. W. T. Baxter (London, 1950).

158

It may be said, and with truth, that the differences between accounting income and economic income are only short-run differences, i.e. if we take a sufficiently long period in the life of an enterprise the changes in the value of equity which distinctively enter into economic income will also be reflected in accounting income. Thus MacNeal's second investor will have his wise investment reflected in his profit when eventually he sells his stock in a later period, if by then it has not fallen in value. That over the whole life of an enterprise its total accounting income and economic income must be identical cannot be gain-said. But this is poor consolation for short-run defects in our measure of income. *All* the problems of income measurement are the result of our desire to attribute income to arbitrarily determined short periods of time. Everything comes right in the end; but by then it is too late to matter.

Having cast some doubt on the effectiveness of accounting income as a gauge of managerial success, we have to recognize that it emerges satisfactorily from the other test, that of practicality. In so far as objectivity is regarded as an indispensable quality of an income concept which is to have any claim to being practical, accounting income is practical enough. But this is of little moment if it does not measure what we want to measure. Objectivity without relevance is not much of a virtue. The question is whether we can retain some or all of the objectivity of accounting income while answering the question which accounting income palpably fails to answer: How much better off has the accounting entity become during the period?

In passing, we might notice a contrary point of view on the relevance of the two income concepts we are comparing in a statement by Professors Hill and Gordon.[1] Rejecting the idea that unrealized profits should be included in income, they argue that 'information as to what management *expects to make* on the things it *has not sold* is no substitute for information as to what management *has made* on the things it *has sold*'. The answer to this is that neither is the second kind of information a substitute for the first, and it is only the second kind which accounting conventionally provides. Both kinds of information are necessary to assess managerial success. As I have already tried to show, to look at realized profits and losses only may be to ignore an important part of the total picture.

In advocating their particular brand of business income, economists have usually argued that the increase in net worth of the enterprise, which constitutes income, must be arrived at by valuing the whole enterprise at the beginning and the end of the period whose income we wish to measure.

[1] T. M. Hill and Myron J. Gordon, *Accounting: a mangagement approach* (2nd ed. 1960, Homewood, Ill.), p. 143.

These valuations, they say, must be made by discounting, at each date, the expected stream of receipts less the expected stream of payments of the enterprise as far into the future as possible, to arrive at the present value of the net stream. Any amounts distributed by the enterprise to its proprietors during the period must, of course, be added back to give the increase in net worth which, in this view, is synonymous with income. Expressed in this way, the concept looks quite unpractical, for it seems to demand a superhuman degree of foresight, not only about the broad sweep of events but also about the details of day-to-day transactions.

I do not think that too much should be made of this difficulty. We do not allow uncertainty about the future entirely to inhibit us from valuing property on the basis of expected net receipts, or at least on the best estimate we can make of them. Moreover, there are simplifying assumptions we could make which would render the valuation process more manageable. Nevertheless, the difficulties are still somewhat formidable.

A second difficulty about the concept of economic income is that in successive discounting of expected future receipts and payments, effect will have to be given not only to real foreseeable changes in the enterprise's future, but also to changes in human expectations about this future. Thus, suppose that at the beginning of the period a large receipt is foreseen as coming in in three years' time. At the end of the period (of, say, a year) the receipt is thought to be much less certain, and in any case probably smaller than was previously expected. The net worth of the enterprise will have apparently shrunk during the year, then, not because of a real change in the future but only because of a change in expectations about the future. Thus economic income will react both to real future changes and to changes in human expectations, and the effects of these two sets of factors will be inextricably combined.

THE CONCEPT OF VARIABLE INCOME

The concept of 'variable income' attempts to eliminate the effect of a change in expectations from our measure of economic income. Alexander, it will be remembered, approaches the problem of measuring business income by considering first the income from a bond, indeed from quite a variety of bonds. He starts with a perpetual bond which pays no interest in the ordinary sense, but whose owner annually receives $10 if, on the toss of a coin, it comes down heads and nothing if it comes down tails. As a matter of fact this example is hardly more bizarre than the British premium savings bonds which have been in issue since 1956 and which, while securing the investor's capital, pay no interest in the ordinary sense but offer the chance, after a qualifying period of a prize in a monthly lottery. The amount of the prize fund is determined by calculating interest, at the rate prescribed from time to time, on the bonds eligible for the draw. In the case of Alexander's perpetual bond, he argues that, assuming a 5 per cent rate of interest, the bond would maintain a steady value of $100, whatever the results of the tosses from year to year, for an even chance of receiving $10 or nothing is equivalent to an expectation of receiving $5 each year, giving a capital value, at 5 per cent of $100. As a matter of fact, according to the strength of the gambling instinct in the community in question, the bond might just as easily be worth more or less than $100; but so long as its value is accepted as being unaffected by the results of each toss, it does not matter just what that value is. And of course, since each toss is a separate event, the chances of success next time are unaffected by past results, so there is no reason why the value of the bond should be affected by the incidence of heads or tails. The income from the bond in any year is then equal to its owner's receipts from it, $10 or nothing according to the result of the toss.

We get closer to real life with Alexander's second bond, which is like the first but has a life limited to 20 years. This bond at the outset will have a capital value of $62.70, this being the present value, at 5 per cent of a 20-year annuity of $5 annually (the expectation of receipts from the bond). A year later, regardless of the outcome of the toss, it should be worth only $60.42, the present value of a 19-year annuity of $5, and each year, as the bond's expectation of life diminishes, its value will continue to fall. In this case the bondholder enjoys an income which is always less than his receipts by the amount of the diminution in the value of his security The loss of capital value in the first year was $2.28, so that if the coin came down heads his receipts were $10 and his income was $7.72, while if the coin came down tails his receipts were zero and his income was − $2.28. This illustration leads us straight to Alexander's first definition of variable income, at least as it applies to income from securities, which is that variable income is equal to the net receipts from the security plus or minus any change in its value which was, *at the beginning of the period*, expected to take place during the period.

This, it must be noted, is a first approximation to the definition of variable income, for the full definition has to provide for the possibility that the net receipts of the period may themselves cause future expectations of receipts to be modified during the period, as where a particularly large distribution to owners of a security during the present period is made at the expense of distributions to be made in future periods. In such a case, variable income has to be defined as the net receipts from the security plus or minus any change in its value during the period which was expected at the beginning of the period, plus or minus the discounted present value of any consequential change in expected future receipts brought about by the level of current receipts. This modification of the definition to take account of consequential change in the value of the security will be seen to be of some significance when shortly we consider the determination of the variable income of a business enterprise.

Because changes in the value of a security which result from changes in expectations which occur during the period are excluded from the definition of variable income, this does not mean that they must be neglected altogether. What it does mean is that they are considered to be best kept separate from income, to be reported separately as unexpected gains. Here, another of Alexander's illustrations makes the point clear. Suppose, he says, the amount paid on the perpetual bond is suddenly raised from $10 or nothing on the toss of a coin to $12 or nothing. At a 5 per cent rate of interest this announcement will raise the value of the bond from $100 to $120. There is an unexpected gain of $20, quite apart from any variable income there may be during that year.

This is perhaps a suitable point at which to compare the informativeness of the three income concepts we can choose from in this case. Accounting income would be reported as $10 for the year if the coin came down heads. The change in the terms of the bond would not be regarded as having any relevance to the determination of current income. Economic income would be reported as $30, the receipts for the period plus the increase in the value of the bond. Alexander's proposal is that we should report a variable income of $10 and an unexpected gain of $20. There seems to me to be no room for doubt that this last method of reporting is more informative than either of the others, if our purpose is to assess the success of the bondholder's investment policy for the year.

Incidentally, the relationship between economic income and variable income can be expressed symbolically quite simply, if we write V as the value of the asset whose income we are considering, R for the net receipts from it, use the subscripts o and 1 for the beginning and end of period 1, and the further subscripts a and e for actual magnitudes and expected magnitudes respectively. Then:

Economic income = Variable income + unexpected gain

$$V_{1a} - V_{0a} + R_a = (V_{1e} - V_{0a} + R_a) + (V_{1a} - V_{1e})$$

However, it has to be admitted that this formulation is incomplete in so far as it excludes from variable income and leaves in unexpected gain the consequential changes in V_{1a} which have already been referred to.

THE VARIABLE INCOME OF A BUSINESS ENTERPRISE

It is easy enough to separate the receipts of the owner of a security from the security itself. When we turn to a business enterprise, we cannot use the amounts distributed by the enterprise to its proprietors to help us in determining the income of the enterprise; and the net receipts of the enterprise will include the proceeds of converting non-cash assets into cash, which proceeds we obviously cannot reckon as income. What corresponds to R_a, in the case of an enterprise, is the change in net tangible assets during the period, all assets being valued at cost. This is equal to accounting net income before charging depreciation or providing for inventory mark-downs, and it is the first element in enterprise variable income.

The second element, $V_{1e} - V_{0a}$, is the change in the ex-dividend value of the enterprise during the year which can be predicted with more or less certainty at the beginning of the year. This predictable change in value is, I suggest, what we ought to be measuring when we provide for depreciation, that is to say, it is depreciation based more on the expected loss of market value through use of obsolescence of assets rather than on allocations of historical cost.[1] Of course, in a world from which uncertainty had been banished, these two concepts of depreciation would amount to the same thing.

The third and last element in the variable income of a business enterprise, corresponding to the consequential change in the value of a security resulting from the year's distribution to proprietors, could be of major importance. We must include in variable income any change in the value of the enterprise which is the result of managerial activity during the year over and above the predictable change just discussed. Such change may take the form of a change in the value of tangible assets or a change in the value of goodwill. To qualify for inclusion in variable income these value changes must be brought about by the activity of the firm. If they are purely the result of factors extraneous to the firm, such as a change in the law or a change in the market rate of interest, then they are not part of variable income but are unexpected gains.

The distinction which has to be drawn here is between value changes which are merely the result of a change in expectations and value changes which are the result of managerial activity. If variable income is to measure the firm's success in adding to its well-offness, value changes of the latter

---

[1] I must repeat here that I am assuming changes in the value of money. In so far as these must be reckoned with, some form of stabilization would have to be built into the above scheme.

type must be included in it. In his original formulation of the way in which the variable income of a corporation might be determined, Alexander did not draw a distinction between internally and externally generated changes in the value of goodwill, but suggested that any change in its value might be included in variable income. However, this seems to me to be inconsistent with his earlier definition. The principal difference between variable income and economic income, as I understand it, is that while economic income includes all changes in the value of net worth which have taken place during the period, variable income includes only those changes which inevitably result from the passage of time or are the result of the activities of the period. To implement this idea, we have to try to distinguish changes in the value of goodwill which are the result of managerial activity, those which reflect, that is to say, changes in expectations brought about by the management and changes in the value of goodwill which cannot so be accounted for.

We have, then, these three constituents of variable business income:

1. The change in net tangible assets, valued at cost.

2. As a deduction, the expected loss of market value of assets through use of obsolescence.

3. Internally generated differences between the value of both tangible and intangible assets at the accounting date and their cost at date of acquisition (or their value at the previous accounting date), to the extent that these differences have not already been included in (2) above.

It is this third element, and especially the recognition of certain changes in the value of goodwill as constituting part of the firm's net income, which particularly distinguishes variable income from accounting income.

CAN WE MEASURE VARIABLE INCOME?

Variable income is a valuable idea, I think, in clarifying our thinking about what an income concept should give us and in recognizing the limitations of accounting income. But can we, in practice, hope to make the distinction between those value changes which are to be included in variable income and those which are to be included in unexpected gain?

Regretfully, I do not think that we can. We must remember that we have two problems, one of valuation and one of attribution, if we want to implement the idea of variable income for a business enterprise. Even if we are prepared to ignore any but quite substantial divergences between the depreciated cost and the current value of tangible assets, we should as a minimum have first to revalue goodwill at the end of each accounting period and then to apportion any change in its value between that part which was the result of managerial activity and that part which was the result of good or bad luck. One has only to state this difficulty to see that there can never be any simple solution to it. Even in very simple domestic situations we know that we can rarely separate the results of good luck and good judgment. In a complex business situation, how much less likely are we to be able to do so!

This difficulty, which would confront us even if our accounts were kept in monetary units of constant purchasing power, is exacerbated when we have to allow for price-level changes. When an asset is bought for $1,000 and prices in general rise so that a year later the asset, though then partly worn out, is worth more on the market than when it was first bought, is this value change to be regarded as an 'unexpected gain' or are we to attribute it to the good judgment of management in purchasing the asset in anticipation of a price rise? If the use of the variable income idea requires us to answer questions like this, I conclude that we simply cannot use it, except perhaps in simple non-business situations.

CONCLUSION

Just as Hicks was led to the conclusion that income was not an effective tool of economic analysis, so it seems to me that we are led to the conclusion that periodic income is not an effective tool of financial planning or control. This conclusion seems to accord ill with the fact that income measurement has long been a central theme of accounting and the main preoccupation of the accounting profession. Yet this fact need not impress us. The practice of medicine once consisted largely of blood-letting. It may be that we are already witnessing a decline in the importance of income measurement. Certainly there is a livelier sense of the shortcomings of ascertained profit figures than there once was, for most of the purposes for which such figures have traditionally been used. There is a rather striking confirmation of this in the preamble to Recommendation XV of the Institute of Chartered Accountants in England and Wales. This recommendation is concerned with the price-level problem, and the passage I have in mind (paragraph 312) reads as follows:

The Council cannot emphasize too strongly that the significance of accounts prepared on the basis of historical cost is subject to limitations, not the least of which is that the monetary unit in which the accounts are prepared is not a stable unit of measurement. In consequence the results shown by accounts prepared on the basis of historical cost are not a measure of increase or decrease in wealth in terms of purchasing power; nor do the results necessarily represent the amount which can prudently be regarded as available for distribution, having regard to the financial requirements of the business. Similarly the results shown by such accounts are

165

not necessarily suitable for purposes such as price fixing, wage negotiations and taxation, unless in using them for these purposes due regard is paid to the amount of profit which has been retained in the business for its maintenance.

This seems pretty much to throw away the baby with the bath-water.

The fact is that for several important purposes periodic income, either historical or prospective, has already been or is being superseded. For decision-making purposes the idea of 'contribution' has taken over from net income. In the field of taxation, we depart from income as the tax base every time we introduce special allowances for depletion, or provide for accelerated depreciation, or permit an anomalous treatment of capital gains. Even for reporting to stockholders, just as in the first half of this century we saw the income statement displace the balance-sheet in importance, so we may now be de-emphasizing the income statement in favour of a statement of fund flows or cash flows. Each of us sees the future differently, no doubt. But my own guess is that, so far as the history of accounting is concerned, the next twenty-five years may subsequently be seen to have been the twilight of income measurement.

11 The nature of income measurement

by William H. Beaver* and Joel S. Demski†

Financial reporting is heavily concerned with income 'measurement.' Theorists have, for decades, argued the nature of income and how best to measure it. Practitioners define their task in terms of income measurement. In turn, the FASB's reaffirmation of the importance of income (FASB, 1976) raises renewed interest in the measurement issue and provides a motivation for our paper.

In particular, the purpose of this paper is to explore the nature of income measurement. We offer initially a strict fundamental measurement perspective in which income measurement is viewed as the representation of a preference ordering on a firm's production plans. Such a measure exists and is open to a straightforward present-value interpretation in the usual economic setting of perfect and complete markets. Unfortunately, these market assumptions render the measure superfluous. Movement to a setting of imperfect or incomplete markets is necessary for economic returns to such measurement to exist, but the desired measurement does not necessarily exist in such a setting.

Abandoning the fundamental measurement perspective, we then offer a reinterpretation of income measurement as a noisy communication process that may be more useful than a strictly cash flow measure and more cost effective than a more ambitious disclosure policy. In this communication setting, however, we do not view the reported datum as a measure in the fundamental sense.

The paper consists of four sections. In the first we review the traditional notion of income measurement in a conventional neoclassical setting under subjective certainty. In the second section we extend the discussion to an uncertain setting where complete and perfect markets are retained. Incomplete markets and the possibility of fundamental income measurement in such a setting are discussed in the third section. Finally, our

* Professor of Accounting, Stanford University.
† Professor of Information and Accounting Systems, Stanford University.

The authors acknowledge the helpful comments of the participants in the Stanford Summer Research Seminar (August, 1977) on an earlier draft of this paper.

This research was sponsored by the Stanford Program in Professional Accounting, major contributors to which are: Arthur Andersen & Co.; Arthur Young & Company; Coopers & Lybrand; Ernst & Ernst; Peat, Marwick, Mitchell & Co.; and Price Waterhouse & Co.

reinterpretation of financial reporting as a noisy communication process in the light of potentially impossible fundamental measurement is presented in the fourth section.

INCOME MEASUREMENT IN A CERTAIN WORLD WITH PERFECT AND COMPLETE MARKETS

Consider a conventional economic setting in which non-satiating households supply various factors of production and consume various commodities that are produced by various firms employing the supplied factors. The market structure is complete in the sense that *all* consumption goods as well as all factors of production are traded in organized markets. And each such market is perfect in the sense that prices are known by all agents, no transactions costs of any form are present, all agents behave as strict price takers, and the transaction technology is convex.[1] Moreover, we presume the economy is at an equilibrium, in which supply and demand offers are equated at the prevailing price.

Initially, we focus on an instantaneous setting in which some firm acquires resources and instantaneously transforms these factors into saleable consumption goods. Let the m dimensional vector $q = (q_1, \ldots, q_m)$ denote the list of factor quantities acquired by our firm in question. Also let the n dimensional vector $r = (r_1, \ldots, r_n)$ denote the quantities of consumption goods produced. Finally, let P denote the $m + n$ dimensional price vector. We call the receipts less the expenditures of this firm its *income*:

$$I = \sum_{j=m+1}^{m+n} P_j r_j - \sum_{j=1}^{m} P_j q_j \qquad (1)$$

At a fundamental level we would term this an *income measure*. One of the features of the neoclassical setting is that the heterogeneous individual shareholders are unanimous in their rankings of alternative production plans for the various firms in the economy (Radner, 1974b).

This ranking is represented by the income measure in Equation (1). In particular, one production plan is as good as another if and only if it leads to an income measure that is not lower.[2] Each individual is assumed to be non-satiating, (*i.e.*, each prefers more consumption to less). With perfect and complete markets, an increase in the individual's wealth is

---

[1] Fractional quantities of all factors and commodities are available.

[2] In more precise terms, we have (with a given set of endowments and prices) a set of production plans that is rank-ordered in a complete and transitive manner. This is then represented by an income measure mapping the production plans into the real numbers and using the $\geq$ relation defined on the real numbers. See Ijrii, 1967; Coombs *et al.*, 1970; Krantz *et al.*, 1971 and Mock, 1976.

The nature of income measurement

commensurate with more consumption. And with the firm's income increased, each shareholder's wealth is increased. Thus, the income measure is well-defined here—receipts less expenditures—and the firms are described as behaving as if they maximized the income measure.

Extension to a multiperiod setting retains the income measure description, but in a more familiar present-value format. We merely recognize production factors and consumption goods in each period and decompose the initial period measure in the obvious manner: that is, a period's income is now defined as the change in the present-value of the future receipts during that period. This provides a series of income measures, one for each period, such that their sum equals the firm's net receipts over the horizon and such that vector maximization of the measures is equivalent to present-value maximization.[1]

We conclude this brief summary of income measurement in a conventional neoclassical setting with several additional points. First, the emphasis is on fundamental measurement. We have existence of a mapping from alternative production plans into the real line that (using the $\geq$ relation) represents a complete and transitive ranking of production plans.[2] The measure is by no means unique, but it surely exists and is open to straightforward, conventional interpretation. Second, since plans, possibilities, and market prices are all known, no one would pay an agent to report this measure. Income is already known or is costlessly constructable by each agent. This, of course, follows from the assumptions of certainty and perfect and complete markets.

Third, the distinction between *ex post* and *ex ante* measurement is unimportant. At each intermediate point in time, the market value of the firm's assets (and claims against those assets) is known because complete and perfect markets exist. Moreover, an outcome which results in higher market value and higher net income is preferred. Hence, the net

---

[1] An interesting feature of this income measure is that none of the usual income measurement conundrums, such as depreciation in the sense of cost allocation, arise in this setting. To be sure, we may interpret the periodic income measure as consisting of periodic cash flow less depreciation. But it is unnecessary to view the depreciation datum as an allocation of some cost. To see this, consider a situation in which factors acquired in one period produce receipts in several future periods. In a completely rich market setting, any factors carried over from one period to the next are marketable with a known price. In that sense no conventional accrual concepts are involved; nor, for that matter, is any conventional depreciation in the sense of interperiod allocation of a purchase price involved. Moreover, the perfect markets assumption ensures the equivalence among present value, replacement cost, and exit value measures.

[2] Somewhat casually, we say a ranking of elements in a set is complete if all elements in the set are ranked. Similarly, the ranking is transitive when one element is ranked ahead of a second and the second is ranked ahead of a third necessarily implies the first is ranked ahead of the third.

income measure easily and unambiguously performs the role of ranking outcomes as well. Indeed, with subjective certainty assumed, the *ex ante* and *ex post* measures will be identical.

INCOME MEASUREMENT IN AN UNCERTAIN WORLD WITH PERFECT AND COMPLETE MARKETS

Movement to an uncertain world leaves the above argument intact, provided we endow the economy with an appropriately rich set of perfect markets. In such a setting, the precise productive outcome is unknown at the time of production. We model this uncertainty in the usual way, by introducing a state variable, denoted $s \in S$, such that any productive outcome is precisely determined by the productive act chosen and which state of nature obtains (Debreu, 1959, especially Chapter 7).

This provides a basis for trading in factors and consumption goods contingent on which state actually obtains. That is, complete insurance arrangements are possible, through the mechanism of event contingent trading. (Note that we assume all agents eventually learn which state does obtain, otherwise their trade arrangements would be constrained to be equal across state occurrences they are unable to distinguish.)

Return now to our instantaneous production setting in (1). With state indexing, $q^s = (q_1^s, \ldots, q_m^s)$ now denotes the quantities of factors acquired if and only if state s obtains. Similarly, $r^s = (r_1^s, \ldots, r_n^s)$ denotes the quantities of consumption goods produced if and only if state s obtains; and P^s denotes the corresponding price vector. Suppose there are l possible states. Then the firm's production plan is an l dimensional list of input-output combinations:

$$((q^1, r^1), \ldots, (q^l, r^l))$$

and the income of such a firm with such a plan is defined as

$$I = \sum_{s=1}^{l} \left(\sum_{j=m+1}^{m+n} P_j^s r_j^s - \sum_{j=1}^{m} P_j^s q_j^s \right) \tag{2}$$

Note in particular that—with the complete and perfect markets assumption—there is a market valuation of each possible production plan. That is, even acknowledging uncertain returns, the presumed rich set of perfect markets allows for an unambiguous (market) valuation of the firm's production plan. And now repeating the prior argument, we again view this valuation as representing the unanimous preference ordering on the set of possible production plans.

Of course, we have merely expanded the notions of factor and commodity in the original setting. Thus, with such a rich set of markets, all that was said before extends with equal force. In particular, the income measure exists in a fundamental sense, and we would not pay anyone to provide it because the component items are already assumed known. In short, existence of uncertainty in and of itself creates no problems with, or interest in, income measurement.

Further note that the *ex ante* and *ex post* measures are now influenced by the state variable. Before the event, the firm's production plan called for production of r^1 if state 1 obtains, r^2 if state 2 obtains, and so on, using some appropriate state contingent factor schedule and resulting in the contemporaneous income measure in Equation (2). After the fact, state $\hat{s}$ has obtained, $r^{\hat{s}}$ was actually produced, and $q^{\hat{s}}$ was actually used. However, under either perspective, the income measure represents a *unanimous* ranking (of production plans in the *ex ante* perspective and outcomes in the *ex post* perspective). Hence, as in the certainty case, the distinction is a trivial one, because both perspectives can be easily reconciled.

It is clear, however, that such a rich set of markets is incongruent with the existent economic structure. We, therefore, turn to the incomplete markets setting, in which all conceivable state contingent trades are *not* available; rather, only a proper subset are.

INCOME MEASUREMENT IN AN UNCERTAIN WORLD WITH INCOMPLETE MARKETS

A setting of imperfect and incomplete markets is important because it is more realistic than the setting discussed above. Concentration on the incomplete setting is, however, sufficient for our purpose. In this setting, the firm is still envisioned as specifying a production plan consisting of state-contingent inputs and outputs. The only difference is that some of the inputs and outputs cannot be traded in organized markets. At one level, the firm may not have markets for certain assets and liabilities, such as outcomes from research and development expenditures, petroleum reserves, rights to accelerated depreciation for tax purposes on its assets, used equipment and the like (Arthur Andersen, 1977). At another level, the non-existence of futures and insurance markets (except in a limited number of cases) provides *prima facie* evidence of the lack of such completeness.

Without marketability of *all* of the factors and commodities, it is possible to lose the unanimous ranking of alternative production plans. Some share-

171

holders may prefer one plan over another based on nonmarketable commodities. And without trading opportunities, there is no way to resolve, via the implicit compensation mechanism of trade, the differences in taste. That is, in a regime of complete and perfect markets, income maximization is unanimously preferred because it is commensurate with increased consumption. But without access to some markets, irreconcilable conflicts may arise. Shareholders may, for example, display heterogeneous tastes in ranking production plans because of nonmarketable assets which each possesses.[1]

It is, of course, possible to construct settings in which unanimous agreement on production plans does exist in an incomplete market setting. For example, if a proposed production plan is spanned by existing plans (from an existing equilibrium) unanimity will exist and prices can be used to evaluate the proposed plan. Similarly, unanimity exists in the mean-variance world of modern finance. (Ekern and Wilson, 1974; Radner, 1974b.)

But even when unanimity does occur in this setting, it is not necessarily represented by an income measure *in any traditional sense*. Under monopolistic conditions, the firm's owners, for example, may be unanimous in *not* seeking to maximize the firm's market value. And in such a setting representation of the unanimous tastes amounts to representation of subjective tastes. The measure, in other words, becomes entirely subjective; and in this sense it does not enjoy the supposed objectivity of the traditional income measure of resting on observed prices.

The important point, though, is that unanimity in the rankings of pro-

---

[1] To illustrate, consider a three-commodity world (α, β and γ) and a firm that must select one of the three production plans listed below (For example, the three commodities could be consumption in three states of the world.):

Net Production	Plan 1	Plan 2	Plan 3
α	45	40	35
β	20	30	34
γ	8	5	10

Three owners equally share in the returns and no market for either commodity exists. Their respective utility functions and evaluations are:

Individual	U_i ($\alpha\,\beta\,\gamma$)	U_i (45, 20, 8)	U_i (40, 30, 5)	U_i (35, 34, 10)
1	$2\alpha + \beta + \gamma$	118	115	114
2	$\alpha + \beta$	65	70	69
3	γ	8	5	10

Observe that all three disagree on the best plan and that, under majority voting, they will be intransitive.

duction plans is not necessarily present here. In such a case, the firm may simply be unable to select between two alternative production plans. (Game theory solution concepts, for example, often result in exasperatingly rich sets of possible solutions and no basis for distinguishing among them.) Thus, some plans are non-comparable. Indeed the ranking may even be intransitive.

Income measurement, on the other hand, is viewed as a mapping from a set of production plans into the real line (with plans ranked by the magnitude of this income). If such a measure represents a ranking of the alternative production plans, then that ranking must be complete and transitive. The income measure, that is, maps from the entire set of plants and it is surely transitive. Hence, whatever it represents must be complete and transitive. But the ranking of production plans is not necessarily complete and transitive in this setting. Thus, fundamental income measurement, in the sense of representing a unanimous ranking of alternative production plans for the firm, is not necessarily possible here.

Financial reporting cannot, therefore, be described in terms of income measurement in this setting of incomplete markets.

A POSSIBLE REINTERPRETATION

What, then, is the nature of income? One possible answer is available if we more closely examine the nature of the economy with incomplete markets. A particular firm offers a complex set of state-contingent production plans, but many individuals (*e.g.*, investors) do not distinguish among the various states to the extent that the firm's management does. This is a major reason for market incompleteness. Hence, the firm now possesses information that is potentially useful to individuals external to its direct operations.

Such information may be useful in the sense of revising beliefs before decisions (*e.g.*, investment decisions) are made (termed pre-decision information). It may also be useful in terms of providing a basis for contracting, as exemplified by cost-plus payment arrangements, dividend restrictions stated in terms of income, managerial incentive arrangements based on income, and so on (termed post-decision information). Of course, these two roles may occur simultaneously in a multiperiod world (Radner, 1974a).

In transmitting this information, for either or both purposes, a number of options become interesting once we recognize costliness of the communication process. The firm might list its specific (r^s, q^s) realizations, which would be potentially useful because not everyone (or anyone) is presumed to observe $\hat{s}$. But this is a vast undertaking. Alternatively, it might list its ending cash balance, say q_1^s. An intermediate role is to aggregate the (r^s, q^s) realizations with the introduction of various groupings and allocations (which can be interpreted as use of pseudo prices for non-marketable factors and commodities). Presumably, this notion of accrual accounting is a cost-effective alternative.

However, the crux of the argument on behalf of accrual accounting rests on the premise that (1) reported income under accrual accounting rules conveys more information than a less ambitious cashflow-oriented accounting system would,[1] (2) accrual accounting is the most efficient means to convey this additional information, and, as a corollary, (3) the 'value' of such additional information system exceeds its 'cost.'

Income reporting under accrual rules, then, is neither 'good' nor 'bad' as such. Rather, it may be a desirable middle ground between more and less reporting. But interpreted in this light, it derives its support from the information it conveys (at whatever cost) and *not* from such criteria as 'more income is better than less.' Indeed, there is no reason to label the bottom line as 'income.' (Of course, there is no reason not to label it as 'income' either.)[2]

This is further discussed below, where we focus more explicitly on the pre- and post-decision settings.

PRE-DECISION INFORMATION

Consider the pre-decision perspective in the AICPA Objectives Study (1973) and the Tentative Conclusions of the FASB's Conceptual Framework Project (1976). Both studies adopt the view that the primary purpose of financial statements is to provide information to some defined class of users (*e.g.*, investors and creditors in the case of the FASB).[3] At the same time, they also support the usefulness of income reporting as a

---

[1] Note that with cash also reported we can meaningfully speak of 'more' information in this context.

[2] Though the terminology differs, this is the spirit of Sorter's (1969) 'events' approach in which the proper combination of 'aggregation' and 'valuation' is sought so as to balance information demands and cost. And by extending the argument we may find accrual procedures to be that happy medium.

[3] Although portions of the conceptual framework create ambiguity regarding the extent to which the FASB intends to adopt an informational perspective, recent statements by Sprouse (1977) at an Annual Meeting of the American Accounting Association confirm this informational perspective. In answer to advocates of the 'full disclosure' approach to financial reporting, Sprouse responded with a view of income as a cost-effective alternative to a comprehensive disclosure policy.

vehicle for providing the desired information. By implication, they have reached a judgment regarding the three issues noted above.

However, the basis for this judgment is less than clear. As indicated earlier, accounting income rules can be viewed as resulting in aggregations over quantities and prices. If the aggregated number which results is a sufficient statistic, there is no loss of information. In this situation, there is a potential savings in cost of processing, and the income-rule question is resolved on pure efficiency grounds (Feltham, 1977).

In general, of course, there will be a loss of information. In this case, heterogeneity of preferences for income rules may arise because the 'value' and 'cost' of the information may fall differently across users. A lack of unanimity regarding preferences for income rules obviously character-izes many of our popular controversies. This occurs for the same reasons that we lack unanimity with regard to production plans; indeed, it is a byproduct of the basic argument because information is, strictly speak-ing, a factor of production.

In a world where markets (for information) were perfect and complete, this heterogeneity could be accommodated by some market-based or ela-borate contracting mechanism. Gonedes and Dopuch (1974), among others, have alluded to the possibility that accounting information may induce externalities (and in the limit, a type of public good). In such a situation, some form of collective action may appear, either in the form of private sector self-regulation (*e.g.*, FASB) or a public-sector-mandated system (*e.g.*, Securities and Exchange Commission).

Contextually, however, there is one important distinction between the measurement and information viewpoints that is worth noting. For certain classes of controversies over 'most-preferred' income rules, the major alternatives can be reported via an essentially costless disclosure policy. The measurement approach would still attempt to resolve the issue as to which rule results in the 'best' measure of income (within limits imposed by nonuniqueness of the measures). However, from an informational per-spective, the issue is not a substantive one. While this constitutes a special case from an analytical viewpoint, empirically many popular accounting controversies fall into this category. Examples include interperiod tax allocation, accounting for the investment credit, and aspects of accounting for business combinations.[1] From an informational perspective, substan-tive issues occur where disclosure or cost is at least implicitly involved. Examples would be replacement cost accounting, foreign currency transla-tion, segment reporting, and 'fair value' aspects of business combinations.

[1] This implicitly assumes that the format of disclosure does not convey information or otherwise affect the firm's production and financing opportunity set.

In any event, the jump from a desire to supply information to income reporting as a desirable vehicle for such reporting remains unclear. Appeal to fundamental measurement arguments is inadequate. On the other hand, the income orientation may be rationalized with a costly communication perspective. But the studies in question have not professed such a perspective.

POST-DECISION INFORMATION

Essentially the same observations emerge in the post-decision setting of traditional stewardship reporting in which the *ex post* reported income datum is used for contingent contracting purposes. An employment contract based on a target income goal requires *ex post* income reporting, a cost-plus contract requires *ex post* reporting, a current ratio constraint on a lender requires *ex post* balance sheet reporting, and so on. And in each instance, the motivation for reporting rests on the improved allocations which such reporting provides, and not on such criteria as 'more income is better than less.' From an informational perspective we analyse this setting just as the pre-decision setting was analysed.

Accrual-income measures may again be interpreted as a middle ground between extensive reporting of production plans and results and cash basis reporting that can be rationalized on cost-of-information grounds. In special cases resolution of the 'proper' aggregation is straightforward (*e.g.*, when an aggregate datum is a less costly sufficient statistic for the more useful datum). But in general, we expect heterogeneity of preferences for information systems, which are resolved via non-market determination mechanisms. And our basic point remains: choice of an income rule cannot be resolved by applying fundamental measurement arguments.[1]

SUMMARY

In a regime of incomplete markets, income measurement in a fundamental sense does not describe what accountants do. A condition for fundamental measurement may be missing in cases where we would commit scarce resources to production of accounting numbers. An informational perspec-

[1] Recent articles have expressed reservations about various deficiencies in income as a fundamental measure and about present value as a valuation mechanism (Ashton, 1977; Bromwich, 1977; McIntyre, 1977; Peasnell, 1977 and Scapens, 1978. The expressed concerns arise because of some assumed incompleteness (or imperfection) in the markets. Hopefully, the framework provided here will serve to synthesize these concerns and to provide some 'convergence' on this long-standing debate.

tive does, however, describe the accountant's activity. But it raises deep concerns over the role of the income concept. Matching of costs and revenues, for example, is not an underlying notion here. Rather, the case for income rests on the assumption of aggregating more informative but also more costly data such that a cost-effective communication mechanism is obtained. However, this assumption is problematical, and in our view, one challenge to accounting theorists is to address the primitive question of the propriety of the accrual concept of income.

REFERENCES

AICPA Objectives Committee, *Objectives of Financial Statements* (AICPA, 1973).

Arthur Andersen & Co., 'Objectives of Financial Statements: The Conceptual Framework for Financial Accounting and Reporting,' (June 1977).

Ashton, R., 'Objectivity of Accounting Measures: A Multirule-Multimeasurer Approach,' THE ACCOUNTING REVIEW (July 1977), pp. 567–575.

Bromwich, M., 'The Use of Present Value Valuation Models in Published Accounting Reports,' THE ACCOUNTING REVIEW (July 1977), pp. 587–596.

Coombs, C., R. Dawes, and A. Tversky, *Mathematical Psychology: An Elementary Introduction* (Prentice-Hall, 1970).

Debreu, G., *Theory of Value* (Yale University Press, 1959).

Demski, J., 'Choice Among Financial Reporting Alternatives,' THE ACCOUNTING REVIEW (April 1974), pp. 221–232.

Demski, J. and G. Feltham, *Cost Determination: A Conceptual Approach* (Iowa State University Press, 1976).

Ekern, S. and R. Wilson, 'On the Theory of the Firm in an Economy with Incomplete Markets,' *Bell Journal of Economics and Management Science* (Spring 1974), pp. 171–180.

Feltham, G., 'Cost Aggregation: An Information Economic Analysis,' *Journal of Accounting Research* (Spring 1977), pp. 42–70.

Financial Accounting Standards Board, *Tentative Conclusions on Objectives of Financial Statements of Business Enterprises* (Stamford, Connecticut, 1976).

Gonedes, N., 'Information-Production and Capital Market Equilibrium,' *The Journal of Finance* (June 1975), pp. 841–864.

Gonedes, N. and N. Dopuch, 'Capital Market Equilibrium, Information Production, and Selecting Accounting Techniques: Theoretical Framework and Review of Empirical Work, *Studies on Financial Accounting Objectives: 1974*, supplement to the *Journal of Accounting Research*, (*1974*), pp. 49–129.

Ijiri, Y., *The Foundations of Accounting Measurement: A Mathematical, Economic, and Behavioral Inquiry* (Prentice-Hall, 1967).

Krantz, D., R. Luce, P. Suppes, and A. Tversky, *Foundations of Measurement* (Academic Press, 1971).

McIntyre, E., 'Present Value Depreciation and the Disaggregation Problem,' THE ACCOUNTING REVIEW (January 1977), pp. 162–171.

Mock, T., *Measurement and Accounting Information Criteria* (American Accounting Association, 1976).

Peasnell, K., 'A Note on the Discounted Present Value Concept,' THE ACCOUNTING REVIEW (January 1977), pp. 186–189.

Radner, R., 'Market Equilibrium and Uncertainty: Concepts and Problems,' in M. Intriligator and D. Kendrick (eds.), *Frontiers of Quantitative Economics*, Volume 2 (North-Holland, 1974a), pp. 43–105.

——, 'A Note on Unanimity of Stockholders' Preference among Alternative Production Plans: A Reformulation of the Ekern-Wilson Model; *Bell Journal of Economics and Management Science* (Spring 1974b), pp. 181–184.

Scapens, R., 'A Neoclassical Measure of Profit,' THE ACCOUNTING REVIEW (April 1978), pp. 448–469.

Sorter, G., 'An "Events" Approach to Basic Accounting Theory,' THE ACCOUNTING REVIEW (January 1969), pp. 12–19.

Sprouse, R., 'Toward a Conceptual Framework for Financial Reporting in the United States,' (speech delivered at the Annual Meeting of the American Accounting Association, August, 1977).

Vickrey, D., 'Is Accounting a Measurement Discipline?' THE ACCOUNTING REVIEW (October 1970), pp. 731–742.

12 Inflation accounting: retrospect and prospect

by Charles Kennedy*

* Honorary Professor of Economic Theory, University of Kent at Canterbury.

OUTLINE OF THE DEBATE

An interest in inflation accounting goes back at least as far as the time of the Weimar Republic, but in this historical outline I shall be concerned with the more recent debate in the United Kingdom. Even in the (by recent standards) moderate conditions of inflation in the sixties, there was growing concern at the distorting effects of inflation on company accounts when these had been prepared on conventional historic-cost lines. In the case of fixed assets, depreciation provisions based on the historic cost of the assets failed to ensure that capital was being maintained intact in real terms. In the case of stocks, the FIFO convention had the result that a substantial part of reported profits represented stock appreciation, even though such profits were of no real benefit to an on-going company which was having to replace its stocks at higher prices because of inflation.

The initiative in tackling this problem was taken by the accounting bodies. After the publication of a number of discussion papers, the Accounting Standards Steering Committee (ASSC) published an Exposure Draft (ED8) in January 1973, followed by a provisional Statement of Standard Accounting. Practice (SSAP7) based on ED8 in May 1974. The standard was made provisional because in the meantime the government had in January 1974 set up its own Committee of Enquiry into inflation accounting under the chairmanship of Sir Francis Sandilands.

The accountants' proposals in ED8 and SSAP7 were relatively simple and amounted to a form of indexation. The main accounts were still to be presented on a historic-cost basis, but in a supplementary statement these historic-cost accounts were to be converted into units of current purchasing power at the end of the accounting period, by applying the change in the retail price index to earlier figures in the accounts.

The whole system came to be known as CPP accounting. The CPP adjustments were to be made not only to payments and receipts during the course of the period, but also to the figures in the opening balance sheet. This had an important consequence in the case of monetary items

179

in the balance sheet. Since the monetary value of these would not have changed over the course of the period, a loss would have to be shown in the profit-and-loss account in the case of monetary assets and a gain in the case of monetary liabilities.

Although CPP accounting attracted considerable support, it also came in for criticism on two main counts. In the first place, it was argued that the use of a general index of inflation like the retail price index could fail to reflect the experience of actual companies which were faced with specific changes in the cost of their inputs. In the second place, it was held to be quite unsafe to take credit for the gain from monetary liabilities independently of the use to which the borrowing had been put, since the gain could turn out to be illusory.

Meanwhile, events themselves were taking a hand. The year 1974 witnessed a very sharp acceleration in inflation, with emphasis on rises in input prices rather than output prices, since rises in the latter were restrained by the operation of the Price Code. As a result, British industry was running rapidly into a cash crisis of alarming proportions. Historic-cost profits remained buoyant because of the large element of stock appreciation, and the Chancellor, obviously unaware of the true situation, aggravated matters by actually increasing the taxation of companies in the Spring Budget. Nor was the position of industry made any easier by the collapse of financial markets. New equity capital was virtually impossible to raise, and borrowing was made difficult because the banks were adopting a cautious stance following the excesses of the earlier property boom and secondary banking expansion.

Much of the credit for the early recognition of the crisis, and for drawing it to the attention of the public, must go to Professor Merrett and Mr Sykes. A number of early warnings culminated in their famous article in the *Financial Times* of 30 September 1974, which described the workings of a Doomsday machine. Unless policies were changed, the authors argued, British industry was doomed. The increased cost of replacing assets by on-going companies was being treated as a profit instead of as a cost, and these 'wholly fictitious' profits were being taxed as though they were genuine. At the same time, companies were facing an 'immense increase in interest charges resulting both from higher interest rates and additional interest on the extra moneys required to finance working capital and fixed investment under inflation'.

Merrett and Sykes had a strong case, but they had overstated it by introducing an element of double-counting. To the extent that the increased cost of replacing assets was being financed by new borrowing, it could not at the same time be a charge against shareholders' funds.

180

Thus, it was illegitimate to argue that interest payments, as well as the whole of the increased cost of replacing assets, should be deducted from conventional profits. An early challenge to the Merrett-and-Sykes thesis was made in a paper by Wynne Godley and Adrian Wood, 'Stock appreciation and the crisis of British industry', published by the Department of Applied Economics at Cambridge at the end of October 1974. The authors used a model in which stocks were entirely financed by borrowing. In that case, they argued, accounting profit incorporating stock appreciation was both a true measure of profit and a proper basis for taxation.

The analysis was valid on the basis of the assumptions made, but the assumptions themselves, although explicit, were extreme ones. In an article in the *Observer* of 3 November 1974, Professor Alan Day was not slow to point out that the matter would be quite different if instead stocks were wholly financed from shareholders' funds. In that case, stock appreciation should not be considered a part of profit and should be exempt from tax. The argument was not at the time pressed home to its rather obvious logical conclusion, but there is little doubt that this particular exchange had an important influence on later developments.

In the event, Merrett and Sykes were persuasive in the matter of company taxation. In the special measures of November 1974, the Chancellor gave very substantial tax relief to companies whose stocks were increasing in value. The tax was deferred and not remitted altogether, but since the crisis had been one of liquidity, this was not a matter of immediate concern. With the passing of the November measures, the cash crisis of British industry was virtually over. Not so, the debate on inflation accounting!

The Sandilands Committee did their work with commendable despatch, and a unanimous Report (Cmd. 6225, HMSO) was published in September 1975. Even critics of the Report's recommendations will readily admit the valuable contribution made by the Committee in presenting and analysing the main issues. Indeed the Report became the focus for later discussions. In it, the Committee recommended a form of value accounting known as current cost accounting (CCA). Assets were to be systematically revalued in the balance sheet to reflect their 'value to the business' or 'deprival value', which in effect meant either replacement cost or economic value, whichever was the lower.[1] In the profit-and-loss account inputs were to be valued also at their 'value to the business', or current cost at the time of the sale of the output. To achieve this,

[1] There has been a good deal of discussion of the Sandilands approach to the valuation of assets, which I shall not attempt to cover here.

two adjustments were necessary to the historic-cost profit figures: a depreciation adjustment so that depreciation provisions would be based on current cost rather than historic-cost, and a 'cost-of-sales' adjustment roughly equivalent to deducting stock appreciation. In paragraph 535, the Committee claimed in bold type that, so far as the profit-and-loss account was concerned, these two adjustments, and these two alone, would constitute a 'comprehensive system of accounting for inflation'. The effect of the proposals was to split the total monetary gains of a company during the accounting period into two components: operating profits, which alone were to appear in the profit-and-loss account, and holding gains, which were to be taken straight to reserves.

No special treatment of any kind was to be given to monetary liabilities and assets. Since these also were to be valued at their 'value to the business', which in their case would be their monetary value, no gain or loss on them could arise. Interest payments were nevertheless to be a charge against operating profit, so as to arrive at what can best be called 'Sandilands profit' (although the Committee continued themselves to use the term 'operating profit').

In their terms of reference, the Committee had been asked to consider the CPP proposals, and they were severe in their criticism of them. One complaint was that SSAP7 was proposing the use of a new unit of measurement, the unit of current purchasing power, whereas the Committee themselves argued in favour of the retention of the monetary unit. Since the unit of current purchasing power is currently a Pound, I have never myself been able to attach any great significance to this distinction. A more substantial criticism was concerned with the use in CPP of a general index of inflation like the retail price index. The Committee argued with some force that what companies were interested in was not the rise in prices in general, to which in any case the Committee were unable to give any precise meaning, but rather the price changes relating to their specific inputs, since it would be these that would affect their cash flow.

Adherents of CPP have accused the Committee of undue dogmatism and even pedantry on this issue. While the use of specific price changes, or of specific indices of price change, may be appropriate for some purposes, for example in the revaluation of assets in the balance sheet, for other purposes, for example for showing the inflation-corrected gain in the shareholders' interest in the income statement, the use of a general index would be preferable.[1]

---

[1] See, for example, W. T. Baxter in the *Journal of Business Finance and Accounting*, Spring 1976, an issue of the journal that contains a useful collection of papers on the whole subject.

The Committee's purist attitude to the problem of measuring inflation had a curious consequence. It led to a widely held view that the Sandilands proposals, far from constituting a comprehensive system of accounting for inflation, were not about inflation accounting at all. But the really interesting thing about this view is that it has not been confined to critics of the Report—snipers from the CPP citadel like Professor D. R. Myddleton.[1] Even staunch supporters like Professor Merrett and Mr Sykes (*Financial Times*, 15 October 1975) have argued that the Report was not trying to identify a measure of *real* profit, but rather a *realistic* measure of money profit. Once started on this semantic slide, it is only too easy to find oneself landing up in the absurd posture of maintaining that a current-cost rate of profit is somehow comparable with a money rate of interest. This is certainly wrong. Current cost accounting is a method of correcting for price changes, and any comparison of a current-cost rate of profit with a money rate of interest is manifestly illegitimate.

As in the case of SSAP7, the main debate on the Sandilands Report centred on the treatment of monetary assets and liabilities. That treatment, or rather non-treatment, seemed to follow logically from the principles the Committee had established earlier, but the principles themselves were insufficiently general, since they had been derived from an analysis in Chapter 4 of the Report of different concepts of profit relating to a hypothetical company that was entirely financed from shareholders' funds. This line of criticism was developed in an article in *The Times* of 1 October 1975 by Wynne Godley and Francis Cripps, who also proposed a solution to the problem of monetary liabilities.

The solution was in fact the logical outcome of the earlier exchange between Godley and Wood and Professor Day. If a company was partly financed by borrowing, not all holding gains needed to be stripped from profits along Sandilands lines but only a proportion of them, the proportion relating to assets financed from shareholders' funds. The geared gains, on the other hand, could be brought back into profit and were in principle distributable to shareholders. New borrowing would be required for the purpose, but even if the whole of the geared gains was distributed, the company's gearing ratio would be simply maintained and not increased.

The geared gains proposal has been supported by the present writer[2]

---

[1] See his paper in the same number of the *JBFA*, Spring 1976, as well as a number of letters to *The Times* and the *Financial Times*.

[2] An unpublished paper making the identical proposals was written at the same time as the Godley-and-Cripps article and independently of it. I would not, however, claim any originality for the proposal, because I had been very much influenced by the earlier exchange between Godley and Wood and Professor Day.

C. Kennedy

and also notably by Mr Martin Gibbs of Messrs Phillips and Drew.[1] It has also been recommended in the Report of the Richardson Committee to the New Zealand government. It has come under criticism for assuming the existing level of gearing to be 'right'. This is a travesty. No supporter of the geared gains proposal has ever assumed the existing level of gearing to be right. All that is done is to take the level of gearing in the opening balance sheet as a point of departure for the purpose of measuring profit. In the adoption of this procedure, no new principle of any kind is being invoked. It has always been the case that the facts of the opening balance sheet have been taken as a point of departure for the measurement of profit. Moreover, it is clear that it is not the absolute value of the liabilities in the balance sheet that is of significance, but rather their value in relation to the value of the company's assets, the company's gearing ratio. The Sandilands proposals for measuring profit also took the facts of the opening balance sheet as a point of departure, but assumed instead the maintenance of the absolute value of monetary liabilities, a figure of no significance whatsoever when asset values are changing. The Godley–Cripps approach to monetary liabilities is definitely superior to the Sandilands approach.

In the same article, Godley and Cripps made the point that their proposal was fully consistent with a CPP calculation of the gain on monetary liabilities, and in fact embraced the latter. The point did not perhaps emerge very clearly from a rather complicated numerical example, but the principle is a simple one. So long as the asset in question is revalued at current cost at the end of the accounting period, a CPP calculation of the real gain on an asset financed by borrowing will always be identical with the monetary holding gain on the asset, *whatever may have been the change in the retail price index during the period*. This is because equal but opposite CPP adjustments will be made to the sum borrowed and to the historic cost of the asset financed by the loan. The two adjustments will therefore cancel each other, and we shall be left with the holding gain on the asset itself.

The Godley–Cripps proposal not only results in an acceptable measure of proprietary profits for a company partly financed by borrowing. It also effectively synthesises two quite separate strands of thinking: on the one hand the CCA idea that non-monetary assets should be systematically revalued at their current cost and on the other the CPP insistence that

---

[1] Mr Gibbs' distinctive contribution has been to point out that to the extent that working capital is financed by trade credit, the extra finance required will be generated virtually automatically in the course of business. For a description of the 'Gibbs' system, see the *Background Papers* to ED18. Numerous research publications of Phillips and Drew have also done a very useful service in quantifying the likely effects on reported profits of the various proposals.

there is a gain to be had from monetary liabilities at a time of rising prices. Moreover, it incorporates the figure for the gain from monetary liabilities in a way that renders it immune from some of the earlier criticisms. As we have already noted, one of the main criticisms of the original CPP treatment of monetary liabilities was that credit was taken for the gain on them quite independently of the use to which the borrowing had been put. The geared gains approach sidesteps this objection by linking the gain on the liability to the holding gain on the asset. This has the added advantage that if an asset falls in value over the period, this will show up in the accounts, as it rightly should, as a geared holding loss.

Godley and Cripps had been concerned with monetary liabilities, but there was also strong criticism of the Sandilands attitude to monetary assets. This criticism came notably from the banks, who argued that the Sandilands proposals were quite unsuitable for application to financial institutions.

The government gave its general blessing to the Sandilands Report and asked the accounting profession to work out a detailed programme for the introduction of CCA, a task that was given to a Steering Group under the chairmanship of Mr Douglas Morpeth. The vexed question of monetary items was left open, and the Steering Group were asked to give it further consideration.

Like the Sandilands Committee, the Morpeth Group worked with commendable speed, and in November 1976 an Exposure Draft for a Proposed Standard on Current Cost Accounting (ED18) was published under the authority of the Accounting Standards Committee (ASC). At the same time there were published *Background Papers* and a somewhat formidable *Guidance Manual*.

It is evident from the *Background Papers* that members of the Group were not in full agreement amongst themselves on the question of monetary items. In the event they resorted to a compromise. In this they took the lead from a qualification in the Sandilands Report itself. Although the Sandilands Committee had fixed on Sandilands profit as the most suitable measure of profit for most purposes and for the great majority of companies, they were prepared to allow some discretion to directors in making transfers to and from the revaluation reserve in particular circumstances. ED18 now gave formal recognition to this discretionary element. Sandilands profit was retained as the central concept of profit, but the holding gains, relabelled revaluation surpluses, were then to be brought back into an appropriation account, and directors were to be allowed to decide what sum should in the end be appropriated to the revaluation reserve. The sum could be greater or less than the revaluation surpluses, and the only requirement was that the directors should explain the reasons for their decision.

In addition, and no doubt as a concession to the CPP viewpoint, ED18 also recommended that there should be a supplementary note to the accounts showing the inflation-corrected gain in the net equity interest of a company over the accounting period.[1]

The last recommendation encountered predictable opposition from opponents of the use of a general index,[2] while the proposed reintroduction of an appropriation account met almost universal criticism. Even so, it was probably not these recommendations that brought about the downfall of the Morpeth enterprise, but rather the complexity of the draft and especially of the *Guidance Manual*. It was felt that the draft had attempted to cover a number of peripheral areas of accounting, areas which were important enough in themselves and which had long troubled accountants, but which would have been better tackled in separate standards. As a result, there was a successful revolt against ED18 amongst the membership of the English Institute of Chartered Accountants, which rejected it by a vote at a special meeting.

Although it was clear that the preparation of a mandatory standard based on ED18 was no longer feasible, the leaders of the profession were reluctant in spite of the rebuff to relinquish all the ground gained in the lengthy struggle for inflation accounting, and in November 1977 the ASC published an Interim Recommendation on inflation accounting, commonly referred to as the 'Hyde Guidelines'. Since at the time of writing they represent the current state of play, I shall give them a section on their own.

THE HYDE GUIDELINES

The Hyde Guidelines, like ED18, bear all the hallmarks of a compromise. Though no-one's ideal system, they have received widespread support, largely one feels because they are thought to be better than nothing, and, depending on one's point of view, not so bad as some of the other proposals that have been put forward.

In other respects, the Hyde Guidelines present a marked contrast to ED18. They are extremely modest by comparison, and of course not

[1] The Consultative Committee of Accountancy Bodies (CCAB) had pressed for this in their initial reactions to the Sandilands Report. For a description of the CCAB 'ideal' system, see *Background Papers* to ED18.

[2] See, for example, the *Submission on ED18* by the London and District Society of Chartered Accountants (LDSCA).

mandatory. They recommend that three adjustments should be made to the conventional historic cost profit figures in a supplementary statement. The first two are the familiar current cost adjustments to depreciation and cost of sales as proposed by Sandilands. The third adjustment, the gearing adjustment, is the one that deals with monetary items. It takes two alternative forms, depending on whether a company's monetary assets exceed its monetary liabilities or *vice versa*.

When the monetary assets of a company exceed its monetary liabilities, an adjustment is recommended that would reflect the increase in the net monetary assets needed to maintain its scale of operation. An appropriate index is to be used for the purpose, which need not be the retail price index.

When monetary liabilities exceed monetary assets, the recommendation is more controversial. Like Godley and Cripps, the Hyde Guidelines recommend that a geared proportion of holding gains should be brought back into profit, but the difference between the proposals is substantial. Whereas Godley and Cripps wished to apply the gearing proportion to all holding gains, the Hyde Guidelines recommend instead that it should be applied only to those holding gains represented by the adjustments to depreciation and sales. This is a very considerable emaciation of the original proposal, and the logic behind it is not immediately apparent. Nor do the Hyde Guidelines present any arguments in its justification. For these we must turn to the LDSCA Submission on ED18, in which as far as I know the Hyde compromise was first recommended. It is clear from paragraph 91 of the background papers in that document that the working party concerned rested their case on the dictates of prudence, and in particular on the principle that no element of *unrealized* revaluation surpluses should be brought into the profit-and-loss account.

The latter is of course a longstanding accounting principle, reaffirmed in SSAP2. It is doubtful, however, whether it can be sustained in a period of inflation. In the first place, it is one of the characteristics of inflation that holding gains will be predominantly positive and that a very substantial part of them will be unrealized. To exclude the geared proportion of these from the profit-and-loss account on the grounds of prudence involves too great a departure from realism. In the second place, for an ongoing manufacturing company, the distinction between realized and unrealized holding gains is of little, if any, significance.

The worry in people's minds, no doubt engendered by the property debacle of 1972–4, is that geared unrealized holding gains may represent a profit of poor quality, which it would be unwise to distribute. While this may be true in some circumstances, it is an insufficient reason for

187

their general exclusion from profits. Their suppression, as recommended in the Hyde Guidelines, will result in a systematic and substantial understatement of company profits attributable to shareholders.

WHAT NEXT?

It is still the intention of the ASC to formulate proposals on price level accounting for promulgation as a standard or standards. So the obvious question to ask is: what next? Part of the answer is simple. The Hyde recommendations were confined to the profit-and-loss account, and the next step must surely be to make corresponding current cost adjustments to the balance sheet. The calculation of the depreciation adjustment and of the gearing proportion will in any case require the systematic revaluation of a large part of a company's assets, so that the extra labour required in extending this to cover all assets should not prove excessive. While there is room for argument as to what is the ideal approach to the valuation of assets, there is no doubt that the adoption of the Sandilands proposals based on deprival value would make for an *improvement* in the balance sheet over the present system based on historic cost, as well as over the CPP proposal that the historic-cost figures should be revalued by applying the retail price index to them.

When it comes to the profit-and-loss account, it is difficult to see how the Hyde recommendations can be used as a point of departure. To make progress we must take a step backward—*reculer pour mieux sauter*. The first requirement for progress is to rid ourselves of the notion that there is a single measure of profit suitable for all purposes and for all users of accounts. In their Submission on ED18, the LDSCA were particularly critical of the discretionary element introduced into ED18, but they still hoped to retain the notion of a single measure of profit. Paragraph 61 of the background papers in the document begins: 'A clear wish exists that current cost accounts should identify one line as the "profit of the year" and that this amount should be quantified by clearly defined rules.'

It is a wish that should not be encouraged. There are all sorts of purposes for which a measure of profit or gain is required: for management accounting, for the calculation of the return on capital employed, for wage negotiations, for pricing policy, for dividend distribution policy, in the calculation of price-earnings ratios or preferably earnings yields,[1] for investment ana-

---

[1] Why should we follow slavishly the deplorable transatlantic practice of turning the earnings yield upside down and using the reciprocal? It is not only that we may want to compare the earnings yield with a rate of interest. When earnings yields are low, the price-earnings ratio is much too sensitive to small changes in the yield. In the extreme case, zero or even

lysis, for determining the inflation-corrected gain in the shareholders' interest, and as a basis for company taxation. One has only to list these purposes—and I do not claim the list to be exhaustive—to realize that no single measure of profit will be suitable for them all; and that if one insists on a single measure it is more than likely to be a compromise unsuitable for any of them.

REAL AND MONEY MEASURES OF PROFIT

In an attempt to sort out the various measures of profit that are required, and that should be presented in the accounts, two main distinctions have to be kept in mind. The first is the distinction between real and money measures of profit or gain.

I have argued earlier that CPP and CCA are both methods of correcting for price changes, and hence of establishing real measures of profit. The difference between them is concerned with the type of price index to be used. In the choice of index, dogmatism is out of place. For some purposes a specific index will be appropriate and for others a general index.

But it is also a mistake to suppose that a correction for price changes is always required. For some purposes, e.g. in the calculation of rates of profit on capital and of earnings yields, it is not obvious that a correction for price changes needs to be made at all. Certainly, no correction should be made if the intention is to compare the rates of return or yield with the uncorrected money rate of interest.[1] Admittedly, there is no harm in calculating real rates of return on capital or real earnings yields, provided it is understood that these are strictly for comparison only with a real rate of interest.

AN ENTITY VIEW AND A PROPRIETARY VIEW

The second, and even more important, distinction that has to made is that between an *entity* view of the company and a *proprietary* view. On an entity view, the company is regarded as an entity in itself. Both shareholders and creditors are thought of as being outside the company. Both

negative earnings yields are perfectly comprehensible. An infinite or negative price-earnings ratio is a nonsense.

[1] In the case of earnings yields, I have argued this point in more detail in a paper in the *Journal of Business Finance and Accounting*, Spring 1976. It is not of course conventional historic-cost earnings that should be used, but rather figures for total money gain. Historic-cost earnings are rightly suspect, not as is commonly supposed because they are too high but because they are too low!

provide finance for the company and require to be compensated, but no distinction has to be made between their separate interests. On a proprietary view, the company belongs to the shareholders.

It is perhaps the most serious criticism of the Sandilands Report that this distintinction was completely muffed. By charging interest payments against operating profit, so as to arrive at Sandilands profit, the Committee were taking neither a consistent entity view nor a consistent proprietary view. On an entity view, interest payments, which are a transfer from shareholders to creditors, should not be brought into the account at all: to deduct them as well as the whole of the adjustments to depreciation and cost of sales amounts to double-counting. On a proprietary view, the fault is one of not-counting: interest payments have to be deducted from profits, but something should have been brought in on the credit side to account for the real gain on the monetary liabilities, which is in effect a gain by shareholders at the expense of creditors.

The Committee (para. 536) justified the deduction of interest payments from operating profit on the grounds that they are an actual cost in money terms, in other words an outward cash flow. This is true, but they are not the only element of cash flow associated with debt finance. In an inflationary period, nominal debt can be expected to rise, and in fact does rise. The net new borrowing that this implies represents a cash inflow, a continuing cash inflow so long as the inflation continues. In short, Sandilands profit is a miscreation. Far from being used as the central concept of profit, it should not find a place at all in the income statement.

I shall conclude this section by indicating in Table 1 what I think is the appropriate view of the company for the various purposes listed earlier. I have not made an allocation as far as the basis for taxation is concerned, since this would require a discussion of the whole rationale of company taxation, a subject that would require a paper on its own. Some of the allocations in the table may be thought open to question. The important point however, is that the matter should be discussed and agreed, so

TABLE I.

Entity view	Proprietary view
Management accounting (non-financial aspects)	Management accounting (financial aspects)
Rate of return on capital employed	Dividend distribution policy
Wage negotiations	Earnings yields
Pricing policy	Investment analysis
	Inflation-corrected gain in the shareholders' interest

that the appropriate measure of profit can be used for the particular purpose in hand.[1]

THE TREATMENT OF MONETARY ITEMS

The CPP proposal for the treatment of monetary items was to use the retail price index to calculate the real gain from net monetary liabilities. The desirability of presenting in the accounts both an entity view and a proprietary view points instead to the need for a separate and asymmetrical treatment of monetary assets and liabilities. I refer here only to liabilities represented by borrowing. Trade creditors are almost certainly better thought of as negative monetary assets and set off against monetary assets (which include trade debtors), so as to arrive at a figure for net monetary assets, which could of course be negative.

Then, if we take as our starting-point the preinterest current cost operating profit, we would first of all bring into profit any net interest received from net monetary assets and then make a deduction, to be transferred to reserves, to allow for the maintenance of net monetary assets in real terms, using specific indices of price changes where this is appropriate. This would give us a figure for what we may call *entity profit*.

From entity profit we would first deduct interest payments and then bring into profit the geared proportion of all holding gains (including the implicit holding gains represented by the transfer to reserves in respect of net monetary assets suggested in the preceding paragraph), and so arrive at a figure for what we may call *proprietary profit*. This latter would be the most suitable figure for use as a *basis* for dividend distribution policy, which does not of course imply that it would always be prudent to distribute proprietary profit in full.

It has already been established that the figure for geared gains is equivalent to a CPP calculation of the real gain on assets financed by borrowing. It follows from this that if we wish, as I certainly do myself, to show in the income statement a measure of the inflation-corrected gain in the shareholders' interest, as shown for example in the last line of the CCAB 'ideal' system, all that we have to do is to add to proprietary profit the inflation-corrected element of ungeared holding gains, using the retail

---

[1] A case in point concerns the pricing policies of nationalized industries. On an entity view, prices would not be expected to cover interest costs. If they are expected to cover them, and especially if in Sandilands fashion no account is taken of the substantial real gains on monetary liabilities, the inevitable consequence is that when nominal interest rates rise with accelerating inflation, nationalized industry prices have to rise disproportionately compared to other prices. Since many of the nationalized industries provide essential services, the effect is equivalent to that of the most undesirable kind of indirect taxation, an indirect tax on essentials.

price index for the purpose. At this stage, however, I prefer to make a small detour, so as to be able to show in the statement a figure for *total proprietary gain*, for use in the calculation of earnings yields. We can obtain this figure simply by adding the ungeared proportion of holding gains to proprietary profit. We can then deduct the inflationary element of ungeared holding gains so as to arrive as before at the inflation-corrected gain in the shareholders' interest.

A SIMPLIFIED INCOME STATEMENT

I can best summarize the proposals of the preceding section by setting down in Table 2 a simplified version of the income statement, simplified because tax, minorities and extraordinary items are ignored.

TABLE 2.

	Current cost operating profit	X̲
plus	Interest received from net monetary assets	X
minus	Adjustment for maintenance of real value of net monetary assets	(X̲)
equals	*Entity profit*	X̲
minus	Interest paid on monetary liabilities	(X)
plus	Geared holding gains	X̲
equals	*Proprietary profit*	X̲
plus	Ungeared holding gains	X̲
equals	*Total proprietary gain*	X̲
minus	Inflationary element of ungeared holding gains	(X̲)
equals	*Inflation-corrected proprietary gain*	X̲

Note: A minor error in the original printed version of this table, and the associated text, has been corrected. In the original version the penultimate line erroneously included *all* holding gains instead of merely ungeared holding gains.

I would claim for this presentation one virtue of omission, and four virtues of commission. The misconceived Sandilands figure of profit is by-passed altogether. Instead, four significant measures of profit or gain are presented in Entity profit, Proprietary profit, Total proprietary gain and Inflation-corrected proprietary gain.[1]

[1] Mr Martin Gibbs would wish also to include in the statement a line showing 'maintainable cash profit' without recourse to borrowing (as distinct from trade credit). The concept is

Inflation accounting

The suggestion that more than one measure of profit in the main statement of the accounts will confuse the users of the accounts has been
greatly exaggerated. A user of the accounts can simply pick on the line
in the statement most appropriate for his purpose. In any case, even
if he is confused, it is definitely preferable that he should remain so than
that he should be misled by a single profit figure that he has not properly
understood.

THE TRUE AND FAIR VIEW

The syndrome of the middle seventies has been a kind of accountants'
anorexia nervosa, a desire to present the profitability of companies in
the slimmest possible light. It was carried to its extreme in the Sandilands
Report. I believe it has had a debilitating effect on the health of the
economy, by restraining the recovery of the market capitalization of the
equity interest in companies to reasonable levels after the stock market
collapse of 1973–4. The result has been that, in spite of a very large
fall in the real rate of interest to substantially negative levels, the average
real cost of capital has perversely risen. If inflation accounting is to play
its part in curing this malady instead of aggravating it, what is wanted
is a much smaller dose of 'prudence' and a much larger dose of 'the true
and fair view'.

POSTSCRIPT*

The purpose of this postscript is threefold: first, to bring up to date
the development of inflation accounting—or, as it is now more fashionable
to call it, accounting for the effect of changing prices—since the original
article was written; secondly, to comment briefly on the most recent proposals for an accounting standard outlined in Exposure Draft 35; thirdly,
to discuss an issue that was deliberately ducked in the original article,
namely what the basis of company taxation should be in conditions of
inflation. The justification for introducing a quite new issue into a postscript is that, arguably, the failure to make any headway in the adaptation
of company taxation to inflation, and indeed the determinedly backward

---

rather too close to Sandilands profit for my own taste, but if it were thought desirable to
include it, this could be done by interposing a line after the deduction of interest payments
from entity profit but before bringing in the geared holding gains. I would have no serious
objection to this procedure, provided it were understood that proprietary profit was a figure
of much greater significance.

* Final version received from the author in December 1984.

step taken by Mr Lawson as Chancellor in his Budget of March 1984, constitute one of the most important features of the last five years.

The Statement of Standard Accounting Practice No. 16 (SSAP16), introduced in March 1980, predictably followed the path indicated in the Hyde Guidelines, which were discussed in the original article. The statement provided for current-cost information to be included with annual financial statements as a supplement to historical-cost information. A current-cost Balance Sheet was to be provided as well as a current-cost profit-and-loss account. In arriving at current-cost operating profit, the same three adjustments were to be made as in the Hyde Guidelines: a depreciation adjustment, a cost-of-sales adjustment and a monetary working capital adjustment. Again, as in the Hyde Guidelines, the gearing adjustment was applied only to the realized holding gains comprising the above three adjustments.

The standard applied to all listed companies and other 'large' entities, with the exception of wholly-owned subsidiaries and of value-based companies such as insurance companies and investment trusts.

Finally, the Accounting Standards Committee (ASC) stated its intention that, as far as possible, it should make no change to SSAP16 for three years, so as to enable producers and users to gain experience in dealing with practical problems and interpreting the information.

Towards the end of the three-year trial period, there appeared to be a general feeling that changes in SSAP16 would be necessary if adherence to the current-cost principles embodied in it were to continue to command respect. There was some delay, however, in the appearance of proposals for a replacement to SSAP16, presumably because of differences of opinion with the ASC itself. Nevertheless, a Statement of Intent on SSAP16 was issued in March 1984. ED 35, based on the proposals contained in the Statement of Intent, followed in July 1984, and this Exposure Draft represents the current state of play at the time of writing.

Changes in ED 35 from SSAP16 can conveniently be listed as changes of scope, presentation, substance and one apparent change of status. As far as change in scope is concerned, the application of the proposed standard is to be restricted to public companies other than wholly-owned subsidiaries and value-based companies. As far as presentation is concerned, the current-cost information is no longer to be presented in supplementary accounts, but is to be shown in the notes unless the full accounts are drawn up on a current-cost basis.

There are two main changes of substance. Current-cost Balance Sheets are no longer required, though the current costs of fixed assets and stocks still have to be shown. The more important change of substance concerns the gearing adjustment. Instead of prescribing a single method of calculation, the proposed standard offers a choice of three methods. The first is the method used in SSAP16, based on the Hyde Guidelines. In the second, the gearing ratio is applied to total holding gains and not restricted to realized holding gains. The third method is essentially a CPP calculation of the gain on net borrowing, a general index of price changes being used for the purpose.

The change of status is that it is laid down that, for companies within the scope of the proposed standard, compliance is essential to give a true and fair view. No such explicit statement was contained in SSAP16, even though it may have been implied.

It would be unfair to form too harsh a judgement on these somewhat lacklustre proposals. The ASC have essentially been conducting a holding operation, designed to preserve the principles of current-cost accounting in the face of what at best can be described as a lukewarm reception of SSAP16 on the part of producers and users of accounts. Most of the changes have been introduced with a view to meeting specific criticisms of SSAP16. In particular, the proposals for the gearing adjustment have been designed to accommodate the disparate views of three different schools of thought: the adherents of the original Hyde Guidelines, with their insistence that only realized gains should be brought into profit; those who, like the present author, accept in principle the geared gains approach but think it should be applied to all holding gains; and the proponents of a CPP treatment of the gain on financial liabilities. At the same time, it must be said that the provision of choice will result in a lack of uniformity of treatment, that will make comparisons between different companies extremely difficult if not impossible.

For the present author, it is disappointing, though not perhaps surprising, that no progress has been made towards the kind of eclectic profit statement that was advocated in the original article.

At the time of writing (December 1984) it is beginning to look unlikely that the ASC's holding operation will succeed. A factor contributing to the general lack of conviction concerning current-cost accounting has been the reluctance of the Government and Inland Revenue to make any move towards the adoption of current-cost profit as a basis for company taxation. It is this question of company taxation that must now be considered.

Whittington (1983) correctly observes that in the original article the present author avoided any commitment on the issue. One reason for this is that he has never been convinced of the justification for any taxation of companies at all. On reflection, however, this was probably an inadequate reason for avoiding the tax question altogether, since even someone

195

who would prefer to see no company taxation can nevertheless form a judgement as to what features of a company tax system are particularly undesirable. For example, there would be very general agreement that spurious profits, arising from the impact of inflation on historical-cost accounts, ought not to be taxed. Indeed, it was the taxation of such spurious profits that led to the clamour in 1974 and to the eventual measures of stock relief introduced by the Chancellor in November of that year.

It will be recalled, however, that the tax was not to be remitted altogether but deferred, and it was not difficult to foresee that the stock relief provisions, together with the system of capital allowances that had been introduced earlier, would result in a rapid build-up of deferred tax liabilities for the great majority of companies. This prospect was viewed with considerable equanimity, not to say complacency, at the time.[1] There would appear to have been two reasons for the prevailing lack of concern.

In the first place, it was recognized that the company tax system in operation from November 1974, though it had been put together very much on an *ad hoc* basis, approximated quite closely to a system of cash-flow taxation. There was a school of thought that very much welcomed this development, and argued that it should be extended into a thorough-going cash-flow tax system. The most detailed advocacy of a cash-flow tax system is to be found in the Meade Report (1978), but reference can also be made to Scott (1976) and to Kay and King (1983). To this school of thought, the fact that deferred tax would have to be paid by a company running down its operations did not constitute an objection, since it was entirely consistent with the principles of cash-flow taxation.

Advocates of cash-flow taxation are to be found mainly amongst the academics. The attitude of the accountancy profession, on the other hand, was rather different. For them, deferred taxation did not need to be taken too seriously, because for the vast majority of companies the deferred tax *would never have to be paid*. In terms of accounting policy, deferred tax could be swept under the carpet. And this was just the procedure that the ASC legitimized in 1978 in their remarkable standard SSAP15. Only if it expected to have to pay the deferred tax in the reasonably near future was a company obliged to charge it against profit and show it as a liability in the Balance Sheet. In all other cases, deferred tax could be shown as a contingent liability in the notes.

For a long time, it appeared that the profession was going to get away with this uncharacteristic lapse into never-never land. When in 1980, as a result of the recession, it looked as though a large number of companies

---

[1] Though not by the present author. In Kennedy (1976) a serious view was taken of the build-up of deferred tax liabilities.

were going to run down their stocks and thereby suffer a clawback of past stock relief, the Chancellor came to the rescue by postponing for a year the operation of the clawback. In his 1981 Budget, Sir Geoffrey Howe went even further: there was to be no clawback of past stock relief unless a company were to cease to trade, and even in that case the clawback was to be limited to the relief that had been given during the preceding six years. Perhaps the profession had been right in thinking that for most companies deferred tax would never have to be paid, but no-one had counted on the 'reforming' zeal of the new Chancellor, Mr Lawson.

In his 1984 Budget statement, Mr Lawson announced the phasing out of stock relief and capital allowances accompanied by a phased reduction in the *rate* of tax. To the present author, the reduction in the rate of tax is of course not unwelcome, but the phasing out of stock relief and capital allowances would appear to be a retrograde step, since it would perpetuate a system in which spurious profits arising from the impact of inflation on historical-cost accounts would be subject to tax. Part of Mr Lawson's argument was that the Government had been so successful in reducing inflation that the relief measures that had been necessary in the seventies were no longer required in 1984. This argument is scarcely tenable, for three reasons. First, a rate of inflation of four or five per cent per annum can hardly be regarded as insignificant. Secondly, and this is a point made with some force in Kay and Mayer (1984), even if from now on the inflation rate were to be zero, the legacy of past inflation would linger on and continue to distort the figures for the depreciation of fixed assets. Thirdly, the company sector would be defenceless against an upsurge of inflation, unless relief measures on 1974 lines were reintroduced.

It remains to consider what the basis for company taxation ought to be, given that companies are still to be taxed. Superficially, the idea of cash-flow taxation is attractive since, as its advocates claim, it results in a 'neutral' tax system: the company's decision to invest, for example, would be unaffected by the tax. Unfortunately, the idea does not stand up to closer analysis.

Consider first the application of a cash-flow tax system to a newly-incorporated company. During the build-up phase, the company would receive credits either in the form of subsidies or of tax credits accumulating at some appropriate rate of interest. If subsidies were used, this would be equivalent to the Government taking a stake in the equity of the company. No contribution would be made to the Exchequer from the private part of the company, but the Government would receive revenue to the extent that the profit earned on its investment exceeded the interest on

197

the sums borrowed to finance the subsidies. If this were the Government's aim, it could well be asked whether it would not be simpler and less costly for the Government openly to acquire shares in the company rather than to rely on an elaborate system of subsidies and taxes to achieve the same result.

Suppose, instead, a system of tax credits were used. In order to achieve the goal of neutrality, the tax credits would need to accumulate at some normal rate of profit rather than at a bond rate of interest. Eventually, a successful company would contribute to the Revenue to the extent that it earned a rate of profit in excess of the normal rate, but there could be a considerable lapse of time before it paid any tax. An unsuccessful company would probably make no contribution to the Revenue at all over its life. Even the sale of its assets on liquidation would be likely to be covered by its outstanding tax credits. All in all, it seems doubtful whether a cash-flow tax system on these lines, when applied to newly-incorporated companies, would cover the cost of collection.

Existing companies, on the other hand, would not have received any subsidies in the early stages or have accumulated any tax credits. In consequence, the application of a cash-flow tax system to existing companies would result in a substantial contribution to the Revenue; but the imposition of such a tax system would amount in effect to an *expropriation* of part of the equity of every company. Exactly the same result would be achieved more simply and almost certainly at less cost if the authorities were to compel every existing company to make a free issue of non-voting shares to the Government. If the expropriation were to be carried out in this more overt way, it would surely be recognized as being unjust and undesirable.

To the extent that the tax system has approximated to a cash-flow system since 1974, this expropriation has already been taking place, alleviated only by the introduction of the six-year cut-off period in Sir Geoffrey Howe's 1981 Budget. By absolving companies in SSAP15 from showing deferred tax liabilities in their Balance Sheets, where emphatically they belong, the Accounting Standards Committee have been ostrich-like in preventing themselves from seeing what has been going on.

Even though it means a departure from the ideal of neutrality, in the writer's opinion it would be much healthier for British companies to make their contribution to the Exchequer as they go along, keeping their Balance Sheets clean, rather than to suffer a build-up of deferred tax liabilities. This implies that the tax should be on profits on an accrual basis. Spurious profits arising from inflation should of course be excluded from taxable profit, and to this end current-cost profit could serve as a tax base as satisfactorily as any other measure of profit. On its adoption, existing deferred tax liabilities would need to be remitted altogether.

Further consideration ought to be given, however, to the question of holding gains. In the case of personal taxation, capital gains are subject to tax only when realized, and there would appear to be no good reason why companies should be treated more severely in this respect than persons. If this is accepted, only the geared proportion of realized holding gains should be subject to tax, and not the geared proportion of unrealized holding gains.

As a consequence, the income statement proposed in the original article would need further elaboration. The geared proportion of realized holding gains and the geared proportion of unrealized gains would have to be brought into profit separately. There would of course be no difficulty in accommodating this further informational refinement within a single-column income statement. Indeed, quite apart from the taxation issue, the writer now thinks, partly in response to a criticism in Whittington (1983) of the original proposal, that it would be an improvement for the two types of geared gain to be shown separately. Within reason, the more information presented the better.

REFERENCES

Kay, J. A. and M. A. King (1983), *The British System of Taxation*, Oxford University Press, third edition, 1983.

Kay John and Colin Mayer (1984), *Inflation Accounting: A Re-Examination of Alternative Proposals*, IFS Report Series No. 10, The Institute for Fiscal Studies.

Kennedy, Charles (1976), 'Sandilands and the taxation issue,' *The Times*, 14 January, 1976.

Meade, J. E. (1978), *The Structure and Reform of Direct Taxation*, (The Meade Committee Report), George Allen and Unwin.

*Scott, M. FG. (1976), *Some Economic Principles of Accounting: A Constructive Critique of the Sandilands Report*, IFS Lecture Series No. 7, The Institute for Fiscal Studies.

Whittington, Geoffrey (1983), *Inflation Accounting: An Introduction to the Debate*, Cambridge University Press.

* The revised version of this paper, which is the next paper appearing in the book, excludes the discussion of taxation.

13 Some economic principles of accounting:a constructive critique of the Sandilands Report[1]

(A lecture given to the Institute for Fiscal Studies, 18 May 1976)
by M. FG. Scott*

I. INTRODUCTION AND SUMMARY

The Report of the Inflation Accounting Committee[2] (hereafter called 'the Report'), by a Committee under the chairmanship of Sir Francis Sandilands (hereafter called 'the Committee'), has rightly aroused widespread interest and criticism. Although entitled 'Inflation Accounting', it is, in fact, a critical analysis of many of the basic principles of accounting, and much of it would be of interest even in a non-inflationary situation. The two main changes which it recommends in the existing system of company accounting might be presented as a triumph for economists, since they amount to the application to company accounts of the procedures followed by the economist statisticians who devised the Blue Books on National Income and Expenditure. These two changes are the calculation of depreciation on fixed assets on the basis of current replacement cost, and the elimination of stock appreciation from operating profit. It may, therefore, seem ungrateful for an economist to question the basic principles underlying these recommendations.

It is, however, the writer's contention that the Report lacks the firm foundation which a set of principles would provide, and that this has resulted in some serious mistakes. The most notable of these relates to the treatment of monetary assets and liabilities, where the Report has completely failed to appreciate that inflation *does* make a difference, and

* Fellow in Economics at Nuffield College, Oxford University.
[1] The writer is grateful for comments received from Sir Alexander Cairncross, J. S. Flemming, J. Kay, J. Pemberton, D. Usher and those attending a seminar at the Institute for Fiscal Studies in May 1976. None of these necessarily agrees with the views expressed here, or is responsible for errors which remain.
[2] *Inflation Accounting*, Report of the Inflation Accounting Committee, Cmnd. 6225, H.M.S.O., September, 1975.

that the existing accounting procedures are highly unsatisfactory. This mistake has attracted widespread criticism, but some others have received less attention. Thus the Report's advocacy of replacement cost depreciation is based on no cogent argument and would, if accepted, introduce a quite unnecessary degree of complexity into company accounts. On the other hand, the Report fails to grapple with the very real complexities surrounding the problem of valuing changes in stocks. It is much too simple to say that stock appreciation must always be deducted in calculating profits, yet this is the impression the Report conveys.

The main purpose of this paper is to suggest principles which should be followed in drawing up accounts for an enterprise's management and shareholders. We accordingly start by considering what it is that the accounts are trying to measure. What do we mean by 'profit' and why do we want to measure it? It is essential to have a clear answer to this question if one is to see how the problems raised by inflation are to be tackled. The Report attempts to give an answer, but it is confused, and the mistakes mentioned above are the result.

The concept of profit which we advocate is similar to the Report's concept of 'operating profit', but we have tried to clarify it so as to avoid these mistakes. In doing so, we emphasize the extent to which profits are dependent on expectations about the future, and are therefore inevitably subjective. Some will be inclined to dismiss our concept for this reason alone. However, we ask readers not to jump to this conclusion too hastily. We are well aware of the need for objectivity in accounts, and of the potentially conflicting interests of shareholders, management and other users of them. Any workable system must be a compromise between what is theoretically desirable and practicably attainable. But that is no reason to dismiss all consideration of what is theoretically desirable. It does mean, however, that one must go beyond the principles in order to see how they can be applied to particular problems—which is what we attempt to do. However, there is an enormous variety of enterprises which need to draw up accounts, and we have neither the space nor the knowledge to provide more than a few examples. These show that in at least one case our suggestions are, indeed, *more* practical than those of the Report. We favour depreciation based on historical costs (adjusted by changes in the index of retail prices) rather than replacement costs. We believe that practical ways of applying the principles described here can be worked out in other cases too. Nevertheless, this paper is mainly concerned with principles, and leaves the practical problems to those with better knowledge of them.

While our main concern is with the accounts for an enterprise's manage-

201

ment and shareholders, we also consider the problem of taxation and inflation accounting more briefly.* Since our thesis is that the most useful concept of profit for management and shareholders alike is one which does depend upon expectations, including the expected rate of inflation, we have to meet the criticism that this must be a quite unacceptable basis for taxation. Profits for tax purposes must surely be more objectively defined. Our answer is to suggest a system of company taxation which would not be based on profits at all, and which would thereby avoid all the difficult problems of inflation accounting. This probably sounds a more radical suggestion than it really is. As we point out, it is only a continuation of an existing trend in the system of company taxation.

The following is a summary of the main points:

1. There are two important and different concepts of income or profit. One is 'gain', the increase in the present discounted value of assets over a period plus the 'take-out' in that period (i.e. dividends plus net capital distributed). The other is 'standard stream' income or profit, the maximum amount which could be taken out in each period for the indefinite future. Concepts similar to these are discussed in the Report, and 'operating profit', which is similar to standard stream profit, is preferred—rightly, in our view. However, the distinction between them is not clearly drawn. Both concepts rest on expectations, so that they are inevitably subjective. But that is equally true of any set of accounts which aims to give a 'true and fair view' of a company's position.   (Section 2)

2. The Report does not recognize that both concepts require a forecast of rates of inflation, so that the size of standard stream profit, for example, depends on the expected rate of inflation. If the concept is to be useful in a time of rapidly rising prices it has to be expressed in terms of constant purchasing power, and this inevitably means choosing some particular price index with which to measure inflation. There is no escape from this, and, if different price index numbers are chosen, different sets of accounts must result. For shareholders in the U.K. the best practical choice is the official retail price index (RPI). The failure of a Report on Inflation Accounting to appreciate these points is astonishing.(Section 3)

3. If company accounts could be designed so as to report estimated standard stream profits in real terms, they would serve the following purposes:

(*i*) Standard stream profits would be a guide to the amount which could be prudently distributed to shareholders.

(*ii*) Standard stream profits, if capitalized at a shareholder's rate of discount, would be a guide to the value of his shares.

* Not included in this reprint.

(*iii*) The difference between standard stream profits and actual take-out would represent the net amounts saved. By relating profits to cumulative net savings (measured in real terms) one could obtain various measures of company performance. These measures could be adapted to judge the performance of nationalized industries. (Section 4)

4. A company's estimates of standard stream profits could be checked in various ways and, in particular, by its auditors and by relating them to the net realizable value of its assets. (Section 4)

5. There are three ways in which one might approach the problem of estimating standard stream profits for a company:

(*i*) As the discount rate multiplied by the present discounted value of its assets.

(*ii*) As total gain less that part of the increase in value of its assets due to expected changes in discount rates or to changes in expectations.

(*iii*) As net current receipts less depreciation.

(Section 5 and, for (*ii*), Section 2)

6. Method 5(*ii*) is similar to that adopted in Chapter 4 of the Report, but the Report does not recognize that some 'holding gains' should be included in standard stream profit, or that depreciation (which it includes as a negative item) is indeed a 'holding loss', and that its counterpart, 'appreciation', should be included for assets such as land, forests, wine or some minerals. (Section 2)

7. Methods 5(*i*) and (*ii*) require explicit forecasts of net cash flows, and are not well related to existing forms of accounts. They may not, therefore, be practical in most cases. Method 5(*iii*), which starts from the profit and loss account rather than the balance sheet, is preferable. In its practical recommendations the Report does, in fact, opt for this approach, but the system proposed, Current Cost Accounting, CCA, would not generally provide good approximations to standard stream profits for a number of reasons. (Section 5)

8. The Report fails to discuss the distinction between current and capital transactions, although this is essential for Method 5(*iii*) (and for the Report's own method). The distinction must be drawn in a way which is consistent with that used in estimating the depreciation of assets.

(Section 5)

9. Net current receipts equal (gross) savings (i.e. capital expenditures less capital receipts) plus take-outs. Depreciation is that rate of gross savings which permits standard stream income to be taken out.

(Section 5)

10. The only method of valuing assets which is directly relevant to calculations of gain or standard stream profit is the present value method

('economic value' in the Report's terminology). The Report considers two other methods, replacement cost and net realizable value, and believes the former to be most generally useful in company accounts. However, they are only relevant indirectly as a means to estimating economic value.

(Section 6)

11. So long as expectations are broadly fulfilled, and expected real discount rates are constant, depreciation should be based on the historic cost of assets such as buildings, machinery, and vehicles, adjusted by reference to the RPI, and *not* to replacement cost (as the Report recommends).

(Section 6)

12. Whether stock appreciation should or should not be deducted in order to arrive at an estimate of standard stream profit depends on the circumstances. Examples are given which show that it may generally be correct to deduct stock appreciation due to general inflation, but that where stock appreciation is due to a *relative* price change it should only be deducted if selling prices are quickly adjusted to reflect that change.

(Section 7)

13. The Report recommends that no adjustment need be made to existing systems of accounting for monetary assets or liabilities. While this recommendation would be broadly acceptable if there were no inflation it is dangerously misleading in an inflationary situation. (Section 8)

14. The Constant Purchasing Power (CPP), method of adjusting monetary assets and liabilities is not satisfactory if the rate of inflation fluctuates. Nor is the average real gain made on holding monetary assets in the past a very useful guide to the standard stream income from them.

(Section 8)

15. In order to estimate standard stream income from monetary assets, including ordinary shares as well as cash, deposits, bonds, etc., we must consider those held for liquidity reasons separately from those held for income. As regards the latter, we must further distinguish 'holding income' from 'dealing income'. Suggestions for estimating each of these kinds of income are made.

(Section 8)

2. TWO CONCEPTS OF INCOME OR PROFIT

There are two concepts of an enterprise's income or profit which are used by economists and others, both of which are to be found in the Report. The first of these, which we shall call the 'gain concept', or just 'gain', is the increase in wealth achieved in a given period plus the net amount taken out in that period from the enterprise by its owners. This is effectively the definition in paragraph 100 of the Report, where it is stated that 'A company's profit for the year may therefore be defined in economic terms as:

'The discounted net present value of all future net cash flows at the end of the year, less the discounted net present value of the future net cash flows at the beginning of the year, plus the net cash flow arising within the year after making adjustments for the introduction of new capital during the year.'

In this definition, the 'net cash flows arising within the year after making adjustments for the introduction of new capital during the year' are what we have called the net amounts taken out from the enterprise by its owners. They would be dividends plus any capital distributed to or less any capital subscribed by the owners. Let us call this 'take-out' for short.

The second concept, which we shall call the 'standard stream concept'[1] is the maximum amount which could be taken out of the enterprise by the owners in a given period without impairing their ability to take the same amount out in all future periods of equal length. This is close to the concept of 'operating profit' in the Report. Thus, in para. 95, we find:

'"Profit for the year" is a practical business concept used as a guide for prudent decision making by companies. It may usefully be defined as the amount of the total gains arising in the year that may prudently be regarded as distributable. It is thus a subjective concept. . . . Gains that are legitimately regarded as profit by a company in a given set of circumstances might not be regarded as profit by another company operating in different circumstances.'

And in paras 166 and 167:

'. . . an accounting system can at least ensure that the profit figure reported is such that, if the profit for the year were fully distributed, it would not prejudice the ability of the company to continue to generate the same profit in future years if revenues earned and costs incurred in future years were the same as in the year of account.

. . . This concept of profit is identical to operating gains as defined in Chapter 4, since if the conditions affecting a company's operations are exactly repeated from one year to another, the amount of operating gains will also be repeated.'

While these quotations show that 'operating gains', which is the main concept of profit favoured in the Report, is similar to the standard stream concept, they leave much unexplained. In the first place, it is not clear what meaning can be given to the quotation from paras. 166 and 167, since *if* revenues and costs are unchanged, the net revenues must be unchanged, and this blanket proviso seems quite independent of the amount distributed. If everything is the same—well, then, everything *is* the same! If the definition is to mean anything the proviso must surely be dropped.

---

[1] This is the term used by Kaldor, 1955.

We then get the standard stream concept.[1]

Secondly, the Report does not make clear that the two definitions of profit are not the same. Thirdly, although the quotation from para 95 could be taken to imply that in some circumstances it would be right to include some holding gains (i.e. the increase in value of an asset held by an enterprise) in distributable profit, in practice the Report defines operating profit to exclude all holding gains or losses (apart from depreciation, which it does not treat as a holding loss).

In order to explain these last two points, it is useful to consider a simple arithmetical example. This enables us to clarify both definitions of profit, to see in which circumstances they coincide and in which they differ, and to understand how, despite the Report, some holding gains should be included in the standard stream concept.

Imagine an enterprise which consists of a fruit tree that bears (and is expected to go on bearing into the indefinite future) a hundred pieces of fruit each year which sell for £1 each, or £100 in all. The average price of consumer goods (as measured by the Retail Price Index RPI) is expected to remain constant for the indefinite future, as also is the price of this fruit. There are no other costs or receipts involved in the enterprise. Then, if the owner of the enterprise discounts all future benefits at a constant rate, say 10 per cent per annum, and if he takes out only the £100 of fruit each year, no more and no less, the enterprise will have a discounted net present value at the end of each year of £1,000. According to the gain concept, the profit of the enterprise will be the increase in net present value over the year, which is zero, plus the take-out, which is £100. So £100 will be the gain. According to the standard stream concept, the profit of the enterprise will be £100, since this is the take-out which can be indefintely repeated. Hence, in this simplest of all cases the two definitions of profit coincide.

Now let us make one difference in our assumptions. Imagine we are standing one year in advance of the harvest of fruit, and that we discount future benefits for *that* year by 20 per cent, but that for all later years we use the constant rate of discount of 10 per cent. We do this, we may suppose, because we expect market rates of discount, currently 20 per cent per annum, to fall to 10 per cent per annum after a year and then to remain constant. The discounted net present value of the tree is then

[1] In para. 739 we find the same puzzling tautology. 'Current cost profit (='operating profit') is the figure of profit that could be repeated in future years if all conditions surrounding the company's operations remained unchanged.' But, if *all* conditions remained unchanged, then *any* distribution could be repeated, since the proviso breaks all connection between the distribution and the future conditions. Of course, the Report does not really intend this, but its authors do not seem to have realized the full implications of a more meaningful definition.

£916·6,[1] and it will rise to £1,000 at the end of the year. The two concepts of income now differ. According to the gain concept, our income is £183·3 (i.e. £100 plus £1,000 less £916·6), whereas according to the standard stream concept it is still £100. Note that if the owner of the enterprise consumed £183·3 (by selling off a right to some future portion of the harvest, let us say), his wealth at the end of the year would be the same as at the beginning, namely, £916·6. But he would then have to cut back his consumption in future years if he wished to maintain his wealth intact. In other words, if interest rates fall, your wealth may rise, but not your standard stream income, since the yield of wealth has fallen. It is clear that, if we want to estimate the standard stream profit of the enterprise, we must exclude holding gains which arise from expected changes in interest rates.

Next, we make allowance for changes in expectations.[2] We revert to our first set of assumptions, but now suppose that, at the end of the year for which we wish to measure profit, expectations are changed in one respect only, namely, that the price of fruit in all future years will be £2 instead of £1. We assume that £2 was also the price realized for the fruit which has just been harvested, although at the start of the year it was expected to be only £1. According to at least one version of the gain concept, the profit for the year is then £200 plus the increase in the value of the tree. At the beginning of the year the tree was valued at £1,000, but at the end of the year it will be valued at £2,000. Hence, the total gain or profit will be £1,200. According to the standard stream concept, however, the profit will be £100 at the start of the year (when the price of fruit is expected to be £1) and £200 at the end (when it is expected to be £2). Once again, it is clear that if we want to estimate the standard stream profit of the enterprise we must exclude holding gains which arise from changes in expectations.[3]

[1] This is the sum of $\frac{£100}{1·2} + \frac{£1,000,}{1·2}$ the first term being the discounted value of the crop for the coming year, and the second being that of all subsequent crops. Standing at the end of the first year, the discounted present value of all subsequent crops is £1,000. In order to discount this back to the beginning of the first year, we must divide by 1·2, the discount rate for the first year being 20 per cent.

[2] The definition of profit given in para 100 of the Report, and quoted above, explicitly assumes that expectations are fulfilled. The Report does not discuss how it is affected if they are not.

[3] Some might wish to modify the gain concept so that assets are revalued according to the same consistent expectations at the beginning as at the end of the period. It is hard to see the merit in this, since one then has a concept which does not refer to gain as shown by anything approximating to market valuations, whereas it is the appeal to such valuations which makes the gain concept attractive, as referring to more objective magnitudes than does the standard stream concept. If one wants to revalue assets one might as well adopt the standard stream concept in the first place. It has a clear and useful meaning, whereas the 'revalued gain' concepts is a hybrid with no very useful meaning. It is not *equivalent* to the standard stream concept, because of the possibility of expected changes in interest rates.

207

Thus far our examples have consistently shown that holding gains should be excluded in estimating standard stream profits. However, this is only true in so far as holding gains result from the two causes identified above, namely, expected changes in interest rates and changes in expectations. All other holding gains should be included. This conclusion seems so much at variance with the Report that it deserves a careful explanation.[1]

Let us continue with our example, with our first set of assumptions, but now assume that the price of fruit is expected to fall steadily at, say, 2 per cent per annum for the indefinite future. This is because of competition from more luscious fruit which is being developed elsewhere. Our tree-enterprise is then in a similar position to that of a typical manufacturing enterprise, with competition from newer assets continually lowering the returns to older assets. The result is that the discounted net present value of the tree falls. If we take as our first year one in which the value of the crop is £100, then it can be shown that the fall in discounted net present value of the tree over that year is £16·6.[2] If we further assume that depreciation funds can always be invested to yield 10 per cent per annum (our discount rate), no more and no less, then it can be shown that the standard stream profit is indeed £83·3, the value of the crop less depreciation of the tree.[3] Hence, in order to estimate standard stream profit we must *not* exclude this holding loss, but must deduct it from the value of sales. This is, of course, perfectly in accord with the Report, which also requires depreciation to be deducted before arriving at operating profit. However, for some inexplicable reason it is not called a holding loss, and this seems to have led the Report into error.

Thus suppose we reverse our assumption of a fall in the price of fruit,

---

[1] The conclusion is only true (a) once all figures for the year have been expressed in terms of constant purchasing power, in the way described below, and (b) if all amounts saved earn the rate of discount. If the latter assumption is not fulfilled (as may well be the case), there is no simple relation between 'gain' and 'standard stream' income, and we must use the approach described later, which is to estimate the latter as net current receipts less depreciation.

[2] At the start of the year, value of the tree is:

$$A_0 = \frac{100}{1 \cdot 1} + \frac{100 \times 0 \cdot 98}{1 \cdot 1^2} + \frac{100 \times 0 \cdot 98^2}{1 \cdot 1^3} + \ldots$$
$$= 833 \cdot 3$$

At the end of the year, the value of the tree is:

$$A_1 = \frac{98}{1 \cdot 1} + \frac{98 \times 0 \cdot 98}{1 \cdot 1^2} + \frac{98 \times 0 \cdot 98^2}{1 \cdot 1^3} + \ldots$$
$$= 816 \cdot 6$$

So $A_0 - A_1 = 16 \cdot 6$

[3] If depreciation funds are invested each year to yield 10 per cent per annum then the enterprise will consist of assets which are always worth £833·3, yielding 10 per cent per annum, and it will always be possible to distribute £83·3 each year.

and now assume that the price is expected to *rise* steadily at 2 per cent per annum. A company owning land, forests, wine, or perhaps oil, in the long run could reasonably hold some such expectation. Furthermore, a rise in the value of its assets *for a time* could be expected by, for example, a company opening up a new mine, or developing a new product. In all such cases of expected appreciation in the value of its assets, this appreciation should be added in to get the standard stream profit, just as depreciation must be deducted in the opposite case. So, in our example, £16·6 should be added to the value of sales, giving £116·6 as the standard stream profit.

It might be objected that this anticipation of future gain is 'unsound'. It would certainly be more conservative to omit appreciation, while including depreciation (which is simply the anticipation of future loss). However, the Report lays emphasis on the need for realism in company accounts, and equates this requirement with the legal requirement that they should show a 'true and fair view' (para. 235). It speaks of the 'overriding importance of the "true and fair view" requirement' (para. 238) and says that 'care should be taken to avoid the concept of prudence being applied with an excessive degree of conservatism, which could give rise to inconsistency with the concept of realism' (para. 240). In view of these remarks, there would seem to be a strong case for including appreciation as well as depreciation in company accounts, at least in certain circumstances.

We may sum up this discussion of fundamental concepts in the following propositions about the way in which changes in the discounted net present values of assets (holding gains) should be brought into an estimate of standard stream profit:

(*a*) Changes in value due to expected changes in interest rates should be excluded.

(*b*) Changes in value due to changes in expectations should be excluded.

(*c*) All other (expected) changes in value should be included.[1]

Hence standard stream profit is equal to total gain *less* increases in asset values due to (*a*) and (*b*). This is therefore one way in which it might be estimated. However, as we argue in Section 5, it is not the most useful way, and it rests on an assumption which we have made throughout the above examples but which may not always be fulfilled, namely, that all savings earn the rate of discount (i.e. 10 per cent per annum above). We therefore propose a different approach, which is to measure standard stream profit as net current receipts less depreciation (or plus appreciation).

[1] But see footnote 1 on preceding page.

M. FG. Scott

Perhaps the single most important conclusion which emerges from the above discussion is that *both* the gain *and* the standard stream concept of profits depend, implicitly or explicitly, upon expectations about the future, and are therefore inevitably subjective. This conclusion will be anathema to many, but there is no escape from it. A set of accounts which is merely an objective record of cash transactions, however useful for some purposes (such as the detection of fraud), cannot give a 'true and fair view' of a company's performance or position. There is all the difference in the world between one company whose net cash receipts have been obtained while its net assets have depreciated and another with the same net cash receipts and appreciating assets. Both depreciation and appreciation look to the future, and so must any accounting concept of profit.

3. THE NEED FOR A 'REAL' INCOME OR PROFIT CONCEPT

Thus far, in our examples, we have assumed that there is no inflation in the sense that the RPI is constant and expected to remain constant indefinitely (but note that we have *not* assumed that *all* prices are constant. On the contrary, relative price changes will inevitably occur, but do not affect our conclusions). We must now tackle the problems which result from the existence of inflation, since they are, after all, the problems which led to the setting up of the Committee, and its Report is entitled 'Inflation Accounting'.

Here we come to a very surprising feature of the Report. It discusses the unit of account which should be used (paras. 148–150 and 203–207) and lists five criteria by which any unit should be judged. It points out that money (the pound) satisfies all of these except one—it fails to represent a constant value through time. Nevertheless, it recommends firmly that money should be retained as the unit of account, despite this failure, and it explicitly rejects (paras. 407–415) the Constant Purchasing Power (CPP) unit of account on the grounds that it fails to meet the first four criteria and satisfies the fifth only very imperfectly.

The explanation for the Report's conclusion may be as follows. It seems to have accepted that the system of accounting used in the Blue Books of National Income and Expenditure is both 'correct' for the national and for company accounting.[1] Following these principles leads to a profit

---

[1] This is the writer's interpretation of the Report's recommendations. The only two adjustments which it proposes to existing systems of accounts are those made in the Blue Books, namely adjustments to depreciation (to give capital consumption on the basis of replacement cost, see Section 6) and to the valuation of stocks (to eliminate stock appreciation, see Section 7).

figure which can be expressed each year in money at the prices of that year. It is then open to any user of the accounts to convert these current price figures into profits at constant prices by dividing through by whatever price index is most appropriate for his own purposes. Since different users will have different needs, it is best to present the accounts in this way, rather than to pick on a particular index, such as the RPI, and so to produce profits at constant prices, which do not suit many users of the accounts.

Unfortunately, this reasoning contains a flaw which is fatal to the Report's recommendations. The flaw is that in general the profit figure, properly calculated, should depend on the rate of inflation which exists and is expected. *One cannot in general produce a useful figure of standard stream profit which is independent of the rate of expected inflation*, at least so long as the enterprise concerned holds any assets, or incurs any liabilities, which are fixed in money terms. Hence, in order to produce a useful profit figure one must make some explicit assumptions about expected inflation, and this implies selecting some price index with which to measure inflation. It is true that such a selection will not satisfy all possible users of the accounts. Nevertheless, this difficulty cannot be avoided—to produce a useful set of accounts some *particular* index must be selected. The only way to please users with very different needs would be to produce different sets of accounts for each of them.[1]

To elaborate the point just made, let us consider an enterprise (e.g. an Oxford College!) whose income is derived entirely from the interest received on fixed interest securities.[2] Suppose that this interest amounts to £100 each year on securities whose market value is £1,000, and that both interest and market value are expected to remain constant in money terms. Can the owners safely take out £100 each year from the enterprise? According to the definition of operating profit recommended in the Report, they can. However, while this recommendation would be quite

---

[1] The difficulty is a very real one for companies substantial proportions of whose shareholders live in different countries, unless changes in exchange rates approximately correspond to changes in purchasing power measured by their respective RPI's. For such companies there may indeed be a case for producing more than one set of accounts.

[2] It might be thought that this example is unfair to the Report, since most of it is addressed to the accounting needs of a manufacturing enterprise. It is indeed a criticism one can make that the problems of other types of enterprise are insufficiently considered. The Report claims, however, that 'Current Cost Accounting (i.e. the Report's recommended system) is also appropriate for use by a wide range of other types of company' (para. 718). It explicitly states 'Thus in the extreme case of a company whose assets consist entirely of cash and debtors, the Current Cost Accounts would be the same as the historic cost accounts, indicating that for such a company historic cost accounting is a satisfactory form of value accounting, and no adjustment is required' (para. 719), and in footnote 3 on p. 217 it includes charities as amongst those to whom CCA would be applicable.

appropriate to an enterprise in the 19th century, it is certainly not appropriate today. The owners might indeed be able to spend £100 a year for ever, but in today's and tomorrow's circumstances that would be a recipe for fairly rapid extinction. With inflation at only 5 per cent per annum, the real purchasing power of £100 would sink to one tenth of its current level in as little as 47 years. With inflation at 10 per cent per annum, it would take only 24 years. Hence it would be very dangerous for the owners of an enterprise of the kind just mentioned to follow the Report's recommendations, and to act on the belief that its standard stream profits could be calculated independently of the rate of expected inflation.

The truth is that the standard stream concept must be interpreted in *real terms* if it is to be a useful guide to prudent distribution. It is the amount which one can take out this year without prejudicing one's ability to take out the same *real* amount in future years which one would like to know. In the example just given, £100 would certainly exceed the enterprise's standard stream profit in present conditions. By way of contrast, in our earlier example of the fruit tree yielding £100 worth of fruit this year, so long as one expected the price of fruit to keep pace with the RPI, £100 would equal its standard stream profit. Now we have already seen that, according to the Report's concept of operating profit, £100 would be that profit in both of these examples. Yet in the case where money income is constant this would provide a highly imprudent guide to distribution, while in the case where it is a safe guide to distribution money income is not constant, but expected to increase in line with the RPI. One can only conclude that the Report's concept is faulty and dangerous, and that in the inflationary circumstances which the Report was designed to deal with any useful and prudent concept has to be based on some constant purchasing power unit of account.

What of the Report's objections to the use of the RPI? The main answer to them has already been given. Since, to be of any use at all as a guide to prudent distribution, standard stream profit has to be expressed in real terms, i.e. in terms of constant purchasing power over *some* bundle of goods and services, the only material question is what bundle? If inflation is at all rapid, almost any bundle is better than money itself. Since this point was clearly not appreciated in the Report, its somewhat fastidious objections to the use of the RPI must be seen from this perspective. Given that some price index must be selected, the practical arguments in favour of the RPI are strong.

Furthermore, it is quite irrelevant to argue as in para. 409 of the Report that 'While movements of the RPI may be representative of the changes in the "purchasing power" of money held by individual shareholders they are unlikely to be indicative of changes in the "purchasing power" of money held by institutional shareholders, companies or other organizations which make use of the annual accounts of companies. The RPI covers few items of goods and services normally purchased by companies and is not an appropriate index to use as an indicator of the changing "purchasing power" of money spent by companies.' This quotation betrays considerable confusion of thought. Companies etc. are not persons, and only exist, or should exist, to satisfy the wants of persons. Companies' purchases are all intermediate transactions. What matters is not the quantities of goods a company buys or sells, but (so far as its shareholders are concerned) the amount of real consumption it affords its shareholders, either now or in the future. From the wider community point of view, it is still the amount of personal consumption provided by a company which matters, and not (except in so far as it is a means to that end) the number of tons of steel or whatever else it may produce or consume.

We conclude, therefore, that standard stream profit should be expressed in terms of constant purchasing power using the RPI. In later sections we discuss how this can best be done, but, before getting down to details, we give a conspectus of the system of accounts to which our conclusions have led us. This enables the detailed discussion which follows to be seen as a coherent whole.

4. A SYSTEM OF ACCOUNTS BASED ON THE REAL STANDARD STREAM CONCEPT

In this section we put on one side the practical issues of estimating standard stream profits in order to see what system of accounts we are trying to achieve. Before we can play the ball where it lies, let us first determine the direction of the hole.

Let us imagine, then, that we have some way of estimating standard stream profits in each year. How would we use these estimates? We do not wish to assume that they are faultless. On the contrary, they will always be subject to error, and we may have to revise the expectations on which they are based each year. However, we do the best we can, and arrive at a series of profit figures for years $1, 2, 3 \ldots n$ which we may label $R_1^1, R_2^1, R_3^1 \ldots R_n^1$. Each year's profit is expressed at the prices of that year, and shows the amount which the directors of the enterprise estimate could be prudently taken out in that year without prejudicing the ability of the enterprise to take out the same real amounts (in terms of purchasing power as measured by the RPI) in future years.

213

Let us now assume that the actual amounts taken out are V_1^1, V_2^1, V_3^1 ... V_n^1. These will normally be dividends, but include capital repayments to and (as a negative item) capital subscriptions by shareholders. For the present we confine attention to accounts for shareholders, although subsequently we also consider accounts which would be of more interest to the community at large and which would be more suitable for a nationalized industry.

The difference between profits and take-out is the net amount saved and invested by the enterprise, I_1^1, I_2^1, I_3^1 ... I_n^1.

Suppose, now, that we are standing at year n. In order to present us with comparable figures over the past n years, the directors adjust all the above figures so that they are in terms of constant year n prices.[1] Let us denote these adjusted figures by R, V and I. They can then provide us with a further set of figures showing the *cumulative* amounts invested, *in real terms*, at the beginning of each year. The cumulation has to start at some point in the past by taking an initial shareholder's capital stock at that point. We do not consider how this might be estimated here, but, so long as the point is far enough back it does not greatly matter how the valuation is done (within reason). Let us assume that in our example this valuation was done at the beginning of year 1 when the initial capital stock was put at I_0. Consequently, at the beginning of year n we have the cumulative savings, at year n prices, which is:

$$K_n = I_0 + I_1 + I_2 + \ldots I_{n-1}$$

We are now in a position to explain three main ways in which the above set of accounts could be used.

1. The profits, R_n, for year n are a guide to the directors in deciding on the dividend.

2. The profits, R_n, are a guide to those buying or selling the company's shares in deciding on an appropriate price for them. Since R_n is meant to be a real perpetuity, the capital value of a share is R_n/rN, where N is the number of shares and r is the shareholder's real rate of discount (assumed constant). Some further allowance should perhaps be made for uncertainty, and allowances should also be made for taxation, which is ignored here.

3. The performance of the company can be judged by several different indicators:

(*i*) Since K_n is a measure of the estimated cumulative sacrifice of consumption made by shareholders since the initiation of the company and

---

[1] This is done quite simply by dividing each year's figures by the RPI for that year and multiplying by the RPI for year n.

R_n is a measure of the profit which is the estimated permanent fruit of that sacrifice, R_n/K_n gives a measure of the long-term performance of the company which may be compared with similar ratios for other companies.

(*ii*) Instead of estimating this ratio for the whole life of the company, as in (*i*), it can be computed for any period in the past. Thus, if the management changed substantially in year r, it might be interesting to compute $(R_n - R_r)/(K_n - K_r)$, which shows the estimated increase in profit in relation to the cumulative sacrifice of consumption since the new management took over. As a limiting case, one can judge performance in the most recent year by

$$(R_n - R_{n-1})/(K_n - K_{n-1}) = (R_n - R_{n-1})/I_{n-1}.$$

It should be emphasized that, while these indicators are subject to many limitations (some of which are discussed below), they are far superior to the indicators which can be derived from existing accounts or from either CCA or CPP accounts. The reasons for this are implicit in much that has already been said, or in what is said below.

Turning to their limitations, one has to recognize two main reasons for an increase, say, in profits over a period of years which it would not generally be possible to disentangle. Profits might increase because, and only because, of the savings made by shareholders. The indicators above would then give the yield achieved on those savings, and one could judge the management's performance by the yield it was able to achieve. But profits might equally well increase because of a change in expectations, and in an uncertain world this would be bound to be an important factor. If estimated profits were not biased, one would expect that, over a long period of years, underestimates would roughly cancel out with overestimates, so that a measure such as R_n/K_n should mainly reflect the yield achieved on savings. Over a short period, however, changes in expectations could well be the most important explanation of changes in profits, and where profits increase because of improved expectations, the above indicators do not give a satisfactory measure of performance. This merely illustrates the fundamental difficulty in any measure of performance, namely the problem of separating the achievement of the person being judged from the effects of other factors outside his control. It is not surprising if we cannot find a satisfactory and simple way of doing this. It does not exist. The indicators proposed are still useful, if not wholly satisfactory.[1]

---

[1] If expectations change we should, in principle, revise *past* estimates of profits and savings, as well as current ones. This would complicate the presentation of the accounts, and would

A more legitimate worry is that the estimates of profits might be biased one way or another. What would be the likely consequences of that? If, say, profits were consistently underestimated by a roughly constant percentage, the effect would be to leave the proportionate rate of growth of profits unaffected, but to underestimate the absolute amounts of I and K, and the absolute increase in R, by equal amounts.[1] In general, the apparent yield of savings would be increased, and it might be increased substantially.[2] Hence, consistent conservatism in estimating profits would make performance look better than it really was. Is there any way of checking this?

There are, fortunately, several checks. In the first place, the auditors would have to be convinced that the estimated profits gave a 'true and fair view' of the company's position and prospects. Secondly, profits would at least have to equal, or exceed, the dividend in the normal situation. Thirdly, underestimating profits would tend to depress the share price, and directors might be reluctant to do this for a variety of reasons. Finally, one could use the balance sheet as a guide to the existence of either gross underestimation or gross inefficiency in the following way.

For this purpose one needs a method of estimating the value of assets which is independent of estimates of profit since one wants to use the former as a check on the latter. Hence it is no use estimating the value of the company's assets by reference to their discounted net present values in their existing use. To do so is to end up with a capitalized value of profits, and that cannot be used to check estimates of profits. If assets are to be valued separately and reasonably objectively, the best method would seem to be to estimate their net realizable value, i.e. what they would fetch if sold. For a reasonably well-run company, this (net of liabilities) should give an appreciably lower figure than the capitalized value of profits. Hence, if the ratio of profits to the net realizable value of assets was unduly low one would suspect that either profits were being underestimated or else the company was being inefficiently run, and an explanation would be required from the management.

Of course, there might be times when the management would be

---

encounter the difficulty of distinguishing between the effects of changes in expectations and of changes in the total amount saved on profits. Nevertheless, further analysis of this problem seems desirable.

[1] Since $R = I + V$, and since K is the accumulated sum of past V (after adjusting for inflation), it follows that, for given V, underestimating R leads to an equal underestimate in I and so, over the years, to underestimating K.

[2] Since I would generally be smaller than R, an equal absolute cut in both would increase the apparent ratio of R/I, and so it would also increase R_n/K_n or the other ratios mentioned in 3 above.

tempted to overestimate profits, or to manipulate their estimates in various ways. We have not space to discuss all the possibilities here, but perhaps sufficient has been said to show that there are checks to such practices. Much would turn on the degree of objectivity in the methods used to estimate profits, and so on the auditors' ability to check the estimates.

Before turning to the details of these estimates, however, we venture one suggestion as to the way in which the accounts might be drawn up so as to serve the interests of a wider community than that of the shareholders. This would be particularly relevant to nationalized industries' accounts. Instead of calculating profits accruing to shareholders, and relating them to shareholders' savings, one could calculate profits earned on all the company's real assets and which, therefore, accrued to its creditors as well as its shareholders, and one could relate them to the total savings of all of these, that is, to the total investment in the company. This measure of performance would show how successful the company had been in managing its real assets, and would separate its achievement in this respect from its achievement in generating profits for its shareholders through skilful financing.

5. THE DISTINCTION BETWEEN CURRENT AND CAPITAL TRANSACTIONS: STANDARD STREAM PROFIT AS NET CURRENT RECEIPTS LESS DEPRECIATION

It would be possible to estimate the standard stream profit yielded by an asset by forecasting the net cash flow of the asset, discounting and adding it up to get the asset's present value, and then calculating what constant real perpetual stream of receipts would have the same present value.[1] This method draws attention to the fact that any estimate of standard stream income must rest, whether explicitly or implicity, on a forecast of some kind. There is no escape from that. However, the method does not lend itself well to accounting procedures, and so one naturally casts around for alternatives.

One method is that implied in the conclusion to Section 2: standard stream profit is total gain *less* increases in asset values due to expected changes in discount rates and to changes in expectations. This method requires an estimate of the present value of a company's assets, and hence a forecast of net cash flows. It is also therefore difficult to relate to normal accounting procedures. It is, nevertheless, closest to the method which the Report *appears* to advocate in its early chapters, as we show below.

---

[1] In performing this calculation it is essential that the real discount rate used should equal the real return on capital expenditures by the enterprise.

Nevertheless, it does not seem to be very practical, and in its later chapters the Report turns to something more akin to the second method.

This is to define current and capital transactions in some suitable way (discussed below) and then to estimate standard stream income as net current receipts less depreciation. We return to this method, which seems the one most suitable for many companies (though not necessarily for all) after reviewing the Report's recommendations.

In its main theoretical Chapter 4, the Report views the problem of estimating profits as essentially one of estimating the increase in value of a company's assets, i.e. its gain, and then adjusting this increase in various ways (paras. 66 to 78). In fact, it classifies accounting systems under three main headings (para. 78):

(*i*) The unit of measurement used.

(*ii*) The basis adopted for measuring net assets.

(*iii*) The extent to which total gains during a period are regarded as profit.

Unfortunately, the Report's approach suffers from the following disadvantages. If one wants to estimate standard stream profits (and, as we saw in Section 2, this does seem to be the Report's concern, and it is also probably the best concept) the only relevant value of assets is the discounted net present value. This is clear from Section 2 and we discuss, and reject, the Report's arguments for alternative valuations in Section 6. Furthermore, it is the discounted net present value of a company's assets *considered as a whole* that we need. It is difficult to see how this can be estimated other than by estimating profits and then capitalizing them. Adding up replacement costs, net realizable value, or any other value, will give totals which, regarded as estimates of the present value of the company, are subject to wide margins of error. Consequently, the *difference* between such estimates over a year will be subject to even greater proportionate margins of error. Furthermore, as the Report recognizes, one cannot include the whole of such differences in standard stream profits. As we saw in Section 2, those due to differences in expectations, or to expected changes in discount rates, must be excluded. The Report fails to recognize that these are, in fact, the principles on which exclusions should be based (and, of course, fails altogether to recognize the need for adjustments on account of inflation and the need to use a unit of account of constant purchasing power). Hence, for a great many important reasons, the Report's approach is, regrettably, unfruitful.

What we have described is, however, only the Report's apparent approach—that described in the more theoretical Chapter 4. In its more practical recommendations for an accounting system in Chapters 12 and

13, the Report adopts a different approach. It starts from the existing profit and loss account, not the balance sheet, and makes only two adjustments to existing historical profits (depreciation is based mainly on replacement cost, and stock appreciation is deducted—see especially para. 535). We return to these adjustments in later sections. The point which we emphasize here is that this approach, via a firm's current account rather than via its balance sheet, is a good one, provided that we make the right distinction between current and capital transactions.

It must be recognized that there are deficiencies in the accounts presently prepared by companies which relate to the distinction between current and capital transactions. If a 'true and fair view' of a company's position is to be given, it is important that capital transactions should be excluded from the current account (and vice versa). This is especially so if capital transactions are lumpy and irregular, as they often are. If, for example, a large advertising campaign is treated as current expenditure, as it may often be, the result is to understate profits when the expenditure is incurred, and to overstate them in later years. The same is true of unusually heavy research and development expenditure.

It is then rather surprising that the Report does not discuss the distinction between current and capital expenditure. Possibly it was felt to be outside the Committee's terms of reference. The omission may, however, have been the result of the Report's approach *via* the balance sheet in Chapter 4, described above. This approach begs the question, since it assumes that the right classification has been made, and that all assets are included in the balance sheet. As the examples of advertising and research and development expenditure show, this may not always be the case.

How should the distinction be drawn? This is a difficult question which we have not sufficient space to answer properly here.[1] We believe that the main guiding principle so far as *real* assets are concerned should be that capital transactions are those which change the nature of the company, while maintenance expenditures are those which are required to keep it unchanged. If maintenance is fully undertaken, it will be possible to maintain the same physical rates of current output and input indefinitely. This does not mean, however, that net current receipts (including full maintenance as a current expense) will be constant, since prices may change. For a typical manufacturing enterprise, these price changes will generally be adverse because of competition from newer and better methods of production. Consequently, if only maintenance is undertaken, net current receipts will tend to fall. It will therefore not be possible to take

[1] For a fuller discussion, see Scott (1976).

out from the company an amount equal to net current receipts indefinitely. On the contrary, some part of net current receipts will have to be devoted to capital expenditure in order to change the nature of the company. This change will have to increase the earning power of the company's assets, whether by adding new assets or by improving existing assets, in such a way as to counter the tendency to falling net earnings from unchanged assets. There is a certain level of capital expenditure which will be just sufficient to enable a constant real rate of take-out for the indefinite future. This level of capital expenditure is *depreciation*, and it is clear that, by definition, the standard stream profit of the company is net current receipts *less* depreciation, provided expectations are fulfilled.

We may express the same conclusion slightly differently. Net current receipts equal the sum of take-out and capital expenditure ('gross' in the sense that depreciation is not deducted, but 'net' in the sense that capital receipts are deducted from capital expenditures). If we make take-out equal to standard-stream income, then capital expenditure must equal depreciation.

How does depreciation as thus defined relate to the change in value of assets? Consider a company which is incurring capital expenditure equal to depreciation, no more and no less, and let us continue to assume that all expectations are fulfilled. Then, by definition, the real take-out from the company must be constant. If (real) rates of discount are also constant, then the real value of the company's assets (i.e. the discounted net present value of the future stream of take-out, the latter being expressed in real terms by dividing by the RPI) must also be constant. Hence, in these circumstances, depreciation is that level of capital expenditure which keeps the real net present value of the company's assets constant. If, however, discount rates or expectations change, or if take-out is not equal to standard stream income, then depreciation will not, in general, be the level of capital expenditure which keeps the real net present value of the company's assets unchanged. We must then fall back on our basic definition of depreciation given in the last paragraph but one.

The above discussion is unduly condensed and the definition of net current receipts not sufficiently flexible. In practice, some conventions must be devised for deciding which items to call current and which capital. The important point is to make one's estimates of depreciation consistent with these conventions so that net current receipts minus depreciation (or plus appreciation) gives a good estimate of standard stream profit. Which conventions are best for a particular company must depend on its own particular circumstances. Thus, for example, a mining company, a manufacturing company and a company providing research services might find that different conventions suited each of them, since assets which were important for one would be negligible for another. All we can attempt here is to set out some general principles which may serve as a guide.

6. DEPRECIATION AND THE VALUATION OF REAL ASSETS

In Section 2 we used only one method of valuing assets, namely, the discounted net present value method, called 'economic value' in the Report (para. 88). In that same paragraph, the Report lists nine possible measures of the value of non-monetary assets, but reduces these to three; current purchase price, net realizable value and 'economic value'. In Chapter 6, the Report discusses which of these three should be used to obtain what it calls the 'value to the business' of an asset. The Report (paras. 208 and 209) quotes and adopts the following definition of 'value to the business' originally put forward by Bonbright:[1]

'The value of a property to its owner is identical in amount with the adverse value of the entire loss, direct and indirect, that the owner might expect to suffer if he were to be deprived of the property'.

Following this definition, and after some further discussion, the Report concludes (para. 222) that 'We believe it is reasonable to assume, where RC (replacement cost) can be ascertained or estimated, that in the great majority of cases it will correctly represent the value of an asset to a business'. It is this conclusion which leads to the Report's recommendations in regard to the valuation of fixed assets in the balance sheet (paras. 527–530), to the view that land, buildings, ships and aircraft should be valued by independent valuers at 'existing use value' at intervals of three to five years (but annually for property companies) (paras. 567–570), and that other fixed assets should in the great majority of cases be valued at written down replacement cost,[2] although 'economic' value or net realizable value should be used in the few cases where replacement cost exceeds both of them (paras. 570–572). In order to make the estimation of replacement cost as objective as possible, the Report proposes that the Government Statistical Service should provide index numbers of prices 'specific to particular industries for capital expenditure on plant and machinery by those industries' (para. 573). A separate index would be published for motor vehicles.

[1] Bonbright (1937).
[2] Using straight line depreciation, written down replacement cost for an asset with a total life of N years, of which n more years remain, would be $\frac{n}{N}$ times replacement cost new.

The method recommended for estimating depreciation depends on the method used to value the assets in the balance sheet. Thus, for an asset whose total economic life is expected to be N years, depreciation on the straight line basis would normally be $1/N$th of its replacement cost new.

The first point which must be made clear is that it is not necessarily the case that the Report's 'value to the business' is the right concept to use, either for the balance sheet or for the calculation of depreciation and hence of profit. 'Value to the business', as defined by Bonbright, seems to be relevant for purposes of insurance, or for compensation for loss or damage. The Report does not give any clear reason as to why it should be the right concept for calculating profit or as an aid in judging a company's performance. So far as the calculation of either of our two concepts of profit is concerned, discounted net present value, or 'economic value',[1] is the only relevant concept. In certain circumstances, either replacement cost or net realizable value may give the best available estimate of economic value, but that is their only relevance to the estimation of profit.

Let us then consider how depreciation should be calculated in order to arrive at a good estimate of standard stream profit. We shall argue that, provided the expectations held when the asset was purchased are fulfilled, and provided one important additional assumption holds, the correct basis for depreciation is the historical cost of an asset, and not its replacement cost. This is true even if there is inflation, although then we have to adjust the historical cost by the RPI in the way described below. However, to simplify the exposition we first assume that the RPI is constant. The important assumption referred to above is that depreciation funds, when reinvested, earn a constant real rate of return which is the same as that earned by the original asset. While it is unlikely that these assumptions will be precisely fulfilled for any single asset they seem reasonable assumptions to make so far as the average of a wide variety of assets is concerned. Where they are fulfilled, depreciation based on replacement cost is incorrect (unless it turns out to be the same as historical cost), and there seems to be no reason to suppose that, where they are not fulfilled, replacement cost would generally give a better estimate (although it could in particular circumstances). The only general solution then would be to return to the basic definition of depreciation given earlier.

---

[1] However, the Report's definition of 'economic value' does not exactly accord with ours. In para. 88 (*vi*) the Report defines it as 'The present value of all expected future earnings from the asset in discounted terms', but in para. 89 this is qualified by saying that it is 'based on the amount that can be earned by holding the asset'. Our definition would allow for the possibility that the asset might be sold, and would include the discounted value of the sales proceeds. It would thus be improbable that the net realizable value could exceed our definition of 'economic value', although the Report envisages this possibility.

TABLE 1. *Arithmetical example to illustrate depreciation based on historical cost*

Item	Cash flows etc. in £ in years:			
	0	1	2	3
	£	£	£	£
Assuming no inflation				
1. Purchase of asset	100			
2. Net current receipts from asset		60	55	
3. Depreciation		50	50	
4. Income from depreciation fund			5	10
5. Total income (lines 2 − 3 + 4)		10	10	10
Assuming inflation at 100% p.a.				
6. Purchase of asset	100			
7. Net current receipts from asset		120	220	
8. Depreciation		100	200	
9. Income from depreciation fund			20	80
10. Total income (lines 7 − 8 + 9)		20	40	80

The following arithmetical example makes the point. In the top half of Table 1 we consider the no-inflation case, and we allow for inflation in the lower half. Taking the top half first, we see that an asset costing £100 in year o has net current receipts of £60 and £55 in the following two years, and zero thereafter. The net present value of this investment, discounting at 10 per cent per annum, is zero. Consequently, the asset yields 10 per cent per annum. If depreciation of £50 in each of the two years is allowed for, and if these amounts are invested to earn 10 per cent per annum, it can be seen that in each year subsequent to the purchase of the original asset the standard stream income from it is £10. This is equal to net current receipts, including income from the depreciation fund, less depreciation. After the end of the asset's life (i.e. in year 3 and subsequent years) the only income is from the depreciation fund.

It will be noted that the depreciation provisions add up to the historical cost of the asset. In our example we have made them equal, £50 in each of two years. This might not occur in practice, but the result that the sum of the depreciation provisions equals the historical cost would still hold.[1] Thus the correct depreciation provision might not be given by

[1] If, for example, we imagine that net current receipts in line 2 in year 1 are reduced by £1, then we must increase those in year 2 by £1·1 in order to keep the asset's yield unchanged. Depreciation in year 1 must then be reduced by £1 (to keep income in line 5 at £10), and it must be increased in year 2 by *only* £1, leaving the total depreciation in years 1 and 2 together unchanged at £100. The reason it only has to be increased by £1 in year 2 is that income from the investment of depreciation in line 4 is down by £0·1 in year 2. Consequently, income in line 5 is still £10. This argument is quite general, and can be applied to any pattern of net current receipts in line 2. For each there will be a uniquely correct pattern of depreciation in line 3 which will always sum to £100. For a valuable discussion of the general case, see Kay (1976).

223

the straight line method (as in the example). Nevertheless, one would generally not go so far wrong by adopting that method, the important point being that the total of the depreciation provisions over the whole life of the asset should equal its cost.

The illustration assumes that the same return (10 per cent) is actually earned on the original asset as on the reinvested depreciation. This is crucial. If, for example, there were some unexpected change which reduced net current receipts in year 2 below £55, then the calculation would be thrown out. In principle, one would have to recalculate the net present value of the asset on the basis of one's revised expectations and this revised net present value would then become the basis for depreciation instead of the original historical cost. In practice, it would not generally be worthwhile attempting to recalculate depreciation provisions in this way. With a large number of assets and a long period of years one could reasonably hope that errors would mostly cancel out. However, if the errors seemed important enough, it could be worthwhile revising one's estimates.

We have said nothing so far about the replacement cost of the asset for the simple reason that it is irrelevant. It might be higher or lower in years 1, 2 and 3 than the original cost of the asset, but that would in no way affect our argument. The proponents of replacement cost depreciation tend to assume that depreciation funds must be sufficient to replace physically the asset being depreciated. However, this is not the case. Assets are frequently not replaced by identical or even similar assets and, in a changing world, there is no reason why they should be. So long as the depreciation funds can be reinvested so as to earn the same constant return as the original asset, *what* they are invested in is immaterial, and our conclusion holds.

This conclusion is formally correct, but may still leave the proponents of replacement cost depreciation unsatisfied. A firm, they could argue, is not free to invest wherever it likes. It is to some extent tied to its existing markets, products or processes by its history. It will have built up a special expertise and special connections so that its assets cannot be switched costlessly from one form to another. In view of this, a sharp rise in the replacement cost of a particular type of machine (or material) needed by the firm will increase its costs and may very well reduce its profitability, and this should somehow be reflected in the accounts. No-one would deny, for example, that a rise in the cost of tyres increases the cost of motoring since it raises the cost of maintaining a car in working order. Why then deny that a rise in the cost of replacing fixed assets raises the cost of production of a firm since it raises the cost of maintaining the firm in working order?

To answer this, we must distinguish between rising costs of production and falling profitability. There is nothing *in principle* in historical cost depreciation which is inconsistent with the idea that costs may rise. Naturally, if machines are replaced by costlier ones, their historical costs rise. One would perhaps like the system of depreciation used to reflect this more smoothly than would occur under, say, the straight line method, and this could in principle be brought about by allocating more of the depreciation to the later years of an asset's life and less to the earlier years, leaving the *total* still equal to the historical cost. Whether the practical advantage of this would be worth the extra complication is rather doubtful.

The more important worry of the adherents to replacement cost depreciation relates to profitability. An unexpected rise in replacement costs could signal a fall in profitability because selling prices could not be increased enough to compensate for the rise in cost. If depreciation is based on historical costs, accounting profits will only fall after replacement has occurred, whereas if depreciation is based on replacement cost the fall in profits will appear sooner in the accounts. This fall is not necessarily, be it noted, in the profitability of investment in the asset being replaced, or in its replacement, but rather in the total assets of the firm.

This admittedly is a case where basing depreciation on replacement cost could give a better guide to standard stream profits than basing it on historical cost. But one swallow does not make a summer. It is equally possible that a rise in replacement costs presages a rise, and not a fall, in the profitability of the firm's total assets. Since the future is uncertain, it may be better not to anticipate it too readily, and to wait for the fall (or rise) to show up as it eventually will with historical cost depreciation. If, however, one is confident enough to want to anticipate the change in profits, then the better procedure would seem to be to make an explicit provision in the accounts. Such provisions are in any case theoretically desirable to smooth out fluctuations in net current receipts due to fluctuations in demand etc. Whether they are desirable in *practice* depends on a variety of considerations relating to the tolerable degree of subjectivity in accounts and the safeguards which could be imposed on estimation procedures.

So far we have been assuming that there is no inflation. It is only then that the basic issues can be clearly seen. It seems probable that much of the attraction of replacement cost depreciation is in practice due to the existence of inflation, and that historical cost depreciation has been discredited because it makes *no* allowance for inflation. This is a confusion of issues. One can quite easily adapt historical cost depreciation so as to allow for inflation as we show below. There is no need to adopt the complex system of revaluation based on index numbers of doubtful reliability[1] as recommended in the Report. It is true that the system has been used by some companies, but it seems likely that the main benefit has been due, not to the use of replacement cost as such, but rather to the fact that *some* adjustment for inflation has been made. That benefit can, however, be obtained much more easily in the manner illustrated in the lower half of Table 1.

This illustration is really the same as in the top half of the Table, but with an inflation rate of 100 per cent per annum superimposed. Consequently, all figures in year 1 have been doubled, in year 2 quadrupled and in year 3 multiplied by eight. The real rate of return is still 10 per cent per annum, but this, combined with 100 per cent inflation, results in a nominal discount rate of 120 per cent per annum (i.e. $1 \cdot 1 \times 2 \times 100-100$). Historical cost depreciation must now be increased in the same proportion as the increase in the RPI from mid-year to mid-year, that is, at 100 per cent per annum, so depreciation is £100 instead of £50 in year 1 and £200 instead of £50 in year 2. Thus only the RPI is required, and not some special index of asset prices. Line 10 of the Table shows that the correct standard stream income is reached by this method. It is still £10 *at year 0 prices* in each and every year, but in terms of actual prices it doubles each year, as shown.

It will be noted that we suggest the *middle* of the year as the reference point. The CPP adjustment, which is in other respects similar to the one suggested above, is to express all accounts in terms of prices at the *end* of the year. This is not an important difference, but it seems that if primary emphasis is given to the figure of profit (as we propose), while the balance sheet is secondary, it is simpler to use mid-year prices. This has the advantage that sales and purchases for the year need not normally be adjusted, since for most practical purposes one can take them as being evenly distributed over the year. In CPP accounts, by contrast, sales and purchases have to be adjusted to end-of-year prices, and this seems a slight complication which it is desirable to avoid.

---

[1] With the best will in the world it is nearly impossible to define what is meant by, let alone to measure, the replacement costs of plant and machinery where technical change is at all rapid. There has been considerable discussion of the difficulties involved, see, for example, Denison (1957).

7. STOCKS

The Report recommends 'that all companies which are in a position to ascertain the current cost of each sale at the time it is made, including those companies now using the base stock method, should in future use these figures as the basis of the charge for cost of sales in their current cost profit and loss accounts' (para. 594). By the current cost of each sale is meant 'value to the business' which, as we saw in Section 6, is generally assumed to be replacement cost. The effect of this recommendation is, therefore, that withdrawals from stock should be charged at their replacement cost at the time when they are made. The Report recommends that companies 'unable to ascertain the current costs of their stocks in such a precise manner' should 'calculate a "cost of sales adjustment" which, when added to the conventional figure for cost of sales, would lead to an approximation to a charge for cost of sales equal to the "value to the business" of stock consumed during the year' (para. 595). It is stated that these recommendations 'will in practice mean that the so-called "stock profits" (stock appreciation) of recent years will no longer flow through the profit and loss account' (para. 534).

In order to see how these recommendations square with the principles derived in earlier sections, it is helpful to consider some arithmetical examples. We shall see that, while in some circumstances they may be quite acceptable, in others one could easily be misled by them. It is not by any means always correct to deduct stock appreciation and F.I.F.O. based on historical cost (adjusted for the increase in the RPI) could quite well be correct. Furthermore, the Report does not adequately consider the variety of circumstances confronting different companies. To simplify matters, we assume to begin with that the RPI is constant and expected to remain so indefinitely, but relax this assumption subsequently. The figures on the no-inflation assumption are given in Table 2.

TABLE 2. *Arithmetical illustration of accounting for stocks*

Item			Years		
	I	2A	2B	3A	3B
	£	£	£	£	£
1. Opening stock at cost	100	100	100	200	200
2. Purchases of materials	100	200	200	200	200
3. Withdrawals of materials at cost	100	100	100	200	200
4. Closing stock at cost	100	200	200	200	200
5. Cost of processing	20	20	20	20	20
6. Bank interest	0	0	5	0	10
7. Sales	130	240	135	240	240
8. Conventional profit using F.I.F.O. (lines $7-6-5-2+4-1$)	10	120	10	20	10
9. Standard stream profits	10	20	10	20	10

Consider a company with a stock of 100 units of a material costing £1 per unit. We assume this stock remains physically constant throughout our example to simplify matters. It is, however, turned over once in the year, so that 100 units are bought and put into stock and 100 units are withdrawn from stock. The latter are processed at a cost of £20 and then sold for £130, the additional profit of £10 representing a return of 10 per cent per annum on the stock of £100. Let us call this the year 1 situation. At the start of year 2, unexpectedly, the price of the material doubles to £2 per unit. We first consider a case, A, in which the company at once increases its selling price from £1·3 to £2·4 per unit to reflect this increase in cost.[1] In this case, assuming that everything else remains the same, the company's accounts on the conventional F.I.F.O. basis would show profits in year 2 as £120, i.e., sales of £240 less purchases of £200 and less processing costs of £20 plus increase in value of stock of £100 (i.e. from £100 at the start to £200 at the end of the year).

In year 3, and all subsequent years we may suppose, prices and quantities remain unchanged. The firm's conventional profit is then £20 per annum (i.e. £240 sales less £220 costs, with no stock change).

Commonsense suggests that the firm's standard stream profit rose from £10 in year 1 to £20 in year 2, as a result of the unexpected increase in price of the material. A profit of £20 is 'required' to yield the 'normal' 10 per cent per annum on the stock of £200. However, the conventional profit of £120 in year 2 is clearly misleading. In the circumstances described, one could not prudently distribute £120 as dividend in year 2 and expect to go on distributing as much in later years. The prudent distribution for year 2 is £20, and so £100 of the conventional profit should be disregarded in estimating standard stream profit.

This is precisely the effect of the Report's recommendation. The replacement cost of the 100 units withdrawn from stock in year 2 was £200, not the £100 charged under conventional F.I.F.O. accounting. Hence the Report's recommendation would be to charge altogether £220 of costs against sales of £240, leaving £20 of profit in year 2, just as in year 3 and later. The £100 of increase in stocks would be treated as a holding gain, and disregarded in calculating profit.

The principles we have suggested would lead to the same result. The economic value (present value) of the material in stock is the amount it contributes to sales. In year 1 this is £1 per unit but, from the start of year 2, because of the unexpected price increase, it becomes £2 per

---

[1] The cost is increased by £1·1, not by £1·0, because of the 10 per cent interest on the value of stocks held for one year.

Some economic principles of accounting

unit.[1] Consequently, the value of stocks should be written up from £100 to £200 at the start of year 2, but this windfall should not be included in standard stream profit. The value of withdrawals from stock should be the expected economic value lost thereby, which is £1 in year 1 but is £2 in year 2 and subsequently. We can then present the accounts for year 2 as follows (this may seem tedious here, but it is helpful for comparison with the subsequent example). Current sales equal total external sales of £240 less capital sales of £200 (i.e. withdrawals from stock), which is £40. Current purchases equal total external purchases of £220 less capital purchases for stock of £200, i.e. £20. Profit is current sales less current purchases less depreciation (nil in this example), and therefore is £20.

Thus far we find no difference between the Report's recommendations and our own. But now consider the same example with one important (and quite realistic) change in assumptions (see Col. B in the Table). In year 2, following the doubling of the material cost, our firm fails to adjust its selling price immediately to reflect this. Instead, it follows a cost plus method of pricing, using conventional F.I.F.O. accounting. It might wish to do this for a variety of reasons: because its competitors were doing it, because its customers would otherwise be offended, or because of Government price control. Whatever the reason, the result is that the firm needs more finance rising from £0 at the beginning of the year to £100 at the end of the year. We may suppose that it borrows from a bank on the security of the increased stock at a rate of interest of 10 per cent. In order to cover the interest on this loan, the firm must charge prices which bring in sales receipts of £135 in year 2, since the average loan outstanding is £50 and the interest is therefore £5. Against these sales receipts it charges costs of £200 for material purchases, £20 for processing and £5 for bank interest, and it credits £100 of increase in the value of stocks. Its profit, under conventional F.I.F.O. accounting, is therefore £10 i.e. the same as in year 1. Furthermore, this profit remains at £10 in year 3 and subsequently, because then, under the same pricing and accounting system, its sales are £240 and its costs are £200 materials,

---

[1] It might be thought that the discounted present value of the stock, when it is bought, should be £1 in year 1, and its value on withdrawal should be £1·1. This would be the right way to look at the matter if the material, like wine, matured while in stock. If, however, the material is physically unchanged, and if prices are also unchanged, a unit of it cannot be worth more merely because it has been held a year in stock. The explanation for holding stocks must in this case be akin to the transactions and precautionary motives for holding cash, e.g. to ensure a smooth flow of supplies in the face of uncertainty about one's ability to get immediate delivery. In that case, the expected discounted present value of stocks in year 1 is just £1 throughout the year and for all units, and, following the change in expectations in year 2, it becomes £2 per unit.

229

M. FG. Scott

£20 processing and £10 bank interest. It would then appear that in these circumstances the firm's standard stream profits have not changed. They were £10 in year 1 and they continue to be £10 in year 2 and subsequently. Furthermore, the conventional F.I.F.O. accounting system has correctly estimated these standard stream profits.

Were we to follow replacement cost accounting in this case, thereby excluding stock appreciation, we would have to conclude that the firm made an operating loss in year 2 of £90.[1] This is because, against its receipts, we would have to charge exactly the same costs as above, but could not take credit for the £100 increase in value of stocks. Consequently, our profit would be £100 less than on the conventional basis. Yet it has to be recognized that this is a totally misleading figure, since, as we saw above, the firm could prudently distribute £10 in year 2 and expect to continue to distribute the same amount in all subsequent years. Hence, if the exclusion of stock appreciation is meant to be a guide to prudent distribution, it has signally failed in its purpose in this case.[2] Nor is this an unrealistic example. There are many cases where companies have delayed passing on cost increases in their selling prices. According to National Income Blue Book conventions and to many commentators, this has resulted in losses, or small profits. However, while it is true to say that companies' profits would have been bigger had they delayed less, it does not follow that their profits, in the standard stream sense, have actually fallen. One could describe the situation, which is illustrated by our examples, as one in which companies are presented with the opportunity of making a windfall gain which they may take to a greater or lesser extent depending on how fast they adjust their selling prices.[3]

It remains to be demonstrated how our own principles lead to a correct calculation of profit in this case B. According to them, withdrawals from stock should be valued at the economic value of the assets concerned. Given the firm's pricing policy, each unit withdrawn in year 2 contributes

---

[1] The Report's recommendations, strictly interpreted, might not lead to this result, however. It could be argued that the 'value to the business' of the withdrawals from stock was their economic value, not their replacement cost, since the latter exceeds the former. If this is correct, the Report's recommendations are in this case in line with our own. The Report does not, however, point out that this could be quite a common case, so that some readers might easily be misled into thinking that stock appreciation should *always* be excluded from operating profit.

[2] There is, however, a qualification to this relating to gearing. Firm B, in our example, has become more highly geared, whereas firm A has become less highly geared, and this could affect distribution policy. Alternatively, firm B, instead of relying on bank borrowing for all of their extra finance required, could issue some more equity.

[3] The opportunity may not be a real one, however, if, for one reason or another, companies are unable to adjust their prices quickly.

only £1 to profit. Consequently, current sales are £135 less capital sales from stock of £100, i.e. £35. Current purchases are £225 less capital purchases for stock of £200, i.e. £25. Profit is therefore £10.

It must be stressed that these two examples are merely designed to show that stock appreciation should not *always* be deducted. They no more than scratch the surface of the problem. Thus, for example, we have said nothing (nor does the Report) about the question of how goods produced for stock should be charged into stock. They feature as capital expenditures in our system, and there is more than one way in which they could be valued. Nor have we discussed (nor does the Report) the circumstances in which a firm might wish to smooth out the effects of fluctuations in the prices of its materials. Not all firms, even if they passed on cost increases at once, would want to regard this as leading to an increase in their standard stream profit, since they might realistically take the view that sharp price increases would be followed by sharp price decreases. Nor have we discussed changes in the physical volume of stocks in a situation in which firms are actively speculating on price changes. All these difficult cases call for special treatment, and although we believe that the principles already discussed are the right guide, the practical solutions of each problem may well differ.

Before concluding this section on stocks, we must say something about the way in which inflation affects the arithmetical illustration in Table 2. In Table 3 we accordingly show the effect of a 10 per cent rate of inflation. Although this complicates the picture, its broad outlines are unchanged. For firm A, which passes on materials price increases at once, a large deduction for stock appreciation from conventional profits is needed when this occurs. For firm B, which delays passing on the price increase, no such large deduction must be made. The main difference is that now, for *both* firms, some deduction from conventional profits is needed in every year on account of stock appreciation equal to the rate of general inflation. Hence standard stream profits (line 9 of Table 3) equals conventional profits (line 8) *less* 10 per cent of the opening stock and, for Firm A only in the year in which material prices double, year 2A, *less* also stock appreciation of £110 due to this doubling.

Hence the main lesson of this further illustration is that it may be correct to deduct stock appreciation which is simply in line with general inflation (as does CPP) but that whether it is correct to deduct stock appreciation which is due to a *relative* price change depends on whether such a change is quickly reflected in selling prices or not.

TABLE 3. *Arithmetical illustration of accounting for stocks, assuming inflation at 10 per cent per annum*

Item	Years				
	1	2A	2B	3A	3B
	£	£	£	£	£
1. Opening stock at cost	90·9	100	100	220	220
2. Purchases of materials	100	220	220	242	242
3. Withdrawals of materials at cost	90·9	100	100	220	220
4. Closing stock at cost	100	220	220	242	242
5. Cost of processing	20	22	22	24·2	24·2
6. Bank interest	0	0	5·5	0	12·1
7. Sales	130	264	148·5	290·4	290·4
8. Conventional profit using F.I.F.O. (lines 7 − 6 − 5 − 2 + 4 − 1)	19·1	142	21	46·2	34·1
9. Standard stream profits	10	22	11	24·2	12·1

Notes:

1. In years 1 and 3 the closing stock is 10 per cent greater in value than the opening stock because it represents the same physical quantity purchased at prices which are on average 10 per cent higher. In year 2, in addition to the above, the closing stock value doubles.
2. The cash needs of the enterprise can be found on the assumption that the whole of standard stream profits is taken out each year. Then borrowings are lines 9 + 2 + 5 + 6 − 7. These are zero for all years with the exception of 2B, when they are £110. Interest in 2B is at 10 per cent per annum on a loan which rises from zero to £110 and we have assumed it is therefore £5·5. For year 3B we have assumed that the loan is indexed, so that interest is 10 per cent of £110 × 1·1.
3. Standard stream profits, line 9, equal conventional profits, line 8, *less* stock appreciation in line with inflation (i.e. 10 per cent of the opening stock) and *less*, in year 2A only, the balance of stock appreciation due to the doubling of material prices. For year 2B, this second deduction is not required (just as in Table 2).

8. MONETARY[1] ASSETS AND LIABILITIES

As we have already seen, the Report does not consider that any adjustment is needed in the conventional treatment of monetary assets and liabilities. It views this as the logical outcome of its approach: 'Because we are recommending that accounts should continue to be drawn up in terms of monetary units (pounds), it follows that no gains or losses in terms of money can arise solely through holding monetary items when prices are changing. The question of whether such gains should be classed as profit does not therefore arise as it does when accounts are drawn up in terms of current purchasing power units' (para. 537).

The flaw in this argument was exposed in Section 3: No sensible person is concerned to maintain a constant *money* income in a period of rapid

[1] Our discussion in this section covers both assets denominated in money terms (e.g. cash or bonds with a redemption value fixed in money terms) and marketable 'paper' securities which is a wider concept including ordinary shares quoted in a stock exchange.

inflation. Yet, if one's receipts consisted entirely of interest on fixed-interest securities, this would, according to the Report's recommendations, be one's income or 'operating profit', all of which one could prudently consume—until its real value vanished away. Furthermore, the Report's recommendations do not lead to consistent results in this matter, since the operating profit of a company with only real assets, as defined in the Report, would certainly *not* be constant in money terms, but would increase broadly in line with inflation.

It is clear, then, that the Report's recommendations are quite unsatisfactory on this score, and they have indeed attracted much criticism. On the other hand, the main rival system which tries to deal with the problem, CPP, is not wholly satisfactory either. According to that system, the actual decline in the real purchasing power of a firm's monetary assets, as measured by the RPI, should be subtracted from its net current receipts in order to arrive at the CPP profit for the year. Likewise, the actual decline in the real purchasing power of a firm's monetary liabilities should be added. These monetary losses and gains are therefore brought into the calculation of CPP profit.

As compared with CCA, the CPP system has the great merit of making *some* allowance for inflation. It can, however, be criticized on several grounds. Some of these criticisms are implicit in the alternative proposals we make below, and relate to the question of whether interest or dividends on monetary assets would be an adequate measure of the standard stream profit from them even in a non-inflationary situation. So far as inflation is concerned, the main difficulty arises over its irregularity. The CPP adjustment would lead to a highly fluctuating loss or gain, as the actual rate of inflation fluctuated from year to year. This would be an unsatisfactory basis for estimating standard stream income. A better procedure would be to estimate the *average* rate of inflation to be expected over the next few years and to make adjustments similar to those required by CPP, but using this estimated average rate. No doubt the average would need to be revised from time to time, but one might hope to achieve some smoothing out of the more extreme fluctuations.

Apart from CPP, the real return from holding marketable securities (both fixed interest, and ordinary shares) has been estimated in the following way,[1] which takes capital gains or losses fully into account, unlike CPP. It is assumed that some specified portfolio is purchased at a given date, and that the whole portfolio is sold one year later. The real return

---

[1] See, for example, M. J. Farrell, December 1962; A. J. Merrett and A. Sykes, December 1963, and also ditto, June 1966; Royal Commission on the Distribution of Income and Wealth, July 1975, Appendix N. N. Barr, September 1975, uses a somewhat similar method.

(before tax) is then the sum of the dividend or interest received during the year and the capital gain (or loss) realized, but after adjusting (as in CPP) for payment made sufficient to keep the real value, at market prices, of the portfolio intact. Thus if the dividend or interest is 4 per cent of the market value of the portfolio at the beginning of the year, if the market value of the portfolio rises by 5 per cent during the year, and if the RPI rises by 6 per cent during the year, then the real return is approximately $4 + 5 - 6 = 3$ per cent. This real return is then the amount which could be taken out at the end of the year while leaving the real market value of the portfolio the same as it was at the beginning of the year. It therefore corresponds to the gain concept of income, not the standard stream concept.

The resulting estimates of gain fluctuate enormously from year to year, and cannot in themselves provide a useful guide to prudent distribution. It might, nevertheless, be argued that the average gain per annum achieved over some reasonably long period in the past would provide such a guide. However, even such long-term rates of gain fluctuate very considerably.[1] Furthermore, it is questionable whether one can project them into the future with any confidence. For example, the average real rates of gain on the shares included in the FT Actuaries index over the period 1963–74 were 0·3 per cent per annum before tax, and −2·9 per cent after deduction of the standard rate of tax and capital gains tax.[2] The last two years of this period showed very large capital losses on shares, part of which were regained in 1975. Projections based on the 1963–74 performance might give a misleadingly low figure for standard stream income. Even if there had been no subsequent recovery, so long as the market did not continue to fall the future rate of gain would be appreciably better than in 1963–74. We therefore conclude that this method is an unsatisfactory way to attempt to estimate standard stream income.

Let us turn now to our own proposals. It is useful to consider separately two different motives for holding monetary assets: to provide liquidity (Keynes's transactions and precautionary motives) and to provide an income (Keynes's speculative motive).

Take the case of a company which holds monetary assets only for liquidity reasons. They take the form of cash, bank deposits or very short-term securities such as bills or trade debtors. Let us further assume, for simplicity, that the money value of the assets it holds is a constant fraction

---

[1] See, for example, the 5-year moving average of gains on the London Stock market for ordinary shares 1948–74 depicted in Figure 16 of the Royal Commission on the Distribution of Income and Wealth, *op. cit.*, which range from about −12 to +20 per cent per annum (pre-tax).

[2] Royal Commission, *op. cit.*, pp. 66, 69.

of the money value of its standard stream profit. Then, if the company's savings net of depreciation are zero, it must be expecting its standard stream profit to grow as fast as the RPI, and no faster. Consequently, it will need to expand its monetary assets at the same rate, that is, to keep their real value constant. This means that an amount sufficient to achieve this result must be provided before any sums are taken out. The case is closely analagous to the required maintenance of a physical asset. The real amount required for maintenance will fluctuate from year to year, depending on the speed of inflation. We could then define 'net current receipts' from the monetary asset as interest plus the value of the liquidity it yields less required maintenance. These net current receipts will fluctuate in real terms, and we need to replace them by a standard stream with the same net present value. The amount of that standard stream then gives the income from the asset. Provided that the money rate of interest is constant, as also is the rate of yield of liquidity,[1] we can estimate the income by subtracting from the interest a weighted average of future expected rates of inflation multiplied by the current money value of the asset (we assume that the liquidity yield shows up in other net current receipts, and therefore does not need to be separately accounted for). The weights are the real discount factors applicable to future periods (multiplied by the real rate of discount, which is assumed constant for simplicity). The effect is, therefore, to give most weight to expected rates of inflation in the near future, and less to those in the more distant future. A formula which summarizes the above is given in the footnote.[2]

Let us consider, now, marketable assets, which are held not for liquidity reasons but in order to derive an income from them. This income could take the form of interest on dividends or capital gains. We consider both fixed interest securities and ordinary shares in broad terms, but do not

---

[1] By this we mean the ratio of the value of the benefit derived from holding the asset (exclusive of interest) to the money value of the asset. This would be difficult to assess but, fortunately, we do not need to do so as long as the benefit shows up elsewhere in the accounts (as it should) and its ratio to the money value of the asset is constant.

[2] If B is the money value at time $t = 0$ of an asset, say a bank deposit, held for liquidity reasons, and if i is the constant rate of interest paid on it, j is the constant liquidity yield per unit of the asset, p_t is the proportionate rate of inflation at time t, and r is the constant real rate of discount of the firm, then it can be shown that the standard stream income from the asset is given by

$$R = B(i + j) - rB \int_0^\infty p_t e^{-rt} . dt.$$ If inflation is expected to be constant at rate p, and if one ignores the liquidity yield (as it shows up elsewhere in the accounts), this simplifies to $R = B(i - p)$. The subtraction of Bp is similar in purpose to the monetary working capital adjustment of SSAP 16 (see Postscript below).

examine all the many different kinds of marketable asset which exist, such as convertible securities, leaseholds, and others.

For any marketable security we must separate two sources of income. First there is the income which accrues to the owner who intends to hold the asset in perpetuity. If the asset has a redemption date, some standard assumption about the reinvestment of the proceeds, and the yield therefrom, must be made, which is similar to the reinvestment of depreciation allowances on real assets. Secondly, there is the income which accrues to the owner from dealing in such assets. Let us call these 'holding' and 'dealing' income respectively.

Consider holding income from fixed interest securities. For a perpetuity, such as War Loan, or Consols, 'current receipts' may be defined as the interest received each year. For a redeemable stock, there is the interest plus the amount received on redemption. These money receipts need to be deflated by the estimated increase in the RPI to express them in terms of constant purchasing power. After discounting by the assumed real rate of discount, their net present value can be estimated. Assuming that any net capital expenditure involved earns the real rate of discount, the standard stream income of the asset can then be found as that amount which, if received in perpetuity, has the same net present value.

It is interesting to consider a perpetuity such as War Loan or Consols in the simplest case where both the rate of inflation and the firm's real rate of discount are assumed constant and positive. One often hears it said that the 'real rate of return' on such an asset is negative if the inflation rate exceeds the interest yield on the market price. The formula which is used is that the 'real rate of return' is $i - p$, where i is the yield and p is the proportionate rate of inflation. So, when i is less than p, the 'real rate of return' is negative. If this is to be taken as implying that the standard stream income from the bond is negative, it is incorrect. It is easy to show that in the circumstances postulated the standard stream income is $ir/(r + p)$, where r is the constant positive real rate of discount, and it is assumed that the bond holder can earn r in alternative investments. This is clearly positive even if p is greater than i. However, the formula $i - p$ is relevant in considering whether to hold the bond. For this to be worth while we require $i - p \geq r$.

Next, consider holding income from shares. If the companies concerned estimated their standard stream profits in accordance with the principles we advocate, and if their rates of discount were broadly similar to those of their shareholders, then (apart from taxation, which we are ignoring here) the latter could take their share of the profits as the best available estimate of their income from them. However, until that happy day dawns, one may have to make do with cruder estimates. The best the writer can suggest is, first, to multiply the market value of the portfolio by the current average dividend yield on a sample of shares which represents those dealt in the market or markets in which the portfolio is invested. Thus if the portfolio were invested in London one would multiply it by the average dividend yield on the FT-Actuaries index. This would give a notional value of dividends which might exceed or fall short of the actual dividends received depending on whether the portfolio was invested in lower- or higher-than-average yielding shares. The reason for using this notional value, rather than the actual one, is given below. Secondly, to this amount of notional dividends one would add (or from it one would subtract) the estimated future rate of growth (or decline) of real dividends on the relevant sample of shares. Thus to continue with the example, if it was expected that, over the long run, dividends on the FT-Actuaries shares would rise by 1 per cent per annum faster than the RPI, one would add on 1 per cent on the portfolio to the notional dividends. The sum of notional dividends and expected real growth of dividends would give estimated holding income.

In estimating the future rate of growth of real dividends one would naturally look at past performance, and here one encounters difficulties similar to those already mentioned in connection with the projection of past rates of real gain. However, dividends are less erratic than share prices, and so the difficulties should be somewhat mitigated by this. Nor should one make a mechanical projection of the past. For dividends earned on investments in foreign countries, one would have to allow for estimated changes in the exchange rate. 'Real dividends' for U.K. shareholders must mean 'expressed in sterling and deflated by the U.K. index of retail prices'.

The reason for using an average, or notional, dividend yield rather than the actual dividends on the portfolio is that one assumes that, for example, higher-than-average dividend yields compensate for lower-than-average growth of dividends. Since one is estimating the rate of growth of dividends from the behaviour of a representative sample of shares, one should use the dividend yield appropriate to that sample. Were one to take *actual* dividends on the portfolio one would have a very unsatisfactory basis for estimating holding income. Since dividend yields vary enormously, it would be possible for the managers of the portfolio to double or halve the dividends, and so the apparent holding income, by switching shares. With the procedure we advocate, this would not be possible.

So much for holding income. Dealing income results from gains made by buying and selling securities, or by holding a portfolio which does better than the sample which forms the basis for the estimation of holding income. In the case of a portfolio which is entirely invested in ordinary shares, or which is only invested in fixed interest securities as a temporary measure to take advantage of an expected fall in share prices, one could estimate holding income *as if* the portfolio were all invested in shares, even when some of it was not. This would implicitly allow for dealing income on, for example, cash held at a time when share prices were expected to fall. Dealing income might be greater than that, however, and in order to estimate the excess one might consider past performance. One could compare the rate of return earned on the actual portfolio (allowing for take-out) with that which would have been earned by holding the shares included in the relevant share price index (allowing for dividends received). This comparison should, ideally, cover as long a period as possible of the performance of the current management. Even so, it could provide an uncertain guide to future dealing income, since luck inevitably plays a large part in performance. It is difficult to know on what other basis one can estimate future dealing income, however. If one wanted to be conservative, one could assume that it would be a *negative* figure equal to the average sales per annum multiplied by the dealing margin. This, in effect, assumes that, apart from dealing costs, the portfolio performs no better than the index.[1]

We do not consider dealing income for a portfolio invested largely or mainly in fixed interest securities, although it might be possible to use a broadly similar method.

We conclude this section with a brief consideration of monetary liabilities. In general, these either exist for 'liquidity' reasons (e.g. trade creditors) or they are held to maturity (e.g. debentures, bonds). They can therefore be dealt with in just the same way as the corresponding assets. Inflation in these cases provides the enterprise with a real gain, although in estimating standard stream income one should not take the credit for the actual gain in any period but rather for the weighted average expected gain, in the manner already described. (Section 9 on Inflation Accounting and Taxation is omitted. It proposed to shift the basis of company taxation from profits to net cash flow to, or 'take-out' by, shareholders and all creditors and debtors of the company, thereby avoiding the necessity for an objective system of inflation-adjusted accounts for tax purposes, as well as achieving some other desirable aims. The interested reader is referred to Kay and King (1983) Chapter 12, where somewhat similar

---

[1] Some evidence for taking this rather jaundiced view of the expertise of portfolio managers is to be found in Jensen (1968), pp. 389–419.

proposals are made. Section 10, which consisted of a few concluding remarks, is also omitted, and the following Postscript substituted.)

POSTSCRIPT

Eight years after the above was written, the price level having more than doubled meanwhile, the most striking feature of the debate on inflation accounting is the inability of those chiefly concerned to agree on a practical set of reforms. Following the Sandilands Report, in November 1976 the Inflation Accounting Steering Group (Morpeth Committee) produced ED 18, which made proposals for a system of Current Cost Accounting (CCA) broadly in line with Sandilands' recommendations. This encountered much criticism, partly on grounds of its length and complexity, and a resolution rejecting compulsory CCA was passed at a meeting of the Institute of Chartered Accountants of England and Wales. The Accounting Standards Committee was forced to think again and eventually, in March 1980, published SSAP 16 which was mandatory for accounting periods beginning in 1980. This was still based on Sandilands, but made two concessions to the view that monetary assets and liabilities were not adequately dealt with in that Report. These concessions were a monetary working capital adjustment and a gearing adjustment, both of which met further severe criticisms. The system remained very complicated and unpopular, and it was reported that only a minority of the non-quoted companies to which it applied were complying with it. Now (in 1984) the Accounting Standards Committee has produced further proposals (ED 35). The basic methodology is the same, but there is no longer a requirement to produce a complete set of CCA accounts, only a series of notes to the main (historic) accounts. 'Value-based' companies, such as banks and insurance companies, are exempted, as are all private companies: presumably this is to weaken the opposition. Nevertheless, strong criticisms have been voiced already.

One of the main criticisms has been of the complexity and arbitrariness of replacement cost valuation of assets. The 'entity' view of company accounts which underlies this method of valuation does not command universal support and suffers from a complete lack of intellectual justification. Who is interested in the cost of maintaining the precise physical assets of a company when those assets are, for very good reasons, not going to remain physically unchanged? Why, then, make complications for no clear purpose? Another criticism relates to the gearing adjustment, dubbed by Whittington (1983, p. 175) in an illuminating review of the whole debate as 'an awkward compromise between the entity and proprietary approaches'. The refusal to make corrections for changes in the general level of prices (compromised in ED 35, however, where this is allowed as one alternative out of three forms of gearing adjustment) has also been criticized. The original opposition to indexation in any form was reported to have come from the Government at the time when the Sandilands Committee was set up, and when the accounting bodies themselves had put forward proposals (ED 8) in which *only* changes in the general level of prices (measured by the RPI) were allowed for, that is, by means of Constant Purchasing Power (CPP) accounts. Governmental opposition must surely be weaker now that it has itself resorted to indexation of tax brackets, social security benefits, and state pensions, and has issued indexed bonds. From the purely practical point of view there would seem to be much to be said for a reversion to the simplicity of the ED 8 proposals. These at least represented an adjustment of a widely-accepted and well-known system of accounting (i.e. historic cost) for general price inflation and nothing else. Experience suggests that reforming the underlying system itself is highly controversial and requires more time.

My own view is that many of the attempts at reform made thus far have been misdirected. In so far as the profit and loss account is concerned, the only two concepts of profit which make sense to me are those I described earlier as 'gain' and 'standard stream income'. Both are of interest, but both generally require subjective forecasts to be made. Accounts can be prepared in ways which form a more or less useful input into such forecasts, and I have tried to make some suggestions on these lines. Much more work is needed by those familiar with the circumstances of different types of company or other entity. In the last resort, however, the most useful and interesting estimates will usually contain a substantial subjective element, and consideration should, I think, be given to how this can best be provided, made explicit, and monitored, and what the relative roles of accountants and directors of companies in preparing such estimates should be. My own practical experience as Bursar of a charity convinces me of two things. First, that there is a strong practical need for estimates of standard stream income and, second, that useful estimates can be provided—but not, so far, or perhaps ever, by accountants *qua* accountants.

REFERENCES

Barr, N., 'Real Rates of Return to Financial Assets since the War', *Three Banks Review*, September 1975.
Bonbright, J. C., *The Valuation of Property*, McGraw-Hill, 1937.

Some economic principles of accounting

Denison, E. F., 'Theoretical Aspects of Quality Change, Capital Consumption and Net Capital Formation', in *Problems of Capital Formation*, Studies in Income and Wealth, Vol. 19, National Bureau of Economic Research, Princeton, 1957.

Farrell, M. J., 'On the Structure of the Capital Market', *Economic Journal*, December 1962.

Inflation Accounting Committee, *Inflation Accounting*, Cmnd. 6225, H.M.S.O., September 1975.

Jensen, M. C., 'The Performance of Mutual Funds in the Period 1945–1964', *The Journal of Finance*, 1968.

Kaldor, N., *An Expenditure Tax*, Allen & Unwin, London, 1955.

Kay, J., 'Accountants, too, could be happy in a golden age: The accountant's rate of profit and the internal rate of return', *Oxford Economic Papers*, November 1976.

Kay, J. and King, M., *The British Tax System*, third edition, Oxford University Press.

Merrett, A. J. and Sykes, A., 'Return on Equities and Fixed Interest Securities 1919–1963', *District Bank Review*, December 1963.

Merrett, A. J., and Sykes, A., 'Return on Equities and Fixed Interest Securities: 1919–1966', *District Bank Review*, June 1966.

Royal Commission on the Distribution of Income and Wealth, Report No. 2, *Income from Companies and its Distribution*, Cmnd. 6172, H.M.S.O., July 1975.

Scott, M. FG., 'Investment and Growth', *Oxford Economic Papers*, November 1976.

Whittington, G., *Inflation Accounting. An Introduction to the Debate*, Cambridge University Press, 1983.

14   Accounting values: sale price versus replacement cost

by W. T. Baxter*

It has often seemed to me that a book review ought to start with some statement of the book's aspirations. Criticism falls into perspective when one knows whether the author is aiming high or low: an attempt to improve on Einstein may be a failure and yet glorious, whereas proposals for a new kind of petty cash account could well seem excellent and yet not call for extravagant praise.

So let it be said at once that Professor Chambers' new book[1] aims high—very high indeed. He tries to give a new and more worthy stature to accounting, to study it in the light of scientific method, to place it in the general framework of man's knowledge, to find its faults, and to cure them. Scope, concepts, names cited, and vocabulary all proclaim this to be no run-of-the-mill text-book. You are on your toes right from the start. Is this the dawn of accounting's Copernican revolution? Or does the book merely restate the well-known in unfamiliar terms, thereby perhaps helping us to think afresh about something that has grown stale (much as an art critic is supposed to turn a hackneyed picture upside-down to gain fresh insight)? The book is clearly trying to do something ambitious and difficult; and my comment must be read in this light.

There would be some advantage in starting the book at its last chapter (Epilogue) which shows how the whole thing hangs together. An early chapter deals with scientific method (perception, learning, hypotheses, etc.); another summarizes the relevant bits of economics (preferences, means, and so forth). We then move on to the social and market environment, and to the nature of classification and measurement. The middle chapters are more closely concerned with accounting: they set out the grounds for thinking the main purpose of accounts is to give a starting-point for action, and then ask what kind of figures will be most helpful to this end. Later chapters compare the needs of ordinary business (whose success can be appraised in terms of cash receipts) and state organizations (with more nebulous criteria of success). Finally Professor Chambers asks why accounting has fostered, and still tolerates, so many practices

* Emeritus Professor of Accounting, London School of Economics and Political Science.
[1] Raymond J. Chambers, *Accounting, Evaluation and Economic Behavior* (Englewood Cliffs, N.J.: Prentice-Hall, 1966), pp. xiii + 388.

that needlessly lessen its worth as an aid to decision and to social welfare. The answer, he suggests, lies in the conflicts between the many parties interested in the figures—managers at different levels, owners, creditors, and the state. We accountants have never been able to choose between these rival masters, and to think out a set of consistent principles, partly because our energy has mostly gone in mastering intricate tax codes, and partly because we lack the 'education at high tertiary level' that might have enabled us to put accounting on the same footing as the other arts.

Plainly a good many of the early pages are background education rather than new thought on accounting. They deal with matters that the account-ant usually leaves to other specialists—here the philosopher and the eco-nomist. They accordingly raise the question of how far a writer (or lecturer) should trespass onto his neighbours' domains. He certainly is entitled to treat all fences between subjects as artificial, and to show how one discipline illuminates another. But the economies of specialization suggest that he should normally venture into the other fellow's subject only where the latter is highly germane to his own, and even then should confine himself to bits not dealt with adequately in their usual habitats. The reader of this book might reasonably complain that the long prelimi-naries slow down the argument (which is further retarded by some forty pages of chapter summaries).

A few elderly and hide-bound readers (like me) may also be put off by the unfamiliar words. Sometimes these add to understanding, and one is grateful for them; at others, they remind one of M. Jourdain's discovery that he had for more than forty years been speaking prose with-out knowing it. The book-keeper of a firm, it turns out, is engaged in the temporal and subjectival ordering of records isomorphic and isochronic with the past transactions of a homeostatic organism. Good for him. But it seems sad that the brave new thoughts cannot be set out in plain words.

The book's central theme is that accounts should serve as a spring-board for action, and so should give the actor the maximum information about the means at his command. When the actor is the manager of a firm, he is interested *inter alia* in financial constraints. Some of his information on this point is private and subjective, and so can be helpful only to himself. To influence others, the argument runs, he must use objective knowledge that is public property. 'Now the market place is a public place in which many actors have commerce with one another. The only knowledge useful to any actor in commercial intercourse with others is knowledge which is equally useful to all others. If an actor has at a point of time so many monetary units, or by reference to market prices the means of acquiring so many monetary units, knowledge of this quantity is useful to the actor and to all other actors with whom he may deal. One cannot expect others to assent blandly to one's private evaluations ...' (p. 146). So, if wealth must be measured in objective and up-to-date terms, the historical cost of assets is useless; current market quotations must be substituted.

But there are commonly two current market prices, the buying price (replacement cost) and the selling price. We must choose between these. To my mind, Professor Chambers' book is rendering its best service when it focusses attention on this choice, which is likely for some decades to loom large in reformist argument.

He reasons thus:

1. A manager wants to know how much money he could marshall for new projects. But buying price 'does not indicate capacity, on the basis of present holdings, to go into a market with cash for the purpose of adapting oneself to contemporary conditions, whereas the selling price does' (p. 92).

2. Accounts are concerned not only with separate items but with sums of items too. These aggregates should represent 'the combined or resultant effects of numbers of events and transactions' (p. 149). They fail to do so, and lack economic significance if the items are historical costs of different dates and price-levels. But if the items are instead sale prices, they can combine into a meaningful aggregate—the total cash that could at a pinch be raised by scrapping the assets piecemeal. 'Aggregation is a necessary device if overtaxing of the span of attention is to be avoided. ... If the only relevant statement at a point of time about a particular asset is its market selling price at that time, the only relevant statement about a group of assets is the sum of their market selling prices at that time' (p. 150).

3. Replacement cost is irrelevant because 'its reference is to a specific future action which the actor may or may not take' (p. 149). (I should have thought this objection held for sale price too.)

4. In budgets for management decision, sale price is at times a relevant quantity. Thus it measures the sacrifice from consuming existing assets instead of selling them off; in particular, in budgets for showing whether or not a machine should be replaced by a new model, one should put in the old (e.g., as a trade-in) at sale price—here its opportunity cost. 'The criterion of choice is opportunity cost not replacement cost. ... The opportunity cost determines, in part, the sum available to finance replacement and provides the basis for calculating the discounted expected returns from retention of the asset. The replacement price provides the sum to be found to finance the replacement and provides the basis for

244

calculating the discounted expected returns from replacement. Both are necessary to the replacement decision' (p. 202). And there is a lot to be said for keeping ordinary accounts in a way that suits decision-budgets.

5. The sum of the sale prices of the separate assets is likewise an ingredient in the most momentous budget of all: it gives the opportunity cost of being in business (p. 202).

In short, 'the single financial property which is uniformly relevant at a point of time for all possible future actions in markets is the market selling price or realizable price of any or all goods held. Realizable price may be described as *current cash equivalent*.[1] What men wish to know, for the purpose of adaptation, is the numerosity of the money tokens which could be substituted for particular objects and for collections of objects if money is required beyond the amount which one already holds' (p. 92).

As a corollary of this rule for asset measurement, income and cost are also functions of sale price. Thus depreciation is (p. 208) decline in sale price. One must however deal in real quantities, i.e., must eliminate the effect of change in the general price level. The book shows how this can be done, with several numerical examples backed up by algebra that is both clear and elegant.

Most of us are now likely to agree with the view that accounts should be geared to decision-making (in part because of Professor Chambers' earlier *Accounting and Action*), and that they should be adjusted for general price change. But I still find the case for selling price quite unconvincing.

Of course, this question is of scant practical importance when buying and selling prices are close to one another. But often they lie wide apart. Where the asset is merchandise, sale price may (even net of selling costs) be far more than buying price. Where the asset is instead part of the fixed equipment, net selling price may be far less than buying price (particularly if the asset is very specific, or is subject to high costs of dismantling or removal). So our choice of measure will often make a big difference.

Sale price is admittedly important when there is overwhelming likelihood of the asset being scrapped or of the firm being sold up piecemeal. At such times, as we have seen, sale price is the right figure to use in decision-budgets, and there is a strong case for using it in the ordinary

---

[1] 'A man does not value money for its own sake, but for its Purchasing Power—that is to say, for what it will buy. Therefore, his demand is not for units of money as such, but for units of purchasing power. Since, however, there is no means of holding general purchasing power except in the form of money, his demand for purchasing power translates itself into a demand for an "equivalent" quantity of money.' John Maynard Keynes, *A Treatise on Money* (London: Macmillan & Co. Ltd., 1930), Vol. I, p. 53.

balance sheet too. But normally assets are not on their last legs, and firms are not on the brink of liquidation; in these more clement times, we may indeed still like to know our assets' sale prices, but merely as a comforting reassurance in case things take a turn for the worse. So long as all is going well, sale price has little relevance.

Normally the ill consequence of using up an asset is that the asset must be replaced. On a 'what difference does it make?' view, therefore, the right measure of sacrifice is here replacement cost. For example, when a manufacturer is estimating the cost of using materials (already in store or on order) for a job, he should charge them at what he will pay for their replacement; again, if he shortens a machine's life by using it on the job, he should charge an appropriate number of service-units (ton-miles, etc.) at the lowest available replacement cost per unit.

There are times, to be sure, when the alternative budgets throw up a figure other than replacement cost as the 'value to the owner' (to use the term favoured by Professor J. C. Bonbright in what should be the bible of theorists in this field, his admirable *Valuation of Property*[1]). He tells us: 'With most types of property ... the property may be worth to its owner its replacement cost, or its net selling price, or some amount between these two figures.' The correct valuation rule for a manager is thus of the traditional lower-of-x-or-y type: replacement cost (assuming replacement to be possible by the desired time) is the ceiling and the norm; but the present value of the asset's future net contribution should be substituted when it is lower (e.g., when the asset is obsolete). Net contribution can however take many forms—internal services or external hire or sale—and the budgets must use the best of these possibilities; and, to quote Professor Bonbright again, 'even if the property is otherwise utterly useless to the owner himself, it has a value to him for the purpose of exchanging it for money.' So sale price is merely a possible lower limit to a gamut of values.

Replacement cost, qualified in the ways just indicated, therefore emerges as the correct asset value for most decision-budgets. This does not automatically make it the best figure for the balance sheet too, but does make it a strong contender.

Unhappily for the cause of crisp definitions, the balance sheet (unlike decision-budgets) does not try to supply a precise answer to a precise question. It certainly does not answer the major question of what the firm is worth as a going concern; that value is a function of anticipated net receipts. What it does instead is to tell us, in vague but still useful

---

[1] New York: McGraw-Hill, 1937. The quotations are from pages 92 and 91.

terms, something about the type and size of the tools available for winning those receipts. Managers and their critics (investors, analysts, holding company officials, etc.) rightly want to know whether good use is being made of the given kit of tools. They therefore study the relation of net receipts to tools—for instance (as Professor Chambers stresses in his ninth chapter) by finding ratios of income to assets, and by comparing the ratios of different periods or different firms. 'Size' is certainly a rather woolly concept here. Yet the income:size comparisons may prove quite a helpful test of efficiency. To yield maximum service, the measure of asset size must give the best available picture of the asset's potential usefulness in its normal role. The measure is the more likely to succeed where it does not depend on facts such as location and specificity, as it does where it is based on sale price. (A refinery in a remote desert may have an immense array of assets that would cost a fortune to replace, and are confidently expected to earn vast sums. Yet their scrap values may be minute or even negative.)

But what about the firm's ability to raise cash for new projects (argument (1) above)? Admittedly this is to some degree linked with the assets' sale prices. But we can scarcely imagine a manufacturer selling off large chunks of his plant to finance the output; only a fundamental change of role would justify such an upheaval. Normally an extra venture is financed out of the more liquid assets only, or by borrowing; and many classes of potential lenders and investors are likely to be impressed even more by good cash flow prospects than by scrap values (though once again these can be comforting background information). So this argument is hardly decisive.

On balance, then, qualified replacement cost seems the stronger candidate for the balance sheet. It has (for each separate asset, though not for the total) a meaning[1] that is perhaps less obvious than the meaning of sale price, but is entirely logical. It has other qualities that are not found in sale price, and is free from the absurdities that sometimes beset the latter.

When we turn to income measurement, the case against sale price

---

[1] 'When I say, "My house is worth $10,000 to me," I mean (if I am precise in my use of language) that the retention of the house is worth to me as much as the acquisition of $10,000 in cash would be worth to me. But this is the same thing as saying that the anticipated loss of my ownership interest in the house has an adverse value to me of $10,000. Such negative terms as "anticipated loss," "damage," and "injury," when used as quantitative terms to which dollar signs may be attached, are simply the converse of such positive words as "value," "worth," and "importance."' J. C. Bonbright, *op. cit.*, p. 72. Professor F. K. Wright seems to hit the nail on the head when he uses 'opportunity value' in this context ('Towards a General Theory of Depreciation,' *Journal of Accounting Research*, Spring, 1964, p. 82).

becomes overwhelming. Consider again the plant that is costly and successful, but highly specific. By the sale price canon, the whole investment might well need to be written off in its first year—with absurd results on trends of reported earnings.

When Professor Chambers' book comes to deal with each type of asset in detail, it abandons the sale price principle and substitutes replacement cost. In the case of finished goods, this switch is due to the uncertainty of predicting profit margins: 'This uncertainty makes it necessary to attempt the measurement from a different direction. Resale price less the expected margin represents the current cost of the product or of the services embodied in it. This is the sum of money which at the time the firm would have to hold if it had not the goods on hand, but was in a position to acquire those goods; it represents the opportunity cost at that time of a decision already taken to hold goods. We may, therefore, take as the current cash equivalent the initial prices of the goods or services sacrificed in production, transformed to contemporary prices' (p. 232). Work-in-progress, if thrown on the market in its unfinished state, might fetch nothing; if one tried instead to measure it by working backwards from the sale price of finished goods, one would have to estimate the costs of the remaining processes; but the latter are internal, and thus have no market price (p. 233). So cost must again be used, as with finished goods. And the same holds for raw materials.

Fixed assets (the book continues) ought to be appraised at their second-hand sale prices. But the market is often small or non-existent; moreover, firms with highly specialized assets might rebel against showing these at tiny figures. So here too sale price may need to be jettisoned, in favour of historical cost modified by a price index and subjective estimates of depreciation (p. 245).

The book does not enlarge on its defection from the sale price principle until the end of this section, when a paragraph runs:

It has been found necessary, in the light of postulated difficulties, to depart from the originally stipulated ideal of obtaining financial position and increments to residual equity on the basis of current resale prices. But the latter is maintained as a matter of principle; the departures are a matter of expedience, or of necessity, in the face of ignorance of the pertinent price data (p. 248).

This subdued statement, inserted at such a late stage, hardly seems an adequate admission that the central proposal is unworkable. The right course would surely have been to put forward the central proposal as the ideal, but at once to concede that it is impractical; at the least, its failings should have been acknowledged with emphasis as soon as the inventory example brought them to the surface. And in any case, as I

248

have tried to show, the sale price rule does not seem to be the best one even as an unachievable ideal.

The rest of the book analyses problems of finance, communication, governmental accounting, and so forth. On these, the argument is interesting and sound.

There is, Heaven knows, plenty of room for a work that tries to jack accounting up to higher intellectual level; and the problem of valuation cries out for major debate. Perhaps a second edition of this book could hit both targets. But (I venture to submit) it should be slimmer and simpler than this one—and more alert for shortcomings in its central theme.

15 Profit measurement and inflation

by R. Mathews* and J. McB. Grant†

THE MEASUREMENT OF ACCOUNTING PROFIT

The first task that must be performed is the theoretical analysis of the effects of conventional methods of accounting on profits and finances in times of inflation. For this purpose it is necessary to examine the accounting theory of profit.

Profit measurement in accounting may be regarded as a process of matching with the revenue realized during a given period the costs and expenses incurred in producing revenue. This matching concept ensures that profit measurement is a logical process, but there are, nevertheless, a number of postulates and conventions underlying the accounting theory of profit which limit the usefulness of accounting profit as a measure of business surplus and hence as a basis for policy decisions.

Revenue is defined as the current (i.e. the non-capital) gross earnings or incomings of an enterprise. As a result of the realization postulate in accounting, revenue is brought to account only when realized, as for example by sale of goods. Costs and expenses are defined as the non-capital outgoings of an enterprise, incurred for the purpose of earning revenue. The historical record convention requires revenue, costs and expenses to be recorded as historical events with a view to making the accounts factual and objective. However, not all the costs and expenses incurred during a given period involve transactions in the market place with outside parties. Some relate to operations within the enterprise, such as the processing of raw materials or the using up of fixed assets, and therefore have no explicit market valuation. The historical record convention results in these operations being recorded in the books of account as though they were objectively measurable historical facts. The values accorded to such costs and expenses are estimates only, and to this extent a subjective element is introduced into the process of profit measurement.

Other assumptions underlying the accounting theory of profit measurement include the continuity assumption, which postulates that a business maintains continuity of existence for an indefinite period, and the account-

---

* Director, Centre for Research on Federal Financial Relations, The Australian National University.
† Commissioner, Australian Trade Practices Commission.

ing period convention, which assumes that the life of an enterprise can be divided into a number of arbitrary time periods, called accounting periods. For financial accounting this period is usually one year. The continuity assumption has important implications in the valuation of assets for balance-sheet purposes, and this indirectly affects the determination of profit. For example, as a result of the continuity assumption and the historical record convention, physical assets such as stocks and fixed capital equipment are taken into account on the basis of original cost and not replacement or realizable values. It follows that such assets are absorbed into costs and expenses on the basis of their original cost to the enterprise. What is assumed, in effect, is that the original cost of assets reflects their value to the enterprise as a going concern.

The application of the accounting period convention results in costs and expenses on the one hand, and revenue on the other, being allocated to accounting periods in order to measure profits by periods. It will be appreciated that this assumption is unrealistic, since the operations of the modern business are continuous. Costs and revenues relating to any given period can be estimated, but not precisely determined, so that the consequence of applying the accounting period convention is to introduce another subjective element into the process of profit measurement.

Finally, the measurement of accounting profit rests on the monetary assumption, which postulates that the recording processes in accounting are carried out in terms of the monetary unit of account. The application of the monetary assumption means that transactions involving different kinds of goods and services are all recorded in terms of a common unit of measurement. Such an assumption is basic to the whole idea of a systematic accounting record, but it must be recognized that the monetary postulate is responsible for some of the more serious limitations inherent in the measurement of accounting profit. The application of the assumption means that fluctuations in the value of money itself are ignored for accounting purposes. This introduces an unreal and misleading element into the accounting record when the value of money changes. The money values used to record transactions in the accounts do not necessarily reflect the current values of the goods and services entering the transactions. This limitation has particular significance when the value of money steadily falls (or steadily rises), as during a period of inflation (or deflation).

These are the important limitations of the accounting theory of profit measurement. In practice, however, the consistency and usefulness of the accounting records are further impaired by two kinds of financial manipulation having no justification in accounting theory. First, there is the doctrine of conservatism. It may be decided, as a matter of financial policy, to make

251

adjustments to costs and revenues in order to ensure that costs are not understated in the accounts and that revenues are not overstated; or it may even be decided deliberately to overstate costs and understate revenues. This might be done, for example, by means of 'accelerated' depreciation, i.e. arbitrarily increasing depreciation charges above the amounts needed to write off the original cost of a fixed asset over its estimated working lifetime. A further example of conservatism as an accounting policy is the arbitrary reduction in closing stock values with a view to writing up the cost of stocks sold above their historical costs.

Procedures such as these undermine the whole foundation of accounting profit measurement, viewed as a systematic matching of costs with revenues. The practice of conservatism as an accounting policy is inconsistent with the accounting postulates mentioned above. Conservatism distorts profits, particularly as the overstatement of costs in one period will often be followed by the understatement of costs in subsequent periods. Excessive depreciation charges, for example, will inevitably be succeeded by inadequate charges in later periods, when the asset has been fully written off but is still in use. Conservatism, if applied as an accounting procedure, also distorts the relationship between the profit and loss statement and the balance-sheet, and makes the latter useless as a statement of the firm's financial position. The making of excessive depreciation charges or the writing down of stocks in effect transfers portion of the firm's profits to undisclosed reserves. Conservatism may still be justified as a financial policy, but only if its effects are clearly disclosed in the accounts.

The second kind of financial adjustment which has no justification in accounting theory is the revaluation of fixed assets to bring book values into line with current market values. This procedure conflicts with the historical record convention and the continuity assumption. Revaluation primarily affects the balance sheet, but the profit and loss statement may be influenced indirectly if subsequent depreciation charges are based on the revised values. Once again, there may be sound financial reasons for revaluation, but the results of any such procedure must be clearly disclosed if the value of the accounting reports is not to be impaired.

LIMITATIONS OF ACCOUNTING PROFIT

In theory, accounting profit is a reasonably definitive concept and one which can be measured fairly accurately, although in practice it may be distorted by the adjustments that have just been described. It is necessary to emphasize, however, that accounting profit is a measure of business surplus in historical money terms, derived by matching historical money costs with realized money revenues. For many purposes such a measure is unsatisfactory. In particular, there are two reasons why accounting profit cannot be accepted as a unique measure of business surplus, and both result from the application of the monetary assumption.

The first is that, when the value of money is changing, accounting profit does not provide a measure of current income, defined as the difference between revenues expressed in current prices and costs and expenses expressed in current prices. If the unit of measurement is itself fluctuating in value, then the values at which costs and revenues are recorded in determining profit are not consistent. The monetary units used to record revenues at one point of time are different from those used at another point of time. Costs and expenses are likewise valued in terms of monetary units which differ from one another, and also differ from the units used to measure revenue items. In these circumstances accounting profit does not measure current income. For purposes of policy-making in the firm it is the latter concept which is important. Current income is relevant, for example, in deciding upon changes in total output and the product composition of output. It will be shown later that preoccupation with accounting profit rather than current income not only tends to distort resource allocation but in addition changes the pattern of income distribution. Management should also have regard to current income, and not accounting profit, when considering policies affecting the financial stability of the enterprise.

The second defect of accounting profit as a measure of business surplus is that it fails to maintain the real value of the capital of the enterprise during a period of rising prices. Adherence to historical money costs means that the money capital contributed by shareholders is preserved as a result of the profit measurement process, but in times of inflation this original money capital will not command the same volume of stocks and fixed assets. This is the 'capital erosion' effect of conventional accounting procedures in times of rising prices. It may be possible to augment shareholders' funds by retaining portion of the profits in the company, but this will not be easy when taxation, dividends and indirectly wages are all related to the level of accounting profits. Unless profits can be retained the enterprise will become short of liquid funds or undercapitalized, and fresh capital will have to be raised to maintain the same volume of physical assets. Because this undercapitalization occurs as a result of conventional accounting procedures, management may not become aware of its existence until the financial position of the enterprise has been seriously weakened. In the initial stages of inflation many firms finance the replacement of stocks and fixed assets at higher prices by increasing short-term indebtedness. As a result their financial stability is undermined.

253

R. Mathews and J. McB. Grant

FINANCIAL STABILITY

The financial stability of a company depends first on the maintenance of a satisfactory relation between short-term assets and short-term liabilities, and secondly on the maintenance of a satisfactory relation between borrowed funds and shareholders' funds. The first relationship measures the short-term financial position of the company, and is usually expressed as the 'working capital ratio', that is, the ratio of current liabilities. However, because stocks will probably be difficult to realize in a time of financial crisis, it seems safer to use the ratio of quick assets (i.e. current assets other than stocks) to current liabilities as a measure of liquidity or short-term financial stability. Short-term financial safety requires that a company's quick assets should be sufficient to meet all the liabilities that may have to be satisfied on demand.

The relationship between borrowed funds and shareholders' funds, sometimes called the 'gearing ratio', gives some indication of the long-term financial position of a company. The size of the gearing ratio should be related to the degree of risk attaching to the enterprise. However, for any given company the higher the gearing ratio the more likely it is that the company will fail to survive a prolonged recession. The gearing ratio cannot be considered in isolation from the company's asset structure and its short-term financial position. In general, financial safety requires that increases in the value of stocks or fixed assets should be accompanied by such reductions in the gearing ratio as will maintain the liquidity position of the company. Unfortunately there is an inherent tendency for traditional accounting methods, based as they are on the monetary assumption, to produce both short-term and long-term financial instability.

ACCOUNTING PROFIT AND CURRENT INCOME

Despite the limitations imposed by the monetary assumption, accounting profit cannot be wholly discarded as a measure of business surplus. Its particular merit is that it is largely an objective measure derived by reference to actual transactions as they affect an enterprise, and the recording of these transactions on an historical basis means that accounting profit is largely factual or descriptive. While accounting profit must for these reasons be retained, a second concept of business surplus is required for purposes of policy-making. This is the concept of current income referred to above.

We have seen that accounting profit for a particular period is the difference between historical costs and revenues, it being assumed that all

254

changes in the value of money may be ignored. We define current income for a particular period as the difference between costs and revenues, all expressed in current prices of the accounting period. For accounting purposes most items of revenue and cost are automatically expressed in prices of the current period; hence the cause of differences between accounting profit and current income can be narrowed down to the difference in the prices used to value items carried forward from one accounting period to another. The accounting theory of profit measurement requires these items to be valued in terms of historical prices, i.e. the prices of past periods, whereas to determine current income it is necessary that they be valued in terms of prices of the current period.

Certain items brought forward from past periods, such as prepaid and accrued expenses, revenue received in advance and accrued revenue, are so insignificant that for practical purposes they may be ignored. In any case these items usually represent money claims not affected by price changes. This leaves two major items of cost, depreciation of fixed assets and the opening stock element in cost of goods sold, which for accounting profit purposes are recorded in terms of prices appropriate to past accounting periods, but which should be valued on the basis of current prices in order to measure current income.

ACCOUNTING FOR DEPRECIATION

Depreciation as an accounting concept may be defined as the value, in terms of the original money cost, of that part of a fixed asset which is used up in producing revenue during a particular period. It is an expense related to the original money cost of the asset, not an allocation of revenue or profit to provide funds for the replacement of the asset. As a result of the profit measurement process the original money investment in the enterprise is maintained intact. In measuring current income, on the other hand, depreciation may be defined as the current cost of using fixed assets in producing revenue during the period. The current cost may be estimated by reference to the current replacement value of the asset.[1]

If the rate of depreciation conforms with the physical rate of deterioration or using up of a fixed asset, and if prices are stable, the accounting allowance for depreciation equals the current cost of using the asset. In times of rising (or falling) prices the depreciation charge needs to be related to the asset's current replacement cost in order to approximate the current

[1] The current replacement value may be taken to mean the current cost of an identical asset, if available, or if that is not available, the cost of an asset capable of achieving similar performance.

255

cost of using it over the given period. It is often argued that the periodic cost of using a fixed asset is determined only by its historical cost, since this is the only paid-out cost which the firm must bear. Where the enterprise has the alternative of using the asset itself or hiring it to other users, to take one example, this paid-out or original cost is irrelevant; the relevant cost concept is the alternative or opportunity cost, measured by the revenue forgone in using the asset as opposed to hiring it to other users. This opportunity cost will reflect the asset's current replacement cost. A similar argument applies when the company may sell the asset as an alternative to using it. This is one of the most powerful arguments in support of the use of current replacement cost as opposed to historical cost, and one with which economists have long been familiar. It is strange that it has received so little attention in discussion on this problem.[1] Ideally, the depreciation charge should maintain intact the real capital resources, or productive capacity of the enterprise. However, this may be difficult if prices rise continually over a number of accounting periods. To maintain the real value of capital it would be necessary to base depreciation on the replacement value at the time when the asset is replaced. This is not known in advance, and the only practicable alternative would be to make the depreciation charge in any period equal to the sum of the following:

(*a*) depreciation based on the current replacement value of the asset; plus

(*b*) the amount by which previous depreciation charges, based on the lower replacement values prevailing in previous periods, have been insufficient to provide for replacement on the basis of current values.

It is clear that the adjustment for (*b*), if included in the depreciation charge for the current period, would seriously distort the measurement of current income, which by definition equals current revenue minus current costs and expenses. For purposes of estimating current income, therefore, depreciation must be restricted to (*a*) above; that is, it must be based solely on the current replacement value of the asset. Current replacement value for this purpose may be defined as the average replacement value prevailing during the current accounting period, and during a period of steadily rising prices this will be approximately the same as the replacement value half-way through the accounting period. Depreciation calculated on this basis will not necessarily provide sufficient funds for replacement of the asset if its replacement value continues to rise in the future. It may approximately do so if it is invested in assets which themselves rise in value with

[1] This point is ignored, for example, in an excellent survey by A. R. Prest of the arguments for and against the use of replacement cost. See, 'Replacement Cost Depreciation', *Accounting Research*, 1 (July 1950), 385.

the inflation, and not held in the form of cash balances and money claims. This applies, for example, if the business has a number of fixed assets, a constant proportion of which fall due for replacement each year.[1]

The relationship between accounting depreciation and current depreciation may be expressed in the following way:

$$\frac{\text{Current}}{\text{depreciation}} = \frac{\text{Accounting}}{\text{depreciation}} \times \frac{\text{Current replacement value of asset}}{\text{Original cost of asset}}.$$

This relationship holds irrespective of the method of estimating accounting depreciation. A simple example will make this clear. Let us suppose that an asset costs £100, and that on the basis of its estimated working life it is decided to write it off over ten years by equal instalments.[2] Accounting depreciation will therefore be recorded at £10 during each year of the asset's life. If the asset's average replacement value rises to £110 in Year 1 and to £120 in Year 2, the current cost of using the asset in Year 1 and Year 2 may be represented by $(\frac{1}{10} \times £110) = £11$, and $(\frac{1}{10} \times £120) = £12$ respectively.

The formula given above yields the same results:

$$\text{Year 1} \quad £10 \times \tfrac{110}{100} = £11,$$
$$\text{Year 2} \quad £10 \quad \tfrac{120}{100} = £12.$$

If the annual depreciation charge is based on the reducing balance of the asset (i.e its original cost less previous depreciation) the same relationship holds. Let us suppose that an asset costs £100, and that it is decided to write it off by making a depreciation charge of 10 per cent p.a. on the reducing balance of the asset. With this method it will take longer than ten years to write off the asset, but we may assume that the estimated life and estimated scrap value of the asset have been taken into account in determining the percentage to be applied. Accounting depreciation under these circumstances will be 10 per cent of £100, or £10, in Year 1; 10 per cent of (£100 − £10), or £9, in Year 2; and so on. If the average replacement value rises to £110 in Year 1 and to £120 in Year 2, the current cost of using the asset in those years may be represented by 10 per cent of £110, or £11, in Year 1; and by 10 per cent of £108 (£120 *minus* 10 per cent of £120), or £10·8, in Year 2. The general formula gives the same results:

$$\text{Year 1} \quad £10 \times \tfrac{110}{100} = £11,$$
$$\text{Year 2} \quad £9 \times \tfrac{120}{100} = £10·8.$$

[1] See Prest for an explanation of this point.
[2] This method is described as the fixed-instalment or straight-line method of recording depreciation.

R. Mathews and J. McB. Grant

The difference between current and accounting depreciation measures the accounting effect of inflation on company profits that results from rising replacement costs of fixed assets. This effect will be carried into the balance-sheet, thereby affecting the financial structure of the company, unless special steps are taken to offset it by transferring an equivalent portion of the accounting profit to the company's reserves.

ACCOUNTING FOR STOCKS

The other important item of cost, valued for accounting purposes in the prices of a past period, is the opening stock element in cost of goods sold. The accounting concept of cost of goods sold is defined as the original money cost of stocks brought forward from previous accounting periods, *plus* the original money cost of stocks purchased during the period, *minus* the original money cost of stocks carried forward into the subsequent accounting period. Cost of goods sold is deducted from the realized sales revenue in order to determine gross profit on trading, from which net accounting profit is derived by deducting other expenses.

To measure current income, on the other hand, it is necessary to determine the current cost of goods sold. Strictly speaking, this involves ascertaining the current cost price of each item of stock sold, at the time it is sold. However, this is not practicable, and we adopt the simplifying assumption that price changes within an accounting period may be ignored.[1] Current cost of goods sold may then be defined as opening stocks *plus* purchases *minus* closing stocks, all valued at current prices of the period. Since purchases and closing stocks are automatically valued at prices of the current period,[2] it is only necessary to determine the current cost of opening stocks. Current cost for this purpose is taken to be the recorded cost price of stocks most recently acquired. Opening stocks are thus revalued in the same prices as closing stocks, and the appreciation of stock values resulting from the inflationary rise in prices is recorded as a cost, and excluded from current income.

The difference between accounting cost of goods sold and current cost of goods sold is thus measured by the difference between (a) opening stocks valued at original prices and (b) opening stocks valued at current prices, i.e. the same prices used to value closing stocks. The effect of this in relation to the measurement of profit or income may be seen from the following

---

[1] This assumption means that we ignore price changes in respect of any physical changes in stocks during the period. It will be shown later that the practical significance of this omission is small.

[2] It is implicitly assumed that stocks have turned over at least once during the year. We are indebted to Professor H. W. Arndt for this point.

simple example. Suppose a trading enterprise, maintaining a constant physical volume of stocks, has a series of monthly sales revenues:

$$r_1, r_2, r_3, \ldots, r_{12}$$

and a series of monthly stock purchases:

$$c_0, c_1, c_2, \ldots, c_{12}$$

where the subscripts in each case designate the month when the revenue was received or the cost incurred. The cost c_0 can be visualized as the original cost of stocks purchased in month o. These are the closing stocks in month o, the opening stocks in month 1, and are absorbed into cost when sold in that month. Accounting profit for the year is calculated as the sum of the differences $r_1 - c_0, r_2 - c_1 \ r_3 - c_2 \ldots, r_{12} - c_{11}$. Current income on the other hand is the sum of the differences $r_1 - c_1, r_2 - c_2, \ldots, r_{12} - c_{12}$. The difference between accounting profit and current income is thus $c_{12} - c_0$. This is the difference between opening stocks valued at closing prices of the current period and the same volume of stocks valued at original prices.

The same idea may be expressed in language more familiar to the accountant. Let us assume that a company commences an accounting period on 1 January with 1,000 units of stock, valued at the original cost of £1,000. During the year 1,000 units are sold for £1,150 and another 1,000 units are bought for £1,100, so that 1,000 units of stock are carried forward into the subsequent accounting period. What is the difference between accounting cost of goods sold and current cost of goods sold? For purposes of simplicity it is assumed that cost is interpreted on the first-in-first-out basis.[1]

To determine accounting profit, cost of goods sold is calculated from historical values:

	£	£
Sales		1,150
less Cost of goods sold		
Opening stock	1,000	
Purchases	1,100	
	2,100	
less Closing stock	1,100	
		1,000
Accounting gross profit		£150

However, the current cost of goods sold is £1,100, and the current gross income is calculated as follows:

	£
Sales	1,150
less Current cost of goods sold	1,100
Current gross income	£50

---

[1] This method of valuation assumes that stocks are disposed of in the order in which they have been acquired.

Alternatively, current gross income can be calculated by ascertaining the current cost of each element in cost of goods sold:

	£	£
Sales		1,150
less Current cost of goods sold		
Opening stock	1,100	
Purchases	1,100	
	2,200	
less Closing stock	1,100	
		1,100
Current gross income		£50

The difference between accounting and current cost of goods sold, also the difference between accounting gross profit and current gross income, is simply the difference between opening stock at current prices (£1,100) and opening stock at original prices (£1,000), i.e. £100. Another method of calculating current gross income would be to deduct this increment in stock values, or stock appreciation as it is called, from accounting gross profit:

	£	£
Accounting gross profit		150
less Stock appreciation		
Opening stock at current prices	1,100	
less Opening stock at original prices	1,000	
		100
Current gross income		£50

This increment in stock values provides us with a measure of the accounting effect of inflation on company profits (and hence on capital structures) arising out of conventional methods of calculating cost of goods sold. In the above illustration, for example, accounting gross profit may be analysed into two elements: (a) the trading profit arising out of sales, £50; and (b) the stock appreciation, £100. If the whole accounting profit were to be disbursed in the form of taxes and dividends, the capital structure of the enterprise would inevitably be weakened. Additional funds to the value of £100 would be required from some source to finance the holding of stocks at the higher prices. Unfortunately, it is only too often the case that these funds are obtained by increasing short-term liabilities or reducing liquid assets. This means that the ratio of quick assets to current liabilities is reduced, thereby indicating a weakening of the financial position of the enterprise. To avoid this situation it would be necessary to transfer portion of accounting profits, corresponding to the stock appreciation, to the company's reserves.

Profit measurement and inflation

To the extent that stocks and fixed assets are brought into account on the basis of original prices instead of current prices which are higher, accounting profit exceeds current income. Using the stock and the fixed instalment depreciation figures from the above examples, and assuming the same changes in current replacement values noted on pp. 257–9, it is possible to measure explicitly the accounting effects of inflation on the profits and financial structure of a company. For this purpose the following additional data are introduced. The only expenses are assumed to be wages, £20. The assets of the company at 1 January, in addition to stocks £1,000, and fixed assets £100, are cash and debtors £1,000; and the liabilities of the enterprise (creditors) at 1 January are £1,000. Accounting profit may be calculated as follows:

	£	£
Sales		1,150
less Cost of goods sold		
Opening stocks	1,100	
Purchases	1,199	
	2,100	
less Closing stocks	1,100	
		1,000
Accounting gross profit		150
less Expenses		
Wages	20	
Depreciation	10	
		30
Accounting net profit		£120

Having determined accounting profit, it is possible to estimate current income by making the following adjustments:

	£	£
Accounting net profit		120
less Adjustments to bring historical costs up to current costs		
Stock appreciation	100	
Depreciation	1	
		101
Current net income		£19

The adjustments necessary to convert accounting profit to current income measure the accounting effects of inflation on company profits.

If the whole of the accounting net profit is distributed, the balance-sheet at the end of the year may be contrasted with the opening balance-sheet as follows.

Assets	1 Jan.		31 Dec.	
	£	£	£	£
Cash and debtors		1,000		1,010
Stocks (at historical cost)		1,000		1,100
Fixed assets (at cost)	100		100	
less Provision for depreciation			10	
	——	100	——	90
		2,100		2,200
less Liabilities				
Creditors		1,000		1,100
Shareholders' funds		£1,100		£1,100

This example illustrates the balance-sheet effect in relation only to the replacement of stocks at higher prices, but similar results would appear when the fixed assets have to be replaced. The example demonstrates that under the conditions postulated inflation has promoted undercapitalization, since the shareholders' funds at the end of the year no longer finance the same volume of stocks and fixed assets. The increase in stock values has been financed by borrowing from creditors. Alternatively it could have been financed by running down cash or debtors. In either event the short-term financial position of the company has obviously deteriorated. To avoid this result it is necessary to base distribution policy on current income rather than accounting profit. This involves transferring to reserves the amounts of the adjustments made in respect of stocks and depreciation of fixed assets. If this is done, and if the whole of current income is distributed, the balance-sheets at 1 January and 31 December will compare as follows:

Assets	1 Jan.		31 Dec.	
	£	£	£	£
Cash and debtors		1,000		1,011
Stocks (at historical cost)		1,000		1,100
Fixed assets (at cost)	100		100	
less Provision for depreciation			10	
	——	100	——	90
		2,100		2,201
less Liabilities				
Creditors		1,000		1,000
Shareholders' funds				
Capital	1,100		1,100	
Reserves			101	
	——	1,100	——	1,201

Under these circumstances shareholders' funds again finance the whole of stocks and fixed assets, so that the opening position has been restored. The additional £11 in cash and debtors represents the funds made available from the depreciation allowance and the depreciation adjustment, and held, for example, against replacement of the fixed assets. The accounting effects of inflation have therefore been avoided.

The essential differences between the alternative distribution policies, one based on accounting profit and the other on current income, may be illustrated by comparative sources and uses statements:

	Distribution based on	
	Accounting Profit	Current income
	£	£
Sources of funds		
Retained profits (increases in reserves)		101
Depreciation allowances	10	10
Reduction in working capital (other than stocks)	90	
	£100	£111
Uses of funds		
Increase in stock values	100	100
Increase in working capital (other than stocks)		11
	£100	£111

To offset the accounting effects of inflation on both profits and financial structures it is therefore necessary to make the adjustments to accounting profits in respect of stocks and depreciation of fixed assets. The adjustments outlined constitute a general procedure for measuring the accounting effects of inflation on profits and financial structures, and this procedure will be used later in calculating the adjustments necessary for Australian companies in the aggregate.

16 The state of current value accounting[1]

by Edgar O. Edwards*

The demonstrated and likely volatility of prices during this decade suggests a review of current value accounting is in order—where it stands today and what its future might be. The literature indicates a substantial acceptance of current value accounting in accounting theory, but an impressive lack of implementation in accounting practice. The promotion of practical application obviously needs executive direction; why else would a quality product remain on the shelf. Nevertheless, while current value accounting seems to have found a growing number of adherents to its principles, there are yet some major differences, many rough edges, and a few blind alleys exposed in the theoretical literature. I intend first to indicate the currency of the subject, then to bring out some of the conceptual issues involved in current value accounting, next to discuss some of the valuation issues, and finally to identify some of the potential analytical uses of current value data.

THE CURRENCY OF THE MATTER

Economists are agreed that inflation is with us, that it lies ahead, and that it is international in character. To cite some figures (U.S. Department of Labor, 1974) which are undoubtedly familiar to everyone, the Consumer Price Index rose by 6·2 per cent between 1972 and 1973 and by 10·7 per cent between May 1973 and May 1974. The commodity element of that index, leaving services aside, rose by 7·4 per cent and 12·0 per cent respectively during those two periods. During the same two periods, on the other hand, the average spendable weekly earnings of those employed in manufacturing having three dependents rose by only 5·4 per cent and 5·7 per cent respectively, suggesting some latent pressure for further price increases as wage earners seek to recoup their losses. Additional inflationary pressures can be inferred from the comparable increases in the Wholesale Price Index of 13·8 per cent between 1972

* Formerly Henry Gardiner Symonds Professor of Administrative Science and Economics, Rice University, Houston, Texas.
[1] This paper is a revision of one presented at the American Accounting Association Meeting in New Orleans, August 20, 1974. The views expressed are those of the author and are not necessarily shared by the Ford Foundation or the government of Kenya.

and 1973 and 16·4 per cent from May 1973 to May 1974, increases which will almost certainly be soon reflected in the commodity portion of the Consumer Price Index.

What has been less widely discussed, both in the media and the professional literature, is the outlook for *differential* price changes, for changes in *relative* prices. I submit that over the next five years the principal economic and accounting challenge will come from substantial and pervasive shifts in relative prices. For example, between 1972 and 1973, while the Wholesale Price Index was rising by 13·8 per cent, the farm products and processed foods and feeds portion of it rose by 30·0 per cent and the industrial commodities portion by only 7·7 per cent, a difference in rate of increase (which is a measure of dispersion) of 22·3 percentage points. The largest prior difference since 1950 occurred in 1953, and that difference was only 7·3 percentage points—against agriculture. Between May 1973 and May 1974, on the other hand, the farm portion of the Wholesale Price Index rose by only 7·7 per cent while the industrial commodities portion rose by 20·1 per cent.

But the dispersion within the Wholesale Price Index would of course be much larger than the figures for these major groups could suggest. Consider a few components of that index for the May 1973 to May 1974 period: refined petroleum products, up 79·5 per cent; iron and steel, up 51·1 per cent; coke, up 44·7 per cent; coal, up 43·7 per cent; all metals, up 28·1 per cent; rubber and plastic products, up 19·9 per cent; heating equipment, up 8·2 per cent; drugs and pharmaceuticals, up 4·9 per cent; *but* wool products, down 5·0 per cent; eggs, down 8·1 per cent; livestock, down 15·7 per cent; live poultry, down 18·5 per cent; and manufactured animal feeds, down 26·5 per cent. Between the highest and the lowest of those I have cited, the difference in rate of price increase is 106 percentage points. Moreover, this spread is still between *groups* of commodities and must underestimate the dispersion among individual commodity price movements. Finally, these data apply only to the United States; the dispersion of price changes internationally would be substantially greater.

One can see the economic pressures mounting. The heating equipment manufacturer, caught in a depressed housing market and a 51·1 per cent rise in iron and steel prices, has only been able to increase his prices by 8·2 per cent; the drug manufacturer who may be paying 79·5 per cent more for his refined petroleum inputs is charging only 4·9 per cent more for his product; and the steel maker who is getting 51·1 per cent more this year than last must nevertheless pay 45 per cent more for his coal and coke. There lies ahead of us a trying period of substantial economic adjustment as these shifting relative prices open up new and possibly international opportunities for some firms while they squeeze others out of international markets and possibly into bankruptcy. The question is whether or not accounting data should record these events as they occur and thereby flag the coming attractions, or only post the closing notices after the audience has gone.

CONCEPTUAL ISSUES

It is tempting in returning to a subject after a long absence, as I am doing, to take up again what seemed to be the most pressing issues in that earlier era (for those earlier views see Edwards, 1954 and 1961, and Edwards and Bell, 1961). But some—perhaps the most fundamental of those issues—while important to the understanding of current value accounting, have retreated from the arena of active controversy, and a few seem to me to be largely of, if I may use the word, historical interest to accounting theoreticians. Other matters now take precedence over them in the theoretical literature.

The first of these issues is the argument that it is sufficient (as well as necessary) to record accounting costs in historical terms. In the midst of rapidly changing prices and values, it gives most of us little comfort to know that the historic cost of every asset now held by business firms throughout the world has not changed since its acquisition. The dictum, 'Move ahead but keep your feet in one place,' raises serious problems of equilibrium if the head gets too far to the fore. We all know what happens to accounting operating profits during periods of rising prices; they tend to be exaggerated or overstated because the costs charged against current sales are historic and usually lower than current costs. Moreover, the difference between the current and historic cost of inputs will normally be larger the more rapidly prices are rising for two reasons—first, given the time lag between purchase and sale of inputs, prices will rise more; second, inflationary circumstances may lengthen the time lag itself as larger inventories are carried as a buffer against delayed deliveries, the risk of running out, and as a means of making gains in anticipation of higher prices.

Thus, the heating equipment manufacturer whose selling prices have risen by 8·2 per cent while one of his important inputs, iron and steel, has risen by 51·1 per cent may yet show an operating profit by historic cost standards. Yet if prices level off and he can no longer cover current operating losses with holding gains, his competitive inefficiency or lack of opportunity may be revealed. One can argue, of course, that the astute manager or observer will not be misled by overstated operating profits,

266

though certainly the observer and very probably the manager cannot make firm judgments about current costs in a complex firm unless they are actually *accounted for*. In any event, the argument does not justify—or explain—the overstatement. Even the use of the term 'overstatement' suggests a standard other than historic cost, for profits are *not* overstated by that standard. The standard of comparison is current value accounting.

What seems to have been widely accepted is not, however, the whole set of current value concepts, but rather that one, a central one, which suggests that accounting operating profit should be split into two parts— current operating profit, determined by deducting the current cost of related inputs from sales, and holding gains realized through use, defined as the difference between the current and historic cost of the sale-related inputs. Note that no historic cost data are lost in this disclosure; new information has been provided.

The second issue about which controversy seems to me to have diminished is whether or not adjustments for the price level alone without accounting for individual price changes can do much for either the manager or the external analyst. All this adjustment can do is restate historic costs in terms of current or some base year's purchasing power. The real holding gains (or losses) which are realized when the price of a sale-related input has risen by more (or less) than the price level are still reported as an indistinguishable element of real accounting profit. The task of sorting out current operating profit and holding gains remains and can only be done by accounting for current values—how the prices of sale-related inputs have changed since acquisition—and then asking how much of these gains is real. Moreover, the operating profits of different firms or even of the same firm in different periods cannot be meaningfully compared to reveal genuine differences and trends unless this division, which only current value accounting makes possible, is first attended to. This principle, too, has won its share of adherents.

But these adjustments relate only to the income statement and indeed only to its operating profit section as customarily displayed. The position statement remains in historic cost terms, and improvements in position which result from price changes on unused assets and liabilities are not recorded either in the position or income statement. The issue of reporting current values in the position statement and related realizable gains or cost savings in the income statement seems still to be an issue commanding discussion (Davidson, 1966; Bell, 1971; Enthoven, 1973, Chapter 13).

Current value accounting rests on the principle that relevant, objective current events of the period should be reported on both statements. Current events are not only those related to the acquisition and disposition of assets and liabilities; they also relate to assets and liabilities carried *through* the period. In other words, the position of a firm is incompletely decribed if the only changes recorded are those marked by an exchange of assets and/or liabilities—the realization principle—while changes in value not marked by an exchange go unnoted. Of course it is a current event when a gain is realized through the disposition of an asset in the current period; but so too was the accrual of that gain a current event of the periods during which accrual took place. The event of the current period in this example is *not* the *gain*, but its *realization*; the portion of the gain which accrued in prior periods is a current event of *those* periods.

We are touching, of course, on the definition of income. But must we settle on one? There is no reason in my view why an income statement should not reveal both the accrual of income and its realization. Indeed, both are events of the current period and should be reported. It is only that the events are different and must be distinguished. The important issue in this instance is disclosure; labelling is a secondary matter.

The fourth conceptual issue to which I would draw attention concerns the role of subjective values in the accounting process. In some respects, this is also a valuation option. Since, however, I see a role for both subjective and objective values, their conceptual relationship strikes me as more important than the possible competition between them as a basis for accounting measurement. Subjective values depend entirely on future, or *ex ante*, events—expected quasi-rents, interest rates, asset and liability values, and time horizons—and are therefore basic to decision making. The essence of decision making is the choice among alternative progressions of future events contained within the decision maker's set of expectations. That choice being made, never for all time, the chain of expected events associated with it represents the standard which will be tested as actual events unfold. That comparison of actual against expected events is essential to the evaluation of business decisions and of the effectiveness of the decision-making process itself.

Subjective values, depending as they do upon expectations about future events, cannot themselves be objectively measured. But those expectations from which they derive can be stated in objectively measurable and dated *dimensions* so that their accuracy can be tested against actual events as they transpire. It is the task of effective management to see that expected events are recorded in dated, objective dimensions; it is the task of accounting to record actual objective events as they occur. It follows that present values have no role to play in the measurement of actual events, except as they affect decisions and hence demand and supply in the marketplace and the prices established there.

The last conceptual issue I would mention is taxation—which elements of income should be subjected to income tax? First, it is important to draw a distinction between tax *payment* and contingent tax *liability*, along much the same lines as the distinction noted earlier between the *accrual* and *realization* of income. If a firm reports the accrual of income, it should also report the contingent tax liability on that income; otherwise its position statement will exaggerate the welfare of the firm. Second, if capital gains are to be taxed at different rates from other income—and I am not convinced that such a distinction is justified—those holding gains realized through use and product sale should be treated in precisely the same way as those realized through direct sale. Finally, taxes on income should be levied against real, not money, income, if equity considerations prevail over the anti-cyclical effects of taxing money income, as it seems to me they should. The problem here is one of relative equity; it is hard to justify taxing business firms on real income, if other entities, such as families and individuals, continue to be taxed on money income.

ISSUES OF VALUATION

Let me turn now to valuation issues on which even more discussion seems to be focused today than on the conceptual issues mentioned above. To a degree, these, too, are conceptual in nature—I do not intend to discuss precise methods of measurement—but at a different level. Here we do not ask whether current values should be reported but rather which variation of current value should be employed? The issue, however, is not whether one is right and another wrong because the options commonly discussed all have roles to play either in the making of decisions or in their evaluation. Perhaps one day we will be able to account for several concepts simultaneously, but the question today is, if one concept of current value is to be most widely used, which should it be? The options are present or subjective value (already discussed), opportunity cost, and variations of replacement cost.

Opportunity cost can be either subjective or objective in nature. The opportunity cost of an asset is the value it would have in its best alternative use. But that alternative use could be a different pattern of employment of the asset *within* the firm. The value of the asset in that alternative pattern of use can be determined only by resorting to the present value of the quasi-rents expected to be earned in that use, a value which is just as subjective in nature as the present value of the asset in the pattern to which it is committed. If a present value is to be used at all for accounting purposes in these circumstances, it surely should be the highest.

269

E. O. Edwards

If the alternative considered is to *dispose* of the asset on the open market, opportunity cost can for the most part be objectively measured as a potential current event. It is, therefore, in an accounting sense, a legitimate method of current cost valuation; it is, if I read them correctly, the method favoured by both Chambers (1966) and Sterling (1970); it is an exit value, as opposed to an entry value, approach. The issue then is one of entry or exit values in determining current values. Phil Bell and I discussed this matter at some length in our book (1961) and concluded there that entry values were preferable as a normal method of valuation. We did so only after much soul searching and the detailed construction of the concept of realizable profit based on opportunity cost. Our arguments then against the strict application of exit values were essentially as follows:

1. Their use leads to anomalous revaluations on acquisition because of transport costs, installation and removal charges, and imperfect access to markets; immediately upon the purchase, delivery and installation of a new machine or truck its net realizable value is normally substantially less than acquisition cost.

2. Their use implies a short run approach to business operations, posing, as they do, disposition and liquidation values for the position statement; a positive realizable profit only indicates that it is worth staying in business in the short run, not that it is worth replacing assets and inputs and staying in business over the longer term or as long as current price relationships continue.

3. Their use leads to the anticipation of operating profit before sale by valuing finished goods, and possibly nearly finished goods, in excess of the current costs incurred in their production.

I now think that this argument can be sharpened by drawing a clear distinction between exit prices derived from markets in which the firm is usually a buyer and those derived from markets in which the firm is usually a seller. A firm that values its assets at exit prices derived from markets in which the firm is normally a buyer reports *unusual* values—those which would obtain in a liquidation situation, at least so far as the assets being so valued are concerned. To employ such values when liquidation is not contemplated is surely misleading. Yet Argument (1)—incurring immediate losses upon acquisition—clearly assumes valuation by exit values in buyer markets for firms having no liquidation intentions. Indeed, Argument (2) is also premised on the assumption that most of the firm's assets would be valued as though they might be disposed of in unusual markets for the firm, though some, particularly finished products, might be valued as though sold through normal channels. Argument (3), on the other hand, clearly assumes exit prices in seller markets and therefore must be considered on different grounds.

I am not convinced of the merit of adopting, as a normal basis for

270

asset valuation in the going concern, exit prices in buyer markets. These are *unusual* values suitable for *unusual* situations.[1] I would not object in principle to keeping track of such exit prices at all times and, as Solomons (1966) has suggested, substituting them for entry values when they are the lesser of the two *and* the firm has taken a definite decision not to replace the asset or even the functions it performs.[2] Indeed, such substitution is necessary if the recent write-downs of computer-leasing and calculator firms are to be justified in advance of actual disposal and if the real position of firms caught holding outmoded style goods is to be reflected in their accounts.

The point at issue, of course, is not *whether* to value by current entry or exit prices, but *when* to shift from entry to exit values. The extremes are (1) immediately upon acquisition of any asset or liability and (2) when accounts receivable are converted to cash, or when all services have been performed, whichever is later (Davidson, 1966). The realization principle normally rests on the sale event to signal the displacement of entry values by exit values. The valuation of all finished goods at exit values, a principle against which Argument (3) is directed, identifies an earlier stage—one which is close to sale for the manufacturing concern but at the point of acquisition of stocks in trade for the trading firm.

If the principle was adopted that all assets and liabilities of the going concern should be valued at current entry prices except for those that the firm normally sells, Arguments (1) and (2) above would be disposed of. Such a 'usual market' criterion comes close to a rule of 'replacement cost or net realizable value, whichever is higher,' but it is not—as the example of a firm which is temporarily selling at a loss discloses.

We are left with Argument (3) about which I feel much less strongly, though pragmatic considerations may yet leave it some persuasiveness. There is no strong argument in principle against valuing assets which the firm normally sells at some version of selling prices. The question is only whether we seek to account for cost savings or unrealized gains. The problem is encountered in estimating selling prices. If these are determined by appraisal, given the location and accessibility of the goods in

---

[1] It should be noted that exit prices in buyer markets are important to decision making at the micro level, but being *unusual*, such values cannot be aggregated into anything meaningful for a nation as a whole, either as a component of national wealth or as a basis for valuing gross national product. Such values do not represent the normal flow of resources into product, but rather the unusual disposition of resources, a concept which is both undefined and unenlightening in aggregate form.

[2] Note, however, that Solomons would employ present value if that is less than replacement cost but greater than net realizable value, a recommendation I would oppose for reasons given earlier. Parker and Harcourt (1969, p. 18), on the other hand, adopt the Solomons view.

271

question, we assume again unusual disposal. If, on the other hand, prices are estimated by deducting still-to-be-incurred selling and delivery costs from expected selling prices (discounting both appropriately), we encounter subjective elements. These, I emphasize again, rightly belong in the list of expected events to be tested, and should not serve as the basis for valuing actual events, a position in accord with the American Accounting Association's Committee on Concepts and Standards—Inventory Measurement (1964, p. 708).

The issue of which entry values to use also merits discussion, particularly for long-lived assets. For most short-lived assets, replacement cost can be determined, and that therefore reflects the current entry value of the economy's resources being employed in the firm, which is, I think, what we want to approximate as closely as possible. For many longer-lived assets the cost of identical replacement can also be ascertained in regular markets. The problem arises when identical assets are no longer produced—and technological changes ensure that this will often be the case. I confess to being less than happy with the discussion Phil Bell and I offered on this matter (1961, Chapter 3) and also with those I have read since. The options, when the cost of identical replacement is not market determined, appear to be opportunity cost (an exit value), the cost of optimal replacement, or the cost of obvious replacement.

The argument for opportunity cost is that the asset is *not* going to be identically replaced, and that therefore it should be written down to its net realizable value and further depreciation should be determined on that basis. But if this is done, it is quite possible, as noted earlier, that subsequent reported operating profits of the firm will suggest that its outmoded assets are just as efficient as the new assets which will probably replace it. Moreover, the firm *does* intend to replace the *functions* or *services* of the asset in question.

Optimal replacement cost, on the other hand, can be determined only by making a comprehensive, hypothetical investment decision which will not in fact be made until some time in the future. (After all, if our firm decides to replace immediately, our problem evaporates.) Such a decision, when it is made, may also involve the rearrangement of many related functions within the firm and the purchase and replacement of complementary equipment and facilities. The use of optimal replacement cost would not reflect all the value of the nation's economic resources now employed by the firm, but rather the value of a very different and hypothetical set. I don't believe its proponents are many.

The cost of obvious replacement probably comes close to what Parker and Harcourt (1969, p. 19) have called 'the cost of currently acquiring the *services* provided by the asset,' or what the American Accounting Association's Committee on Concepts and Standards—Long-Lived Assets (1964, p. 695) called 'the purchase price of assets which provide equivalent service capacity.' By obvious replacement I mean the clear means currently available for providing the identical physical services, *regardless of the operating costs which the hypothetical asset might entail.* A refrigerator may be replaced by another of the same cooling capacity and temperature range. Very probably this would not represent optimal replacement. There may also be problems of adjusting for size, temperature control, and asset life. Assuming these can be solved or do not exist, the cost of obvious replacement still has theoretical deficiencies.

A new machine, identical in physical performance, may make an old one obsolete in any of three ways: (1) by raising capital costs and lowering operating costs, (2) by lowering both capital and operating costs, or (3) by lowering capital costs and raising operating costs. By valuing the old machine according to the new one, current cost depreciation will be raised in the first case and reduced in the others. Assuming that operating charges will continue to be charged as actually incurred with the old machine, the operating profits now reported for the old machine as compared with a firm actually using the new one will be lower in the first two cases but higher in the third. In that case the firm employing the old machine has adopted the lower depreciation charges associated with the new machine but retained its own, lower, operating costs. The old machine will appear to be more efficient than the new one. This drawback may not be too serious in a practical sense if my guess is right that few new machines are in fact Type 3, but that is a matter for empirical research, not casual observation. In any event, the drawback is a serious conceptual deficiency.

I have not touched on matters of appraisal, price indices, and averaging formulas as means of approximating cost concepts in practice. Frankly, I regard them as marginal, if necessary, matters which will be satisfactorily resolved once the more important conceptual issues have been settled.

THE ANALYTICAL USES OF CURRENT VALUE ACCOUNTING

If the reluctance to employ current value accounting is rooted in the uncertainty which remains about the issues so far discussed, there is reason for optimism because the degree of uncertainty seems to be diminishing with research and the passage of time. It is also possible, however, that the analytical value of current value accounting data is not considered to be high enough to warrant the cost of producing it. Furthermore, several of the advantages of current value data can be realized only if current value accounting is widely practiced; inter-firm comparisons are an obvious example. In any event, a brief review of the analytical potential of current value data seems in order. I suggest its discussion under three heads: the internal evaluation of business decisions, prediction, and the external evaluation of business performance.

I have already noted the essential role of current value data in providing information on actual current events as a means of identifying and analysing variances from expected events. The accumulation of current value data is not in itself sufficient for this purpose; a statement of expected events is also required. Such statements can be found in budgets and standard costs, but the events identified in them may not always be dated or stated in dimensions which promote subsequent comparison with actual events. Furthermore, they normally relate to events which compose current operating profit, not holding gains. Statements of expected holding gains and losses are also of importance if business decisions are to be fully evaluated because decisions about operating profit and holding gains are related, not independent in nature. I was delighted, therefore, to see the article by Petri and Minch (1974) which provides a framework for the evaluation of decisions on holding gains.

The relationship between operating profit and holding gains is most clearly revealed in the case of inventories. In the absence of price changes, inventory levels are usually determined by purchase lags, delivery patterns, and the acceptable risk of running out. If prices of items in inventory are expected to rise, stockpiling is a natural business response both to make holding gains and to protect against anticipated delivery problems. If prices do not rise, current operating profit will nevertheless be reduced because of the cost of carrying excessive inventories; if they fall, current operating profit may rise, but the increase should be more than offset by holding losses. Without full statements of expected events, the precise causes of changing profit patterns cannot be pin-pointed, nor the sources of error identified and the process of decision making improved. Financial decisions require similar analysis and evaluation.

Improving prediction depends upon the definition of better functional relationships between expectations about future events, 'what will be,' and past experience, 'what has been,' in which expectations are rooted. Such functions are the essence of econometric models. But if 'what has been' is defined in strictly historic cost terms and reported operating profit represents an amalgam of current and differently dated historic costs, trends over time and comparisons among firms are distorted and the establishment of probable functional relationships is made exceedingly difficult.

Those who attempt to evaluate business performance from outside the firm normally do so largely to improve either private or public decisions. Those whose interests are largely private include present and prospective stockholders, creditors, customers, suppliers, and competitors, and the consultants and security analysts on whom they depend for information and advice. The makers of public policy and those who provide the analytical base for policy decisions are normally employed by governmental or multinational agencies. Private decision makers outside the firm, like the firm itself, can usually be assumed to be striving to maximize their own incomes; policy makers, on the other hand, are charged with representing wider public interests and promoting the general welfare. These two groups evaluate business performance with different purposes in mind. While their evaluations will have much in common, they also differ in important respects.

Those in the private group share an interest in *comparative evaluations*. The position and performance of a single firm as judged by an absolute standard are normally of considerably less importance to them than its position and performance relative to other firms whether in the same industry, in the same nation, or internationally. It is through comparative evaluations that external investors formulate their expectations about future events, choose their portfolios, and decide on new businesses or lines of activity—and by so doing, collectively influence security prices, interest rates, and the allocation of capital among firms, industries, and nations.

These external evaluations of business firms differ from the internal evaluation process discussed earlier in two important respects. In the first place, they do not involve direct comparisons of management expectations with objective accomplishments. Outsiders do not normally have access to management expectations. They seek to judge, therefore, not *internal* managerial efficiency, but rather *relative* managerial efficiency, by comparing performance among firms and over time.

In the second place, outsiders do not have access to managerial accounting data but must rely for their assessments on published financial reports and supplementary data as sources of current events. Making information available to external investors based on current rather than historic cost data is important as a means of improving external private decisions and hence the allocation of a nation's resources among its firms and industries.

Those who make public policy decisions, on the other hand, cannot normally assess business performance exclusively on the basis of reported business profits. In the first place, these may arise not only from the efficient production of quality products (which is normally in the public interest) but also from malpractices, monopolistic advantages, and situations of unusual scarcity. When such conditions come to light through the evaluation of business performance, various forms of regulation, anti-trust actions, and excess-profit taxes may be employed to protect the public interest.

In the second place, business profits will not normally reflect those benefits which accrue to society from business operations in the form of unmarketable side effects of principal business activities, such as skills former employees take with them. Similarly, business profits will not naturally reflect certain social costs which society may have to bear as a result of business activity because they do not enter the accounts of the business firm; environmental effects are a widely discussed example. When the divergence between social and private costs becomes large, public policy will usually seek to establish systems of incentives and disincentives which will lead business firms to introduce into their private accounts those social costs and benefits which would otherwise accrue to society but not to the business community. Such incentive systems should induce business firms to modify their behaviour in socially desirable directions.

Each firm or industry which is *socially* efficient should be able to cover the full current cost of its operation even though some of those costs may not usually reach the private accounts through existing mechanisms of the market, falling instead on others. To attempt such assessments requires the valuation of excluded social costs once they have been identified and allocated. There are two basic approaches to this problem—to measure social costs by the damages imposed on society by them or to measure such costs by the current value of the resources which would be required to prevent them from occurring. The point is that such social assessments, complex as they are, can be made more effectively if the operating profits, with which the analysis begins, are reported by business firms in current value terms.

I have not mentioned the advantages of current value data based on entry costs for aggregation into national accounts or for decomposition into input-output coefficients. Even leaving aside aggregate considerations, the many advantages of current value accounting seem to me impressive.

The end is in sight. There is only the matter of implementation to consider. Why has the 'quality product' remained on the shelf? I have no illuminating answers, but one suggestion. Is an industry-wide experiment with current value accounting a feasible first step? Is there a trade association or an industry which might lend its cooperation? Would it be appropriate for the American Accounting Association to take the lead in initiating such an experiment?

REFERENCES

American Accounting Association, Committee on Concepts and Standards—Inventory Measurement, 'A Discussion of Various Approaches to Inventory Measurement,' THE ACCOUNTING REVIEW (July 1964).

American Accounting Association, Committee on Concepts and Standards—Long-Lived Assets, 'Accounting for Land, Building, and Equipment,' THE ACCOUNTING REVIEW (July 1964).

Bell, P. W., 'On Current Replacement Costs and Business Income,' in R. R. Sterling, ed., *Asset Valuation* (Scholars Book Co., 1971).

Chambers, R. J., *Accounting, Evaluation and Economic Behavior* (Prentice-Hall, 1966).

Davidson, S., 'The Realization Concept,' in M. Backer, ed., *Modern Accounting Theory* (Prentice-Hall, 1966).

Edwards, E. O., 'Depreciation Policy under Changing Price Levels,' THE ACCOUNTING REVIEW (April 1954).

Edwards, E. O., 'Depreciation and the Maintenance of Real Capital,' in J. L. Meij, ed., *Depreciation and Replacement Policy* (North-Holland, 1961).

Edwards, E. O. and Bell, P. W., *The Theory and Measurement of Business Income* (University of California Press, 1961).

Enthoven, A. J. H., *Accountancy and Economic Development Policy* (North-Holland, 1973).

Parker, R. H. and Harcourt, G. C., eds., *Readings in the Concept and Measurement of Income* (Cambridge University Press, 1969).

Petri, E. and Minch, R., 'Evaluation of Resource Acquisition Decisions by the Partitioning of Holding Activity,' THE ACCOUNTING REVIEW (July 1974).

Solomons, D., 'Economic and Accounting Concepts of Cost and Value,' in M. Backer, ed., *Modern Accounting Theory* (Prentice-Hall, 1966).

Sterling, R. R., *Theory of the Measurement of Enterprise Income* (University Press of Kansas, 1970).

United States Department of Labor, *Monthly Labor Review* (July 1974).

17 Current value accounting and the simple production case: Edbejo and other companies in the taxi business

by Philip W. Bell* and L. Todd Johnson†

Although designed to be about as simple a production problem (in this case 'service production' rather than 'goods production') as can be devised, accounting for the taxi business is considerably more complex than would be initially supposed. Given the simple taxi company case as a vehicle, we employ comparative analysis to demonstrate why only one of the major accounting theories espoused, current entry value accounting, can alone best fulfil the evolving standards of accounting as we understand them. In particular, we demonstrate that internal and external users always need current entry value data to evaluate decisions and performance so as to make new decisions. We also show that, even though current entry value data is the sine qua non, it may be usefully supplemented in certain cases by current exit value and/or subjective present value data.

ACCOUNTING STANDARDS TO BE EMPLOYED IN THE PROBLEM

In tackling the problem, we have followed certain accounting 'standards'—as opposed to 'principles,' on the one hand, and 'conventions' or 'rules,' on the other—that we believe are becoming more and more

* Philip W. Bell is Professor of Accounting and Economics, Graduate School of Administration, Rice University.
† L. Todd Johnson is Professor of Accounting, University of Colorado at Boulder.

The authors are indebted to their colleague and collaborator, Edgar O. Edwards, in many ways that include, but go beyond, helpful comments with respect to the thinking that went into this paper. The paper, of course, draws on (Edwards and Bell, 1961). It draws even more on the forthcoming text, (Edwards, Bell, and Johnson, 1979). In many ways we hope the text and this paper will help to clear up some of the myriad misinterpretations and confusions which have crept into the literature since 1961, particularly with respect to the Edwards–Bell book, by (a) stating the Edwards–Bell model in simpler fashion and (b) contrasting it with alternative models in such a way as to bring out clearly the differences. The only basic addition to the Edwards–Bell model we make here is specifically to employ the concept of deprival value and ascertain where it leads in a decision model.

generally accepted within the profession.[1] Certain of our standards are implicit in the following definition of accounting—a hybrid of (American Accounting Association, 1966) and (Study Group on the Objectives of Financial Statements, 1973)—a definition with certain additions over which there would seem to be little or no disagreement, viz:

Accounting is the measurement—usually in monetary terms—of economic events which pertain to economic entities and which are relevant to the informational needs of parties who must evaluate decisions already undertaken and performance in order to make new decisions with respect to those economic entities, parties to whom such measurements must be periodically communicated in timely and intelligible fashion.

Of especial import in this definition is the use of the term 'measurement' as it implicitly encompasses the notions of 'objectivity' and 'comparability.' Objectivity we take to mean agreement by qualified independent observers; by comparability we mean that identical events are recorded in the same manner, regardless of where or when they occur. Furthermore, in our view, measurement also dictates a focus upon empirical rather than nonempirical phenomena.

This definition, then, imposes four standards that accounting data must meet:

1. The only economic events to be recorded should be empirical in nature.

2. All the economic events of a period and only the events of that period should be recorded as they occur; events that occurred in prior periods and events that may occur in future periods are to be excluded.

3. Economic events recorded should be classified in such a way as to identify their cause.

4. Any and all aggregations of data and changes in those aggregations must be internally consistent and interpretable in an empirical sense.

As we shall demonstrate shortly, the meeting of these four standards is crucial to make measurements an operational concept, which, in turn, is essential for effective evaluation of decisions and performance both by managers and outsiders. In addition, these conditions will provide the criteria for acceptance or rejection of certain of the major conventions of traditional accounting. Let us, then, turn to the problem.

---

[1] We accept the term 'principle' to mean a fundamental truth, based perhaps on a tautology, such as in any traffic jam more cars get into the wrong lane than the right lane. A 'standard' is defined as that which is set up or established by authority, custom, or general consent as an *appropriate* or *proper* requirement to be met, a condition to be fulfilled, in meeting the objectives set forth for accounting mesurement. A 'convention' or 'rule' is merely something that is followed, that is done. There are no fundamental, underlying 'principles' in accounting, as (Gilman, 1939) argued. There can be 'standards' based on 'right reason' of 'what ought to be.' 'Conventions' or 'rules,' then, should be consistent with the 'standards' established.

P. W. Bell and L. T. Johnson

STATEMENT OF THE PROBLEM

We approach the problem of accounting for the taxi business by considering how six different companies would account for the same set of expected and actual economic events. These companies and their accounting approaches are as follows:

1. Edbejo—current entry value accounting
2. Gynstamrev—current replacement value accounting
3. Ijirco—traditional historical cost accounting
4. Chaste—current exit value accounting
5. Stauron—discounted future cash-flow accounting
6. Thomco—cash-flow accounting

Of the six, we shall demonstrate that the first—Edbejo's—accounting method is preferable to all of the others, given the standards set forth earlier.

All six companies have been in the taxi business in other locales for some time, but they are all considering entering a new market, each with $100,000 to invest in the new taxi business. Each company is assumed to have a two-year planning horizon—short enough to keep matters manageable but long enough to highlight the differences in the accounting approaches. At the end of each year, dividends will be paid to stockholders in an amount sufficient to maintain the original monetary investment of $100,000 intact. The objective of each company is to maximize such dividends.

The companies are all contemplating the purchase of standard automobiles for use as taxis—Dodges, in particular. Past experience with these cars as taxis indicates that, purchased new, they have a service life of two years in normal use, at the end of which time the cars are worthless. Halfway through that life, the cars are typically regarded as being in 'average condition' for purposes of 'Blue Book' valuation. At present, 31 December, 19Xo, the prices of Dodges are as follows:

	New	Used (one-year-old, average condition, with typical taxi mileage)
Retail Price (which taxi company would pay)	$5,000	$2,500
Wholesale Price (which taxi company would receive)	$4,630	$2,315

280

Thus, the initial $100,000 investment is sufficient to buy either twenty new cars or forty used ones.

Based on prior experience with similar cars in other cities, the companies are able to make cash-flow projections with respect to the new market. They expect that a new car will generate positive net cash flows (fares collected less outlays for wages, gas, oil, repairs, and maintenance) of $3,500 during its first year of service and $3,000 during the second year. If a one-year-old used car is purchased, it would generate the same cash flows as a new car in its second year of service. These cash flows can be given probability weightings and, if so desired, a risk aversion factor in order to arrive at a 'certainty equivalent' (see below). Moreover, the demand for taxi service in this new market is sufficiently great so that the addition of taxis in the numbers being contemplated by these firms would not influence the cash-flow figures anticipated. Finally, none of the companies anticipate any changes either in specific prices (taxis, wages, and so forth) or the general price-level. (This assumption is not critical to our analysis but does simplify the statement of the problem somewhat.)

Given the foregoing data, two options emerge as being preferable. The first option requires spending the $100,000 to acquire twenty new taxis at 31 December, 19X0. These taxis are expected to generate positive net cash inflows of $70,000 (20 new taxis @ $3,500/new taxi) during 19X1 and $60,000 (20 used taxis @ $3,000/used taxi) during 19X2. Of the first year's cash inflows, $50,000 might be reinvested in taxis and $20,000 distributed to stockholders. The $50,000 reinvested would be sufficient to acquire, say, twenty used taxis that would generate an additional $60,000 of cash inflows during 19X2, at the end of which time they—like the other twenty taxis originally purchased new—would be worthless. Thus, this option would permit distributions to stockholders of $20,000 at the end of 19X1 and $120,000 at the end of 19X2.

An alternative option that is equally preferable would entail investment all in used cars. The $100,000 initially available would allow the purchase of forty used Dodges (40 used cars @ $2,500/used car). These taxis would generate net cash inflows of $120,000 (40 used cars @ $3,000/used car) during 19X1, $20,000 of which could be distributed to stockholders at year-end, leaving $100,000 to purchase forty more used Dodges to replace those originally purchased. These forty taxis would again generate net cash inflows of $120,000 during 19X2. Thus, under this option, $20,000 could be distributed to stockholders at the end of 19X1 and $120,000 at the end of 19X2, the same as under the first option.

Because both options would produce identical expected cash flows, they both must provide the same internal rate of return. An initial investment of $100,000 which generates $20,000 after one year, $120,000 after two years, and nothing thereafter has a 20 per cent internal rate of return. Thus, both options have the same rate of return and the companies should be indifferent as to the one selected. For purposes of comparability in the subsequent discussion, however, we will assume that all companies elect the first option, that of initially buying twenty new Dodges for use as taxis. The question of reinvestment at the end of the first year—which now appears to be desirable—will be re-examined at that time before any further commitments are made. This option, because it leaves non-monetary assets on hand at the end of the first year, also raises an interesting accounting question not inherent in the second option. Let us now put the initial purchase of twenty new Dodges and the subsequent cash flows arising from their use as taxis into a formal plan for, say, the Edbejo Taxi Company.

PLANNING BY THE EDBEJO TAXI COMPANY

As noted earlier, this company opts for an accounting method based upon current entry values. Edbejo based its decision to invest in twenty new taxis on the Subjective Goodwill engendered, this being the difference between the Subjective Value (V_0) of the new taxis as seen by the firm and their current entry value (M_0)—their purchase price—both at 31 December, 19X0. That Subjective Goodwill was determined as follows:

$$V_0 - M_0 = \left(\frac{\$70,000}{1 \cdot 1} + \frac{\$60,000}{(1 \cdot 1)^2} \right) - \$100,000$$
$$= (\$63,636 + \$49,587) - \$100,000$$
$$= \$13,223$$

The anticipated future cash flows were discounted by the risk-free lending rate of interest which we have assumed to be 10 per cent. If uncertainty is brought into the analysis, the net cash flows can be adjusted by means of probability weightings and attitudes toward risk so that our numerator(s) can be considered to be the certainty equivalent for the expected cash flow each period. We could also build a risk factor into the discount rate, thereby creating a 'target' rate of interest as suggested below. This target rate would normally exceed the risk-free rate and would be the minimum rate of return that the firm would accept given the element of risk involved. The precise means of handling risk and uncertainty in our cash-flow projections does not concern us; to keep matters as simple as possible, we assume that a certainty equivalent of future expected cash flows is measured and a risk-free lending rate is used as the discount factor.

Current value and the simple production case

Edbejo's plan calls, then, for turning the Subjective Goodwill of the assets acquired into market value over the life of the plan. If there were perfect competition and perfect certainty in the product and capital markets, V_0 would always, in equilibrium, equal M_0, but then there would be no net new business investment in the economy (but rather only replacement investment, i.e., we would have a stationary state). The existence of positive Subjective Goodwill represents the anticipated reward for risk-taking, which can be measured by the excess of the target rate over the risk-free lending rate, as well as the possible existence of entrepreneurial acumen, possession of some monopoly element, or whatever, which factors are reflected in an excess of the expected rate of return over the target rate.[1]

If Edbejo's expectations regarding the course of future events are correct, the market value of its total assets will increase over 19X1 from $100,000 to $120,000 (cash increasing from zero to $70,000 and taxis decreasing from $100,000 to $50,000 at current entry prices). The cash available at the end of 19X1 could either be distributed to stockholders, reinvested in taxis, or some combination of the two. Although the initial two-year plan calls for $50,000 to be reinvested and $20,000 distributed, no action will be taken until an assessment is made of the results of 19X1's activities. For now, let us focus only on the twenty new taxis acquired at the end of 19X0, ignoring the reinvestment option and assuming all $70,000 in cash is distributed to stockholders at the end of 19X1. Edbejo would then expect the market value of its total assets to increase during 19X2 from $50,000 (the current entry value of its twenty now-used cars at the beginning of 19X2) to $60,000 (the cash generated by the twenty used cars, the cars themselves being worthless at year-end).

These increases in market value over each of the two years we shall call *Current Income*, which is composed of two parts. One part is the *implicit interest* on the investment, that which could have been earned simply by investing the $100,000 in risk-free securities rather than taxis. The other part, which we will call *Excess Current Income*, represents the return for 'outguessing the market.' Over the life of the plan, the firm expects to convert its Subjective Goodwill into market value, this conversion giving rise to Excess Current Income. Thus, we have for Edbejo:

---

[1] We disagree with writers like Joshua Ronen and Lawrence Revsine (see references in Appendix B), who associate a positive $V_0 - M_0$, and indeed the size of $V_0 - M_0$, solely with the presumed element of risk involved in the investment. Positive Subjective Goodwill for a particular entrepreneur may be certain of realization, but that entrepreneur perhaps is the only one to see these prospects (an important element of 'entrepreneurship'), or he may have some degree of monopoly power.

P. W. Bell and L. T. Johnson

	Year	
	19X1	19X2
Expected Current Income (Change in market value):		
M_1 (before distributions) $- M_0 =$		
$\quad$ \$120,000 $-$ \$100,000 $=$	\$20,000	
$M_2 - M_1$ (after distributions) $=$		
$\quad$ \$60,000 $-$ \$50,000 $=$		\$10,000
Less Implicit Interest on Assets at Beginning of Period:		
$\cdot$10 $(M_0) = \cdot$10 (\$100,000) $=$	10,000	
$\cdot$10 M_1 (after distributions) $=$		
$\quad \cdot$10 (\$50,000) $=$		5,000
equals Excess Current Income	\$10,000	\$5,000

The present value of this stream of Excess Current Income discounted to 31 December, 19X0 is:

$$\frac{\$10,000}{1\cdot1} + \frac{\$5,000}{(1\cdot1)^2} = \$9,091 + \$4,132 = \$13,223$$

which is exactly equal to Subjective Goodwill. Thus, if events during 19X1 and 19X2 unfold as expected, Edbejo will just turn its Subjective Goodwill into market value.[1] Let us see what events (some expected, some not) unfold for 19X1.

EVENTS UNFOLD FOR 19X1

On the very first day of business in 19X1, the major auto companies (including the Dodge Division of Chrysler Corporation) announce a 20

---

[1] Robert Anthony (1975) has urged that imputed interest on owners' investment in the firm be deducted, along with any actual interest paid to creditors, from entity income in arriving at ownership income. If the interest rate chosen for this purpose is the same as that used in the discounting exercise, i.e., the interest that could be earned on risk-free securities, his proposal for defining ownership income is the same as our Excess Current Income. Such a measure, which is a measure of the firm's ability to 'outguess the market,' has its function, as seen above. It is indeed the concept of profit used by economists traditionally in all work in price theory—their average total cost curve includes implicit interest, a 'normal rate of return.' But it is not a measure of the total income earned by owners. One can argue, however (and Anthony does), that the imputed interest factor should not be subject to corporate income tax since it is unrelated to the special firm activity of trying to 'outguess the market.'

per cent price increase on all new cars. This price increase has a secondary impact on the prices of used cars as well, as indicated by the supplement to the used car 'Blue Book' that comes out immediately following the announcement. The newly-posted prices for new and used Dodges are as follows:

	New	Used (one-year-old average condition, with typical taxi mileage)
Retail Price	$6,000	$3,000
Wholesale Price	$5,000	$2,500

The margin to dealers was widened because their old margin was insufficient, causing many dealers to go out of business. Thus, there was an easing of a situation that had developed into cut-throat competition.

(We emphasize that we could have just as readily assumed that prices rose gradually over the period or in discrete jumps over the year. Computations would have become more cumbersome, but our analysis of the problem would not have been fundamentally affected.)[1]

These prices for both new and used cars remain unchanged throughout 19X1, nor are there any changes in the general price level during that time. The projected net cash inflows of $70,000 for 19X1 occur exactly as anticipated. Thus, the change in car prices was not the consequence of altered expectations regarding the cash flows generated in the taxi business. Let us turn now to how various companies adopting differing accounting approaches would treat these sets of expected and actual economic events.

ACCOUNTING BY THE EDBEJO TAXI COMPANY

By using current entry values as the basis for its accounting, Edbejo would report assets of $100,000 (20 new taxis @ $5,000/new taxi) on 31 December, 19X0 and $130,000 before distributions to stockholders ($70,000 cash plus 20 used taxis @ $3,000/used taxi) on 31 December, 19X1. Assets (and equities), therefore, increased by $30,000 during 19X1, this amount being Edbejo's Current Income. If we dichotomize Current Income into Current Operating Income and Holding Gains (technically, we feel the latter should be termed Cost Savings based on having purchased assets at less than current cost, but we will use the more common

---

[1] See (Edwards and Bell, 1961, Chapters 3, 7 and 8), or, more simply, (Edwards, Bell, and Johnson, 1979, Chapter 12) for illustrations of how the effects of gradual specific price changes and general price level changes can be incorporated into accounting records.

terminology), listing both expected and actual results side-by-side to yield variances, we have:

Edbejo Taxi Company
Income Statement
For the Year Ended 31 December, 19X1

	Expected	Actual	Variance
Revenues less Expenses (other than depreciation)	$70,000	$70,000	–o–
Depreciation Expense	50,000	60,000	+$10,000
Current Operating Income	$20,000	$10,000	–$10,000
Holding Gain	–o–	20,000	+20,000
Current Income	$20,000	$30,000	+$10,000

By dichotomizing income in this fashion, we are able to isolate the causes of the change in Edbejo's total assets during 19X1 as between changes resulting from service production activities and from price changes.[1] The taxis rose in price on the first day of the year from $100,000 to $120,000, resulting in a Holding Gain (unexpected) of $20,000. The cash rose from zero to $70,000 (as expected) during the year as a result of the taxi services rendered, but the decline in value of the taxis themselves from $120,000 to $60,000 as a result of their use during the year was greater than expected, thereby leading to a Current Operating Income $10,000 below the planned amount.

What does all of this tell Edbejo's managers and owners? First, it tells them that the investment in taxis is no longer a profitable one in terms of current prices. Had Edbejo acquired twenty new taxis either today or one day later than they in fact were acquired, they would have cost $120,000. In terms of current entry prices, this amounts to a rate of return over cost of 8·33 per cent ($10,000 ÷ $120,000) for 19X1 and—if expected net cash flows remain as before—o per cent for 19X2, both

---

[1] The argument that operating income and holding gains may be intertwined (that, for example, a firm may have to suffer some holding losses in order to maintain minimum inventory levels needed for efficient operations) and that the interrelationship of the two negates dichotomization does not seem to us to hold water. Indeed, one of us has argued that it is all the more reason to dichotomize, in the case of inventories, so as to be able to measure to what extent each dimension of expectations were realized; see (Bell, 1975). At any rate, the fact that operating and holding gains may be interdependent does not seem to us to provide any reason not to try to measure each independently in order to better understand why change occurred, i.e., to what extent the total income or loss is attributable to each factor.

less than the risk-free interest rate of 10 per cent. Clearly, Edbejo should not reinvest in this type of business, even though reinvestment was part of the original two-year plan.

On the other hand, the original investors have not fared badly, as the total Current Income figure shows. Indeed, they are better off than they expected to be at the end of 19X1 since actual exceeded expected Current Income by $10,000. The decision to invest in the taxi business turned out to be a wise one, but, as is now apparent, the reasons underlying the investment are no longer valid. Edbejo should not reinvest in taxis, and the question now arises as to whether Edbejo should continue to use its existing fleet as taxis for another year, put them to another use, or liquidate them now. We shall return to this question later; first, let us see how the other companies are viewing the situation.

ACCOUNTING BY THE GYNSTAMREV TAXI COMPANY

Let us turn first to an approach to current value accounting that is frequently espoused in place of—and not infrequently confused with—the approach adopted by Edbejo. The Gynstamrev Taxi Company, confronted by the same events as Edbejo, would report total assets at the end of 19X1 in the same amount as Edbejo (cash of $70,000 and taxis of $60,000) but would report as total income for 19X1 only the $10,000 that Edbejo reported as Current Operating Income, excluding the $20,000 of Holding Gain. Thus, Gynstamrev's managers and stockholders, like Edbejo's, would be aware that reinvestment in the taxi business would be unprofitable. However, Gynstamrev's stockholders would be told that their income for 19X1 was only $10,000—$20,000 less than Edbejo's. Why?

The notion that underlies Gynstamrev's approach (termed Current Replacement Value Accounting, or CRVA, for short) is that only the amount over and above that necessary to 'maintain the existing physical capital' of the firm is 'distributable' and, therefore, may be reported as income. Gynstamrev's capital at the beginning of 19X1 consisted of twenty new Dodge cars. To replace those cars at year-end would require $120,000. During 19X1, Gynstamrev generated $70,000 in cash and had on hand at year-end twenty one-year-old Dodges valued at $60,000 (at current replacement cost), for a total of $130,000. Since it would take $120,000 to break even in Gynstamrev's terms, then only $10,000 of the $130,000 can be regarded as income. (The year-end position statement is brought into balance by means of a 'reserve for replacement' in the amount of $20,000 which is added to the equities side.) Should Gynstamrev distribute $10,000 to stockholders at the end of 19X1, it would have $60,000 cash with which it could buy twenty one-year-old taxis. Suppose that, erroneously expecting greater cash flows than $3,000 per used taxi in 19X2, Gynstamrev decides to buy twenty more used taxis. Its fleet of 20 used taxis would then generate cash flows of $120,000 (40 used taxis @ $3,000/used taxi) during 19X2. Since current cost depreciation for 19X2 would also be $120,000, Gynstamrev would have no 'distributable' income for the year but would have enough cash at year-end with which it could purchase twenty new Dodges, thereby just maintaining its physical capital.[1]

At this point, Gynstamrev would have to assess its expectations as to cash flows for 19X3 and 19X4 in order to decide whether or not to reinvest. There are, of course, two possible scenarios: (1) that expected future cash flows will be the same as in the past (i.e., $3,500 for a new taxi and $3,000 for a year-old one) or (2) that expected cash flows will be greater than in the past, say 20 per cent more (i.e., $4,200 for a new taxi and $3,600 for a used one).

In the first case, if Gynstamrev's management acts rationally, the firm will not reinvest either in new or used taxis because the rate of return associated with the taxi business would be less than that which could be earned from riskless securities. Gynstamrev could then either invest the $120,000 cash in other assets promising a higher rate of return or distribute the cash to its stockholders. Consider the distribution case. If Gynstamrev distributes all $120,000 to its stockholders, they will have received a total of $130,000 from an initial investment of $100,000, yet the only income reported by Gynstamrev to date was the $10,000 in 19X1. Where did the firm get the extra $20,000 from? Did it steal the money? Moral: It can hardly be argued that the holding gains are not a component of income because they must be devoted to replacement *when replacement is clearly not going to take place.*

---

[1] Such is the way it *might* work out. In fact, if Gynstamrev invested its $60,000 current cost depreciation at the end of 19X1 in ten *new* Dodges rather than twenty *used* Dodges, it could generate some 'Distributable Income' in 19X2 [because new cars are more profitable than used cars, i.e., a new car earns $3,500 ($70,000 ÷ 20) whereas a used car earns $3,000 ($60,000 ÷ 20)] and actually expand its physical stock of assets in a fairly short space of time to a stable, even-age pool of twenty-six cars by continuing to reinvest its current cost depreciation in new cars in this manner each year (assuming no further price changes). On the other hand, if there is a further increase in prices in 19X2, the company might not be able to maintain its stock of physical assets under any circumstances (without new contributions of capital)—'back-log depreciation' might be required. There is no magic 'matching' of reinvestment of current cost depreciation and maintenance of the physical stock of capital at all, hence, no magic correctness to the concept of 'Distributable Income' over and above the necessary to maintain physical capital. See (Edwards, Bell and Johnson, 1979, Chapter 13) and references therein and, especially, (Edwards, 1961).

Current value and the simple production case

Let us now consider the alternative scenario—one more favourable to Gynstamrev's CRVA approach—where reinvestment of $120,000 in twenty new Dodges is justified in light of greater expected future cash flows. If the cash flows are 20 per cent greater than before, then Gynstamrev would report income as follows for 19X3 and 19X4:

	19X3	19X4
Revenues less Expenses		
(other than depreciation)	$84,000	$72,000
Depreciation Expense	60,000	60,000
Income	$24,000	$12,000

Thus, Gynstamrev would have a 20 per cent rate of return in each year on its reinvestment in new taxis ($24,000/$120,000 in 19X3; $12,000/$60,000 in 19X4). Is Gynstamrev no better off than it was before since it has only twenty taxis to operate in 19X3 and 19X4? We think that it is better off, based on the following considerations.

Recall that reinvestment of the $120,000 available at the end of 19X2 became profitable when projected cash flows increased by 20 per cent. Suppose, then, instead of projected cash flows increasing by 20 per cent, the prices of taxis decline by 20 per cent (i.e., to the original prices of $5,000 retail new, and so forth). In such a case, reinvestment of $120,000 would be equally as profitable. However, a $120,000 investment would buy *twenty-four* new Dodges ($120,000 ÷ $5,000/new car) in this case. These twenty-four new Dodges would generate cash inflows of $84,000 in 19X3 (24 new taxis @ $3,500/new taxi) and $72,000 in 19X4 (24 used taxis @ $3,000/used taxi), exactly the same as above. Depreciation would also be the same per year as above, yielding *identical incomes* as above on a CRVA basis. Yet a CRVA advocate would argue that Gynstamrev would be better off with *twenty-four* taxis as in this case rather than with *twenty* above even though both situations entail *identical investments* generating *identical cash flows*. In contrast to Gynstamrev's accountants, we agree with Professor Baxter [1976, p. 120] who argues:

Surely the right criterion of asset expansion is that the outlay is expected to improve the cash flow. Dearer units are just as likely as more units to do this (unless the firm is queerly placed). Both types of outlay are investment in extra resources, and so bring expansion in the economic sense.

If a firm does replace—and this is the only circumstance relevant for CRVA—in the face of higher asset prices, it will do so presumably because

289

of expected increases in future cash flows; this is just as much an expansion as if there were physical expansion with unchanged asset prices and future cash flows. It will involve some expansion even if cash flow increases do not keep pace with rising asset prices (hence, the rate of return falls) so long as it is profitable to replace at all. In this case, there is even a stronger argument that stockholders should be informed of the holding gain and the lower rate of return so that they may decide whether or not to continue their investment in the firm.

The arguments that underlie Gynstamrev's CRVA approach are: (1) it reflects an 'entity' rather than 'proprietary' view of income, i.e., the *firm* rather than its *owners* must be made better off for income to be recognized; (2) any 'holding gain' on assets the firm already owns is a mythical one that does no more than offset the added 'suffering' that the firm must incur if its input prices rise; (3) the 'holding gain' is not something that can be prudently distributed because the firm must retain an amount of cash inflows equal to current cost depreciation in order to replace existing assets as they wear out, thereby maintaining intact the firm's physical capital. Although these arguments tend to intertwine with one another, we will treat them one by one.

Central to all of these arguments is the fallacious assumption that the firm must continue to reinvest in the same kinds of assets it presently owns. We are not aware of any dictum or law that generally requires companies either to remain in the same line of business or to continue to use its existing assets in the same fashion in which they have been used. Thus, appealing to the entity versus proprietary approach seems to us an empty argument.[1] The *firm* may very well be better off not to continue investing in the same kinds of assets in the same fashion. To the best of our knowledge, Studebaker (for example) no longer manufactures automobiles, yet it continues to exist as an operating entity.

With regard to the 'mythical' holding gain that does no more than offset subsequent 'suffering,' consider the following. Suppose two individuals, A and B, each have $100,000 cash and each plans to buy a house. A, anticipating a price rise, buys one quickly for $80,000; B procrastinates and ends up buying a like house for $100,000. As a result, A has both a house *and* $20,000 cash; B has only a house. Is not A $20,000 'better off' than B? If so, then why is it that CRVA enthusiasts would show

---

[1] The issue has been put in these terms by R. S. Gynther (see Gynther, 1966, pp. 141–42 and elsewhere); by the Sandilands Committee (Inflation Accounting Committee, 1975), which argues (p. 140), 'The concept of capital maintenance adopted in the profit and loss accounts by replacement cost accounting is invariably one which regards capital as the capital of the company, rather than of the shareholders'; and by many others.

zero income for *both* A and B? Moreover, when and if they both decide to replace their present houses, who is still better off, A or B?

Finally, consider the argument that it would be imprudent to distribute a holding gain as income. This argument, we think, confuses what is properly a question of present or future *liquidity* with the measurement of 'well-offness.' What Professor William Baxter (1976, p. 120) said in criticizing the Sandilands Committee is germane to this point:

> Cash distributions may be imprudent for all manner of reasons; where do we draw the line in deciding on whether imprudence changes income? If I commit myself to buying a car, the budgetary strain may be agonizing; but does it cut down my salary?[1]

Measurements of 'well-offness' are quite separate and apart from matters of liquidity; indeed, extensive holdings of monetary rather than non-monetary assets very often will make one relatively less well-off as time passes.

ACCOUNTING BY THE IJIRCO TAXI COMPANY

The Ijirco Company starts business with the same investment as Edbejo and is subsequently confronted by the same set of economic events, but its accountants formulate their reports in terms of historical costs. Traditional Accounting Income for 19X1 would be reported as follows:

Ijirco Taxi Company
Income Statement
For the Year Ended 31 December, 19X1

	Expected	Actual	Variance
Revenues less Expenses (other than depreciation)	$70,000	$70,000	–o–
Depreciation	50,000	50,000	–o–
Traditional Accounting Income	$20,000	$20,000	–o–

[1] Interestingly, the Sandilands Committee (Inflation Accounting Committee, 1975, p. 29) worked toward its definition of income by drawing the business analogy to Hicks' definition of income for the individual: 'A company's profit for the year is the maximum value which the company *can distribute* during the year and still expect to be as well off at the end of the year as it was at the beginning' (italics ours). And the Committee then opted for a definition of 'well-offness' identical to ours, i.e., a firm will be just as well off at the end of the period as at the beginning if it has the same *market value* of assets, or shareholders will be just as well off if the total market value of assets minus liabilities are unchanged. But then it makes a subtle shift subsequently and ends up defining income or profit as 'the amount of total gains arising in the year that *may prudently be regarded as distributable*' (p. 37; italics ours) and arguing that 'prudence' requires, in effect, the maintenance of *physical* capital.

P. W. Bell and L. T. Johnson

The primary accounting problem confronted by Ijirco is how to allocate the historical cost of the taxis as between 19X1 and 19X2 (a problem not encountered by Edbejo since its accountants focused only on current market prices). All of the choices are rather arbitrary; of the arbitrary methods, we believe the preferable one to be the internal rate method which, in this case, posits straight-line depreciation.[1] This method yields (in the absence of price changes) a depreciation figure that is at least consistent with the pattern of cash flows initially projected, thereby making the rate of return constant over the life of the asset(s). With this method, older assets will not generate a different rate of return than newer ones and, under certain conditions (no price changes, perfect markets, firm's anticipation of year-to-year cash flows must be in the same relative pattern as the market's), the book values yielded would reflect used asset market prices. Regardless of the historical cost depreciation method adopted, no variances of actual from expected depreciation will emerge so long as the service life is not altered.

What, then, does this tell the managers and owners of Ijirco? Everything is apparently exactly on course. The original wise decision to invest in the taxi business has been confirmed; moreover there is no reason to believe that reinvestment in taxis would not also be an equally wise decision. Certainly no consideration need be given the possibilities of either putting the existing fleet of taxis to an alternative use or liquidating the fleet (as Edbejo's managers and owners would now be contemplating).

There is also the matter of comparability (not an issue with Edbejo's current entry value accounting) with companies reporting on an historical cost basis. Suppose another company, call it Ijirco II as opposed to Ijirco I above, was exactly the same as Ijirco I except that it acquired its taxis on January 1, 19X1 for $120,000 (perhaps erroneously anticipating 20 per cent higher cash flows of $84,000 in 19X1 and $72,000 in 19X2). Assuming that the two companies were equally efficient in rendering taxi services (and that both adopt internal rate, straight-line depreciation methods), their income statements for 19X1 and 19X2 would be as shown on the following page.

It should be apparent that the historical cost approach adopted by these

[1] Under this method, the expected internal rate of return (in this case, 20 per cent) is applied to the unallocated historical cost of the asset(s) at the beginning of the period so as to compute a hypothetical figure for income (in this case, $20,000 for 19X1). This figure is then subtracted from the net of revenues less expenses other than depreciation to yield the depreciation number (in this case, $50,000 for 19X1). See (Edwards, Bell and Johnson, 1979, Chapter 6) for extensive discussion and illustration of the internal rate of depreciation applicable to assets of differing efficiencies, i.e., differing patterns of revenues less expenses other than depreciation over the their useful lives.

Current value and the simple production case

	Ijirco I		Ijirco II	
	19X1	19X2	19X1	19X2
Revenues less Expenses (other than depreciation)	$70,000	$60,000	$70,000	$60,000
Depreciation Expense	50,000	50,000	60,000	60,000
Traditional Accounting Income	$20,000	$10,000	$10,000	–o–

two companies has masked their equal operating efficiency, something that cannot occur under Edbejo's current entry value accounting. Ijirco I's holding gain of $20,000 in 19X1 becomes part of operating income in 19X1 *and* 19X2, $10,000 in each year. And, at the end of 19X1 (but before distributions to stockholders), even though both companies possess identical assets ($70,000 cash plus twenty one-year-old Dodges), they would report different asset totals, Ijirco I reporting $120,000 and Ijirco II, $130,000. Again, this could not occur under Edbejo's approach. Ijirco I has violated the second and third standards set out at the beginning (pp. 278–9) because it has not reported all of the economic events of 19X1 in that period; it has reported in 19X2 (as an economic event of that period) an economic event that occurred in 19X1, and it has classified in both periods a realized holding gain as operating income. The violation of these two standards leads to noncomparability, hence, unreliable interpretability of the accounting results (i.e., a violation of the fourth standard).

But the deficiencies of Traditional Accounting Income, based on historical costs and the application of the realization convention, are fairly well known. Indeed, the only serious claim for it would seem to be based on the erroneous belief that historical costs are somehow more 'objective' and more 'verifiable' than current values; such is not the case. Only at one point in time are historical costs even *equally* as objective as current values, that being when the two are identical—at the time the asset is purchased. At any subsequent date, historical costs are almost certainly *less* objective than current values because they must be allocated as between expired and unexpired by means of arbitrary procedures. 'Objectivity' cannot be achieved by recourse to arbitrary procedures any more than 'comparability' can.

ACCOUNTING BY THE CHASTE TAXI COMPANY

A somewhat different variant of current value accounting has been adopted by the Chaste Taxi Company. This company prices its assets in terms of current exit values, the amount that could be obtained for them were they to be sold either immediately or in the near-term future. Income is then measured by the changes in those values over the period. Owning the same kinds of assets and projecting the same future cash flows as Edbejo, Chaste's expected incomes for 19X1 and 19X2 are as follows:

	19X1	19X2
Revenue less Expenses (other than depreciation)	$70,000	$60,000
Depreciation Expense	53,700	46,300
Income	$16,300	$13,700

Like Edbejo, Chaste began with $100,000 in cash. When it purchased twenty new Dodges, its assets—valued in terms of 'cash equivalents'—dropped to $92,600 (20 new cars @ $4,630/new car). By the end of 19X1, total assets were expected to be $116,300, comprised of $70,000 cash generated during the year plus twenty one-year-old taxis valued at $46,300 (20 used cars @ $2,315/used car). Thus, income for 19X1 would be the difference between the ending and beginning cash equivalents, $116,300 − $100,000 = $16,300. Assuming no reinvestment at the end of 19X1, the twenty used taxis would generate cash flows of $60,000 during 19X2 while declining in value from $46,300 to zero, thereby yielding income for 19X2 of $13,700.

Given the price changes that occurred at the beginning of 19X1, a comparison of Chaste's expected results with actual would be as follows:

Chaste Taxi Company
Income Statement
For the Year Ended 31 December, 19X1

	Expected	Actual	Variance
Revenues less Expenses (other than depreciation)	$70,000	$70,000	–o–
Depreciation Expense	53,700	50,000	−$3,700
Income	$16,300	$20,000	+$3,700

Rather than pointing to difficulties (as did Edbejo's Current Operating Income and Gynastamrev's Income figures) or suggesting that everything

294

was going exactly according to plan (as did Ijirco's Traditional Accounting Income), Chaste's reports suggest that things went better than expected in 19X1. An investment of $100,000 generated income of $20,000 for a 20 per cent rate of return; this is further reinforced by the expectation that the twenty now-used taxis valued at $50,000 will generate cash flows of $60,000 in 19X2, another 20 per cent return. There is certainly no reason indicated to suggest liquidation (even though its accounting approach is predicated on the assumption of liquidation—just as Gynstamrev's is predicated on the assumption of reinvestment). Chaste's management and stockholders—and *potential* stockholders—would have no reason to believe that the firm will not do as well in the future as in the past.

But will it? Thus far, Chaste's *original* investment in taxis has gone well, just as Edbejo's, and the *original* stockholders should feel quite sanguine. But Edbejo's stockholders, both original and potential, have been forewarned that the taxi business is not *currently* profitable and that reinvestment is not justified nor should potential stockholders invest in the business. Chaste's stockholders—both original and potential—have received no such warning from Chaste's financial statements. Thus, they may be erroneously induced to either invest or reinvest.

The Chaste approach to current value accounting appears to be quite popular these days, at least among academics who eschew the going concern convention in the belief that business firms should re-think their options continuously. Indeed, Chambers calls the approach 'continuously contemporary accounting,' arguing that a firm that maximizes the change in current exit values in each period (i.e., in the short-run) will inevitably maximize in the long-run as well. Appendix A demonstrates, however, that such short-run maximizations do not necessarily lead to an equivalent maximization in the long-run.

The central difficulty with Chaste's approach—as well as with Gynstamrev's—is that of putting the cart before the horse. Both assume that the firm is *sentenced* (in Chaste's case, to liquidation of its existing assets; in Gynastamrev's case, to replacement of its existing assets) before a *verdict* is arrived at. Moreover, the sentence influences the verdict! Such is an Alice in Wonderland approach:

'No, no!' said the Queen. 'Sentence first—verdict afterwards.'
'Stuff and nonsense!' said Alice loudly. 'The idea of having the sentence first!'
'Hold your tongue!' said the Queen, turning purple.
'I won't!' said Alice.
'Off with her head!' the Queen shouted at the top of her voice. Nobody moved.[1]

[1] Chapter XII of *Alice's Adventures in Wonderland* on 'Alice's Evidence.'

P. W. Bell and L. T. Johnson

ACCOUNTING BY THE STAURON TAXI COMPANY

This company takes a very different approach to current value accounting, the 'discounted cash flows approach' which is based essentially on the Hicksian concept of 'Economic Income.' Hicks (1946, p. 174) defined income as 'the maximum amount which an individual can spend [consume] this week and still be able to spend [consume] the same amount in real terms in each ensuing week.' The Stauron Taxi Company, with the same assets purchased at the same time and with the same projected cash flows over a two-year planning period as Edbejo, would report its expected Economic Income as

$$EI_1 = V_1 - V_0 = iV_0.[1]$$

We have already found that V_0 is equal to \$113,223. We can find V_1 by adding to the first period's cash flows of \$70,000 the present value of expected cash flows in the second period discounted to the end of the first period, i.e.,

$$\frac{\$60,000}{1 \cdot 1}.$$

Thus,

$$V_1 = \$70,000 + \frac{\$60,000}{1 \cdot 1} = \$124,545$$

and from the above

$$EI_1 = \$124,545 - \$113,223 = \cdot 1(\$113,223) = \$11,322.$$

If the firm received \$70,000 in 19X1 as expected and distributed Economic Income of \$11,322, it could buy \$58,678 of securities with the remainder and earn \$5,868 interest in 19X2. In the second year it would then receive \$60,000 + \$5,868 = \$65,868. It could again distribute Economic Income of \$11,322 and purchase \$54,546 in securities, which, with the \$58,678 of securies carried over from 19X1, would give it \$113,224 in securities (equal to its original Subjective Value); and it could, assuming no change

---

[1] We have:

$$V_0 = \frac{E_1}{(1+i)} + \frac{E_2}{(1+i)^2},$$

$$V_1 = E_1 + \frac{E_2}{(1+i)},$$

and

$$V_1 - V_0 = \frac{E_1 + iE_1 - E_1}{(1+i)} + \frac{E_2 + iE_2 - E_2}{(1+i)^2} = iV_0.$$

296

in the rate of interest, then continue to distribute Economic Income of $11,322 forever. Our *expected Economic Income*, which we could pay out in 19X1, 19X2, and forever, was based on expected receipts *during the plan period*—which was as far as we could see in thinking of 'outguessing the market.' After that, we had to count on just matching the market, i.e., earning interest on risk-free securities.

It is useful to view expected Economic Income in one further sense. If we add and subtract the total market value of our assets at the end of 19X0, M_0, and add and subtract the total expected market value of our assets at the end of 19X1 (the taxis valued at current entry prices), M_1, and rearrange terms, we obtain the following:

$$EI_1 = V_1 - V_0 + [M_1 - M_1 + M_0 - M_0],$$
$$= [M_1 - M_0] - [(V_0 - M_0) - (V_1 - M_1)]$$

At the outset there is a certain Subjective Goodwill $(V_0 - M_0)$ which, it is expected, will be turned into market value by the end of the plan. Expected Economic Income in 19X1 consists of the increase in market value which will have been achieved in 19X1 (if expectations are fulfilled), i.e., $[M_1 - M_0]$, less the decline in this Subjective Goodwill which remains to be realized in the future as the plan continues to unfold $[(V_0 - M_0) - (V_1 - M_1)]$—this decline occurring because some of the initial Subjective Goodwill has already been turned into market value.

But everything up to now has been in terms of subjective expectations, and this violates our standard of accounting for measurable empirical phenomena. Then can we in some way measure Economic Income ex post and compare it with ex ante Economic Income? Let us define ex post 19X1 values with a prime ('). Then,

$$EI'_1 = [M'_1 - M_0] - [(V_0 - M_0) - (V'_1 - M'_1)]$$

and subtracting ex ante Economic Income from ex post Economic Income we obtain:

$$EI'_1 - EI_1 = [M'_1 - M_1] + [(V'_1 - M'_1) - (V_1 - M_1)]$$
$$c \quad = \quad a \quad + \quad b$$

Given the rise in asset prices at the beginning of the period, coupled with fulfilment of cash flow expectations and unchanged future cash flow expectations, Stauron's comparison of actual with expected Economic Income would suggest that everything is right on course, for $c = 0$ in the above. It must be—there are no deviations of actual from expected cash flows in 19X1, nor future expected cash flows in 19X2 as were expected at the end of 19X1, from those same future expected cash flows in 19X2 which had been expected in 19X0. *If* deviations are broken down as above, however, we have:

$$c \qquad = \qquad a \qquad + \qquad b$$

$$\$11,322 - \$11,322 = [\$130,000 - \$120,000] + [(\$124,545 - \$130,000)$$
$$- (\$124,545 - \$120,000)]$$

$$0 \quad = \quad \$10,000 \qquad - \qquad \$10,000$$

The discounted cash flows/Economic Income approach deals only with cash flows, not at all with changes in asset prices. If cash flows are generated as expected and there is no change in further expectations about the future (hence, $V'_1 = V_1$), Economic Income ex post always equals Economic Income ex ante (i.e., $V'_1 - V_0 = V_1 - V_0$). Further, even ex post Economic Income necessitates using subjective forecasts of the future, again violating our standard of measuring only empirical phenomena. It is only the *a* component of *c* above that can serve as an objective measure to evaluate decisions and performance; the *b* component involves V'_1 relating to forecasts of future cash flows. There is simply no way that Economic Income per se can become a valuable tool in evaluating past decisions and performance.[1]

Many discounted cash-flow enthusiasts, of course, look upon their approach more in terms of an attempt to arrive at some form of accounting information which will serve to *predict future cash flows* than as information that may be useful in evaluating past decisions and performance (which may be useful in making new decisions about the future). *Forecasts* of future cash flows may be useful to predict future cash flows, and actual cash flows *in a period* may serve as a useful check on the forecast *for that period*. But we then have only *part* of the information necessary to evaluate decisions and performance, and we are not strictly using Economic Income or a discounted future cash flows approach but rather only a projected and actual one-period cash flows approach. Using objectively

---

[1] George Staubus, one of the foremost proponents of using the discounted cash flows approach in accounts, knows this and has been promoting objective 'surrogates' for his V_1, V'_1, and V_0—replacement cost (current entry value) in the case of materials and use-assets, net realizable value (current exit value) in the case of inventories, and simply the total (exit value) of accounts receivable; see (Staubus, 1967, 1971). But then Staubus simply has a combination of entry and exit values to measure M'_1 and M_1, and his 'Economic Income' bears no real relationship to discounted cash flows but is really *a* version of $M'_1 - M_0$ unless one assumes perfect markets, i.e., $V_1 = M_1$ for use-assets, in which case there would be no investment in use-assets because one could do just as well by buying risk-free securities.

determined market value 'surrogates' for the V's or portions of the V's that we cannot measure objectively, as both Staubus and Ronen suggest we do, essentially yields a polyglot measure of $M'_1 - M_0$ but does not necessarily get us very close to an ex ante $V_1 - V_0$ or ex post V'_1. And a higher than expected M'_1 value does not necessarily predict larger-than-originally expected cash flows in the future, as our taxi illustration clearly shows. The rise in taxi prices coupled with no increase in cash flows over those expected is squeezing out the 'excess profits' originally foreseen by our taxi company, as suppliers and/or competitors awaken to what Edbejo envisaged at first. Even higher-than-expected cash flows in the present, a part of $M'_1 - M_0$, may mean lower-than-originally expected cash flows in the future since the high present flows may have been produced by using assets up faster. We are left with the unsatisfying, but we believe necessary, conclusion that objective accounting data for the present and past is of little use to predict the future. Appendix B expands upon the foregoing discussion.

ACCOUNTING BY THE THOMCO TAXI COMPANY

By far the simplest of the accounting approaches posited—and it is not a current value approach—is the one adopted by Thomco. Exasperated by the arbitrary allocations of revenues and costs as between periods (a requirement indigenous to historical cost accounting as well as to some forms of current cost accounting) and opposed to the subjectivities inherent in discounted future cash flow accounting, the Thomco Taxi Company elects simply to report annual cash flows.[1] Since Thomco experienced the same events as Edbejo and the others, its lone financial statement for 19X1 would be simply:

Thomco Taxi Company
Statement of Cash Flows
For the Year Ended 31 December, 19X1

	Expected	Actual	Variance
Cash Flows (revenues les expenses other than depreciation)	$70,000	$70,000	—o—

---

[1] See (Thomas, 1969, 1974). Appendix C in this book contains further comments on these works.

As a consequence of such reporting, not only would Thomco's management and stockholders not have any tip-off that anything was wrong (because everything was in accordance in terms of cash flows expected and achieved), they simply would have no measure of performance or 'accomplishment.' Any change in the value of its use-assets, either up (as with a price rise) or down (as with a price drop and/or depreciation) was simply ignored. Can it then be said that Thomco did as well (or as poorly) as the other companies?

Suppose that during 19X1 Thomco's drivers drove their taxis harder and further, thereby generating cash flows of $75,000 instead of the $70,000 initially projected. Was the decision (perhaps unconscious) to do so a wise one? It would appear so, given Thomco's reporting method which would show a 'favourable' variance of $5,000 ($75,000 actual cash flows minus $70,000 expected). It also would appear that Thomco did better than its competitors who only produced cash flows of $70,000.

But what if at the end of 19X1 Thomco's year-old taxis were in 'very rough' condition as a result of hard use and high mileage? (Recall that the other companies' year-old taxis were regarded as being in 'average' condition.) Suppose that the year-end prices for year-old taxis in 'very rough' condition were $1,500 retail and $1,250 wholesale as opposed to $3,000 retail and $2,500 wholesale for cars in 'average' condition. In terms of Edbejo's accounting, Thomco's situation would then be depicted as follows:

Thomco Taxi Company
Income Statement
For the Year Ended 31 December, 19X1

Revenues less Expenses (other than depreciation)	$75,000
Depreciation Expense	90,000
Current Operating Income (Loss)	($15,000)
Holding Gain	20,000
Current Income	$5,000

Consider also Thomco's circumstance in terms of Chaste's current exit value accounting:

Current value and the simple production case

Thomco Taxi Company
Income Statement
For the Year Ended 31 December, 19X1

Revenues less Expenses (other than depreciation)	$75,000
Depreciation Expense	75,000
Income	$–0–

In neither context could it be said that operating taxis in the manner Thomco did during 19X1 was desirable. An investment of $100,000 in riskless securities bearing interest at 10 per cent would have been preferable. Thus, we conclude that Thomco's accounting approach is inadequate since it excludes information essential to the evaluation of past decisions and performance.

EVALUATION OF RESULTS FOR 19X1 AND DECISION MAKING FOR 19X2

The Edbejo, Gynstamrev, Ijirco, Chaste, Stauron, and Thomco Taxi Companies all ended 19X1 with $70,000 in cash generated from operations plus twenty one-year-old Dodge taxis that had been purchased new. Based upon the results reported in their respective financial statements for 19X1, each must decide upon a course of action to take for 19X2. Should they acquire additional taxis with the available cash, reinvest but in some different line of activity, distribute the cash but continue to use their existing taxis, or sell the taxis and distribute all cash, thereby liquidating the company? Presumably each company will use the information provided in its own financial statements to evaluate its past decision to invest in the taxi business and to help in formulating a course of action for 19X2 (certainly a failure to do so would be an indictment of the accounting approach adopted).

Based on the accounting data reported for 19X1, several of the companies should be quite sanguine about their initial decision; what is more, the data indicate no reason not to reinvest the available cash in more taxis. Ijirco's results, for one, indicate that everything is going in accordance with the original plan; actual income for 19X1 was exactly as expected with a 20 per cent rate of return on investment. Therefore, on the basis of the information reported to them, its managers and stockholders should have no qualms about reinvestment. Stauron's expectations for 19X1 have also materialized; and if its original projection of cash flows for 19X2 still holds, then Stauron's *subjective* view of 'well-offness' is as anticipated

301

and the firm is right on course. So, too, for Thomco whose cash flows for 19X1 are good and exactly as expected. Thus, on the basis of their annual reports, there should be no cause for concern for anyone associated with these three companies, nor is there any apparent reason to deviate from what they are now doing.

Chaste's management and stockholders, on the other hand, are presented with data indicating that the firm generated a 20 per cent rate of return on its original investment. For those who were privy to Chaste's forecasts, this was somewhat greater than expected. And its present fleet of taxis, valued at $50,000, is expected to generate cash flows of $60,000 in 19X2 for another 20 per cent rate of return. Although expected income for 19X2 is slightly lower than originally anticipated in the plan, it is exactly offset by the unexpected increase in 19X1's income. This is hardly the sort of news that incites panic. Thus, it appears that the activity the firm is presently engaged in—the taxi business—is going well, hence, there should be no cause for concern at Chaste either.

The accounting data generated by Edbejo and Gynstamrev, however, suggest cause for concern. The taxi business that the firms are engaged in is not *currently* profitable, providing a rate of return of less than 10 per cent in terms of the *current* purchase prices of the assets essential to run the business. Gynstarmrev presumably has already made its decision to reinvest in taxis—at least its income figure is dependent upon that assumption—even though such a move would be unwise. If Gynstamrev does not replace under the circumstances, this would suggest its approach to measuring income was based on an erroneous assumption, hence, was in error.

What about Edbejo? Its accounting data indicate that the taxi business is unprofitable and reinvestment in taxis is not justified (although the original stockholders have fared well because of the wise decision to purchase taxis prior to the price increase). Should Edbejo sell its taxis or continue to use them for one more year? An examination of used car 'Blue Book' prices indicates that, in terms of 19X1's performance and the original expectations for 19X2,

$$\begin{matrix} \text{current} & & \text{present} & & \text{current} \\ \text{entry} & > & \text{value} & > & \text{exit} \\ \text{value} & & & & \text{value} \end{matrix}$$

In other words, Edbejo's taxis have a value in use greater than their value in liquidation, even though their purchase today would not be justified.

Upon restructuring its thinking in the above terms, Edbejo might consider adopting the concept of *deprival value* for purposes of valuing its

Current value and the simple production case

assets. Basically, this approach begins with the asset's *present value to the business* (its discounted future cash flows) modified by ceiling and floor constraints as follows:

1. If an asset's present value to the business is greater than its current entry price, then the deprival value of the asset is its current entry price. This is because if the firm were deprived of the asset, the current entry price defines the maximum amount of cash the firm would have to sacrifice in order to restore itself to its previous status.

2. If an asset's present value to the business is less than its current exit price, then the deprival value of the asset is its current exit price. This is because the current exit price defines the minimum amount of cash that the firm would have to accept for the asset.

No difficulties arise, therefore, when an asset's present value is either greater than its current entry price or less than its current exit price because, when such is the case, *objective* market values are used as the basis for valuation. However, when the asset's present value falls between the two, then deprival value is equal to present value which is a *subjective* value.[1] But we must reject this type of valuation for the same reasons as stated earlier with respect to the Stauron Taxi Company. How, then, can the deprival value concept be adapted to Edbejo's needs?

By introducing certain rate of return criteria, we can modify the deprival value concept so as not only to meet the accounting standards enunciated earlier but also to provide the basis for decision rules with respect to reinvestment, use, and liquidation of an asset. To do this, we utilize the following rates of return:

$$\rho = \frac{\text{Current Operating Income}}{\text{Current Entry Value}}$$
(on current entry value basis)

$$\rho' = \frac{\text{Income}}{\text{Current Exit Value}}$$
(on current exit value basis)

It seems to us that *ex post Current Operating Income* and ρ are the appropriate *primary accounting concepts* to use in first evaluating the

[1] For a use-asset (such as taxis), current entry value will almost inevitably exceed current exit value so there are only the three possible combinations of current entry value, current exit value, and present value suggested here. For an inventory asset, current exit value normally exceeds current entry value so we have three other combinations possible, the two sets of combinations together making up the six cases normally treated in the recent revival of Bonbright's notion of the deprival value (which was initiated by David Solomons in 1966). See (Solomons, 1966), (Parker and Harcourt, 1969, esp. pp. 17–19), and (Inflation Accounting Committee, 1975, p. 58).

original decision to enter the taxi business so as to assist in arriving at a decision as to what to do next. Managers and stockholders are evaluating this business—the taxi business—and, say, Edbejo's performance in this business. In the long-run, holding gains resulting from rises in the entry and/or exit value of most use-assets should be tied to operating income. It may be that car (hence, taxi) prices will increase again in 19X2, thereby giving rise to new holding agains, either because cash flows do go up or because perhaps of factors wholly unrelated to the taxi business (cars are obviously used for other purposes). If rates of return which are based on data fusing holding gains and operating income are used in evaluating business decisions—as is the case with exit value accounting and the ρ' concept—firms may be misled about the long-run profitability of their particular activity. The same holding gains might be achieved by employing the use-assets in some more profitable line of *operating* activity as we suggest below.[1]

But given these two rates of return, then Edbejo's taxis might be accounted for as follows:

1. On a current entry value basis from date of acquisition so long as $\rho > \cdot 10$ (our risk-free interest rate).

2. On a dual basis, using both current entry and exit values so long as $\rho \leq \cdot 10$ and $\rho' > \cdot 10$.

3. On a current exit value basis when $\rho' \leq \cdot 10$ (although for reasons given below, we would not expect to find assets valued on this basis on financial statements).

Thus, these three simple criteria serve as the means to adapt the deprival value approach to Edbejo, keeping all values in terms of objective market prices.

Having a dual set of rates of return also provides Edbejo with a set of decision rules with respect to reinvestment, use, and liquidation of its taxi fleet.[2] These rules can be stated in terms of traffic signals, viz:

1. $\rho > \cdot 10$ = green light (reinvestment in autos as taxis is still profitable).

2. $\rho \leq \cdot 10$ but $\rho' > \cdot 10$ = yellow light (reinvestment in taxis is no longer profitable, but use of existing autos as taxis is preferable to their liquida-

---

[1] It is the different numerator in the two expressions that bothers us more than the different denominators. In (Edwards, Bell, and Johnson, 1979, Chapter 13), we show that using a *common* numerator can lead to identical and sensible frameworks for decision rules, one using *only* ρ (which is what we espouse) but in certain cases exit values as well, the other using ρ and ρ'. The former, which entry value proponents might prefer, and the latter, which exit value proponents might prefer, come to the same thing.

[2] See (Edwards and Bell, 1961, p. 101), which initially suggested these decision rules, using current entry and exit value rates of return.

tion; consideration should be given, however, to alternative uses of the autos).

3. $\rho' \leqslant \cdot 10$ = red light (neither reinvestment in autos as taxis nor continued use of existing autos as taxis is preferable to their liquidation).

Thus, the adoption of the modified deprival value approach would provide Edbejo not only with a means for evaluating past decisions and performance but also with a related set of decision rules regarding its present assets and activities. The green/yellow/red light signal pattern articulates with the data contained in Edbejo's financial statements (although the red light signal should prompt immediate liquidation of the autos—assuming there is no other profitable use to which they could be put—thereby eliminating the assets that would otherwise be valued in terms of current exit prices).

In terms of the foregoing, Edbejo at the end of 19X1 received a yellow light signal ($\rho \leqslant \cdot 10$ but $\rho' > \cdot 10$). Thus, Edbejo has been warned that reinvestment in autos as taxis is no longer profitable but that continued use of its 20 existing Dodges as taxis is preferable to their immediate liquidation. At this time, Edbejo should give serious consideration to alternative, more profitable uses of its present fleet. In that regard, it should be apparent that

Current entry value to a taxi operator	=	Current exit value to a used car dealer	>	Present value of autos as taxis	>	Current exit value to a taxi operator	=	Current entry value to a used car dealer

Edbejo's 20 Dodges are worth more as *inventory* assets if Edbejo were in the used car business than as *use* assets in the taxi business (because of differing access to different wholesale and retail markets). Thus, Edbejo should give serious consideration to getting out of the taxi business and into the used car business.

But that is a whole different ballgame. Were space available, we believe that we could demonstrate that even in the case of a *trading* rather than a *production* company, the modified deprival value approach (with current entry values as the primary valuation basis) is still the preferable means of accounting.[1]

[1] One final footnote postscript. We have not had the space to consider the further adjustment to our current entry value figures to take account of changes in the general price level, an adjustment that we believe is essential if accounting reports of income and position are to be fully comparable one to another. There is still some considerable confusion on this matter, the Sandilands Committee, for example, reviving the old either/or error—either specific asset prices adjustment or the general price level adjustment, but not both. Sandilands, as we

P. W. Bell and L. T. Johnson

APPENDIX A

A demonstration that maximization of short-run changes in current exit values need not result in long-run maximization

Implicit in most exit-value theorizing is the notion that one wishes to re-think all decisions, starting from scratch, at the beginning of every new period, on the basis of cash-equivalents existing at the end of the previous period. If one plans at least hypothetically to liquidate each period, it seems to follow that one will want to maximize the increase in cash-equivalents earned each period. To do so maximizes the optimal potential gain (in terms of increased cash-equivalents) for the next period, and the next, and the next. However, doing this will *not* necessarily result in maximizing the increase in cash-equivalents over a longer period.

To illustrate this point, consider the following example. An investor has $10,000 to invest and wants cash dividends of $1,000 per year. Beyond this basic requirement, he wants to maximize the increase in market value of shares held, which he interprets as maximizing the change in current exit values. Only two securities are available, A and B. Security A, whose market price is expected to remain constant, pays a dividend of $4 per share at the end of each period; Security B, whose market price is expected to increase, pays $1. The current entry and exit prices (which differ because of a brokerage commission) over a three-year period are as follows:

	End of Period			
	0	1	2	3
Security A:				
Current entry value	$10·00	$10·00	$10·00	$10·00
Current exit value	9·00	9·00	9·00	9·00
Security B:				
Current entry value	10·00	13·10	17·32	24·00
Current exit value	9·00	11·80	15·60	21·60

read it, argues for no further adjustment once current cost figures are arrived at essentially on the physical maintenance of capital argument as we document in (Edwards, Bell and Johnson, 1979, Chapter 13). We cannot accept that argument and believe that Current Income and its components as well as position statement data must be put into 'real' terms, adjusted by using a general consumer price index so that (1) ownership income can be measured in 'real' terms for any one period, (2) both entity and ownership incomes can be compared over time, and (3) perhaps most importantly of all, Current Income data between firms can be properly compared for a single period. Firm A and Firm B might report the same total Current Income for a period, but if there has been inflation and Firm A's Current Income is mostly Current Operating Income while Firm B's Current Income is heavily Holding Gains, with, say, Firm B having a larger total asset base, then Firm B's total Current *Real* Income would likely be smaller than Firm A's and certainly would be different from Firm A's except in rare circumstances.

Current value and the simple production case

If the investor invested his entire $10,000 in either A or B at the beginning of the first period, he would have acquired 1,000 shares in either case. Let us see how each of these investments would have fared over the three-year span (assuming any reinvestment in shares is made on the first day of the next period):

	Security A Period			Security B Period		
	1	2	3	1	2	3
Investment at beginning of period (cash and cash-equivalents committed)	$10,000	$12,000	$15,900	$10,000	$11,800	$15,600
Number of shares held	(1,000)	(1,300)	(1,720)	(1,000)	(1,000)	(1,000)
Dividends received	$4,000	$5,200	$6,880	$1,000	$1,000	$1,000
Dividends withdrawn	1,000	1,000	1,000	1,000	1,000	1,000
Dividends reinvested	$3,000	$4,200	$5,880	–o–	–o–	–o–
Investment at end of period (cash and cash-equivalents committed)	$12,000	$15,900	$21,360	$11,800	$15,600	$21,600
Change in current exit value of investment	+$2,000	+$3,900	+$5,460	+$1,800	+$3,800	+$6,000

Clearly, the investor would have been better off with Security A in each of the first two periods; however, over the three periods as a whole, he would have fared better with Security B. What is more, even if he had switched from Security A to Security B between the second and third periods, he still would not have fared as well as if he had been in B all along. (This is because he would have had only $15,900 with which to purchase Security B, enough for only 918 shares at a purchase price of $17·32 apiece; by buying Security B at the outset, he would have had 1,000 shares). Thus, attempting to maximize changes in current exit values in each period will not necessarily result in maximization of exit values for all the periods taken together.

APPENDIX B
On the notion of 'Economic Income' as a viable and meaningful goal for accounting: comments on Revsine's and Ronen's approaches

The writer who perhaps tries the hardest (though we think unsuccessfully) to link 'Current Income' (change in market value) with what he calls 'Economic Income' and thus make the latter concept relevant for accounting is Lawrence Revsine (1973, Chapters 4 and 6). He defines 'Economic Income' as rV_i, where r is defined as 'the market rate of return,' (pp. 97, 101), later indicating that this is the 'cost of capital' (p. 106). V_i is the present value of future expected earnings discounted using r. In a perfectly competitive frictionless economy, he then argues, ρ, the internal rate of return on the asset of the firm, will always equal r, and C_i (the market value of the asset) will always adjust to equal V_i. Not surprisingly, then, with appropriate internal rate depreciation such as we employ, 'Current Income' will always equal iV_i, his 'Economic Income.' Where $V_i \neq C_i$ because of cost or revenue differences among firms in an imperfectly competitive economy and/or cost of capital differences among firms, the equality between 'Current Income' and 'Economic Income' is only 'an approximation' (p. 107). Revsine's objective in this exercise is to try to link 'Current Income' with expected future earnings, which are based on forecasting the future. If Current Income rises, he argues, it 'may' be a reflection of an increase in expected future earnings and a rise in Economic Income, hence, have 'predictive significance to investors' (p. 117). It may reflect this, or it may not. A rise in an asset's market value, hence, increase in Current Income, may simply reflect the market becoming aware of the potential of the asset that only our firm foresaw initially—a squeezing out of excess profits. Indeed, Traditional Accounting Income, in our case, better reflects the unchanged expectations of future earnings on our asset than Current Income in 19X1. The case for Current Income over Traditional Accounting Income relies on its greater effectiveness in evaluating past performance, not on its greater effectiveness in predicting the future.

A prolific and ardent proponent of the discounted cash flows approach and Economic Income, and their use in the development of accounting data, is Joshua Ronen. We are not entirely sure that we understand all of Ronen's various and sundry publications on the subject, but consider his contributions to Volume II of the *Trueblood Report, op. cit.* Ronen seems, first, not to understand Edwards and Bell (1961). He identifies (Ronen, 1974a, p. 143n) their concept of 'Business Profit' (equals what we here call Current Income which is clearly $M'_1 - M_0$ as depicted in the text) with Hicks' 'Economic Income' ($V_1 - V_0$ or $V'_1 - V_0$). (A number of writers have taken to calling $M'_1 - M_0$ 'Economic Income,' which we think is unfortunate.) But Ronen is definitely trying to deal with true 'Economic Income,' i.e., with ex ante discounted future cash flows in period o and ex ante and ex post discounted future cash flows in period 1. In (Ronen, 1974b), he attempts to establish $V_1 - V_0$ by investigating a firm which has made future cash flow estimates, *annually*, i.e., each *successive* year, for 1971, 1972, 1973 and 1974. He takes these annual (i.e., updated) forecasts for 1972, 1973 and 1974, adds the exit value of all assets for the end of 1974 as a 'surrogate' for future cash flows beyond that date, and, in effect, calls it V_1. He does the same thing for these annual forecasts for 1971, 1972 and 1973, and adds the exit value of all assets for the end of 1973 as a 'surrogate' to obtain what he in effect calls V_0. Since these annual forecasts have been updated each year, based on whatever new information the firm had at the time, it is difficult to see how these can be thought of as V_0 and V_1 values (aside from the difficulties of using exit values at the end of the three-year period as a 'surrogate' for future cash flows thereafter). Clearly, they are *not* the view of the future as seen by the firm in period o (1970).

Be that as it may, Ronen (1974b, pp. 211–12) then says, in his only referral to ex post considerations, 'Such cash flow estimates should reflect management's expectations to be validated and assessed as a result of comparison with actual cash flows.' Go through the above exercise, compare these expected future cash flows with actual cash flows, and you 'have it'! What do you have? At the *end* of the three-year Ronen planning period, 1971 to 1973, we could obtain V_0, V_1, V_2 by discounting future cash flows expected *at the beginning of each successive year* (X_{1e}, X_{2e}, X_{3e}, and the exit value of assets at the end of 1973, EV_3), and we could compute the actual value of cash flows in 1971, X_{1a}. But all we then have is:

$$V_0 = \frac{X_{1e}}{1+i} + \frac{X_{2e}}{(1+i)^2} + \frac{X_{3e}}{(1+i)^3} + \frac{EV_3}{(1+i)^3};$$

$$V_1' = X_{1a} + \frac{X_{2e}}{(1+i)} + \frac{X_{3e}}{(1+i)^2} + \frac{EV_3}{(1+i)^2}.$$

We have $X_{1a} - X_{1e}$ but since the rest involves *future* expected cash flows, forecasted annually, since one cannot even arrive at all of these until 1973, *and* since there is no allowance for any change in expectations along the way, it is hard to see that (Ronen, 1974b) involves anything more than a simple, one-period statement comparing expected and annual cash flows—which, following his elaborate framework, one could not arrive at until the *end* of the three-year planning period, not quite meeting the needs for producing accounting reports in a 'timely manner.' There is simply no way, in our view, that an ex post discounted cash flows statement can be objectively determined and made useful in the fashioning of accounting reports purportedly explaining present and past economic events.

APPENDIX C

Allocation problems when there are aggregation difficulties and/or no used asset market exists: further discussion of Thomas' analyses

Professor Arthur L. Thomas (1969, 1974) has developed extensive, careful, and rigorous arguments as to why any scheme for allocating an unexpired cost among periods (either in historical cost or current cost terms) has serious shortcomings. We have great respect for Professor Thomas, but we do not see that allocation of revenues between periods offers any substantive difficulties just because revenue in one period may depend on a build-up of quality of service in a previous period or on the presumption that service will continue in a future period. The revenue of a period is the revenue of the period, and if it is higher in the second period because lower prices to build a market were charged in the first period, so be it. There does not seem to us to be any reason to consider allocating part of the second period's revenues to the first period simply because one reduced first-period revenues to enhance second-period revenues. Allocating costs between periods does offer more difficulties, although Professor Thomas seems to agree with us that there are fewer difficulties if market value depreciation is applied as we do here. There is no need, then, to allocate costs to particular revenues. We are left only with the Objective Goodwill problem, when the value of a group of assets (as when a firm is bought out) exceeds the value of the assets considered separately. As Edwards and Bell (1961, p. 45*n*) once wrote, 'In general, however, the market for goodwill is a slumbering one, awakening only occasionally when *bona fide* offers for the firm as a whole (or major part of it) are made.' One may not even understand the source of Objective Goodwill—why one paid more for the firm than the sum of the value of the individual assets. Hence, one may have no idea over what period Objective Goodwill should be amortized if at all. We see nothing to do but to use internal rate depreciation in such cases, computing an internal rate of return for the Objective Goodwill on the basis of earnings of the firm as a whole minus earnings if the assets had been acquired separately and applying that rate to the beginning-of-the-period value of Objective Goodwill to get income which, when subtracted from the differential earnings pattern, will yield amortization.

Suppose, for example, we had bought out another cab company with a fleet of twenty new Dodges for $110,000 rather than acquire the Dodges separately for $100,000. Suppose our expected earnings pattern was now $77,000 and $66,000 over 19X1 and 19X2, rather than $70,000 and $60,000. Solving for ρ, the internal rate of return,

$$\text{Objective Goodwill } \$110,000 - \$100,000 = \$10,000 =$$

$$\frac{(\$77,000 - \$70,000)}{\$7,000} + \frac{(\$66,000 - \$60,000)}{\$6,000}, \text{ and } \rho = 20\%$$
$$\frac{\$7,000}{1 + \rho} + \frac{\$6,000}{(1 + \rho)^2}$$

(Note that we do not have to assume that the life of Objective Goodwill is the same as the life of physical assets if we have some real reason to believe that the two lives differ; the difference might be as shown plus $2,000 in 19X3.) The *assumed* income derived from Objective Goodwill in 19X1 is $2,000 (20 per cent of $10,000), and the amount to be amortized is Earnings minus Income = $5,000. And *assumed* income derived from Objective Goodwill in 19X2 is $1,000 (20 per cent times the remaining value of $5,000), and Earnings minus Income = $5,000. This is *not* very satisfactory, but better than nothing we feel, where no active market with currently active bid and ask prices exists at all for that which has to be amortized. If the market's assumption about the *pattern* of earnings (but not necessarily of ρ) is the same as the firm's, internal rate amortization *should* give you an approximation of what market value would be if an active market existed. Professor Thomas argues that 'elementary business experience assures us that (barring manipulation) uniform annual profitability is most unlikely.' Surely true in practice, but in theory used assets should not yield, say, greater rates of return than new assets because everyone would prefer and buy used assets. If our actual earnings pattern diverges from our expected, we must re-fashion our internal rate depreciation pattern period-by-period, ending with a residual.

We recognize and concede the difficulties of allocation where no active market exists for an asset, such as might be the case of Objective Goodwill. As argued in (Edwards and Bell), 'though theoretically (the steps followed in depreciation) are necessary only for historical cost' (p. 171), 'markets for many used assets are at best sporadic in nature' (p. 77). Hence, when out of our idyllic 'Blue Book'/taxi world, some depreciation method is essential based on the, perhaps estimated, current purchase price of a comparable new fixed asset. Unlike Arthur Thomas, we believe that we simply cannot get along without some estimate of 'accomplishment' each period, imperfect as that estimate may be in some cases, and so opt for imperfection in those cases where we cannot be precisely accurate.

REFERENCES

American Accounting Association, *A Statement of Basic Accounting Theory* (1966).

Anthony, R. N., 'Let's Account for Interest,' *Proceedings of the American Accounting Association* (1975), pp. 268–71.

Baxter, W. T., 'The Sandilands Report,' *Journal of Business Finance and Accounting* (1976), p. 120.

Bell, P. W., 'On Optimizing Inventory Gains and Losses In the Face of Price Changes,' *Proceedings of the American Accounting Association* (1975), pp. 435–51.

Edwards, E. O. and Bell, P. W., *The Theory and Measurement of Business Income* (California, 1961).

Edwards, E. O., Bell, P. W. and Johnson, L. T., *Accounting for Economic Events* (Scholars Book Company, 1979).

Gilman, S., *Accounting Concepts of Profit* (Roland Press, 1939).

Gynther, R. S., *Accounting for Price-Level Changes—Theory and Procedures* (Oxford University Press, 1966).

Hicks, J. R., *Value and Capital*, 2nd ed. (Oxford University Press, 1946).

Inflation Accounting Committee, *Inflation Accounting* (HMSO, Cmd. 6225, 1975).

Parker, R. H. and Harcourt, G. C. (eds.), *Readings in the Concept and Measurement of Income* (Cambridge University Press, 1969).

Revsine, L., *Replacement Cost Accounting* (Prentice-Hall, 1973).

Ronen, J., 'Discounted Cash Flow Accounting,' in J. J. Cramer, Jr., and G. H. Sorter (eds.), *Objectives of Financial Statements* (American Institute of Certified Public Accountants, 1974a), pp. 143–60.

Ronen, J., 'A Test of the Feasibility of Preparing Discounted Cash Flow Accounting Statements,' in J. J. Cramer, Jr., and G. H. Sorter (eds.), *Objectives of Financial Statements* (American Institute of Certified Public Accountants, 1974b), pp. 202–12.

Solomons, D., 'Economic and Accounting Concepts of Cost and Value,' in M. Backer (ed.), *Modern Accounting Theory* (Prentice-Hall, 1966).

Staubus, G., 'Current Cash Equivalent for Assets: A Dissent,' THE ACCOUNTING REVIEW (October 1967), pp. 650–71.

Staubus, G., 'The Relevance of Evidence of Cash Flows,' in R. Sterling (ed.), *Asset Valuation and Income Determination* (Scholars Book Co., 1971).

Study Group on the Objectives of Financial Statements, *Objectives of Financial Statements* (American Institute of Certified Public Accountants, 1973).

Thomas, A. L., 'The Allocation Problem in Financial Accounting Theory,' *Studies in Accounting Research No. 3* (American Accounting Association, 1969).

Thomas, A. L., 'The Allocation Problem: Part Two,' *Studies in Accounting Research No. 9* (American Accounting Association, 1974).

18 Why use general purchasing power?

by Reg S. Gynther*

This paper is really the third in a series. The first paper[1] examined behavioural factors which underlie different perceptions of the firm and of the way in which accounting for the firm should be carried out. The second paper[2] showed how these different perceptions of the firm are closely related to different perceptions of the capital that should be maintained intact before profit can emerge when accounting for changing prices. The second paper went on to demonstrate that accounting for the effects of changing prices is more directly concerned with capital maintenance than with periodic asset valuations and short-term profit determinations. In order to prevent confusion, it also urged that discussions in this area should be careful to distinguish between capital maintenance concepts and methods on the one hand, and asset valuation concepts and methods (and their related profit determination ideas) on the other. The various combinations of capital maintenance concepts and asset valuation methods were displayed in a matrix.[3]

The purpose of this (third) paper is to analyse critically the different reasons given by those who want to use general purchasing power in their proposals for accounting and/or reporting reform—i.e., for asset valuation and/or capital maintenance. These reasons are classified under five headings and are examined in turn. Some of the arguments used here by this writer are scattered throughout his book in this area,[4] and in some related papers.[5] These arguments are now drawn together, and it is hoped, made clearer. New arguments are added, and some support is drawn from some of the other people who have criticized the advocated

---

* Emeritus Professor, University of Queensland.

[1] Reg S. Gynther, 'Accounting Concepts and Behavioural Hypotheses', *Accounting Review*, April, 1967, pp. 274–290.

[2] Reg S. Gynther, 'Capital Maintenance, Price Changes and Profit Determination', *Accounting Review*, October, 1970, pp. 712–730.

[3] Ibid., p. 720. A development of this matrix is included as Appendix 1 to this paper.

[4] Reg S. Gynther, *Accounting for Price-Level Changes: Theory and Procedures* (Oxford: Pergamon Press, 1966).

[5] For example: Reg S. Gynther, *Accounting for Price Changes—Theory and Practice* (Society Bulletin No. 5) (Melbourne: Australian Society of Accountants, 1968); and 'Accounting for Price-Level Changes—One General Index or Several Specific Indexes?', *Accountancy*, July 1962.

314

use of general purchasing power.[1] A clearer exposition of what this writer advocates in lieu of general purchasing power will have to be the subject of a fourth paper. Some indications are included below, but in the meantime anyone interested would obtain a fair idea from his book.[2]

At the outset it should be stated that none of this writer's arguments will be based on the practical problems that surround the actual construction of a general index (or an index of prices of consumer goods). That is, they will not be based on problems such as those of selecting the items to be included in the basket of commodities for the index, of choosing individual prices, and of deciding on the weighting to be given to each item.[3] An attempt will be made to adhere to conceptual matters.

I. A 'UNIT OF MEASUREMENT'

Many advocates of accounting reform in times of rising prices argue for the incorporation of changes in general purchasing power into accounting and reporting processes in order to provide a 'unit of measurement'. Moonitz is one of these advocates. He recently wrote:

What we are searching for is either a type of money which is constant in its power to command other goods and services (and that type has never appeared) or a method which enables us to measure the *different* exchange-values of money, at different points in time, and therefore to restate them in terms of a single unit of constant exchange value. The latter cannot be done directly—there is no market-place for dollars of different dates (and purchasing-powers). It can be done indirectly, provided we have a measure of the things money can buy at different points of time. This measure is present in an index of prices in general, and the more general the better.[4]

In all fairness, the reasoning that underlies statements like this should be presented here, and this can be done best by someone who believes in what he is saying. We therefore quote again from Moonitz:

Among other matters, measurement theory concerns itself with different 'scales' of measurement and their inter-relationship. To measure the length of an object, for

---

[1] For example: R. L. Mathews, 'Price-Level Changes and Useless Information', *Journal of Accounting Research*, Spring, 1965, pp. 133–155.

   L. S. Rosen, *Current Value Accounting and Price-Level Restatements* (Toronto: The Canadian Institute of Chartered Accountants, 1972), especially Chapter 4.

   John B. Ryan, 'Baying the Moon: Myth of Purchasing Power as a Constant Unit of Measure', *The Australian Accountant*, November, 1972, pp. 383–388.

[2] Op cit.

[3] *If* it were conceptually correct to use a general type index (or some other index) for accounting reform, accountants would need to press, in the construction of the index, for those improvements that they perceived to be necessary. In the meantime, the use of the existing index would, most likely, result in much better information than would be the case if they used no index at all.

[4] Maurice Moonitz, 'Price-Level Accounting and Scales of Measurement', *Accounting Review*, July, 1970, p. 469.

example, we need a scale based upon a unit such as a metre or a foot. If the length is 10 metres, the same identical length may also be expressed in terms of a different unit, and the result expressed as 33 feet (approximately). To measure the weight of an object, we need a scale based upon a unit such as kilogram or a pound. A weight of 10 kilograms for a given object is identical with a result of 22 pounds (approximately). The attribute 'length' or the attribute 'weight' may be expressed in one unit or in another. Once expressed, the result may be transformed from one unit to the other. But the difference in the numerals has no significance ...

A similar result follows in price-level accounting where we are trying to measure the change in the 'exchange-value of money', the change in the unit employed in accounting to measure the power of money to command goods and services in the market. ... For example, a rise in an index of general purchasing-power from 100 to 200 is interpreted as a reduction in the exchange-value of money by one-half. The dollar in its function as the unit used in our scale of measurement has shrunk by 50 per cent.

A balance sheet restated for this effect, and for this effect alone presents a restatement (transformation) of the underlying financial data from one unit of measurement to another; for example, from the 'dollar at end-of-year 1965' to the 'dollar at end-of-year 1970'. But this restatement from one unit to another does not reflect any change at all in the attribute measured. The difference between the two numerals, e.g., 'total assets in terms of dollars at end-of-year 1965' versus the same total in terms of 'dollars at end-of-year 1970' has no significance, any more than the difference between metres and feet or between kilos and pounds had any significance in the earlier examples.[1]

Similar 'unit of measurement' statements have been made by The Research Foundation of The Institute of Chartered Accountants in England and Wales,[2] the Accounting Principles Board of the American Institute of Certified Public Accountants,[3] Chambers,[4] Stamp,[5] Heath[6] and others.

However, this implicit assumption that we can obtain a standard 'unit of measurement' based on general purchasing power does not stand up to critical analysis. It might be *physically possible* to calculate a general index in any country, but it would have no real meaning to any one entity (e.g., person, firm, company, etc.). For example, at any point

---

[1] Ibid., pp. 465–466.

[2] *Accounting for Stewardship in a Period of Inflation* (London: The Research Foundation of The Institute of Chartered Accountants in England and Wales, 1968), pp. 5–8.

[3] *Financial Statements Restated for General Price-Level Changes* (Statement No. 3 of the Accounting Principles Board) (New York: The American Institute of Certified Public Accountants, June, 1969), p. 3.

[4] Raymond J. Chambers, *Accounting Evaluation and Economic Behavior* (Englewood Cliffs, New Jersey: Prentice-Hall, Inc., 1966), pp. 93–96; and his 'Measurement in Accounting', *Journal of Accounting Research*, Spring, 1965, pp. 32–62.

[5] Edward Stamp, 'Income and Value Determination and Changing Price-Levels: An Essay Towards a Theory', *The Accountant's Magazine*, June, 1971, pp. 277–292.

[6] Loyd C. Heath, 'Distinguishing Between Monetary and Nonmonetary Assets and Liabilities in General Price-Level Accounting', *Accounting Review*, July, 1972, pp. 458–468.

of time the USA dollar does *not* mean the same thing to the many managers of entities in the USA, and the pound sterling does *not* mean the same thing to the managers of entities in Great Britain. People in those countries do not *see* themselves holding 'general purchasing power' when they have money in their pockets; they *see* themselves holding specific purchasing power for those relatively few things (out of a huge range of available goods and services) that they are likely to buy.

On the other hand, these same people do know exactly what standard measures like metres or kilograms represent. If they don't, they *can* obtain standard rulers and weights to give them the exact meaning. The precision of their metre rulers can be checked in Paris by comparing them with the distance between two microscopic lines on a specific bar of platinum-iridium kept under specific physical conditions—i.e., as a standard measurement of length called a 'metre'.

But nobody in the USA, for example, would ever know what was meant by a measure called 'a dollar of general purchasing power' even if one were decreed to exist. A dollar 'of general purchasing power' can never be a standard unit of measurement alongside metres and kilograms, etc.

Dollars serve merely as a convenient means of exchange but money values and market prices reflect individual subjective valuations.[1]

It is no use saying that any entity *could* purchase any item of goods anywhere in the USA. They don't and won't. It is also no use saying that the USA dollar *should* mean the same thing to each and every entity in the USA; the fact is, it doesn't and it never will. *Further, the meaning of a dollar to each entity changes in different ways through time.* On the other hand, unless the standards are changed by decree, the metre and kilogram will always mean the same thing to every entity in the USA (and elsewhere too).

Even within an overall average condition of zero inflation in a country, prices of many different commodities would be changing (some significantly) in different directions and at different rates. These changes would be affecting different entities in different ways. A perfect price index is purely a personal concept and is applicable only to one entity. Thus, changes in wealth, when prices of commodities change in a non-proportional manner (and this is the way they *always* change), are purely personal measurements. As Sterling says about this matter, 'Any attempt to generalize is prone to a wide margin of error'.[2] (This writer argues that we

---

[1] A. A. Alchian and W. R. Allen, *University Economics* (Belmont Wadsworth Publishing Co. Inc. 1964), p. 248.

[2] Robert R. Sterling, *Theory of the Measurement of Enterprise Income* (Lawrence: The University Press of Kansas, 1970), p. 338.

do not have to worry about calculating an index for each entity in order to get the correct theoretical results. We merely need to account for individual, specific changes in those prices that concern each entity. This procedure is easier and more accurate in practice—and it is being practised.)

In support of his 'unit of measurement' statements (above) Moonitz said this:

A sum of US $1,000 will buy $1,000 of clothes, shoes, coal, limestone, oil, hammers, saws, advertising space, etc., in any combination we choose, provided the total does not, of course, exceed $1,000. Furthermore, this power to buy goods and services is available in New York or Chicago, San Francisco or Fargo, and it makes no difference who holds the $1,000, where they got it, how they got it, or what they intended, at some time in the past, to do with the money. Money is *generalized* purchasing-power.[1]

This is not correct. The power to buy those goods varies from city to city in the USA, just as the purchasing power of a sum of money will vary from city to city in almost any country. (In some places, prices of identical commodities even vary significantly between working-class suburbs and top executive suburbs in the one city). The following USA Labor Department figures taken from the *Wall Street Journal* of March 17, 1969 substantiate this point.[2] They show 'how much it costs an urban family of four to live' in 1967 'for three different standards of living':

Metropolitan Area	Lower Budget $	Moderate Budget $	Higher Budget $
Total USA (*the 'general average'*)	5915	9076	13050
Boston	6251	9973	14568
New York	6021	9977	14868
Philadelphia	5898	9079	13131
Pittsburgh	5841	8764	12551
Chicago	6104	9334	13325
Cleveland	5915	9262	12997
Detroit	5873	8981	12911
Minn-St. Paul	6058	9399	13348
St. Louis	6002	9140	12813
Atlanta	5597	8328	11846
Dallas	5607	8345	12157
Washington DC	6133	9273	13419
San Francisco	6571	9774	14079
Denver	5905	9080	13011
Los Angeles	6305	9326	13645

[1] Op. cit., pp. 469–470.
[2] 'Government Gears Index of Family Costs to Three Separate Standards of Living'. No doubt later figures are available.

318

The 'purchasing power' of the dollar *does* vary from place to place, and significantly so in some cases. It is *not* 'generalized'. The purchasing power of the dollar is even different for two people living side by side and for two companies trading side by side in New York City. They have different spending patterns.

Professor Chambers bases his 'unit of measurement' ideas on invalid assumptions similar to those of Professor Moonitz. He states:

> From the viewpoint of the market, a given sum of money has the same significance no matter who tenders it or who receives it. Its significance subsists in the fact that it *can* be offered in exchange for *any* collection of goods desired by any holder up to the amount he holds; it represents command over marketed goods and services generally, or general purchasing power.[1]

The 'market' does not have a viewpoint. The individual managers of entities operating in the market have viewpoints and these differ one from the other depending on their individual needs, value systems, etc.—in the way already mentioned above. Further, it is no use stating that a given sum of money 'can' be offered in exchange for 'any' collection of goods when individuals in the real world do not in fact have this sort of ability. They all have horizons beyond which they cannot see (nor do many want to). But Professor Chambers actually says (above), 'any collection of goods *desired by any holder up to the amount [of money]* he holds'. The goods 'desired by any holder' limits the range of goods for each individual to a considerable degree—and to a different degree in each case. The result is not '*general* purchasing power' but '*individual* purchasing power'. This seems to be admitted by Professor Chambers for in the very next paragraph of his book he goes on to say:

> Men seek to have stocks of money adequate to meet *their* daily demands for goods, as a precaution against unforseen events, including the possibility of taking advantage of relative changes in prices of the kinds of goods *they* want.[2]

As no unit of measurement based on general purchasing power can exist at a point of time and through time with common meaning to all people, it would be sheer fantasy to decree that an overall unit of measurement *does* exist, i.e., in the way that metres and kilograms exist as common, standard, observable units of measurement. We would have a tremendous problem solved if we really did have a standard unit of measurement for accounting, but we don't.

It would be terribly wrong to prescribe a model of accounting based on the fiction that general purchasing power constitutes a 'standard unit of measurement'. 'Standard units of measurement' are precise things

---

[1] Op. cit., p. 70. Emphasis added. [2] Ibid. Emphasis added.

that can be checked by all (like the measure of a metre in Paris). An examination of the way various specific indexes fluctuate widely around their average movement shows that general purchasing power can not even *approximate* a 'standard unit of measurement' to many or most entities. Any attempt to improve conventional accounting by an additional invalid convention can only result in accounting getting further away from reality.

2. 'ACCOUNTING FOR INFLATION' AND 'ACCOUNTING FOR THE CHANGING VALUE OF MONEY'

Much of what was said in the previous section could be said here too (but it won't be). This section is included because several people have argued that we should be 'accounting for inflation' or 'accounting for the changing value of money' without actually mentioning anything about 'a unit of measurement'. Exposure Draft ED8 issued on the 17 January, 1973, by the Accounting Standards Steering Committee[1] is typical. In paragraph 8 we are told that 'the method proposed in this Statement shows the effects on annual accounts of *inflation*'; and in paragraph 10 we are told the purpose of the Statement is 'to measure *changes in the value of money*'.[2]

Maybe the 'unit of measurement' arguments are just sophisticated extensions of the accounting 'for inflation' and 'for the changing value of money' arguments. The first quotation from Professor Moonitz on page 315 above suggests this.

Although there are various economic theories about pure inflation being caused by increases in the overall supply of money, about demand-pull inflation, and about cost-push inflation, etc., the term 'inflation' has come to be used in direct association with increases in the Consumer Price Index and similar indexes. These indexes are averages based on many sorts of prices, and these prices change for a variety of reasons. Who is to say just why individual prices relevant to individual entities vary widely around some general index average?

Advocates of accounting 'for inflation' and 'for the changing value of money' argue for the use of one general purchasing power index (usually the reciprocal of the value of money or a surrogate thereof) in their accounting reform methods. But how can we account 'for inflation' using just

---

[1] Accounting Standards Steering Committee, *Proposed Statement of Standard Accounting Practice—Accounting for Changes in the Purchasing Power of Money* (Exposure Draft ED8) (London: The Institute of Chartered Accountants in England and Wales, 17 January, 1973).
[2] Ibid.

one price index series when inflation affects every entity in a different way? And how can we use just one index to account for *the* 'changing value of money' when money means something different to every entity, especially through time. We can speak of the changing value of money from a national viewpoint, but not from an individual entity viewpoint.

If we are to measure changes in *the value of money* by examining changes in the prices of particular goods and services, we have to choose the goods and services and the weight which we shall attach to each. It is clear, therefore, that the conclusions which we draw as to movements in the purchasing power of money depend on the choice of data. The importance of a given index number may be quite different to different individuals. To a poor man a rise in the index number due to a rise in the price of tea and sugar is probably much more important than it would be to a rich man, while a rise in the number due to the price of Rolls-Royce cars means nothing to the poor man. *Can an index be framed which will give the right significance to all commodities for all people? Clearly not—the importance of price changes depends on how you spend your money.*[1]

The meaningfulness of any index varies inversely with the degree of deviation from the assumed pattern of purchases. The pattern is unlikely to fit *any* particular person perfectly, *and it may vary widely.* The consumer price index includes meat and milk which have little relevance to a vegetarian or to a playboy who consumes wine, women, and song.[2]

This discussion is not merely highlighting a practical difficulty in constructing a suitable general index series to show the effects of 'inflation' on the 'purchasing power of money'. It has been demonstrated that no matter how carefully we go about this task the result will not depict the effects of price changes as they affect *any one entity* in a nation. As the Assistant Government Statistician for New Zealand said in 1969:

The New Zealand Consumers' Price Index, for example, is based on the average consumption expenditure pattern for all persons living in urban households whose composition is broadly 'family' in nature. The CPI does not claim to measure the changing relative level of consumer prices paid by, say, a merchant seaman.

Before using an official or ad hoc price index for price level accounting, therefore, the first question that needs to be answered is: is the index appropriate for the proposed application, . . .?[3]

This question gets to the crux of the matter. What are we trying to do with these accounting reports? What is the objective of the whole exercise? Surely it isn't merely to 'account for inflation' or to 'account for the changing value of money'. Surely we should be trying to account

---

[1] Ronald S. Edwards, 'The Nature and Measurement of Income' in W. T. Baxter (ed.), *Studies in Accounting* (Sydney: Law Book Co. of Australasia Pty Ltd., 1950), p. 243. Emphasis added.

[2] Robert R. Sterling, op. cit., p. 339. Emphasis added.

[3] Stephen Kuzmicich, 'An Economic Statistician's Background Comments on Changing Price Levels', an unpublished paper presented at the Victoria University of Wellington, NZ., 1969, p. 6.

321

for entities of all kinds (people, firms, companies, organizations, etc.) and their specific and different price changes in order to assist them and their shareholders, etc. with their individual planning, decision-making, and control problems. We must face up to the fact that 'inflation' affects them all differently, and that the overall use by all entities of one general-type index will *not* assist for these purposes.[1] (More will be said about this later in this paper.)

3. 'THE STANDARD OF COMPARISON OF RESOURCES (ASSETS)'

The notion of a 'standard of comparison' is very similar to that of a 'unit of measurement' (already discussed above). With one, the emphasis is on 'measuring'; it is on 'comparing' with the other. It is included here as a third reason for using general purchasing power in accounting reform because it introduces this new objective of using general purchasing power adjustments to 'make *comparisons of resources*'. In a recent paper Mr Rosenfield of the staff of the Accounting Research Division of the American Institute of Certified Public Accountants argued for this 'standard of comparison' for the purpose of comparing resources. He wrote:

General price-level restatement addresses the question of *the standard* that should be used in accounting *to compare diverse resources*. ... Individuals or enterprises often wish to *compare collections of resources* ... Money is used as the *standard of comparison* in more specialized economies ... Money is used as the standard because it is accepted widely in exchange for other resources and can therefore be readily related to them. But money has a defect that makes it less than ideal as a standard: the general purchasing power of money—its command over goods and services in general—is notoriously fickle. An increase in money may not indicate an increase in general purchasing power. General purchasing power itself is a resource that is widely prized. ...*A unit of general purchasing power may be devised* ... *and collections of diverse resources may be compared on their relationships to that standard*.

General price-level restatement is the accounting process of *changing the standard used to compare diverse resources from units of money to units of general purchasing power*. ...

General price-level restatement does not change the relationship emphasized between resources and the standard of comparison. For example, a balance sheet prepared under present GAAP [generally accepted accounting principles] emphasizes historical cost. After general price-level restatement of that balance sheet, the relationship emphasized is still historical cost, although *the standard* has been changed from units of money to units of general purchasing power.'[2]

---

[1] At this point it might be necessary to remind some readers that any general index constructed would be an *average* of all the specific price changes in the community in question. The overall, general price movements and the individual specific price movements are related; they are not separate and unrelated things.

[2] Paul Rosenfield, 'The Confusion Between General Price-Level Restatement and Current Value Accounting', *The Journal of Accountancy*, October 1972, pp. 65–66. Emphasis added.

First of all, it is necessary to point out some invalid assumptions adopted by Rosenfield. He says that money is used as a 'standard.' It is not. It is used as a means of exchange. It is not a common 'standard' to the people who use it. As has been pointed out above, it means something different from person to person. Further, even if we were to calculate a 'unit of general purchasing power', it, too, would not be a 'standard'. It would not be meaningful to any one person and therefore could not be a 'standard', i.e., in the way that 'metre' and 'kilogram' are standards.

Secondly, *general* purchasing power is *not* 'widely prized'. Nobody can feel or understand *general* purchasing power. *Specific* individual purchasing power might be prized in many cases. If there were a change tomorrow in a calculation of 'general purchasing power', caused solely by changes in prices of tobacco products, it would not affect the specific purchasing power that this writer prizes because he does not smoke.

Now let us examine this matter of comparisons *of resources*. The whole Rosenfield paper is built on his statement.

Individuals or enterprises often wish to compare collections of resources. For example, a person may wish to compare his present stock of resources with his stock a year previous or with his anticipated stock a year hence. Or, he may wish to compare his resources with the resources of others.[1]

This mentions two kinds of comparisons: (a) inter-period comparisons for the one entity, and (b) comparisons between entities in the same period. The use of general purchasing power is not suitable for either purpose.

(a) Inter-period comparisons of resources for the one entity

Rosenfield is not alone in suggesting that the restatement of resources in accordance with changes in general purchasing power will enable meaningful inter-period comparisons to be made. The Research Foundation of The Institute of Chartered Accountants in England and Wales, for example, said this:

Over a period of years even a gradual fall in the value of money, will, if progressive, have significant consequences. Unless these are quantified, *comparisons of results and net assets for a number of years* fail to indicate to investors the real growth (or lack of it) in the business, and management remains ill-informed, if not uninformed, of the extent to which their policies have procured benefits or the reverse from the general effect of inflation as distinct from the circumstances inherent in the particular business or trade.[2]

No evidence was supplied to support this statement. It is believed that no evidence could be supplied to prove that such figures would 'indicate real growth'.

---

[1] Ibid., p. 65.

[2] *Accounting for Stewardship in a Period of Inflation*, op. cit., p. 6. Emphasis added.

R. S. Gynther

The authors of Accounting Research Study No. 6[1] used the following example to support the use of a general index to facilitate the comparison of resources over time. Like Mathews,[2] this writer will use this same example to demonstrate that general index adjustments do nothing to assist such comparisons.

At three points of time three blocks of similar land (of 10, 15, and 5 acres—and in that order) were purchased for $10,000 each. At the time of each purchase the general price index stood at 100, 125, and 75 respectively. By time 4 it had risen to 200. In Table 1 the unadjusted and adjusted (to time 4 general purchasing power) costs are presented.

The authors of Accounting Research Study No. 6 went on to claim that the adjusted figures (see columns 5 and 8, Table 1) show 'the cost of each parcel of land in *proper* relation to the cost of others, that is, the adjusted amounts indicate *the relative sacrifice* which the purchaser made in acquiring each parcel.'[3] However, this writer (like Mathews) claims that the purchaser is not likely to be the least bit interested in comparing his 'relative sacrifices' expressed in this way. What would this tell him—and for what purposes? The purchaser would be interested in competently compiled estimates of the net present value of the land (from its intended uses—e.g., from long-term leases), and he would be interested in the land's current market price. These figures would be helpful for planning and decision making.

If, at time 4, the estimated net present value of the land is $3,500 per acre (total of $105,000 for the 30 acres), and the current market price is $3,000 per acre (total $90,000), the purchaser would be badly misled if he measured his 'sacrifice' in using or selling the different pieces of land by reference to the adjusted figures in columns 5 and 8 above. The general-index-adjusted cost of $5,333 per acre for the third purchase can only confuse him. The same applies to the other adjusted figures. They supply him with data (definitely not 'information') that is no more relevant for his decisions than the original historical costs of the land were. And how could comparisons of the net assets (of say a steel company) adjusted in this way by a general index 'indicate to investors the *real growth* (or lack of it) in the business', and how could such figures make management 'informed'—i.e., in the way claimed above by The Reserarch Foundation of The Institute of Chartered Accountants in England and

---

[1] The Staff of the Accounting Research Division, *Reporting the Financial Effects of Price-Level Changes* (Accounting Research Study No. 6). (New York: American Institute of Certified Public Accountants, 1963), pp. 25–28.

[2] Op. cit., pp. 144–146.

[3] *Reporting the Financial Effects of Price-Level Changes*, op. cit., p. 26. Emphasis added.

TABLE I.

Purchase	Historical cost	General index when bought	Multiplier to adjust to time 4's general index of 200	Historical cost adjusted to time 4's G.I. of 200	No. of acres	Cost per acre— in Year 4	
						Historical cost	Historical cost adjusted to G.I. of 200
1	2	3	4	5	6	7	8
	$			$		$	$
First	10,000	100	200/100	20,000	10	1,000	2,000
Second	10,000	125	200/125	16,000	15	667	1,067
Third	10,000	75	200/75	26,667	5	2,000	5,333
Totals	$30,000			$62,667	30	$1,000	$2,089

Wales?[1] In any case, how could the shareholders and management of a steel company obtain any worthwhile information from having the unallocated historical costs of its assets restated by a general index which included weights for price changes for items such as meat, bread, underwear, shoes, saws, etc.? And what sort of profit figures would inter-period comparisons of such figures produce for a steel company?

The authors of Accounting Research Study No. 6 tell us that these general-price-level adjustments enable us to compare *dollars* 'at different points of time'.[2] But once the dollars *are* invested in assets of some kind, why should our objective be to compare the general purchasing power of those *dollars*? It is meaningless to look upon stocks of resources (particularly as at past dates) as being stocks of generalized purchasing power (of *dollars*) when the purchasing power of the firm was *not* used for the purpose of buying all the goods and services included in the regime of the general purchasing power index. What does become meaningful is specific information relating to the *assets* that *were* purchased (with those dollars).

Those who want to make inter-period comparisons of resources can best do this by comparing the *specific values* of those assets that *were* actually purchased by companies. To do this the specific values as at past dates need to be expressed in present day prices—i.e. with the aid of *an index relevant to the person making the comparison* wherever he may be situated. Table 2 demonstrates how such comparisons can be made. (The estimated net present value and current market values of the land at time 4 in the above land example are used, and time 3 figures are now introduced for this purpose.)

The valid inter-period comparison is between the figures in lines 3 and 4, Table 2, i.e. between the restated specific values for year 3 and the specific values for year 4. The general index was merely used here as *a* means of expressing past *specific* values of *assets* in current prices. There is no useful purpose in comparing the *general* purchasing power of *dollars* invested in assets over time.

Before concluding this section it should be mentioned that valid inter-period comparisons of profit figures can be made only in a way similar to that indicated above. That is, profit for each entity must be determined taking into account the specific, individual values of the assets, depreciation, costs of goods sold, etc. of each entity—for the way it actually operated and was actually situated and deployed in the period concerned. Anyone wishing to make inter-period comparisons of an entity's profit

---

[1] *Accounting for Stewardship in a Period of Inflation*, op. cit., p. 6. Emphasis added.
[2] *Reporting the Financial Effects of Price-Level Changes*, op. cit., p. 24.

TABLE 2.

Item	Net present values		Current market prices	
	Per acre	Total for 30 acres	Per acre	Total for 30 acres
	$	$	$	$
1. Specific values as at Time 3	1,800	54,000	1,500	45,000
2. Multiplier (for a user who considers the General Index is relevant for him)	200/75	200/75	200/75	200/75
3. Time 3 specific values (in line '1' above) expressed in Year 4 prices (using the multiplier in line '2')	4,800	144,000	4,000	120,000
4. Specific values as at Time 4	3,500	105,000	3,000	90,000

figures (calculated in this way) would need to use some index, relevant to him, to express past profits in current terms. Incidentally, like several others, this writer has always claimed that inter-period comparisons can best be carried out by the use of ratios and percentages—and not by the use of absolute figures.[1]

(b) Comparisons of resources of different entities in the same period

This is the second of the two sorts of comparisons of resources that Rosenfield said (above) would be made possible by general purchasing power restatements. As these between-entity comparisons are invalid for reasons similar to those mentioned in the preceding paragraphs, they can be dealt with fairly quickly.

Suppose that on the same day in 1960 two parcels of land were purchased for £100,000 each by two different purchasers—one in Kent and the other in Yorkshire. In any subsequent year they would be shown by each purchaser at identical figures if they were left at their historical cost, or if they were restated using the general price index for England. Yet, in 1973, the land in Yorkshire could still be a remote semi-wilderness on a moor while the land in Kent could now be on the fringe of an expanding town. What could a comparison of the identical restated *pounds* invested in these two parcels of land tell anyone? Why would anyone 'wish' to make such a comparison—and for what rational purpose?

Before producing figures for people to make comparisons of resources, accountants need to know the objectives of such comparisons. However, whatever these objectives might be, this writer cannot think of any valid

---

[1] For example, Reg S. Gynther, *Accounting for Price-Level Changes: Theory and Procedures*, op. cit., pp. 204–206.

327

R. S. Gynther

reason for using unallocated historical costs adjusted by a general purchasing power index.

4. 'MAINTAINING THE GENERAL PURCHASING POWER OF SHAREHOLDERS' CAPITAL'

This is a fourth type of reason put forward by many who advocate the use of general purchasing power (in one way or another) in accounting and reporting reform. All of those who advocate using an index of general purchasing power for restating assets also advocate its use for restating shareholders' capital. Whether it is their main aim or not, they are advocating the maintenance of the general purchasing power of shareholders' capital—i.e., before profit can emerge.[1]

In addition to these there are many others who advocate using a general purchasing power index (e.g., a Consumer Price index) for the maintenance of shareholders' capital even though they use some other base for restating resources (assets). Edwards and Bell,[2] Chambers,[3] and the American Accounting Association[4] are typical of such reformers. They advocate the use of some other method for valuing assets. Any differences between the way in which their assets are revalued and the way in which shareholders' capital is restated (using the general-type index) are treated as holding gains and losses (or similar). (A chart showing many combinations of asset valuation methods and capital maintenance concepts forms Appendix 2 to this paper.[5]) For example, Chambers, who advocated the use of something akin to net realizable values for the valuing of assets, says:

> The maintenance of opening capital at the closing date will be effected if the measure of the opening residual equity is transformed by a general index of prices (i.e. of the purchasing power of money) to its equivalent in units of the dimension prevailing at the closing date.[6]
>
> Income shall be measured by reference to the maintenance of capital, as capital is measured in the new scale.[7]

---

1 For example see L. A. Wilk, *Accounting for Inflation* (London: Sweet & Maxwell Limited, 1960).
2 Edgar O. Edwards and Philip W. Bell, *The Theory and Measurement of Business Income* (Berkeley and Los Angeles: University of California Press, 1961).
3 Op. cit.
4 Committee to Prepare a Statement of Basic Accounting Theory, *A Statement of Basic Accounting Theory* (American Accounting Association, 1966) see example 2.2.
5 This chart first appeared in this approximate form in Reg S. Gynther's 'Accounting for Changing Prices: Some Recent Thinking, Recommendations and Practice', *The Chartered Accountant in Australia,* December, 1971, pp. 12–23.
6 'Measurement in Accounting', op. cit., p. 58.
7 *Accounting, Evaluation and Economic Behavior,* op. cit., p. 227.

Chambers, like the many others, definitely has the firm's shareholders in mind when he advocates using an index of consumers' goods (as his general index of prices) for the purposes of maintaining the purchasing power of shareholders' capital. As one of his two reasons he says:

The role of the firm in relation to its constituents (i.e., owners, shareholders) is to provide them with gains or incomes. Whether these incomes will be devoted to consumption or to further investment, we do not know; nor, indeed, do we know what the magnitudes of those incomes will be, for the constituents may choose not to withdraw in any year the whole of the increase in the firm's residual equity (i.e., after restatement by the C.P.I.). But insofar as any part of this increase withdrawn is to be devoted to consumption, a consumers' goods index is relevant; and insofar as any part is left in the firm or invested in other forms, the considerations of the first argument above make a consumers' goods index equally relevant.[1]

(His other argument was that 'all production and trading operations are geared to the final objective of making available consumers' goods'.)[2]

There are several reasons why a general-type price index should *not* be used for the restating of shareholders' capital (or 'residual equity') when prices are changing. For the first of these we can do no better than quote from Rosen. He says this in the recent study he completed for the Canadian Institute of Chartered Accountants:

A common argument given in favour of price-level restated reports is that financial reports eventually must account for the purchasing power of shareholders. The reasoning is that shareholders' investments are only 'temporary'; in time, the shareholder will receive cash for his investment, and spend the money on consumers' goods. Thus, a consumer price index should be used to restate historic costs (or capital)—at least, for those reports to be sent to shareholders. (As some institutions are large shareholders, other people argue similarly for the use of a general price-index that also includes weights for non-consumer goods.)

The weakness of this argument is that in those companies where there is a continual turnover of shareholders, the sum paid by the shareholder is unlikely to correspond with the sum recorded in the company's accounts (whether adjusted or not). Hence, for the objective noted it is pointless to account for the *original* investment in the company by restating all accounts for consumer purchasing power changes. The shareholder would be best advised to restate *his* investment for consumer purchasing power changes from the date he acquired the shares (i.e., in his *own* set of accounts). The restated sum could then be compared to the current market price of his shares if he wished to see whether or not he at least maintained general purchasing power.[3]

After all, it is from the market that he will receive the proceeds if he sells his shares; he will not receive these from the company.

But in any case, how can we use just one, overall, general index to maintain the capital of shareholders? As was pointed out earlier in this paper, every individual has a different spending pattern. Prices often vary

---

[1] Ibid., p. 229.   [2] Ibid.   [3] Rosen, op. cit., p. 67. Emphasis added.

329

significantly from city to city, and in any case, money means something different to each and every shareholder even if they are residing side by side in the same city. Further, many shareholders are large entities of various kinds; their 'consumption' patterns cover a wide range of items, very different in each individual case.

And for what geographical area is such a general index to be calculated? As Moonitz says, 'the assumption is made, *usually implicitly*, that we are concerned solely with a *domestic* currency and with changes in its exchange-value in the *domestic* economy'.[1] But what about the French shareholder who lives on the German border and who makes most of his purchases in Germany? And what do we do if all the shareholders in a company operating in England pack up and move to Argentina to live? Will this mean that we must now completely restate the shareholders' capital in accordance with movements in a general index for Argentina— i.e., even though the company still continues to operate in England? If the answer to this last question is 'yes', it will mean that the company would report different profits from the identical company next door that has all its shareholders residing in England! (Chambers and others are looking at shareholders as consumers; they can only consume where they reside.)

Further, what do we do in a case where most shareholders of a company are spread across most European countries, many are in Asia, and others are in the Americas? Do we calculate one overall general index (with weights for the different countries) to maintain the capital of the shareholders of such a company? If so, does this mean that we must recalculate this index each year as shares are sold from country to country (and thus changing the weights for each country)? If we follow this through to a logical conclusion we would end up calculating a general index for the whole world. After all, some people argue that money represents *general* purchasing power, and with the world 'shrinking' it is possible for an increasing number of people (maybe everyone) to use their money to purchase goods and services from all parts of the world. It is also evident that an increasing number of foreign shareholders are appearing in the share registers of companies in many countries.

In view of what has been said in the last few paragraphs, the ideal solution for those who want to 'maintain the purchasing power of shareholders' capital' in times of price changes (i.e. those who want profit to be determined only after such capital has been maintained) might be to prepare a separate set of financial statements for each and every shareholder. Only in this way could the individual value of money to each

[1]Moonitz, op. cit., p. 470. Emphasis added.

shareholder be taken into account when restating shareholders' capital. If we were to do this we could have a shareholder in Paris expecting a dividend from the profit reported to him, while a shareholder in Rio de Janeiro was lamenting the loss reported to him by the same company for the same period.

However, this writer is convinced that the ideal solution is a far more practical one.[1] It is one which has theoretical validity because of its realistic behavioural underpinnings, and it is the one which will meet the objectives of providing decision-making information to shareholders, managements and others. The ideal solution is for each entity to calculate its profit for a period after restating capital in accordance with individual movements in those specific prices which relate to the operating capacity it actually had for that period. Here 'capital' relates to the specific capital funds necessary to support the basic assets of the entity—i.e., in the form they were actually deployed during the period concerned. As these funds also include forms of long-term capital such as preference shares and debentures, profit for any period of rising prices cannot include any 'holding gains' on long-term debentures or on any other form of long-term capital. Nor can it include any of the Edwards-and-Bell-type gains (or losses) on holding non-monetary assets during periods of price changes.[2] It can be demonstrated that so-called gains of this nature can only be shed (as dividends) if the operating capacity is run down (e.g. by selling some of the basic assets) or if additional capital is raised—and that, therefore, they are not gains to the entity itself. (See Appendix 2 for such a demonstration.)

In our environment today, the roles of producing, distributing, servicing, financing, etc. are performed by entities, whether they be government departments, local government authorities, companies, partnerships, individuals, household units, clubs, associations, etc. Each shareholder or member or participant of any of these entities is a separate entity (e.g. an investing entity) in his own right. The focus is on the actions and performance of entities, and in order to evaluate the performances of each of these entities in what they are endeavouring to do, it is essential that we separate the performances of each entity from those of any member entities it may have (e.g., shareholders of a company).[3] If this separation is not made a misleading hybrid results.

[1] It has, for example, been employed by relatively small companies with which this writer is associated, and (except for some relatively small variations) by the (large) Philips Electrical group of companies on a world-wide basis for many years.

[2] Edwards and Bell, op. cit.

[3] This paragraph is adapted from a paper presented to the 18th Victoria University of Wellington (New Zealand) Advanced Accounting Seminar in August, 1969.

R. S. Gynther

In this writer's solution to the accounting-for-changing-prices problem, the focus is on each entity. Only in this way will both managers and shareholders obtain information which is relevant to their decisions about each entity. Instead of endeavouring to account for the shareholders *in* the books of the entity (i.e. by endeavouring to maintain the general purchasing power of shareholders' funds before arriving at company profits) the shareholders must do their own individual accounting (as separate entities) in their *own* books of account (at home or in their own offices, etc.). With profit calculated after maintaining capital funds needed to support the basic assets of each entity (after noting the relative specific price movements), each user of the resultant financial statements will be able to evaluate growth in each entity's profit, its resources, etc. To express past profit and asset figures in current prices for comparison purposes, each user can use the price index that he believes to be most relevant to him for this purpose—i.e., in the way outlined in Section 3 above. This is something that management might like to do as an exercise, for example, to see if increases in profits or dividends have kept pace with increases in a consumer price index.

However, to attempt to incorporate these user indexes *into* the accounts and the financial statements of each entity can only distort the reported performance of each entity—i.e., in the operations it was actually carrying out.

If meaningful asset valuation methods are used (see previous section) in conjunction with capital restated by a *general*-type index, it results in the incorrect reporting of profit. In such cases reported profit includes 'holding gains and losses' that are of a *capital* nature to the entity, and which suffer from the serious deficiencies highlighted by Drake and Dopuch.[1]

For the reasons given in this section it is incorrect to use any sort of a general price index to restate capital contributed by shareholders. The use of such a general-type index for this purpose can only ensure that a company will not unwittingly distribute divideds to an extent that erodes the real *historic cost* of shareholder capital. This is something very different from an entity's real operating capacity capital.[2]

[1] David F. Drake and Nicholas Dopuch, 'On the Case for Dichotomizing Income', *Journal of Accounting Research*, Autumn 1965, pp. 192–205.
[2] Edwards and Bell said something like this: op. cit., p. 22—and then proceeded to advocate a method of accounting for changing prices which did exactly that on the capital side!

5. 'ACCOUNTING FOR STEWARDSHIP' OR TO MEET 'FIDUCIARY ACCOUNTABILITIES'?

In the four sections above we have examined the proposed usage of general purchasing power in accounting reform in conjunction with four reasons given for doing so. A valid reason has yet to be found. However, we have not yet examined the real reasons which underlie recent important documents issued by two professional accounting bodies, i.e., the American Institute of Certified Public Accountants' Accounting Principles Board Statement No. 3[1] and the recent Exposure Draft ED8 issued by the Accounting Standards Steering Committee in Great Britain.[2] We noticed that the former mentioned that the main difference between general price-level and historical-cost statements 'is the unit of measure'.[3] We also noticed that the latter indicates (almost as an aside) that 'the purpose is to measure changes in the value of money'.[4] However, neither document supplies its real underlying objectives for advocating the use of a 'unit of measure' or the current 'value of money'.

The Accounting Principles Board, in its Statement No. 3, says at the outset that 'general price-level financial statements *should* prove useful to investors, creditors, management, employees, government officials, and others who are concerned with the economic affairs of business enterprises',[5] but no attempt is made to demonstrate just how and in what way these users 'should' be assisted by such restatements. The first footnote in this Accounting Principles Board Statement No. 3 makes this writer believe that it merely adopts the main recommendations of the American Institute of Certified Public Accountants' Accounting Research Study No. 6.[6] This seems to complete a circle because the constraining directions given to the authors of Accounting Research Study No. 6 came from the Accounting Principles Board itself. The authors were merely told to 'set up a research project to study the problem' caused by 'fluctuations in *the value of the dollar*' and 'to prepare a report in which recommendations are made for the disclosure of the effect of *price-level changes* upon the financial statements'.[7] In other words, the Accounting Principles Board assumed at the outset (in 1961) that all adjustments should be by one general purchasing power index. Their real reasons were not supplied.

---

[1] *Financial Statements Restated for General Price-Level Changes*, op. cit.
[2] *Proposed Statement of Standard Accounting Practice—Accounting for Changes in the Purchasing Power of Money*, op. cit.
[3] Op. cit., p. 3.   [4] Op. cit., paragraph 10.   [5] Op. cit., p. 4. Emphasis added.
[6] *Reporting the Financial Effects of Price-Level Changes*, op. cit., p. 2.
[7] Ibid., p. 1. Emphasis added.

R. S. Gynther

In Great Britain, the Accounting Standards Steering Committee's recent Exposure Draft ED8 also does not supply any real objective. In paragraph 1 it states this:

The purpose of this Statement is to establish a standard method for calculating the effect of changes in the purchasing power of money *on conventional historical cost accounts*. It does not suggest the abandonment of the historical convention, but simply that historical costs should be converted from an aggregation of historical pounds of many different purchasing powers into approximate figures of current general purchasing power ...[1]

But why? Presumably for the same reasons (?) that have existed for the issuing of 'conventional historical-cost accounts'.

To this writer it is incredible that the 'programme' of this Accounting Standards Steering Committee only lists in 19th place for some 'future' action, a study entitled, 'Fundamental Objects and Principles of Periodic Financial Statements'.[2] How can this committee issue any 'Statement' or 'Exposure Draft' on any aspect of financial statements *before* establishing what these 'objects and principles of periodic financial statements' are? Surely this projected 'objects' study should not be in 19th place. It should have been the first one undertaken so that all the statements that followed could aim at the 'objects' decided upon, and so that they could comply with the underlying 'principles'. As it is, the 'Statements of Standard Accounting Practice' and 'Exposure Drafts' (like ED8) can only float about aimlessly in mid-air, and quite likely in different directions.

As the contents of Exposure Draft ED8 are fairly consistent with the report of The Research Foundation of The Institute of Chartered Accountants in England and Wales (which report preceded it), and as that report was titled, 'Accounting for *Stewardship* in a Period of Inflation',[3] it could be assumed that the objective of Exposure Draft ED8 relates to 'stewardship'. This assumption is supported by the following extract from an official 'Statement' issued by The Institute of Chartered Accountants in England and Wales in 1952:

The primary purpose of the annual accounts of a business is to present information to the proprietors, showing how their funds have been utilized and the profits derived from such use.[4]

This is a common version of the so-called stewardship objective of accounting.

---

[1] Op. cit., paragraph 1. Emphasis added.   [2] Ibid., see back cover.   [3] Op. cit.
[4] The Institute of Chartered Accountants in England and Wales, Statement N 15 on 'Accounting in Relation to Changes in the Purchasing Power of Money', 30th May, 1952, paragraph 1.

Paul Grady, when compiling his inventory of accounting principles for the American Institute of Certified Public Accountants said something similar early in his study—i.e., after studying all of the past pronouncements, etc. of that Institute:

The separation of ownership from management of the business entity is a primary factor in imposing on the entity the fiduciary accountabilities to its shareholders. The summary of generally accepted accounting principles later set forth is classified in relation to these fiduciary accountabilities.[1]

If these similar matters, 'stewardship' and 'fiduciary accountabilities', are the main objectives of the two documents that are now being discussed, they should have been defined in some detail. The Research Foundation of The Institute of Chartered Accountants in England and Wales in its *Accounting for Stewardship in a Period of Inflation*[2] did not define what is meant by 'stewardship', nor did it explain how its general price-level recommendations would improve stewardship.

Further, if the objectives of issuing financial statements were the *narrow* versions of 'stewardship' and 'fiduciary accountabilities' that are often espoused, they would merely relate to reporting on what managers and directors have done with the funds that were entrusted to them by shareholders and others. As Edey says, this calls for nothing more than a summarized cash-flow statement, a list of liabilities incurred, a list of non-monetary assets purchased and still on hand, and a list of monetary assets possessed on balance day. There would be no need for any attempt to value the non-monetary assets, nor would this narrow version of 'stewardship' call for an attempt to determine a profit figure.[3] As there is no need to put a value on assets, there would be no need to consider revaluations or restatements using a general (or any other) index.

Probably 'stewardship' and 'fiduciary accountabilities' are seen by most to go further than the above narrow interpretation. (For example, see the above extract from the 1952 Statement issued by The Institute of Chartered Accountants in England and Wales). This slightly wider view sees the necessity to produce an historical-cost balance sheet which includes the unallocated costs of non-monetary assets along with the monetary items, as well as a profit figure determined after deducting allocations from many past expenditures. However, this writer has never been able

---

1 Paul Grady, *Inventory of Generally Accepted Accounting Principles for Business Enterprises* (Accounting Research Study No. 7) (New York: American Institute of Certified Public Accountants, 1965), p. 26.
2 Op. cit.
3 Harold Edey, 'The Nature of Profit', *Accounting and Business Research*, Winter, 1970, p. 54.

to see how financial reports built on mere arbitrary allocations[1] of past payments of funds to purchase assets (and the resultant balances of unallocated costs) can fill any meaningful stewardship role. Directors have much latitude in determining the ways in which they make allocations (many of which can be large) of past expenditures.[2] This is no real way to report on the honesty with which funds invested in a company are being managed. It follows that the restatement of such allocations and the resultant unallocated historical-cost balances of non-monetary assets (i.e., by a general purchasing power index) will *not* improve the possibilities of attaining any such stewardship objective. Such restatements will inherit all the deficiencies of historical-cost accounting. From a pure stewardship viewpoint such restatements might even hide or disguise some uses of *funds*.

Some might argue that a true interpretation of 'stewardship' and 'fiduciary accountabilities' would require the production of financial statements (for shareholders and other suppliers of funds) showing the *efficiency* with which the funds have been managed by the directors, and supplying information on how the employment of funds is expected to affect *the future* of the entity. Reporting of this kind calls for something far more than the mere general index restatements of conventional historic-cost financial statements. It requires the reporting of values of resources actually deployed, with such values reflecting as much of the future as is possible. (The current value of *money* invested in those resources is useless for this purpose. See Section 3 above). It also calls for periodic profit to be determined taking into account (*a*) the resources valued in this way, and (*b*) capital maintained to support the operating capacity of the specific basic assets of the entity. (See Section 4 above).

Therefore, if the two professional bodies have a narrow, a somewhat wider, or a very wide view of 'stewardship' or 'fiduciary accountabilities' in mind as the main objective of their recommendations for the restatement of conventional historical-cost accounts (to include the effect of changes in the general purchasing power of money), they will not achieve their objective. General index adjustments are not valid for this purpose.

6. CONCLUDING REMARKS

The purpose of this paper was to analyse critically the different reasons given by those who advocate the use of general purchasing power in their proposals for accounting and/or reporting reform—i.e., to cope with the

---

[1] See Arthur L. Thomas, *The Allocation Problem in Financial Accounting Theory* (Studies in Accounting Research No. 3) (American Accounting Association, 1969). Thomas claims, with much force, that *all allocations* are arbitrary no matter how much thought is put into them. [2] Ibid.

inadequacies of conventional historical-cost accounting in times of rising prices. The different reasons found in the literature were classified under five headings and they were examined in turn; all were found to be invalid. The five headings were:

1. A 'Unit of Measurement',
2. 'Accounting for Inflation' and 'Accounting for the Changing Value of Money',
3. 'The Standard of Comparison of Resources (Assets)',
4. 'Maintaining the General Purchasing Power of Shareholders' Capital', and
5. 'Accounting for Stewardship' or to fulfil 'Fiduciary Accountabilities'.

General purchasing power changes should not be used in any way in such accounting and/or reporting reform. They do not result in the production of information useful to internal or external people for decision or control purposes. It is hoped that the professional bodies in the USA and Great Britain will give much further thought to this matter before directing their members to implement accounting or reporting involving changes in general purchasing power. Rosen, in the study he carried out for the Canadian Institute of Chartered Accountants, also 'urged' that this Institute '*not* pursue this avenue in future research and pronouncements'.[1]

Although this paper is a 'destructive' one, the writer does have his own 'solution' to the problem of accounting in times of changing (i.e., rising and falling) prices. Indications of the theoretical nature of this 'solution' were given in Sections 3 and 4 above and will be the subject of a fourth paper. In the meantime, his book[2] gives a reasonable exposition of what he advocates. This 'solution' is being applied in a fully integrated fashion in a relatively small way in Australia. The somewhat similar Philips Electrical system shows that it can be applied in large entities.

Lastly, despite what might have been said elsewhere (and by this writer too), the words, 'It is better to be approximately correct than precisely wrong' do not justify the use of an index of general purchasing power. The use of such an index will produce financial statements that are not even *approximately* correct in most cases. Prices that affect individual companies (and specific indexes) fluctuate *widely* around and from the general index 'average'. The whole general purchasing power approach needs to be shelved and the matter approached from a different direction.

---

[1] Rosen, *Current Value Accounting and Price-Level Restatements*, op. cit., p. 8 and Chapter 4.

[2] R. S. Gynther, *Accounting for Price-Level Changes: Theory and Procedures*, op. cit.

R. S. Gynther

ACKNOWLEDGEMENT. An earlier version of this paper was presented at the National Conference of the Association of University Teachers of Accounting in Edinburgh in April, 1973, when the author was a Simon Visiting Professor at the University of Manchester.

APPENDIX I

The Treatment of Borrowing When Accounting for Changing Prices

The purpose of this appendix is to demonstrate that the inclusion in profits of so-called holding gains on long-term borrowings (and other forms of long-term capital), i.e. when prices are rising, results in the overstatement of profits of the entity concerned. It will be shown that these 'holding gains' can only be shed as dividends (*a*) if the operating capacity is run down (e.g. by selling off some of the basic assets) or (*b*) if additional capital is raised—and that, therefore, they are not gains to the entity itself.

This is a matter to which this writer devoted much space in Chapter 11 of his book,[1] one that Kirkman was concerned about in a recent paper,[2] that Parker and Harcourt recognized in their book,[3] and that Mathews[4] and others have endeavoured to make clear in their writings and examples. Further it is not a minor matter. Cutler and Westwick have clearly demonstrated that these so-called gains on long-term borrowings would be one of the largest adjustments to profit in absolute terms—i.e. if included in a system of accounting for changing prices.[5]

An example

Let us suppose that a company owns land which it rents to farmers, that it distributes all of its profits to its shareholders, and that tax is paid immediately. At the end of its first year of operations the following financial statements were prepared:

[1] R. S. Gynther, *Accounting for Price-Level Changes: Theory and Procedures* (Oxford: Pergamon Press Ltd., 1966).

[2] P. R. A. Kirkman, 'A Weakness of ED8? Long-term Debt and Distributable Profits', *The Accountant*, April 19th, 1973.

[3] R. H. Parker and G. C. Harcourt, *Readings in the Concept and Measurement of Income* (Cambridge: Cambridge University Press, 1969). See footnote p. 24.

[4] R. L. Mathews, 'Income, Price Changes and the Valuation Controversy in Accounting', *Accounting Review*, July, 1968.

[5] R. S. Cutler and C. A. Westwick, 'The Impact of Inflation Accounting on the Stock Market', *Accountancy*, March, 1973, pp. 15–24. Incidentally, the fact that the stock market has not responded to the changes in company profits that they estimated in this paper, could indicate that interested parties consider general price-level adjusted information to be irrelevant.

Profit and Loss Statement for Year 1

Net rents received from farmers	40
Less Interest on Debentures (say 10%)	10
	30
Less Tax (say 50%)	15
= Net Profit	$15

Balance Sheet at End of Year 1

Ordinary Share Capital	100
Debentures (20 year Term)	100
= Total Funds Employed	$200
Represented by:	
Land rented to farmers	$200

Let us assume that early in Year 2 the prices of all commodities and services doubled overnight![1] (That prices might only increase by a few per cent in the real world is granted. The doubling of prices helps to establish a point; any lesser increases merely involve a matter of degree).

The financial statements for Year 2 are prepared with two columns. Column 1 includes holding gains on the Debenture capital (i.e. in the way recommended by many people) while Column 2 does not.

Profit and Loss Statement for Year 2

	1 Including holding on Debentures	2 With no holding gains on Debentures
Net rents received from farmers	80	80
Less Interest on Debentures (still at 10% on amounts received from Debenture holders)	10	10
	70	70
Less Tax (50%)	35	35
= Net operating profit	35	35
Plus Holding Gain on Long-Term Borrowings (When prices increased by 100%)	100	NIL
= Net Profit	$135	$35

[1] By assuming that *all* prices double we obviate clouding the matter at hand with a debate of a different (but related) matter—i.e. the treatment of variations between movements in specific prices of non-monetary items and in prices of all goods in general.

339

Balance Sheet at End of Year 2

	1	2
Ordinary Share Capital	100	100
Capital Maintenance Adjustment	100	200
Undistributed Profits		
(After the Distribution of the Operating		
Profit of $35)	100	NIL
= Total Equity Interest	300	300
Debentures	100	100
= Total Funds Employed	$400	$400
Represented by:		
Land rented to farmers	$400	$400

(The Capital Maintenance Adjustment item of $100 in the Column 1 Balance Sheet above can be calculated in two ways: (i) As the focus here is on maintaining the general purchasing power of *shareholders' funds* (only), the adjustment equals the rate of price change multiplied by the opening balance of shareholders' funds; i.e. 100% of $100. (ii) The second way looks at the effects of the doubling of prices as if these were actually included in the accounting system; then there would be two entries:

(a) Land   *Dr.* $200

    Capital Maintenance Adjustment   *Cr.* $200

    (To revalue the land)

(b) Capital Maintenance Adustment   *Dr.* $100

    Holding Gain on Long-Term

    Borrowings   *Cr.* $100

The *Net* Capital Maintenance Adjustment is a credit of $100.

The Column 2 presentation includes only the first of these two entries, i.e. from revaluing the land. The Capital Maintenance Adjustment A/c therefore has a balance of $200.

Now let us look at some of the aspects of the Year 2 financial statements. The Column 1 Balance Sheet shows 'Undistributed Profits' of $100 (a result of creating a holding gain on the long-term borrowings). *As the only way in which these 'profits' could be distributed would be either to (a) sell one-quarter of the land, or (b)* raise additional long-term capital funds of $100, *they cannot be profits to the company itself.* To include this amount of $100 in 'profits' in the Year 2 Profit and Loss Statement and Balance Sheet can only mislead. The $100 is needed to maintain the *same* level of business. (Incidentally, short-term borrowings of $100 would need to be replaced constantly, and therefore would really be akin to raising additional capital of some form.)

The fact of the matter is, that on the morning after the night in which all prices doubled, the company possessed the same quantity of land. It had not increased in size. The company itself was no better off and no worse off. It now required *capital* funds of $400 (in the new current prices) to continue doing what it was doing. The second column above shows the correct results and position of the entity to which the shareholders subscribed their money.

When prices rise, 'profits' or 'gains' cannot be made from holding funds needed to support the basic assets of a company. It does not matter whether those funds come from ordinary shareholders, preference shareholders, debenture holders, or were raised from an issue of convertible notes. If it is ever decided to reduce the size of the operations of a company, long-term borrowings can be repaid at due date (without replacement) and/or refunds of shareholder capital can be made. In the meantime it gives a false picture to record 'holding gains' on *any* form of long-term funds needed to support basic assets.

Many readers will now protest, 'But the shareholders are better off'. And so they probably are. An inspection of the second column above shows that after-tax profits have more than doubled. They have increased from $15 in Year 1 to $35 in Year 2. Further; the second column in the above Balance Sheet shows that shareholders have a three quarter stake in the company's assets at the end of Year 2, compared with only a half stake at the end of Year 1. Therefore, all else being equal, the stock exchange prices of their shares will more than double. As shareholders are separate entities (they are investing entities in our society), they should have their own accounting systems separate from the company's accounting system, and in these they should revalue the shares they own after comparing the relevant share prices at the stock exchange with prices they paid for them.

To endeavour to account for shareholders within the company's accounting system produces a confused hybrid from which misleading financial reports can flow. It produces a double-counting effect. 'Profits' that are not profits to the company itself are included in the company's financial statements, while share prices at the stock exchange automatically reflect the gains that shareholders (as separate entities) make at the expense of debenture holders.

It is believed that more people would quickly become aware of this 'double counting' if the taxation authorities decided to include such 'holding gains' (on company long-term borrowings) in the profit figure to be taxed—i.e. as well as taxing capital gains on share transactions.

341

APPENDIX 2.
Main possible combinations of Net Asset Valuation Methods and Capital Maintenance Ideas with some known advocates for some of the combinations

Capital Maintenance Ideas	Net Asset Valuation Methods						
	1 Historical costs	2 Historical costs × General index	3 Historical costs × Consumer price index	4 Historical costs × Investment price index	5 Current market buying prices (Current replacement costs)	6 Net present values	7 Current market selling prices (Net realizable values, C.C.Es.)
A. Money Capital	Conventional Historical-cost accounting Yuji Ijiri (a)						
B. General Purchasing Power		Accounting Principles Board of American Institute of Certified Public Accountants (b)			American Accounting Assn's Committee to prepare a statement of Basic Accounting Theory (c)	American Accounting Assn's Committee on Concepts and Standards—long lived assets (as an ideal concept) (d)	B. L. Branford (e)
C. Consumer Purchasing Power			Accounting Standards Steering Committee (f)		Edwards & Bell (g)		Raymond J. Chambers (h) Robert R. Sterling (i)
D. Investment Purchasing Power				Eldon S. Hendriksen (when a single index is to be used) (j)	Eldon S. Hendriksen (his main idea for use in practice) (k)	Eldon S. Hendriksen (as an ideal concept in some cases) (l)	

E. Operating Capacity (mainly based on current replacement costs)	Russell L. Mathews (m) Reg S. Gynther (for most practical applications) (n)	Reg S. Gynther (as an ideal concept)	Reg S. Gynther (for some practical applications as a surrogate for net present values)

*This chart first appeared in this approximate form in Reg S. Gynther, 'Accounting for Changing Prices: Some Recent Thinking, Recommendations and Practice', *The Chartered Accountant in Australia*, December, 1971, pp. 12–23. An earlier version appeared in Reg S. Gynther, *Accounting for Price Changes—Theory and Practice* (Society, Bulletin No. 5) (Melbourne: Australian Society of Accountants, 1968).

REFERENCES TO THE LISTED ADVOCATES FOR SOME OF THE COMBINATIONS

(a) Yuji Ijiri, *The Foundations of Accounting Measurement* (Englewood Cliffs, New Jersey: Prentice-Hall, Inc., 1967).

(b) Accounting Principles Board, *Financial Statements Restated for General Price-Level Changes* (Statement of the Accounting Principles Board no. 3) (New York: American Institute of Certified Public Accountants, 1969).

(c) Committee to Prepare a Statement of Basic Accounting Theory, *A Statement of Basic Accounting Theory* (American Accounting Association, 1966).

(d) American Accounting Association's Committee on Concepts and Standards—Long-Lived Assets, 'Accounting for Land, Buildings and Equipment', *Accounting Review*, July, 1964, pp. 693–699.

(e) B. L. Branford, 'Current Monetary Measures in Accounting', *Accounting Bulletin* (Queensland Division of the Australian Society of Accountants), November, 1968.

(f) Accounting Standards Steering Committee, *Proposed Statement of Standard Accounting Practice: Accounting for Changes in the Purchasing Power of Money* (Exposure Draft ED8) (London: C/o The Institute of Chartered Accountants in England and Wales, 17th January, 1973.)

(g) Edgar O. Edwards & Philip W. Bell, *The Theory and Measurement of Business Income.* (Berkeley and Los Angeles: University of California Press, 1961).

(h) Raymond J. Chambers, *Accounting, Evaluation and Economic Behavior* (Englewood Cliffs, New Jersey: Prentice-Hall Inc., 1966).

(i) Robert R. Sterling, *Theory of the Measurement of Enterprise Income* (Lawrence: The University Press of Kansas, 1970).

(j) Eidon S. Hendriksen, *Accounting Theory* Rev. Ed. (Homewood, Illinois: Richard D. Irwin, Inc., 1970) pp. 222 and 225.

(k) Ibid., pp. 225, 268 and 282.

(l) Ibid., pp. 225, 260–264, and 282.

(m) Russell L. Mathews, 'Income, Price Changes and the Valuation Controversy in Accounting', *Accounting Review*, July, 1968, pp. 509–516.

(n) R. S. Gynther, *Accounting for Price-Level Changes: Theory and Procedures* (Oxford: Pergamon Press Ltd., 1966).

19 Second thoughts on continuously contemporary accounting[1]

by R. J. Chambers*

FIRST THOUGHTS

I do have second thoughts on some elements of the argument in *Accounting, Evaluation and Economic Behaviour*. But I would like to begin with some of my 'first' thoughts—the ideas and circumstances which prompted the development of the theory in the first place.

Some twenty-five years ago I was engaged in a government regulatory agency which, for its purposes, required the analysis and comparison of the financial positions, results and costs of business firms in all kinds of industries. For a time this work was my sole preoccupation. The conventional accounting processes on which the financial statements were based made comparisons between firms, even in the same trade, most difficult. The pressing tasks of administration prevented us from seeking a solution which would treat firms of different ages and sizes equitably. But the experience left a great sense of uneasiness, a sense of dealing with something quite undisciplined, subject to no firm principles. When I left that position I was quite disenchanted about accounting, although it had been the major subject of my studies and work for the previous ten years.

For the following nine years I was engaged in the teaching of aspects of management. My main interest was in financial aspects of business; but as these aspects of business touch every participant in the activities of a firm in some way, their study I considered to provide, in microcosm, examples of the whole of the relations between a business entity and its owners, managers, creditors, customers, competitors, and so on. Changes in the attitudes and actions of any of these parties would require changes in the actions, tactics and strategies of the firm. The immediate post-war years provided numerous frequent and varied examples of the shuffling and bargaining and haggling which go by the general description of adaptation.

* Emeritus Professor of Accounting in the University of Sydney, 1960–1982.

[1] This paper owes its origin to a suggestion of Dr Horace Brock, North Texas State University. It was prepared as the basis of a discussion in that University in February 1970. The present text has benefited from comments, objections and doubts expressed on presentation of the paper in several U.S. universities. To my hosts and interlocutors I am grateful.

The idea of a firm which went on doing the same things year by year, or which set up plans and stuck to them—an idea which many describe as the going concern concept—did not match the observable behaviour of the business community. Changes in the environment and in the expectations of businessmen constantly obliged business firms to respond, sometimes aggressively, sometimes defensively. According to my undergraduate economics, all this was 'old hat'. But in learning it anew, by observation, it became clear that the form which adaptation took depended in part, often a crucial part, on the means at the disposal of a firm. Knowledge of the present facts, in particular the present financial facts, of a business was a necessary condition of informed adaptation. And as adaptation is continuous, knowledge of the financial facts must be continuously brought up to date.

Accounting as it was then expounded and practised did not provide this information. Perhaps it could. In any case I had by this time (1950) become disenchanted with the literature, the 'theory', of management. Apart from the works of Barnard and Simon, it was too full of unargued prescriptions, which may well serve as rules of thumb but which one could see 'violated' in almost every firm, and which lacked any coherent, reasoned foundation. I turned back to accounting, as a university teacher, in 1953.

Fortunately for me, there was evidence in Australia to the point that the long-established doctrine of conventional accounting—the initial cost doctrine—was not in fact endorsed and followed in practice. Poring over company reports, prospectuses, loan indentures and press reports, I found that this evidence was substantial. Hundreds of companies had revalued their assets upwards in spite of the cost doctrine. And the terms of issue of preference shares and loan securities made it clear that there were good commercial reasons for doing so. For if one did not know the contemporary worth of the assets of a company from time to time one could not know whether the terms of contracts and indentures were in fact violated.

The observed revaluations were, of course, made on various kinds of evidence; more frequently than not their bases were not disclosed. But they did confirm the view that more up-to-date information than original costs was needed in practice. And as general commercial practice is substantially the same around the world, there seemed good grounds for supposing that up-to-date information was necessary everywhere, notwithstanding extant doctrines and accounting practices. That there were and are good grounds for this belief has since been confirmed by many more observations than I had then made. Even in the United States, where

345

upward revaluation was virtually outlawed in the 'thirties, up-to-date information was regarded by accountants as significant when market prices of assets fell; and by some security analysts as significant in a wider range of circumstances. Why then didn't the textbooks take notice of these things?

They were worth closer analysis. I began to find that they contained vague and inconsistent propositions, that those propositions did not constitute coherent systems of ideas from which rules could be deduced, that particular terms had widely variant meanings as between texts, that firmly stated propositions were virtually cancelled by appended provisos, and that there were numerous other difficulties.

For some years I had no clear idea of what should be regarded as contemporary information. That it should be contemporary was the main thing. I wrote of replacement prices sometimes, of price-level adjustments at other times and of the present value of expected proceeds at other times.[1] It was not until I began (in 1963) to put the product of my past thinking into comprehensive and systematic form that the solution of the problem occurred to me. Neither replacement prices nor price-level adjusted costs nor present values provided the *generally* usable premises of financial calculations. The argument I developed in *Accounting, Evaluation and Economic Behaviour* led to the conclusion that resale prices were the kind of contemporary information which was useful in making *all* judgements about the past and *all* plans for the future of business firms.

I have given this brief account of some twenty years' thinking—about practical experiences, about observed financial events and about the state of accounting doctrine—simply to show that the outcome was not just a novelty. It was a conclusion to which everything pointed—provided one could only free oneself from the 'sanctity' of established doctrine long enough to allow the evidence to accumulate. I had in fact taken some steps to free myself from existing dogma. About fifteen years ago I tried diligently for some years to find some common core in the principal expositions of accounting, the expositions of the conventional mode and of modes of accounting which would reduce the alleged flaws in conventional accounting. I had little success. I had also meanwhile, read the accounts of the histories of a number of business firms, and of mergers, disputes, frauds and failures; accounts written by lawyers, journalists, and businessmen themselves, and thus free of the overtones or verbal uses of accountants. I concluded that only by the persistent attempt to construct a theory

[1] Examples will be found in the articles brought together in *Accounting, Finance and Management*, Butterworth, Sydney, 1969.

independently of the existing dogma, but with an open eye to commercial and financial events, could one circumvent the contradictions and inconsistencies of existing expositions and recommendations on accounting practices.

Old habits die hard, however. I will indicate presently some respects in which I failed to shake off old ideas. And I will give examples of points where attempts to add force to my argument led me into improper extensions of my chosen set of ideas.

But first may I say that my second thoughts on continuously contemporary accounting have only served to confirm my belief in the validity of the main ideas. Critics have attacked my exposition. I invited this. In the Preface I foreshadowed that others would judge whether the development of my ideas had been in the direction of 'maturity or senility'; and in the Epilogue I said: 'We have not come to the end of the road. In a very real sense, much of the journey lies ahead'. But none of the critics has attacked the main features of the argument. These are (a) that informed choice of future actions and informed appraisals of past actions depend on present knowledge of a present state; (b) that in respect of financial information there is no business function other than accounting which accumulates such knowledge; and (c) that such knowledge is only part of the premises of choice of judgement, the other parts being presently available external information and the (subjective) expectations of managers, investors and others who exercise choice and judgement. If these points remain unchallenged, and as they are the main grounds for the details of the whole system, I can only feel that my critics have left the main part of the structure unscarred.

Perhaps the most pointed way of proceeding will be to consider some of the criticisms to which my work has been exposed. I hope I can convey the burden of the criticisms fairly. I will acknowledge their propriety in some cases. But, in respect of other criticisms I will offer some defences, the better to show that, in the more significant particulars, my original position is unaffected. I acknowledge the generous remarks of reviewers and others on the general character of my exercise. What I may say in rebuttal of particular objections I hope will be taken as an attempt to clarify what I must have left in doubt, and without any suspicion of animosity on my part.

ALLEGED INCONSISTENCY

The most widely noticed element of my exposition is its treatment of inventories and durable assets. After developing the case for the use of resale prices, I introduced the possibility of using replacement prices and indexed calculations. This move was interpreted variously. After the establishment of 'a consistent theoretical rationale for using realizable price', McDonald found the 'switch ... less than compelling'.[1] Wright suggested that I was obliged to use replacement prices because the use of current resale prices 'fails to deal satisfactorily with the problem of inventory measurement', and that I was led to 'present two quite different methods of accounting for durable goods, without being able to provide any useful criterion for choosing among them'.[2] Baxter alleged that when my argument comes 'to deal with each type of asset in detail, it abandons the sale price principle and substitutes replacement cost'.[3] Benston implies a charge of inconsistency. 'It would seem that ... Chambers would favour accounting statements in which assets are valued on several bases. But he rejects this notion emphatically, on the grounds that only one method can be correct'.[4] Hendriksen points to inconsistency in my firm adherence to resale price for durables while demanding the application of the 'rigid realization rule' for inventories: '... current output prices are more consistent with Chambers' postulates than are current input prices'.[5] Iselin pointed out that to use any other price than net realizable value would be inconsistent with my own definition of financial position.[6]

To some of these 'charges' I plead 'not guilty'; to others 'guilty—but under extenuating circumstances'!

Had I been content to develop a theory without regard for the availability of the information which the theory presumed to be available, I could have avoided the possibility of charges of inconsistency. But I believe that theory is closely related to practice, and I did not wish to evade the practical difficulties which might stand in the way of endorsement. That is why I undertook the discussion of different kinds of inventories and durables in some detail. And it is on just those parts of the analysis that critical attention has focused, relatively few pages in Chapter 10.

But I did make one serious mistake; it is hinted at most directly by Hendriksen, and it had, before that, been pointed out to me by my own colleague, W. P. Birkett, in Sydney. The mistake was to make use of

[1] Daniel L. McDonald, review in *The Canadian Chartered Accountant*, August 1966, pp. 78–9.
[2] F. K. Wright, 'Capacity for Adaptation and the Asset Measurement Problem', *Abacus*, August 1967, pp. 74–9, at p. 77.
[3] W. T. Baxter, 'Accounting Values: Sale Price versus Replacement Cost', *Journal of Accounting Research*, Autumn 1967, pp. 208–14, at p. 213.
[4] George J. Benston, review in *The American Economic Review*, March 1967, pp. 297–9, at p. 299.
[5] Eldon S. Hendriksen, review in *Journal of Business*, April 1967, pp. 211–13, at p. 213.
[6] Errol R. Iselin, 'Chambers on Accounting Theory', *The Accounting Review*, April 1968, pp. 231–8, at p. 233.

the idea of realization, in the conventional sense, in discussing the relation between inventory values and income. The conventional idea is that profit should not be anticipated. The balances which turn up in the balance sheet are what they are because this dictum is applied. My own system strictly has no use for this notion. Asset balances are indicative of the present prices of assets on hand; income is the difference between residual equities at two dates based on assets at prices ruling at those dates.

How did I come to make this mistake, especially as I regarded 'realization' as a term relating to revenues only and made this point even after perpetrating the inconsistency under examination? Looking back, it seems due, in part, to inadvertent adherence to an old verbal habit, an old and familiar formula. The difficulties of shaking off old habits are notorious. But I suspect also that I was intimidated by the novelty of the resale price idea which, to my knowledge, has no respectable antecedent in the literature. Perhaps, too, I was cowed by the possibility that a strict use of the resale price rule would entail the elimination of monetary representations of many assets. Whatever the cause of causes, I was inconsistent in this respect. I can scarcely blame my critics for the appellations they gave—'switch', 'defection', 'abandons ... and ... substitutes'—to what I did. And I can scarcely blame them for alleging that I countenanced the use of two kinds of contemporary price. Certainly I said repeatedly that I was seeking resale prices and that any other device was merely an attempt to approximate resale prices, and that their use did not mean I was departing from the principle of resale price. But the deliberate use of the old test of realization properly confused the matter. I will presently indicate what I now see as the way through the dilemma which then confronted me.

RESALE PRICE

A number of critics have challenged the propriety of using resale prices. Baxter, even after listing five of my arguments without any hint of real objection, still found 'the case for selling price quite unconvincing' (p. 211). He was in favour of 'qualified' replacement price. Benston said that the measurement of assets and the derivation of income by reference to contemporary prices 'differs from the present value approach favoured by most economists' (p. 298). Staubus put up an extensive defence of the use of discounted values as a counter to my proposals.[1] Solomons

---

[1] George J. Staubus, 'Current Cash Equivalent for Assets: A Dissent', *The Accounting Review*, October 1967, pp. 650–61.

said that in his view 'it is "value to the owner" that is relevant'.[1] I
am not sure what this phrase 'value to the owner' means exactly. Baxter
(p. 212) attributes it to Bonbright; both Baxter and Solomons, following
Bonbright, suggest that value to the owner has the limiting values, replacement price and selling price. This does not give us a clear warrant for
supposing that value to the owner is the discounted value of expected
net proceeds, favoured by 'most economists' (Benston) and Staubus. But
Baxter said 'the present value of the asset's future net contribution' should
be expanded' (p. 78); otherwise his views on the 'relation' between resale
presume that value to the owner is the net present value for purpose
of our later analysis. Wright contended that 'resale price measures capacity
for adaptation if existing activities are to be contracted, whereas replacement cost measures capacity for adaptation if existing activities are to
be expanded' (p. 78); otherwise his views on the 'relation' between resale
price, replacement price and value to the owner are substantially the same
as those of Baxter and Solomons. Dein contended: 'The proposed statement of financial position seems to emphasize for the continuing entity
approximately the dimension which the statement of affairs emphasizes
for the financially embarrassed entity'. As for contemporary financial
information, he said, 'a cash projection schedule extending several years
into the future' would be more informative than the proposed balance
sheet. He himself is content with accounting as it now is.[2]

How does one come to grips with the criticisms of so many who among
themselves are champions of quite different proposals? I will try—by
indicating the general drift of *Accounting, Evaluation and Economic Behavior* and by treating generically the objections.

In the book I tried to set out all the kinds of figures which would
be usable in any judgement, on financial grounds, of past actions or future
possibilities. I indicated the necessity of calculating net present values
for *prospective* projects.[3] I indicated that the purchase price of a new
asset (whether or not it was a 'replacement' of an old asset) was necessary
information in the calculation of net present values. I indicated that resale
prices of assets were necessary information in the calculation of the net
present values of prospective projects. I indicated that resale prices were
necessary to the determination of any present position and hence to the
assessment of past performance and to the estimation of the betterment
to be expected from any future action. It should be noticed that my

---

[1] David Solomons, review in *Abacus*, December 1966, pp. 205–9, at p. 208.
[2] Raymond C. Dein, review in *The Journal of Accountancy*, October 1966, pp. 89–90.
[3] For a subsequent and different statement of the case, see my reply to Staubus: 'Measures
and Values', *The Accounting Review*, April 1968, pp. 239–47.

analysis of the range of specific calculations and assessments included specific uses of all the kinds of information (present values, replacement prices, and resale prices) the need for which has been the justification of systems other than my own. I rejected present values and replacement prices as bases for the preparation of factual financial statements, on the grounds (a) that they are both transient or ephemeral in character and are ascertainable directly at any time, and (b) that they do not in any case yield an indication of the present state of the financial affairs of a firm at any time—information which is necessary to every retrospective and prospective judgement.

As for the criticisms, consider first the idea of the value of an asset to a firm. We must consider Solomons' reference to 'value to the owner', cited above, as meaning value to the firm, since we are dealing with representations of assets in the accounts of firms. If the value of an asset to a firm means the net present value or discounted value of the expected proceeds *of an asset*, the term can only be used of assets which yield identifiable incomes without the aid of other assets or inputs. There are some assets of this kind; but they can be few only, for even the occasional attention which must be given to such things as leased property or security holdings entails that the *net* proceeds is not a figure independent of the net proceeds of other activities. In the typical case revenues arise from the use of assets in combination. In this case it is not possible to assign a significant net present value to each of the assets used in combination.

Usually, of course, net present values are calculated for *projects* which require the use in combination of plant, inventories and labour-service. But even in this case the net present value of a project must be considered in an incremental sense; it is the present value of a project to be undertaken given the existing state of the firm. It is contingent on that state. It follows that the present value of any project cannot be related to anything else than the present value of an alternative project given the same state of the firm. It also follows that to obtain the values of all the projects of the firm, each would have to be considered as if the firm were a different firm. Thus, to obtain the present value of project J of a firm whose projects are J, K, L, M, N, PV_J would have to be obtained by recourse to assumptions about the firm in the absence of J: similarly for each of the other projects. The interdependences of the variables stand in the way of making any unequivocal statement about any asset.

Yet it is demonstrable that some firm indication of the present financial characteristics of particular assets or classes of asset is of interest and use to firms, their managers and their creditors. Specific assets can be, and are, mortgaged or pledged. A charge may be given over a class of assets or a collection of assets, never over a project (unless it corresponds with an identified collection of assets). Some asset values enter directly into calculations made to indicate drifts in efficiency. It is difficult to imagine what meaning could be assigned to a receivables turnover, inventory turnover or working capital turnover rate, in which the numerators were present values of the relevant assets. No proponent of the use of present values has suggested what tests may be applied, when attempting to assess drifts in efficiency, if present value figures alone were available for analysis. The long-established practice of accounting for assets in terms other than their values to the firm is not lacking in claims to legitimacy.

But suppose we could calculate the net present values of assets. What of the assertions of Baxter, Bonbright, Solomons, and Wright to the effect that this value has as its limiting magnitudes resale price and replacement price, assuming rational behaviour. We may consider four possible combinations of the magnitudes.

Let A be the asset now held. Let B be the best alternative use of the proceeds of A; B may be a replacement of A, or an entirely different asset, or either of the former plus the investment of the surplus cash (if any) at interest or in an additional asset. Let PV_A be the present value of holding A; and PV_B the present value of the course of action B, i.e., the present value of investing $800 in B.

	Resale price A	Replacement Price A	PV_A	Indicated action
(a)	$800	$1,000	$1,200	Invest in B if $PV_B > $1,200
(b)	$800	$1,000	$ 900	Invest in B if $PV_B > $ 900.
(c)	$800	$ 600	$1,000	⎧Course B should already have
(d)	$800	$ 600	$ 750	⎨been taken.

Note first, that it may be said that cases (c) and (d) are not feasible, assuming rational behaviour. There is, however, a difference between rational behaviour and rational *and informed* behaviour. If resale prices are not somehow kept under observation, it is quite possible for cases (c) and (d) to occur.

In cases (a) and (c) the present value of A exceeds both the resale price and the replacement price of A. These are quite feasible situations. But they are certainly not covered by the view that these two prices are outside limits to the value of A to the firm. In cases (b) and (d), the present value of A falls between the resale price and the replacement price of A. But in case (b), if the asset A were shown as $900 (i.e., PV_A), or as $1,000 (replacement price of A) these figures would be of no use in deciding whether B was a possible alternative (i.e., whether $800 would be available to invest in B) and hence, also, no use in discovering what PV_B is: for both depend on knowledge of the resale price of A. And in case (d), if the asset A were shown as \$750 (i.e., PV_A) or as \$600 (replacement price of A), neither of these figures would be of use in deciding the feasibility of alternatives.

In respect of cases (c) and (d) where resale price exceeds replacement price, it should be remembered that the replacement of A is only one of the forms course B can take. To discover which form B should take, it is necessary to know how much is available (i.e., \$800), not only the replacement price of A; for some other course than the replacement of A could have a greater present value.

Now consider Wright's contention that the use of resale prices represents 'capacity for adaptation if existing activities are to be contracted' (p. 78). It will be noticed that we made no reference whatever, in the case used above, to contraction or expansion. The criterion of choice between holding an asset and doing other things (including replacing the asset) is simply which has the greatest present value (other considerations being equal). If a firm knows its position on a resale price basis it knows approximately what cash it can lay its hands on; and that is one of the facts which determine whether a firm can expand or must contract.

The constancy with which the resale price of A occurs in the discussion of the example indicates its necessity and the variety of its uses. Replacement prices and new goods prices and present values are used in all such choice-making deliberations; but the one thing to which all are tied is the resale price of the present asset. This is a different and more extensive role than Solomons' description of it—'an occasional surrogate' for replacement cost (p. 208)—suggests.

We take up, next, an objection raised by Baxter, Solomons, and Benston. Suppose an asset is bought which immediately has a low or zero resale price to the firm. Said Solomons: 'The use of resale prices in this situation leads to what I can only regard as an absurdity and a flagrant failure to measure up to the criterion of correspondence with the economic events which are being recorded' (p. 208).

Suppose a firm buys a specialized asset A for \$10,000, the present value of its expected net proceeds being \$20,000. The purchase for \$10,000, an economic event, will be recorded. If the resale price to the firm becomes zero immediately, that too is an economic event. The loss of the firm's adaptive capacity is an economic event for the firm. To record it is to measure up fully to the criterion of correspondence with events which occurred. But we need to follow through the example to see whether it produces absurdities.

Suppose the firm's net trading income for the first year is $5,000. Its balance sheet at the end of the year would appear thus:

Asset A (cost $10,000)	0	Owners' equity 1 January	10,000
		Less investment in non-	
Cash	5,000	vendible asset	10,000
			0
		Plus net trading income	5,000
	$5,000		$5,000

The mere fact that the resale price of A is zero has no necessary effect on the firm's income expectations. For the firm could have anticipated that the asset would have no resale price. Or, if its sale was estimated to be at some distance, the expected proceeds would have only a slight effect on the present value calculation; for the discount rate on such a specialized asset would tend to be high. We may suppose that the only factor affecting income expectations at the end of the first year is that $5,000 of the originally expected income has already been yielded.

The way in which the firm's affairs are reported puts investors on notice of several things. First, it indicates that the firm has a high rate of return on the sum of money it can invest in any alternative; an infinite rate of return even if the net income is only $1, for the sum it could invest (apart from retained income) is zero. Second, it indicates that the firm has no means of securing a continuing income, if the asset becomes exhausted or obsolete, other than by retaining and reinvesting some of the cash generated each year. If the asset were shown at cost less amortization, investors would be entitled to suppose that the asset (by association in the balance sheet with other money-like assets) is saleable and that continuity of the firm's income may be secured otherwise than by retaining profits. Third, it indicates that the firm has no property-base for borrowing, though it might be able to borrow on the strength of its expected earnings. If the asset were shown at cost less amortization, there would seem to be a property-base for borrowing when in fact there is not. Fourth, it indicates that the firm's original cash is now locked in. Investors will be prepared to pay less for a share in this firm than in other firms having saleable assets and the same income expectations, because of this lack of asset-coverage. Whatever they pay they will know they are paying for *their* share in the firm's income prospects only.

I have used an extreme example, stripped of complexity. It may be worth pointing out that, by appropriate arrangement, all the background information given in the balance sheet for the first year could be carried into the balance sheet of a subsequent year. It may be objected that the immediate depreciation charge of $10,000 should be shown as a charge in the income account, resulting in a net loss of $5,000. But the manner in which it has been represented is logically identical and informationally superior in the extreme circumstance I have chosen. There can surely be no grounds for refusing to show an unusual event in an explicit if unusual manner.

In short, the mode of reporting is not unrealistic, though it may seem odd when we have long been accustomed to something else. It is certainly not 'absurd'. It discloses some things which conventional balance sheets do not disclose, things which are pertinent to investors. It enables investors to distinguish between this firm and other firms having the same income prospects but saleable assets also. It does represent the firm's financial position, and it does represent its capacity for adaptation.

It is difficult to forbear quoting observations which are intended to be critical but which merely strengthen my case. Solomons observed: 'The failure to recognize that the owner of an asset which is not for sale does not directly suffer if its resale price drops, unless this change is associated with some change in his expectations (as indeed it may be, indirectly, or in the long run) must be regarded as a serious flaw in Chambers' theory' (p. 208). If we recognize what Solomons said I failed to recognize, there is no reason to be squeamish about accounting for the drop. That I proposed to account for it indicates that I did recognize the point, and on Solomons' own grounds my treatment has strength rather than a serious flaw. My treatment also covers the proviso which begins with 'unless . . .' in the sentence cited. The firm owning the asset does suffer indirectly (as does every firm whose assets fall in resale price), in the sense that its adaptability and its property-base for borrowing are reduced. (No automobile buyer is thought to be foolish when he pays $3,000 for a car which, immediately on leaving the showroom, has a cash value of, say, $2,700. But it would be foolish to assert that nothing had happened to the buyer's financial position in the same circumstances.) What is more to the point, however, is that unless *investors* in the firm know of the drop in resale price they do not know of these indirect effects on the firm, and can take no account of them in forming or revising *their* expectations. To hold back information which does no direct harm to the firm, but which would have an effect on the expectations of rational investors, is to fail to represent material facts, to fail in disclosure. No mention of the investor's calculations, reflections and choices is made by Solomons, Baxter or Benston, except perhaps in an oblique or vague way.

R. J. Chambers

I introduced this phrase as a generalization which would cover all assets. It would be curious to speak of the resale price of cash; and also, as I contemplated ways of approximating resale price, some general term seemed to be necessary. I do not believe that my exposition made it perfectly clear what I intended; and I know there are several points at which I would now like to make amendments. But what I intended was, I hope, reasonably clear from much of the detail of my argument.

We speak quite generally of *financial* statements and *financial* position. I suspect we often use the adjective loosely. Finance means money, cash or its substitutes. 'Financial' has therefore to do with money. It seems reasonable that a financial statement should deal with money and the equivalents in terms of money of claims and other assets and of obligations. The money equivalent of anything is its price. Things which have no money equivalent, no price, have no present financial characteristic.

When speaking of the money or cash equivalent of assets I did not mean what I or you *expect* or a firm *expects* or hopes to get. What we expect or hope an asset will yield, by use or by sale, is not a characteristic of the asset. What we expect or hope is a characteristic of ourselves. We are entitled to expect or hope what we please. But in any form of calculating which we hope will inform us of our present capacity for action, we would be naïve to suppose that others will concur with the prices we put on things unless there is some evidence to the effect that they do concur. This evidence is the fact that, at any given date, transactions occur or have recently occurred at stated prices. In setting down assets at these selling prices, it is not assumed that the goods on hand will in fact be sold at those prices.[1] Selling those goods is something which will be done after the balancing date. We make no assumptions about what will be done after that date, becase one of the premises of what we then decide to do is the state of affairs as we find it at balancing date. We are simply using the prices quoted in the market as the indicators of present cash equivalents.

The phrase has been interpreted by some as indicating what is expected to be received in cash. And I think there are some points at which vagueness or a poor choice of words on my part contributed to this interpretation. But as early as Chapter 4 of the book it is made clear that the quoted market price is what is intended. One may of course entertain expectations of receiving a market price; but the crucial point for our

---

[1] The point is made more fully in 'Continuously Contemporary Accounting—Additivity and Action', *The Accounting Review*, October 1967, pp. 751-7.

purpose is not the expectations we entertain but the existence of a market price. If the resale price of a good I hold is $100, that is the cash equivalent of the good, regardless of its price in the future and regardless of whether I sell in the near or distant future.

I may have confused the matter somewhat by reference to the discounting of payables on p. 107 and by the implication of my recourse to the authority of Sprouse and Moonitz on p. 196 for abandoning discounting for 'roughly' matched short-term receivables and payables. These are mistakes, due, I imagine, to my difficulties in weaving my way among so many conflicting ideas. Discounting has a place in present value calculations. But it has no place in my notion of a dated financial position. The matter may also have been confused by my treatment of bonds as obligations. For bonds held as assets I suggested market prices; but for bonds as liabilities I suggested their face value. Hendriksen questioned the differential treatment (p. 213). My defence is simply that, at a given time, the issuer owes the bondholders the contractual amount of the bonds, whatever the price at which the bonds are traded.

The contractual amount of a bond at any time may be more or less than the face value, by virtue of redemption provisions in the bond indenture. It can readily be calculated from those provisions. But even if the market price is materially different from this contractual amount, the latter is the relevant figure for assessment of a present financial position. In recent years, in some countries, certain outstanding bond issues have sold at discounts as high as fifty per cent of face value. Suppose that a company has $10,000 in assets, and an outstanding bond the contractual amount of which is $5,000: and suppose that the bond is selling at 60. Certainly no creditor would accept the notion that he was holding a $60 bond if its contractual amount were $100. As long as the company's affairs are reasonably secure, the bond price is a function of the coupon rate and the current market rate of interest. It has nothing to do directly with the equity of bondholders and others in the assets of the company. It is the quite separate function of the balance sheet to show just this.

The position is perhaps analogous to that of stockholders. The equity of stockholders in the assets of a firm is not given by the prices at which the stock is traded. I suppose that in any calculation of the leverage of a firm, the face value of liabilities would be used rather than their market value; and that in any calculation for re-funding or liquidating the loan, the face value would be used in ignorance of the bondholders' reaction to the proposal. In short, equities are not just negative assets, and there is no reason that I can yet see why the same general rule should apply to both assets and equities. The current cash equivalent of the assets or any set of assets can be meaningfully set off against an amount now owing, no matter when the amount now owing has to be paid; this possibility is a significant feature of the utility of figures available for use in financial calculations.

The additivity of current cash equivalents has been called in question by Benston (p. 299) and by Larson and Schattke.[1] Both, however, confuse the notion of additivity of numbers of monetary units assigned to assets with the question of the way in which a seller may combine or group assets in any given sale. The additivity of such numbers subsists in the similarity of what they designate, not in their magnitudes. Numbers of monetary units designating the same kinds of prices in monetary units of the same kind are additive. In what groupings assets will, in fact, be sold, is dependent on the proceeds expected at the time and in the circumstances in which they are offered. As I hold that knowledge of financial position is one of these circumstances, it would be circular reasoning to assume any particular grouping for the purpose of finding out the position which will, in part, influence the grouping at the time of sale.[2] I would be satisfied to consider the prices of assets in the quantities, parcels or combinations in which the firm customarily sells or offers them for sale. If we are concerned with the production of figures which may be embodied in a variety of distinctive calculations, what we seek is their most probable values; or perhaps the values which depend on the fewest *ad hoc* stipulations. It seems to be incontestable that the quantities, parcels and combinations within the usual and ordinary experience of the firm best meet this test.

Refer now to Dein's remark on the utility of a cash projection schedule. Whatever uses a cash projection schedule may have, its preparation entails the use of resale prices—for inventories; for such other assets as may be intended to be sold in the period covered; and, in the event that borrowing is necessary, for such assets as may be pledged as security, and that means potentially any and all assets. Instead of being an argument against the continuous availability of information based on resale prices, the cash budgeting suggestion of Dein and others is a strong argument in favour. Further, it would be useless to offer a cash projection schedule which was inconsistent with the figures appearing in a balance sheet which purports to represent the position at the date from which the cash projection schedule proceeds. No reader of the two could form a legitimate view of the consequences of the projected cash movements from two statements prepared on inconsistent bases.

[1] Kermit Larson and R. W. Schattke, 'Current Cash Equivalent, Additivity and Financial Action', *The Accounting Review*, October 1966, pp. 634–41.

[2] This objection was answered more fully in the article referred to in footnote 1 on p. 356.

One final comment on the relation between the present and the future. Wright alleged that my difficulties arose from my assertion that 'accounting is not concerned with the future'. In pointing out at the same time that I *do* make some assumptions about the future (the firm has at least some future; adaptation itself is future) he implies inconsistency in my premises (p. 77). The juxtaposition of such statements is a caricature. What I held was that *in the derivation of figures* descriptive of a present position no account can be taken of the future. It should be obvious that we always estimate the future from the present, never the other way round. Even in present value calculations we must estimate the future from a known present if the result is to be informative. It is only in that sense that accounting is not concerned with the future. If assumptions are made about the future in deriving a representation of the present, the result will be the same vicious circularity we mentioned when dealing with the grouping of assets for sale. The same objection may be taken to Baxter's observation: 'so long as all is going well, sale price has little relevance' (p. 212). We are required to suppose that all is going well, when we are preparing statements to show whether or not all is going well!

SECOND THOUGHTS

What then are my second thoughts? In a number of respects the criticisms have, in fact, provided occasion for additional arguments in favour of my main argument. And a number of other things have made me more confident than I was six or seven years ago of the feasibility of adhering to the resale price principle in practice.

The accessibility of resale prices At the time of writing I was aware that newspapers and trade periodicals carried classified advertisements from which some idea of contemporary prices could be obtained for a wide range of industrial goods. I knew that in the second-hand motor vehicle business and in the wholesale grocery business there were, in Australia, trade publications giving extensive lists of prices. I have since been informed by my colleague, R. P. Brooker (now deceased), that there are extensive catalogues of used machinery prices available to the trade in the United Kingdom. A recent Sydney graduate[1] has shown that in the mining industry resale prices of minerals, in partly processed and fully processed states, are available for a wide range of basic mineral

[1] George J. Foster, 'Mining Inventories in a Current Price Accounting System', *Abacus*, December 1969.

359

R. J. Chambers

products. A graduate student of Michigan State University[1] has drawn
attention to the existence of extensive catalogues of used equipment prices
in the earthmoving and road-building industry and of used motor vehicles
in the United States. And of course any reader of the newspapers and
business and trade journals will find prices of other primary products
and equipment than those mentioned above. Even if one thinks about
it ever so little, one cannot help believing that knowledge of prices of
all kinds of things, new and second-hand, must be available to people
who use particular kinds of assets for particular kinds of operations. Yet
we are prone to overlook the extensive service industries (specialists,
exchanges, secondhand merchants, trade periodicals) which grow up on
the fringe of the main manufacturing and distributive trades.

The necessity of judgement None of these sources will necessarily give
unequivocal resale prices. But their existence certainly gives assurance
that there is extensive evidence on which informed judgement could be
exercised with the object of approximating resale prices. There may be
some who have supposed that my proposals were so tightly phrased that
I excluded the exercise of judgement. The tightness of my specification,
however, relates to the principles to be used, not to the identity of the
magnitudes derived. I wrote explicitly of approximation, and 'the best
possible approximation to cash equivalents'. These very words imply the
use of judgement.

The exercise of judgement has long been the trump card of those who
favour freedom of choice among the vast array of 'invented' accounting
rules. We are asked to suppose that, from this array of rules, all having
different effects on the computed profit residual and on the statement
of position, the accountant can choose just that set of particular rules
which, in a given firm for a given year, will yield a fair representation
of results and position. But so great is the range of possibilities that this
desired end could only be attained by chance, certainly not by judgement.
Indeed all the usual talk of judgement seems rather hollow in the light
of the common dependence on *managerial* judgement for many of the
figures incorporated in annual statements. How often are we told that
the statements are the statements of management!

But when we set up an ideal type of information, and ask that accountants use their best skill and judgement in approximating it, then there
is a real opportunity for using judgement. Skill and judgement are demon-

[1] James C. McKeown, 'An Application of a Current Market Value Accounting Model'. (Unpublished thesis, 1969.) McKeown also compares the system, to its advantage, with conventional
accounting.

360

strated only when one has to work within limits, or to an ideal. One does not need judgement of a high order to drive a car over an open field. One does when driving under the rules of the road, on a three-lane highway, in the midst of unpredictable traffic.

The inventory problem Now, for the inventory problem which has caused me the greatest consequential trouble. My attempts to suggest a practicable 'second best' when resale prices are not available show that I wished all 'assets' presently represented in balance sheets to have some monetary magnitude (as the main figure in the list of assets, not merely a memorandum figure) under my system. I do not now hold this view, as an earlier illustration in this paper shows.

It is not difficult, I think, to find resale prices for undifferentiated raw materials, (i.e., unprocessed by the present owner). The owner could generally dispose of these materials without substantial loss; but because he occupies a different position from his supplier in the chain of physical distribution, his resale price will generally be lower than his purchase price. Nor is it difficult to assign a selling price to his finished goods in the manner in which they are usually sold, in gross lots, as made up goods, as spare parts, as the case may be. There is, however, a difficulty in dealing with goods in the course of production. For some partly processed goods there are markets from which indications of resale prices in their then condition can be obtained. But for the rest, let them be shown at zero value.

This may seem drastic, but only by reason of our long-standing habits. However, notwithstanding those habits, there must be thousands of machines in daily use across the country which have been written off, or down to a purely nominal value, under existing methods of accounting. No fuss is made about that. Again there are thousands of instances of assets being shown at less than they are expected to produce in cash, now or in the future. No fuss is made about that. But there is the positive argument from my own theory. If, as we claim, the cash equivalents of assets provide the kinds of magnitude which we can presently relate to other financial magnitudes when reflecting on immediate possibilities, then any 'asset' which has no present cash equivalent can properly be shown to have none.

Two other kinds of comfort may be offered. First, there is no reason why the direct cost of work in process which has no resale price should not be shown in parenthesis, without extension.[1] Second, we are prone

---

[1] More generally, there is no reason why 'cost' figures could not be shown in parentheses for all assets, with current cash equivalents in the main balance sheet columns—at least until it is generally realized how useless the cost figures are.

to think of the effect of any such change in methods on the closing values of assets and on the profits of a single year. But as the closing figures of one year become the opening figures of the next it is unlikely that the aggregate of the profit figures over a number of years would differ materially, from this cause, from the aggregate obtained under many other ways of accounting. We would, however, have the advantage of knowing exactly what those figures represented at any time, and the advantage of a consistent general rule.

Method and product Technical features of my argument and theory aside, there are two general observations with which I might close.

Much of the discussion of alternative accounting methods, and most of the reviews and criticisms of my theory, make scanty use of illustrative examples of the substantive choices of managers and investors. I am convinced that unless we ask 'how could this or that piece of information, or this or that calculated magnitude, be used by an investor or manager in judging or choosing?', we will not find out what is worth producing. That is the way in which I have proceeded in deriving my own conclusions and in the above analysis of some contrary assertions. Unless by this means we can be sure that a specific piece of information has a quite specific place in some thought process in a class of imaginable situations, it is vain to attempt to argue its merits.

Finally, as I have said, the critics have left the main structure of my theory unscarred. None saw fit to comment on the way in which my theory provides a synthesis in which there is a fit and proper place for all the kinds of information which have been said to be needed for informed judgements and choices on financial grounds. There is a place for original prices—at the original point of purchase. There is a place for replacement prices—not in periodical reporting, but in the course of reflections on future alternatives. There is a place for present values of expected proceeds—again, not in periodical reporting, but in the course of reflections on future alternatives. There is a place for corrections for general price level movements—in the calculation of the capital maintenance adjustment and net income. And there is a place for resale prices—in *every one* of the contexts just mentioned. To fit these various pieces of information together into a coherent system does not require me to deny the utility of any one of them as pieces of information. But any theory which neglects the utility of knowledge of resale prices in all problem contexts leaves out of account the one kind of information which is a necessary premise of all judgements and choices. I should like to know of any other systematic way in which these different kinds of information can be reconciled. Until

362

I hear of any such alternative I have no second thoughts on this, the distinctive characteristic of my theory.

ADDENDUM (1984)

The preceding selection was a response to reviews of the book there named. The reviews and the response focused more on asset valuation than on income calculation. The author's views on income calculation have not changed since the book was published, but he has supplied the following note on the process.

Continuously contemporary accounting was devised not only to elimi-nate the heterogenous bases of valuation of conventional and some alterna-tive forms of accounting, but also to cope with the effect of shifts in the prices of assets and in the general purchasing power of the money unit. It is, indeed, arguable that the many bases of valuation endorsed in the literature or used in practice arose because of shifts in the prices of goods and in the purchasing power of the money unit.

The periodical income accounts and balance sheets which are the pro-duct of accounting are not temporally isolated or *ad hoc*. The very process of progressive accumulation which has long characterized accounting entails that these statements are integral parts of a continuous financial history of the relationships between a firm and the rest of the world. Further, the dated financial statements from time to time are expected to be serviceable, at or about the dates they bear, in appraisals of past performance and speculative consideration of future prospects. They must therefore be expressed in appropriately-dated dollars, i.e., in dollars of the same general purchasing power as the dollars in circulation at succes-sive balance dates. Further still, as the balance sheet amounts of one date are expressed in dollars of general purchasing power different from the balance sheet amounts of a subsequent date (all being derived from dated observations or dated contracts), the accounting must provide a systematic and plausible adjustment for the effects of the difference. Con-tinuously contemporary accounting was devised to satisfy these condi-tions.

The complete generality of the system and the systematic derivation of statements of position and results under it may be illustrated for a single period.[1] The demonstration runs in terms of money amounts or

---

[1] Some elements of the notation and argument were developed in 1961. The following demon-stration embodies a number of refinements after the publication of *Accounting, Evaluation and Economic Behaviour*.

dated money equivalents (net resale prices) of assets, liabilities and equity. Monetary assets are all assets of fixed money amount; non-monetary assets are all assets whose money equivalents are market selling prices. Liabilities are (with few exceptions) obligations of fixed money amount.

Let $\$_1$ and $\$_2$ represent dollars of the general purchasing power of the dollar at dates t_1 and t_2, the opening and closing dates of a period. Let $\$_1 M_1$ and $\$_2 M_2$ be the amounts of net monetary assets (monetary assets less liabilities) at the two dates. Let $\$_1 N_1$ and $\$_2 N_2$ be the sums of the money equivalents or net resale prices of non-monetary assets at the two dates. Let $\$_1 R_1$ and $\$_2 R_2$ be the amounts of the residual equity of the firm in its assets (and be equal, therefore, to the amounts of net assets) at the two dates. Let p be the proportionate increase between t_1 and t_2 in an index of changes in the general level of prices, so that, in terms of general purchasing power, $\$_1 = \$_2(1 + p)$. Then, at t_1,

$$\$_1 M_1 + \$_1 N_1 = \$_1 R_1 \qquad [1]$$

and at t_2,

$$\$_2 M_2 + \$_2 N_2 = \$_2 R_2 \qquad [2]$$

Let $\$_2 Y_2$ be the net income (or profit) of the period ended t_2; it is the amount of the increment in the residual equity:

$$\$_2 Y_2 = \$_2 R_2 - \$_1 R_1$$

And, since $\$_1 = \$_2(1 + p)$ in general purchasing power,

$$\$_2 Y_2 = \$_2 R_2 - \$_2(1 + p)R_1 \qquad [3]$$

Substituting $(M_1 + N_1)$ for R_1 and $(M_2 + N_2)$ for R_2 in [3],

$$\begin{aligned}\$_2 Y_2 &= \$_2(M_2 + N_2) - \$_2(1 + p)(M_1 + N_1) \qquad [4]\\ &= \$_2(M_2 - M_1) + \$_2(N_2 - N_1) - \$_2 p(M_1 + N_1).\end{aligned}$$

To this point we have an expression for net income which is wholly in $\$_2$. And, since all the amounts are amounts observable or discovered independently of the internal calculations of the company, the amount of income is authenticated simply by authentication of the components of [4], which embrace all assets and liabilities. The argument is extended to cover the transactions and other events which occurred during the period. Let T represent the nominal amount of the difference between the total sales proceeds (in cash or credit) of goods and services sold and the total purchase prices (whether settled in cash or credit) of goods bought during the period.

Let I represent, in respect of all non-monetary assets (inventories and other assets) sold during the period, the sum of the nominal differences between their selling prices and their purchase prices (or their recorded money equivalents at t_1, for non-monetary assets in possession at that date). Let E represent the aggregate nominal amount of all payments in the nature of expenses during the period (i.e., all payments which do not give rise to possession of non-monetary assets). Let V represent the sum of the differences between the discovered money equivalents of all non-monetary assets at t_2 and their book values (before adjusting to discovered values). V is thus inclusive of the accrued changes in money equivalents of all non-monetary assets at t_2. Then, in nominal amounts,

$$M_2 = M_1 + T - E$$
$$\text{and } N_2 = N_1 + I + V - T$$

Substituting these values of M_2 and N_2 in [4] above,

$$\$_2 Y_2 = \$_2[(M_1 + T - E) + (N_1 + I + V - T) - (1 + p)(M_1 + N_1)]$$
$$= \$_2[(I - E) + V - p(M_1 + N_1)]$$

And, since $M_1 + N_1 = R_1$,

$$\$_2 Y_2 = \$_2[(I - E) + V - pR_1] \tag{5}$$

The expression for net income in terms of changes in amounts of assets and net assets [4] has thus been converted to an equivalent expression in terms of transactions and accrued changes in the money equivalents of assets. The terms of [5] are interpretable in the following way.

The amount $(I\text{-}E)$ is the realized net proceeds (in cash or accounts receivable) of the period from all transactions in goods and services. It is the firm's net revenue. It is obtained by the usual process of accumulating the amounts of transactions in appropriate accounts. The amount V is the algebraic sum of all particular price variation adjustments, including the variations in money equivalents signified by depreciation and appreciation. The term $(-\$_2 pR_1)$ is a capital maintenance adjustment that allows for the effect of the change in the general purchasing power of the money unit on the opening amount of equity. Under deflationary conditions, p itself will be negative, and $(-\$_2 pR_1)$ will be positive. The other half of the double-entry corresponding to $(-\$_2 pR_1)$ in the income account is an entry of the same amount in an equity account that may be described as an inflation adjustment account or a capital maintenance reserve. $\$_2 Y_2$, then, is the firm's real income expressed in $\$_2$.

Note that the amounts T, I, E and V are described as nominal amounts. In fact, any instance of a transaction or price variation is a dated event expressed in its specific dated dollar. But it is impossible to follow the day-by-day shifts in the general purchasing power of the dollar. This is not only because of the multitude of transactions and price variations that are the daily experience of any firm, but also because the value of p (the shift in an index of the general level of prices) becomes available only infrequently. However, the demonstration indicates that the adjustments of the system fully compensate for the use of nominal amounts for events between opening and closing dates of a period. Thus, the day-to-day processes of accounting for transactions of every kind are no different from those of traditional accounting. The difference of continuously contemporary accounting lies in the terminal adjustments, which secure that the closing balances summarized in the balance sheet correspond with observables, and that the balance sheet is a mathematically valid and practically serviceable indicator of the financial relationship of the firm with its environment. An income account identifying the three main components mentioned above may be amplified to report net revenues and price variation adjustments in as many sub-categories as may be desired. It clearly distinguishes between the realized and the accrued elements of the gross increment in net assets. As the system's description implies, its object is periodically to bring to up-to-date terms all the features of a firm's financial affairs.

Index

Index

Index